MAKING A PSYCHOPATH

MAKING A PSYCHOPATH

My Journey into
Seven Dangerous Minds

Dr. Mark Freestone

ST. MARTIN'S PRESS
NEW YORK

Library of Congress Cataloging-in-Publication Data

Names: Freestone, Mark, author.
Title: Making a psychopath : my journey into seven dangerous
    minds / Dr. Mark Freestone.
Description: First U.S. edition. | New York : St. Martin's Press,
    2022. | Originally published in Great Britian in 2020 by
    Ebury. | Includes bibliographical references.
Identifiers: LCCN 2021046519 | ISBN 9781250277978
    (hardcover) | ISBN 9781250277985 (ebook)
Subjects: LCSH: Psychopaths—Case studies. | Criminal
    psychology—Case studies.
Classification: LCC RC555 .F74 2022 | DDC 616.85/82—dc23/
    eng/20211005
LC record available at https://lccn.loc.gov/2021046519

Of course, this book is for Lotte,
Edward, and Albert

CONTENTS

contents

PREFACE

"We want your help with a character: it's a TV show about a female assassin. Who's also a psychopath."

My face rested slowly into the palm of my hand. Fortunately for everyone, this wasn't visible to the very lovely and well-meaning person on the phone.

"Umm . . ." I stalled, trying not to sigh too audibly. Everyone knows (don't they?) that women are rarely psychopaths and almost never assassins. Apart from anything else, male assassins have the "killing game" tied down hard and tend to give horrible new meanings to the phrase "rampant misogyny."

Wait, though: there was Ulrike Meinhof, right? Brigitte Mohnhaupt? Aileen Wuornos? They were women, and they killed a lot of people—for political reasons at least. Sort of. Maybe I could work with this: a misunderstood, isolated weirdo who is recruited into a strange sect on the fringes of society.

"We also want her to be really glamorous and sexy."

I made a funny noise like someone who had spent two years studying for an A-level English paper on Shakespeare only to turn over their exam and find questions about Emily Dickinson. I had to make this wish list into a real, credible psychopath. Why did I ever get involved in working with TV anyway?

The beginning of this story reaches back to the early 2000s, when I—clutching my just-printed sociology PhD—secured some research funding to do an investigation study of the Dangerous and Severe Personality Disorder (DSPD) Program in England and Wales. DSPD was supposed to be a shining new hope of treatment for people with severe personality disorders, especially antisocial personality disorder (sociopathy) and psychopathy. There was a huge sense of therapeutic optimism back then, and a dose of apparently healthy arrogance: no other country in the world had managed to reliably treat psychopaths before, but that was only because the British hadn't tried it on this kind of scale.[1]

Ignoring several pointed statements of concern from highly experienced psychiatrists and psychologists, between 2002 and 2005 four new special high-security units in prisons and hospitals in the UK were opened to some of Britain's most dangerous and uncontainable men and women . . . and me. Between 2004 and 2013, I worked in and around these new units, talking to hundreds of prisoners and staff and trying to understand what this system was and how it was going to make a difference where nothing else had. Being neither a forensic psychologist nor a psychiatrist, I had no real concept of what a psychopath was when I began, and I had to learn from the ground up what made these prisoners different.

Over these years I gained a huge amount of experience with men diagnosed with psychopathy, and with the brave people who volunteered to work with them through the DSPD Program and beyond. Some of the work was formal, meeting with patients and prisoners to conduct assessment or treatment under the supervision of a psychologist or psychiatrist, or my own research; and some of it was informal, meeting patients and staff on the ward and talking about whatever was on the wind, playing chess or guitar with inmates.

It was being contacted to work on *Killing Eve,* and drawing on my experiences with psychopaths, some of which made their way into the television series in one form or another to help the writers shape the story and characters, that made me think about these experiences again. Villanelle is such a curiously compelling character. Both in the series and Luke Jennings's original Villanelle novellas, she is a terrible, terrible person: devoid of warmth, empathy, relationship skills, humility, or genuine emotion, who not only kills people for money but also because she thinks it's funny, or simply because it's more convenient than having to tolerate relationships with them. Yet, something about her draws people in: perhaps people identify with parts of her character, or perhaps they envy the chaos she brings with her.

Of course, Villanelle is fiction. And although we tried to make her as real as possible, I realized that my own stories could give a window into what it's like interacting with people with a diagnosis of psychopathy, and that they could also show that psychopaths are not all one and the same. Although it does seem that criminal psychopaths have no problem acting out in detail some of the darkest things that would make most of us feel guilty if we only dreamed them, one of the few things about psychopaths I'm absolutely sure of is that psychopathy in itself is not a *reason* or a *cause* for doing anything.

I hope this book gives people whose interest, of whatever kind, was piqued by Villanelle and characters like her, a chance to understand a bit more about the very misunderstood disorder—or, more likely, disorders—we call psychopathy. Taking a chapter each for seven types of patient, I am going to show how very diverse criminal psychopaths are in their backgrounds, their characters and their ways of being dangerous. From the horrifically violent gang leader to the man who always ends up hurting those who help him, what the people in this book all have in common is that they have done at least one terrible thing to another person and they can't quite understand why the rest of society is making such a fuss about it.

INTRODUCTION

Does the world need another book on psychopaths?[1] After all, it seems we have heard or read just about everything there is to say about this most misunderstood of characters. Are they evil from birth? Are they created by perverse or abusive family dynamics? Why do some psychopaths make for such compelling fictional characters? Is my ex or boss a psychopath?

I am not a psychiatrist, someone who diagnoses and treats mental disorders, nor a forensic psychologist, who studies the minds, brains, and behavior of criminals, although I have worked extensively with some of the most influential and experienced members of both professions. My background is a bit different: I originally trained in sociology, a discipline mainly concerned with understanding patterns of relationships and social interaction and which rarely deals with the individual. However, I have worked directly with criminal psychopaths in secure hospitals and in the community for over fifteen years. I have eaten with psychopaths, laughed and cried with them. I have seen them bleed and, in one case, die. They have manipulated me; I have probably manipulated them. And many words have been said—usually not by me—that should never be said by one human to another.

Throughout this time, conducting research, performing assessments and running treatment groups, I have built up both a wealth of experience of how psychopaths interact with people, and a resolute skepticism about the way that psychiatry and forensic psychology views psychopaths. Today I work in a psychiatry department that prides itself on a bio-psychosocial understanding of mental disorder, which means that we always try to understand what influence the circumstances in which people grew up have on their adult lives, when thinking about mental disorder. This is critically important in formulating a treatment plan that can help to persuade a person that there are positive reasons to change, and to avoid re-creating the traumatic, abusive, or neglectful environments of their childhood.

My belief is that to understand people we should always focus on relationships rather than traits and diagnosis, and so I feel I can offer a slightly different perspective on this most misunderstood of personalities. Psychopaths don't exist in a vacuum; their disorder is about the way they understand and interact with other people, about the relationships they form. One of the questions I sometimes ask my students is whether a psychopath would be able to survive on a desert island far away from other humans. My answer to this is: yes, absolutely. Someone with a diagnosis of, say, schizophrenia or dementia would be unlikely to cope in such an isolated setting on their own and would probably perish. I think a psychopath would thrive.

I also hope I can offer some clarity about what makes a psychopath and whether they can change. There are too many contradictory statements about what the term "psychopath" means and whether treatment always makes psychopaths worse rather than better. There's a smorgasbord of stubborn misconceptions about people with a psychopathic disorder that come partly from our tendency—and this was certainly the perspective I had when I first started working in secure mental health services in 2004—to think of psychopathy as a footnote for a kind of supervillain, bereft of a moral compass and totally Machiavellian in their expert manipulation of others. In fact, years of experience have taught me that the reality is less dramatic, but perhaps far more unsettling: that psychopaths are, in the vast majority, not experts in much at all, and certainly not intellectual puppet masters like Thomas Harris's Hannibal Lecter. Rather, they are individuals who, through a toxic and statistically unlikely combination of genetic bad luck and a desperate emotionally, physically, or financially deprived upbringing, have come to lack some of the most basic social skills, powers of reasoning, and emotional responses that contribute so much to making us human. This, I aim to show, is what makes a psychopath.

I want to show how a single word, "psychopath," is far too narrow a term to capture the diversity of people who have attracted the label. I want to highlight the kind of disturbed environments that create psychopaths and the "containers"—prison and, to a lesser extent, psychiatric hospitals—that perpetuate their social and personal dysfunction, allowing them to hone their skills of manipulation and sadism.

My hope is that the anonymized case studies in this book, each one an amalgamation of the characters whom I have come across in my professional life, help to humanize psychopaths, and help the reader understand why it is so difficult for these men and women to form the kinds of social and emotional relationships we take for granted.

I am interested in whether it is fair to morally judge psychopaths and whether there is a degree of complicity between all of us, professionals and the general public alike, in consigning them to the dustbin of humanity. I think that, more often, professionals working in mental health and criminal justice systems adopt the easier and attractive judgmental perspective on psychopaths, perceiving them as "impossible to rehabilitate" or "naturally evil." This way, when things go wrong and someone loses their job for a breach of professional ethics for allowing themselves to be manipulated by a psychopath, we comfort ourselves with the notion that the psychopath is simply a genetic aberration we cannot help but can only be intimidated or controlled by. Similarly, if clinicians have nothing to offer someone with psychopathy, this becomes a self-fulfilling prophecy: "I can't help you, so you must be bad."[2]

Combine this with the psychopath's tendency toward violence, manipulation and controlling behavior, and you'll find that working with them is very rarely a straightforward or satisfying task. Psychopaths tend to reoffend more prolifically and more quickly than other offenders: one study says that up to 90 percent of psychopathic offenders will be reconvicted of a violent offense within twenty years.[3] Diligence and persistence are often rewarded with disappointment and frustration, and sometimes a complaint or a colorful metaphor about your parentage.

This book describes composites of people I have dealt with in my career and some publicly visible ones. They include Danny, a man who is more of a danger to himself than to anyone else. Eddie, who has a terrifying history of violence but has turned away from that life and found empathy and remorse. And Angela, a woman who perhaps scares me more than any of the men I describe. In some way each story challenges the misconceptions about psychopaths, and they will hopefully give you a different perspective on the disorder and the kind of person that springs to mind when we use the word.

CHAPTER ONE

The Masks of Psychopathy

Although psychopathy has been one of the most important and written-about topics of forensic psychiatry and psychology over the last thirty years, it's astonishing how little we really understand it. In part, this makes sense: psychopaths are not common, the largest group of them are in the criminal justice system, and increasingly doing research in prisons and forensic hospitals is expensive, complex, and often unrewarding. Not to mention, of course, that most psychopaths in prison are probably quite bored and, well, psychopathic: meaning that some of them will be entirely uninterested in engaging in research at all—after all, what would they gain?—and another group will see any research project as an opportunity to present themselves in a particular, usually favorable, light that doesn't have any basis in reality. Or they'll just tell some fantastic whoppers and watch the researcher squirm as they try to weigh social convention against the urge to laugh, scream, or slap their research participant (or all three). This is a bit of a shame, because in the early 2000s a lot of progress was made in trying to understand that there were probably several different kinds of psychopath, and that using a single word to describe them all was increasingly problematic.

I want to tease apart the idea that the word "psychopath" or the diagnosis of "psychopathy" refers to a single type of person, instantly recognizable from just about every television program with a one-dimensional bad guy (or gal, more of which later): in fact, people with a diagnosis of psychopathy can differ quite fundamentally from one another in several significant ways. Understanding this and why it might be will prepare you a bit for the variety of presentations—the variety of "masks" that psychopaths wear, or that we project onto them—that we'll meet in the chapters that follow.

Fifteen Thousand Paper Psychopaths

How can one diagnosis mean many things? Well, for a start, we might want to think about the Psychopathy Checklist, Revised (PCL-R)[1], the gold standard psychopathy assessment used by forensic psychologists and psychiatrists across the world, which consists of twenty items relating to distinctive traits of a psychopath, each rateable between 0 and 2. If we take the more conservative threshold used in the United States, someone needs a score of 30 on the PCL-R to be diagnosed as a "clinical psychopath." This means, as Jon Ronson points out in his terrific book on the subject of the PCL-R, *The Psychopath Test,* that there are 15,504 different combinations of items[2] that would result in someone meeting the threshold, each representing a different cluster of different traits: over 15,000 different ways to be a psychopath.

To make matters more complex, there are two very different constellations or factors within the PCL-R. One is a group of traits, or personality features, that relate to antisocial behavior: impulsivity, poor behavioral controls, criminal convictions, and so on. People with this group of traits tend to show antisocial behavior during their early adult life: drug addiction, offending, bankruptcy, homelessness, and a tendency toward making decisions without planning. At around the age of thirty, however, their criminality and antisocial behavior seem to "burn out"[3] and they desist in most cases from this kind of criminal or self-destructive behavior. The second group usually has this antisocial tendency too, but also a further set of personality traits—such as callousness, shallow emotions, and a lack of remorse for their acts—that tend to be more durable over time and which are genetically based.[4] These traits never really change throughout a lifespan,[5] meaning that people with this group won't ever fully find a way of empathizing with others or understanding emotions. This also means that, without treatment, they will never be truly "safe" within society.

One of the biggest questions facing psychopathy research is whether psychopaths are also necessarily criminals. Hervey Cleckley was the first psychiatrist to write about psychopaths in detail, and his book *The Mask of Sanity*,[6] published in 1941, didn't specify anything about criminality or violence in his description of the disorder. In fact, his understanding of psychopaths was very different from ours today. Rather than cool, calculating criminals, Cleckley believed that psychopaths were "morally insane"; that they were unable to tell right from wrong and therefore just as "mad" as people with a psychotic illness like schizophrenia, albeit their madness affected a different part of the brain relating to moral reasoning, not perception. However, he suggested that in a psychopath madness was "concealed" by a mask of social awareness that hid the madness, effectively tricking those around them into thinking they were sane. It was their inability to learn from mistakes, to feel remorse for those they hurt, or to empathize with emotions in others that revealed the deep inner disturbance, marking them out as psychopaths.

Despite acknowledging lack of remorse as a core aspect of psychopathy, Cleckley did not make any association between psychopathy and crime; that only came later with Robert Hare's Psychopathy Checklist[7] in 1980. This was based on Cleckley's work but had several advantages: rather than a theoretical description of a concept, Hare gave a set of clear and measurable criteria, in the form of a checklist, which measured how psychopathic someone was on a scale. Anyone who has worked in applied psychology knows how important this is. Once a concept is "testable" it is usable in clinical practice, and—in the case of a measure that relates to crime as well as mental disorder—forensic and criminal work, too.

It was with the second edition of the checklist, the PCL-R,[8] that Hare did something that has divided understanding of psychopathy ever since: he incorporated both criminal and behavioral tendencies into his checklist. In many respects this was a great decision: it allowed the checklist to be used in courts, where it was not just an assessment of a clinical condition but, as a hybrid measure, could also perform a fair assessment of a convicted offender's chances of reoffending. However, it also leads to a fundamental change in the way we think about psychopaths, from people with a moral deficiency similar to madness, to people who are primarily criminals whose emotional and thinking deficits make them more suited to, and predisposed to, crime.

A Different Brain?

We now have a lot more research available to us about the causes of psychopathy, how it manifests in the brain, and in the genetic profile of people with the disorder, and we know it is not the case that all psychopaths are necessarily criminals. We'll look at the brain first.

The high quality brain-imaging equipment that became available in the early twenty-first century has shown that there are two very specific regions of psychopaths' brains that differ significantly from those of people without psychopathy, and that these brain regions are linked to specific kinds of emotional and cognitive processing that are deficient in psychopaths.

The first of these two regions is the prefrontal

cortex, a region shaped like a half-moon that takes up most of the frontal lobe of your brain, just behind your brows. First-year psychology students almost all get a lecture on the case of Phineas Gage, the nineteenth-century Australian rail worker who took a tamping iron—a two-meter piece of iron used to "pin down" rail tracks—through his eye socket and not only survived, but did so with most of his cognitive abilities intact. However, the iron significantly damaged Gage's prefrontal cortex[9] and as a result his personality was completely altered: he become irritable and prone to aggressive mood swings, although he could still function tolerably in society; enough to hold down a job after his recovery from the injury.[10]

Similarly, I have worked with patients who have a diagnosis of an "organic" personality disorder: this means that the diagnosing doctor(s) believe that they have isolated the cause of the psychopathy or sociopathy to a specific, neurological cause. One patient I worked with had had a very difficult birth where there was damage to their frontal lobe owing to obstetric forceps. (This is a vanishingly rare thing to happen: only around three in a thousand births in the United States will result in brain injury, and the majority of these will be due to oxygen deprivation to the baby's brain,[11] not a direct physical injury.) My patient had terribly dysregulated behavior: they spoke normally and showed good intellectual development (played a mean game of chess), but almost seemed incapable of making rational decisions or sticking to them without being overcome with nearly hysterical levels of emotion: rage, despair, elation, contempt, guilt, anger, sadness, all within minutes of each other.

This is because the prefrontal cortex and its near neighbor, the orbitofrontal cortex ("orbit" being the area around the eye), govern our ability to make good decisions based on available information, and in particular our expectation of how society will respond to us when we fail to conform to social rules and norms, for example by breaking the law.[12] In a psychopath, these areas, absent or severely damaged in Phineas Gage, show significantly lower activation;[13] that is, the neurons in that part of the brain light up less than usual in a brain-imaging machine, indicating less activity, and appear to be linked to an inability to learn from experience.

The second region that is different in psychopaths is the amygdala, a small area in the very center of the brain, right at the top of the brain stem, in what we know as the "limbic" system. The amygdala is closely linked to a lot of brain regions and we think it plays a critical role in our ability to process and understand emotion. I say "we think" because this is a part of the brain that is deep in the gray matter at the base of the skull and we have no lucky anecdotal evidence, such as the case of Phineas Gage, to help us determine its exact purpose.

Any injury that penetrated to the amygdala would almost certainly result in death because of the importance of the surrounding brain tissue to essential things like breathing and keeping your heart beating. Instead, all we have to go on are observational studies that show a link between people with reduced activation—which is a pretty general idea as we don't know how much activation is "normal"—and problems in recognizing emotions, particularly fear, disgust, or sadness, in faces.[14] Clearly, someone who is unable to recognize emotion would have difficulties in expressing remorse or empathy with others because they would not even see why these responses would be necessary; and there we have the "void" at the core of the psychopath.

Touching the Void

Putting this together, we have pretty good, although not definitive, evidence that psychopaths have something different about their brain make-up that probably means they are unable to make calculations about risk, or to recognize and respond to emotions in others. However, even people with quite severe brain abnormalities in these areas can lead perfectly healthy, normal lives, and this brings me to a second fascinating case: that of James H. Fallon, a well-known American neuropsychologist.

James (Jim) Fallon is a family man with a very successful career in neuropsychology. I strongly recommend his excellent, fascinating, and unsettling account of his own experiences, *The Psychopath Inside,*[15] and his compelling TED Talk. To cut a long story short, however, Jim was conducting some standard research using PET scans (a kind of early magnetic resonance imagining or MRI technique) when he noticed that one of the scans showed exceptionally low activity in areas of the amygdala, prefrontal cortex, and limbic system. "Huh, this guy is a regular psychopathic murderer," he flippantly thought, only to realize that the scan was actually from a supposedly "healthy" control. When he checked the patient ID he further noticed that the healthy control was listed as a "Dr. J. Fallon": the neuroscientist himself was a psychopath. He then sought out his genealogical records and realized that he had several ancestors who had been killers, and quite possibly psychopaths. Next, he tested his DNA profile, which revealed he had the "warrior" version of the MAO-A gene, an unusual genetic profile typically found in people who have committed a few murders.

Jim's family had always been aware that he was

emotionally distant, paid little or no attention to social niceties, and was known for a bit of a temper. But he was also a pretty big deal in academic circles before this took place. He had built his scientific career on well-conducted neuroscience, which is, well . . . hard. You can't bluff your way as a neuroscientist (believe me, I've tried): it requires a technical understanding of both physiology and complicated research techniques, an eye for detail, an ability to think in the abstract, and very high levels of patience. None of these things are typically associated with psychopaths, nor any of the patients and prisoners I have worked with. Jim was such a big deal, in fact, that the knowledge that he had all the genetic and physiological traits of a psychopath didn't really hurt his career, except to hook him up with a book deal and a lot of media attention. He explained in one interview: "I know something's wrong [with me]; I just don't care . . . I don't give a shit."

So here we have the first mask of psychopathy: not all psychopaths are the same, and some are unrecognizable from each other. Jim's case highlights some very serious questions about the nature of criminal psychopathy and where it comes from, and why despite all the genetics and the brain structure he would never make the grade on the psychopath test. Yes, brain structure and genes play a part, but experience has taught me that there are some clear regularities about the past of the people I have worked with. I say this because I have never, ever met a psychopathic criminal, much less a killer, who magically sprang from a near-perfect background. Some psychopaths come from relatively (or even very) privileged homes, or families where on the surface all can seem well; however, scratch beneath that surface and there is always something amiss. This can manifest in obvious ways—perhaps a parent with a drinking problem, or a violent relationship between the mother and father—or it can be more subtle—a disproportionate allocation of love for one child at the expense of another, or a paternal figure who believes in discipline at the expense of any human connection. These disruptions target the vital bond or "attachment"[16] between parents and their children, meaning that the children lack a clear sense of who they should be or how they should behave. It seems that when a child's sense of identity and security is absent or distorted in this way, this is fertile ground for the development of a criminal psychopath as the child's genes, their character, interacts with their environment.

Someone recently challenged me on this theory, citing the American serial killer Ted Bundy as someone who was widely believed to be a psychopath[17] but had a "normal" upbringing. However, reading closely between the lines, Bundy's early life shows a pattern of highly distorted role models and relationships: confusion about the true identity of his father—never a stable basis for a young man to develop a secure sense of self—and a grandiose, patriarchal grandfather[18] who provided exactly the kind of callous, remorseless, and aggressive role model that any budding psychopath needs. The great psychoanalyst Phyllis Greenacre, one of the first people to write about psychopaths, noted as long ago as 1945, before Bundy and long before *The Psychopath Test,* how many psychopaths seemed to come from families where the father was "an unusually prominent or respected man."[19]

Now, absolutely, some people have suffered through terrible upbringings far worse than this, sometimes with terrifying parental figures, and yet turned into decent, respectable members of society. I am good friends with someone who has suffered terrible sexual and emotional abuse at the hands of their father and brother, yet they have a life, a partner, two children, and their own business, all of which they are absolutely dedicated to. They wear the marks of their traumatic childhood almost like battle scars: they have an endearingly pragmatic and resolute internal formulation that these awful experiences have made them who they are today, and that was someone to be proud of, not feel guilty about. This friend told me once that because of their own childhood they recognized the value of love and family, and that they would never endanger either now that they are an adult with their own children.

Here is the second mask of psychopathy: whether someone will be a psychopath or not does not depend only on their upbringing but on a complex interplay between early experience and genetics, both of which play a part in the formation of the adult brain. Two particular genetic patterns stand out: firstly, the particular type MAO-A gene that affected Jim Fallon; and secondly, a particular phenotype—that is, an expression of particular genetic patterns—called "callous unemotional traits" that are first noticed in children.

"Callous unemotionality" is a trait in the Psychopathy Checklist, but it's quite rare for it to be applied to children; however, it is children aged twelve or younger who start to show callous unemotional traits—that is, a disregard for the impact of their actions on other people and a general lack of emotional range or recognition—who tend to have the worst outcomes for criminality and adult psychopathy. This tendency is different from those children who don't show callous unemotionality until young adulthood (i.e., as teenagers) and has been shown by studies of twins to be unaffected by social class, education or parenting.[20] This doesn't mean that Lionel Shriver's book *We Need to Talk about Kevin,* where a young boy seems to spring from the womb as a ready-made psychopath, is intended as a cautionary tale to any would-be parents. Not all children with callous unemotional traits develop into an adult psychopath and not all adult psychopaths had these traits as children (or at least, as far as we know). Rather, I think it's the book's ambiguity about whether the mother is an honest narrator about her relationship with her son that is the fundamental conceit: are the parents truly blameless victims of their psychopathic offspring, or have they somehow brought this fate upon themselves? In my experience, and to summarize the findings from research, the answer to this question is almost certainly "the latter": the way parents act toward their children has huge implications for the development of psychopathy.

Killer Women: Psychopaths or Unicorns?

The third and final mask of psychopathy is the way it manifests through gender. A key part of what I think makes *Killing Eve* an effective thriller, and something that took a lot of time and discussion to get right in the early writing meetings, was whether the psychopathic assassin Villanelle could be made out to be a "true"—in the sense of clinically accurate—psychopath. Why was this so challenging? Because "true" female psychopaths are a highly elusive breed. Firstly, there are very, very few of them: when the UK government first commissioned secure prison and hospital places for dangerous people with severe personality disorders for the DSPD Program, they estimated that the population of men they were serving was around 2,000. However, the highest estimate they could come up for women dangerous and psychopathic enough to warrant specialized care for their personality disorder was only 40, or 1 female psychopath for every 50 males. If we accept the (generous) estimate that there are about 3 psychopaths in every 1,000 men, this means that only 6 in every 100,000 women will be diagnosable as a psychopath using the PCL-R checklist, making about 200 female psychopaths in the UK. In other words, they are very rare, if we accept that the PCL-R is a good way of assessing women for psychopathy.

However, current understandings suggest that female psychopaths don't present or behave in the same way as male psychopaths. Scottish forensic psychologist Caroline Logan has written some of the most interesting work on this difference, and in a recent article she summarized our cultural conceptions of the female psychopath as a "femme fatale":[21] not someone who was necessarily physically harmful toward others—although we will look at Angela Simpson, an interesting case that challenges this misconception, later on—but rather who harms and damages relationships and well-being psychologically. Logan talks about how male psychopaths tend to focus their energies on control, or the mastery of their environment and others around them, where female psychopaths are much more focused on the manipulation of relationships. She uses the example of the character of the Marquise de Merteuil in *Les Liaisons Dangereuses* (or Kathryn Merteuil in the 1999 film *Cruel Intentions*) who seeks to carry out revenge by playing characters' desires off against one another to her own benefit. Like a male psychopath, she does this through deceit and lies, without any expression of empathy or remorse, and in apparently full knowledge of the damage her actions will do.

There are dozens of other expressions of this kind of arch female manipulator in fiction: from Hedda Gabler in Ibsen's play of the same name (1896), to Sula Peace in Toni Morrison's *Sula* (1973), and more recently in Tana French's *In the Woods* (2007). Often in these stories there is violence done, but it is rarely, if ever, by the female antagonist: rather, other characters—frequently men—are manipulated into hurting themselves or others with threats or promises.

It's all very well to learn from fiction, but what do we know about female psychopaths in real life? The answer is that research is patchy, probably because there are so few women who meet these criteria. The first observation to make is that yes, there are a small number of women—the forty or so we discussed earlier—who would score highly

enough on the PCL-R to qualify as criminal psychopaths. The second, more complex idea is: it is
very possible that women with psychopathy often
have very different psychological and criminal
profiles from men. Some of the items in the PCL-
R might have very different interpretations when
applied to women rather than men: for example,
the item relating to a "parasitic lifestyle" would be
clearly applied to a man who was financially dependent on a woman, but cultural considerations
might well mean that a woman being financially
dependent upon a man is not convincing evidence
of psychopathy.[22] Similarly, "promiscuous sexual
behavior," another PCL-R item, might have different underlying motivations and meanings between
men and women: for men this behavior might be
about status and sensation-seeking, whereas for
women it might be more related to power and manipulation.[23] So, qualifying the previous answer
of yes, the maybe response cautions us that even
women who score highly on the PCL-R may not
have the same motivations for their behavior or
psychological profile as men.

The third point is that there are probably no "real" female psychopaths who resemble Villanelle's psychopathic assassin in *Killing Eve*. If we mean by that that they use personal violence as well as psychological intimidation and sexual manipulation to achieve their goals, and show no remorse for their violent actions, then the answer is there are no real precedents for this. In fact, there is even some contradictory evidence: a Dutch study found that highly psychopathic women were actually *less* likely to commit homicide than men,[24] which lends some support to the idea that female psychopaths eschew violence in favor of relationship-based manipulation. There are exceptions: Angela Simpson, who we'll discuss in chapter seven, who presents with a very "male" form of psychopathy; and Aileen Wuornos, who murdered six men in the United States in the late 1980s and who was found to have a very high PCL-R score of 32 out of 40.[25] However, up until her execution in 2002 she gave very different and inconsistent accounts of her offending and her feelings of remorse (or otherwise) toward her victims; she was also diagnosed with borderline personality disorder, which is a condition almost incompatible with psychopathy, with symptoms including extreme emotional dysregulation and an unstable self-identity. There is also a plausible narrative for a lot of the killings beyond simple gratification or violence for violence's sake: Wuornos repeatedly stated that the killings were self-defense as she believed the victims were planning to rape her. Whether they were or not, if she perceived this level of threat it would constitute a degree of motivation that would not require someone to be psychopathic in order to act.

Moving Things Forward

What can all these people have in common: a blue-collar worker who becomes sociopathic after a brain injury, a New York professor who is well socially integrated but struggles to relate to other people, a group of kids who start from an early age to show signs of an uncaring attitude toward their peers, and a female psychopath who might not be a psychopath at all? It's not an easy question to answer, but it's not one we can ignore: psychopathy is again and again shown to be so strongly related to the risk of violence,[26] social deviance including risky drug use and financial instability,[27] and poor likelihood of successful treatment, rehabilitation, or "recovery." How is it possible to hit this moving target: to understand what a psychopath is, bring together the seemingly contradictory strands of research, and to try to do something constructive about improving the prospects of people with this most misunderstood disorder?

Psychopathy, as we best understand it, which is an uneasy alliance between a checklist of controlling and antisocial behaviors matched with a number of structural deficits in the brain, explains a fair bit about why some people are more likely to make a risky or interpersonally damaging choice in each situation. However, it doesn't often offer a convincing or satisfying motive for anything: someone with a diagnosis of schizophrenia may have a delusional belief that their friend is secretly plotting to murder them and hear a voice telling them to poison their tea, but psychopathy offers no such clear causal pathways from someone's internal world to their behaviors.

One of the best examples I can think of is one I still go over with my students today: a man I will call Ben, a life-sentenced prisoner. Ben was sent to prison for armed robbery after a failed attack on an armored money van, which had been coordinated by his stepfather. When Ben was released from prison, he was fixated on taking revenge for what he saw as a "setup," where his stepfather had caused to him being sent to prison. After just two weeks on release he put together a "tool bag" of hammers, knives, rope, and a saw, and set off with the very explicit intent of killing his stepfather. However, along the way he met an old friend who persuaded him to come to the pub for a drink. Over a few beers, Ben confessed what he was planning, and the friend persuaded him that it wasn't worth it: Ben had only just come out of a long prison sentence, why was he so keen to go back there? Ben saw sense, and the two of them stayed until closing time, then set off for home. The friend, engaging in what sounds like drunken banter, told Ben he was a "pussy" for being talked out of his murderous plot so easily: so Ben grabbed the hammer from his bag, and beat his friend to death with it.

Now don't get me wrong: Ben was deeply psychopathic. He didn't "get" remorse, was a career criminal (albeit a very bad one as he was always getting caught) and grandiose in his sense of entitlement to be violent to people who wronged him. He planned a very serious offense out of nothing but a misguided sense of revenge for a damaged ego: and on the way to carry this out, he impulsively decided not go to go through with it, until he received another blow to his ego that he responded to with sudden homicidal rage. Knowing Ben was a psychopath doesn't really explain this, though: rather, it's his specific personality, his extreme ego vulnerability and hair trigger that contributed to the murder that day. In other words, the actions of psychopaths still very much need an explanation beyond "they are a psychopath."

It is very, very easy to write bad fictional psychopathic characters: "Ahmed was dangerous . . . because he was a psychopath"; and it is very hard to write good ones. This is because the "void" at the center of the psychopathic mind, the fleeting displays of deep emotion (shallow affect) and cold-blooded nature, isn't very interesting in itself. This "void" has to be overlaid onto a complex developmental history and set of desires and motivations, as it always is in real life. Hannibal Lecter's relationship with Clarice Starling is one example. What does Lecter want from Clarice: a protégé? But she is repulsed by his killing. A lover? He is homosexual. A daughter? This is a psychopath, incapable of attachment. The key, of course, is that this is never made explicit and we are made to guess what Lecter thinks this relationship is.

Psychopathic disorder wears masks on many levels. Psychopathy can hide in plain sight, and our confusion about its core traits makes it very difficult to make a clear determination about whether someone is or isn't a psychopath, unless they are a very "typical" male criminal who had serious behavioral problems as a child. How can we take a concept seriously, though, if the difference between a psychopath and a non-psychopath is simply whether they were or were not convicted of a crime? What bearing can the accurate (or inaccurate) functioning of the justice system possibly have on one person's psychological makeup? *American Psycho*'s Patrick Bateman shows that wealth and privilege can confound our understandings of culpability and personality, and how unfair that is in a world where so many people will have been sentenced to death because of a supposed diagnosis of psychopathic disorder.

The people I describe in the coming chapters are intended to help show that a "psychopath" often has far more to them than a simple diagnosis. Like all of us, they are complex individuals with idiosyncratic motivations, beliefs, desires, and criminal offenses, not reducible to the fact that they are psychopaths. However, it is because they are psychopaths that we need to take notice of them: in every case these men and women have committed very serious crimes, some of them truly horrific, and there is every likelihood that they will do so again.

CHAPTER TWO

Paul, the Hit Man

Working in large institutions—prisons, hospitals, halfway houses—with people who have committed serious crimes is hard, draining work. The people you are working with are at once potentially dangerous, having committed at least one serious crime and being dissatisfied with their incarceration, and yet also highly vulnerable. This means that your job as a professional is incredibly difficult: you are working with people in a place they do not want to be, trying to give them a reason to change that they do not want, and trying to avoid giving them the opportunity to do harm to you, which a number of them certainly do. On top of that, criminals with personality disorders such as psychopathy are hard to rehabilitate: there is no clear treatment for their mental disorder and they are often very keen to re-create the life they came from—usually one defined by drugs and violence—within the prison. This means that prisons themselves are hard places. Most of the older jails with any kind of interesting Victorian architecture are now long gone, victims of health and safety regulations that require plumbing for toilets rather than slop buckets and clear lines of sight around the wings so people cannot get up to nefarious deeds in the shadows. What is left are cold, concrete institutions that are often characterized by bare, whitewashed walls. Maximum-security prisons are perhaps the worst: the walls are higher and supplemented by extra-high wire fences and helicopter wire.

Nobody, in any institution I worked in, was as adroit at bringing their outside life with them into prison as Paul. I first met him in a high-security prison together with a group of other prisoners who were discussing their upcoming treatment with a psychologist. This was a new service, part of the DSPD service, established in a prison to work with serious offenders who had previously been consid-

paul, the hit man

ered "untreatable" because of their psychopathy or other serious personality disorder. My job at the time was to observe meetings like these to try to understand and write about the kind of culture created when you tried to rehabilitate the apparently unrehabilitatable; how relationships were formed between staff and prisoners who might have been in solitary confinement for years or never had a parole meeting where they had a chance of being released from prison.

Most of the prisoners in the group looked anxious, probably rightly, as most of them had life sentences and realized that this might be their last chance to ever get out of prison. However, nobody had any idea about what "treatment" was, beyond a couple of stitches from the nurse after a fight in the cafeteria. One man in the group held the prison's record for solitary confinement: he had been locked up on his own for six years, and now even sitting next to other people caused him to sweat profusely and look nervously at the blank wall behind him several times per minute. I imagined that after a solitary cell measuring eight by ten feet, even this poky, windowless prison meeting room, which barely held eight chairs and a filing cabinet, must have felt impossibly open and exposed. Another man, also sweating, wore a pair of what I came to learn were known as "nonce glasses": glasses with photoreactive lenses that darken in bright light to protect the eyes, and to which sex offenders are inexplicably yet compulsively drawn. I say inexplicably because every other prisoner and staff member seems to know that wearing them is pretty much a membership card to the "nonce club" so nobody else ever does—violent offenders looking to victimize a nonce thus always know exactly where to start.

In the middle of this motley group, sitting in a slump that made him practically horizontal, manspreading like it was going out of fashion, was when I first laid eyes on Paul. His mouth was twisted in the odd, mirthless expression of someone who feels nothing but contempt for anything around him but feels he should probably disguise that fact in his best interests.

"I wonder what everyone's expectations are of

today?" asked the female psychologist, following an approved line of Socratic questioning and doing everyone the courtesy of looking genuinely interested in the answers.

"Get the fuck out of this place," quipped Paul. Nonce Glasses tittered nervously; Solitary Guy's eyes looked like they were fixed on an imaginary eighteen-wheeler driving directly at his head.

"Well, I suppose that's one goal," deadpanned the psychologist.

"And who the fuck is *this*?" inquired Paul, gesturing vaguely at me.

Suddenly, I could very much see the appeal of hiding behind nonce glasses.

I quickly got the feeling that nobody was more at home in the prison, not the staff, and certainly not me, than Paul was. Meetings in prisons tend to be rather tense, difficult affairs, where the agendas of staff and prisoners come into close conflict, but no matter how tense the meeting Paul just slouched through it, arms folded and a near-constant smirk on his face. Except for those few moments when he sensed he had someone in a compromising position—then his face would contort with righteous fury, like a televangelist from the United States, as he let them know exactly how they now *owed* him something and by God was it time for him to collect.

Outside of prison, Paul had been one of those individuals who I am probably asked the most about: a hit man. I am tempted to write "assassin," but "assassin" has all sorts of glamorous connotations: what Paul did was not glamorous in any way. When people owed him or his bosses money, he would either find them, tie them up and torture them, or order any of his spineless yet almost equally brutal underlings, driven by a combination of fear and a desire to become the "big man" themselves, to do the same. Paul's reign of terror extended across several counties in England, aggressively pushing drugs on vulnerable men and women, backed up by his cronies. Nearly all of his cronies were also addicted to the crack cocaine that Paul dealt, giving him nearly absolute control over their lives.

Finally, things went too far: a rival appeared on the drug scene and started threatening business. Paul gathered several younger accomplices—one of them a boy so young he had to be tried in a youth court—and together they ambushed the other dealer and shot him dead with multiple bullets from a submachine gun. At trial, Paul instructed his legal team to blame everything on his young co-defendants, exonerating himself absolutely. After conviction, he used every single appeal attempt allowed to him by the legal system to get this narrative to stick. In a testament to his ongoing power even from inside, the basis of the appeals was that several witnesses to the original trial decided to withdraw their statements or change their stories. Reading through the trial notes, I became deeply impressed with the police who must have moved extremely quickly to secure witness testimony before the apparatus of Paul's klepto-pharmaceutical intimidation machine persuaded them to change their stories. Although it didn't mean a great deal to me at the time, I also saw that Paul had a PCL-R score of 38 out of 40, which meant that he would have been in the most psychopathic 1 percent of all prisoners.[1]

There are many, many men and women for whom prison is a terrible, terrible place: a place full of restriction, bullying, and soul-sapping boredom, where the only constant friends are your own sense of guilt, fear, and loneliness. However, for some—and I have never known anyone to do this so well as Paul—even the maximum-security jail where we met seemed to be a home away from home.

Paul had been born into a criminal family, inducted by his father at a young age into the "con code" of never snitching, never showing respect for authority, and doing your time without ever cracking. He was also good-looking, with a shock of black hair and great cheekbones, only slightly filled out by the relatively slow, sedate pace of prison life, which meant that people tended to give him more leeway than his terrible criminal past suggested they should. Cons and prison officers of all ranks and levels of the hierarchy almost seem to defer to Paul as though the prison was *his* place, his web into which we had all been pulled by a variety of career choices of varying degrees of questionability.

So, it was into this web that I stepped, fresh out of prison security training, trying to understand what "power" meant inside institutions and how psychopaths' unique personalities helped or hindered them in such an environment. Paul could not have been nicer to me: he seemed to be in every prisoner meeting I attended for the first week, and also the guitar club where he was a regular attendee well-known for his zealous, if not harmonically faithful, interpretations of Leonard Cohen classics. Sensing I was a bit lost in the new, complicated and highly rigid prison regime, he made several helpful suggestions for sessions I should attend if I "wanted to know what was really going on in here." Intrigued, I agreed to attend a number of social and treatment activities around the prison over the next couple of weeks.

Mostly, this was a great success: Paul was always gregarious and keen to integrate me, as well as being popular with the inmates and some—but not all—of the staff. I often wonder what might have happened in the prison were it not for Josie, a five-foot-nothing forensic psychologist who looked like she barely came up to Paul's waist, but absolutely had his number. Whenever she was around, she would take it upon herself to narrate the subtext of Paul's every statement: "When you say it like that, Paul, it sounds to me a bit like a threat" or "I don't know why, Paul, but I feel a bit like you're trying to make me look stupid in front of the group. Do you want to explain why that is?" After a while Paul got the message and started being a lot more cautious around Josie.

I came to appreciate the easygoing charm Paul displayed outside of treatment meetings and also his apparent understanding of my naivety and eagerness to understand prison life. Informal groups—cooking classes, playing chess (yes, psychopaths can be great chess players), even just mealtime chats—with Paul present were never dull, as there was always some new, interesting dynamic or juicy piece of prison gossip that surprised everyone, sometimes the staff included. One of his favorite topics and sources of mirth was what he called the "sausage club," an apparently secretive society of sexual transactions that took place between the other prisoners, most of whom self-identified as straight and displayed rampantly homophobic attitudes, but seemed to believe at the same time that sex with other men was better than no sex at all. I say "apparently" because Paul seemed to know exactly who owed who what sexual favor at any moment, and who was jealous because someone got a blowjob from someone else in the shower on Monday, and so on. He would conclude with a robust disclaimer such as, "Of course, I don't ever get involved in those prohibited behaviors myself," which I thought was perhaps there to make the staff feel they were doing their jobs a bit, but at the same time I did wonder why someone who gave so little of a shit about anything or what anyone else thought would bother to dissuade them that he was doing anything untoward.

While this was fun to begin with, the more time I spent listening to Paul the more I came to respect the prison staff, perhaps especially Josie, in their handling of this exceptionally difficult group of men. I also began to see that, far from making everyone's difficult life more enjoyable with a "bit of banter," Paul was effectively spreading poison around the institution: selectively releasing rumor and innuendo to keep the staff on their toes and the prisoners too concerned about their illicit antics being revealed to ever challenge him.

Of course, in time, I became the victim of one of Paul's manufactured dramas.

One of the biggest challenges for me as a non-prison officer within the prison was trying to get access to the things that happened outside the experience of the prison's clinical staff, who were mainly on a nine-to-five shift. Life in the prison for "civilian" staff was a fairly safe and often mundane experience, much like any other job. However, we regularly came to the morning briefing to hear tales of the horrors that had happened during the evening and night shifts, while we were all safe at home. I had decided that the only way to really understand this was to do an "A" shift; to spend a full twelve-hour shift in the prison, 7 a.m. to

7 p.m., and experience what the officers and prisoners did when we weren't there. This would take some planning on my part: for starters, I was in my mid-twenties and not particularly given to 6 a.m. rises. Second, I would need to fill up my day so that I was neither too bored nor too tired to make sense of what was going on. I asked Paul for advice.

"Mate, you need to come along to breakfast and dinner. Everyone's tired and hungry, and that's where the shit really hits the fan."

For a moment, Paul hesitated, apparently thinking about something. This was uncommon for him.

"You also got to come to the wing business meeting, that's at 2 p.m., and the men talking group, that's at 4; I'm in that. There's the treatment session that runs every day, too: that's really important for you to come to. Are you writing this down?"

Yes, as it turns out, I was. I was also taking the advice of this apparently sincere, very psychopathic man quite seriously, perhaps too seriously.

My "A" shift went as well as can be expected: I got up early, came to breakfast and watched semi-serious rows break out over portion sizes. I learned about the "phantom shitter" who fouled the showers every morning, and I was introduced to another inmate, Patrick, who had a kind of insult diarrhea, where he couldn't help but produce blood-curdling dismissals of staff and prisoners at the slightest provocation, delivered so loud and fast that the individual words were indistinguishable. "Fuckyourmotherhopeshe dieso'arsecancer" was a memorable but relatively low-key example. I attended all the security briefings as staff handed over important information about safety between night and morning shifts, then again the next day; and interviewed a couple of prisoners about their particularly upsetting criminal history, one of which involved burning someone to death in a car. It was very hard work, and when I got back to my cold, rented flat at 7:40 p.m. I sat down and fell straight asleep before I'd even managed to type up my notes from the day.

It wasn't until the next day when I attended the treatment orientation group, as usual, with a mix of officers, civilian staff, and prisoners, that

I had the slightest idea something was not right. Paul was there and apparently very, very offended about something.

"Fuck were you yesterday?" He was looking directly at me.

"Err, what . . . I . . ."

"You said you'd come to the men talking group."

I racked my brains: had I said that?

"I was in the treatment session, I thought that was—"

"Nah . . . fuck's sake. You're all the same, you lot. I said I was going to be in the men talking group and you said that you'd come to it."

I was mortified. By the nature of my research project I was there under sufferance of all the staff and prisoners, and if someone thought I had acted unfairly or unethically then my research was all in jeopardy.

"I'm really sorry," I began. "I didn't realize . . ."

The most menacing sneer I can recall ever seeing crossed Paul's face.

"You mean you thought you'd take the easy option and hang out with the staff when you're supposed to be understanding what life's like for cons. I thought you were better than that, mate."

I looked around the group, feeling the depth of my shame. Nobody met my gaze. Paul was shaking his head. Louise, the officer who was running the orientation group, had a rueful look on her face. It seemed that everyone was aware that I couldn't be counted on to follow through on my promises. Who was going to trust me now to tell me important stuff so I could do my job? Fuck.

Later that day I managed to get my head back together and realized that I had been played for a fool with one of the oldest tricks in the book. It was the same trick that Richard Pryor's character falls for in *Moving*: give the punter a mass of banter and irrelevant chat to confuse them and hide among it important pieces of information (like where Paul was actually going to be that day) that you reckon they won't pick out of the mix. Honestly, I was more disappointed with myself than cross with Paul; I had become carried away with the idea of understanding the prisoner experience and forgotten that they were there for a reason.

After all, if in a situation where Paul was detained against his will and had virtually no power at all he could still make a fool out of a man with a PhD, imagine what he could do in the community if he was allowed to do and say whatever he wanted.

As if to reinforce the point, the next day I tried to avoid Paul as much as possible, but when I finally saw him at guitar club he didn't seem to have any ill will, or indeed any memory of shaming me out of existence the day before. He was genial and charming as ever. Only Louise, the officer, seemed to be notably less warm toward me. She was quite an upstanding character, very neat and upright, and not someone who gave the impression of tolerating infractions easily, so perhaps my technically not wrong but arguably immoral behavior had displeased her, as did the slightly immature and over-enthusiastic actions of a large group of younger male officers who were based on the same wing.

Later the next week, Paul and I even had a bit of a rebonding session over a shared love for Radiohead's album *OK Computer*. He asked me if I wouldn't mind printing him off some guitar tablature from the internet, maybe for the song "Lucky"—which just so happened to be both of our favorite tracks from the album—and "Karma Police" too. Sensing an opportunity to return to Paul's good graces, and perhaps reconnect with his stream of gossip and insider knowledge, that night I dutifully downloaded, printed out, and stapled the guitar tabs together, with a bit more care than I might have done if they were for my use.

However, when I got to the prison car park the next day, something made me hesitate. Suddenly the question of whether or not staples were allowed in the prison seemed extremely important and, in the best tradition of criminal justice work, it seemed a better idea not to take the risk. The guitar tablature remained on the seat of my car and I resolved to bring them in later when I'd taken the staples out. Nice and safe.

Fortunately, as it transpired, things didn't quite work out as planned: in the end I had to leave the prison for a few weeks shortly after this, earlier than planned as I had switched my work contracts over. When I came back, I was no longer a university nerd, but employed by the Prison Service as a lead researcher, a *bona fide* member of the (civilian) prison staff. In the melee, I had forgotten all about Paul's tabs and they had become lost in the morass of paperwork all academics hefted about across jobs before cloud storage and digitizing.

The first day back in the prison, things seemed a little off. Everyone looked very tense and nobody stopped to congratulate me on my new job or even acknowledge me. Something was clearly up, but the prison was running exactly as normal: prisoner movement at 7:50, morning meeting at 8:30, work in the morning, treatment sessions in the afternoon. When I went onto the wing, there were a few new prisoners, which was to be expected as the prison was supposed to be filling up to justify our additional funding from the DSPD program—and no sign of Paul. That was odd because he had been on the "lifer" wing where moving was unlikely because so many of the prisoners were perceived as very high-risk offenders with long tariffs (the time before a life-sentenced prisoner is eligible for parole) and/or high levels of psychopathy, like Paul. Together, this meant that nobody on the ward was particularly high priority for treatment: they were going nowhere fast. So, where had Paul gone? Guitar club was not until the following week, and I saw on the timetable that the treatment orientation group was not running either, so I couldn't ask any of the cons or staff.

It wasn't until much later that day that I finally managed to find Jackie, who had been my colleague since my first days in the prison. She was probably, to paraphrase Francis Ford Coppola's *Apocalypse Now,* wrapped a bit tightly for any prison, let alone a maximum-security one full of psychopaths, but she was bright, loyal, knew the prison regulations inside out, and had a good ear for gossip, which made her a great companion.

By this time, I had worked in maximum-security settings across the country for a total of almost two years, so I had seen and heard a lot of crazy stuff: security breaches, deaths in custody, terrible self-harm, and shocking violence. Still, my jaw dropped as Jackie told the story.

The week before there had been a food fight among the rowdy younger officers on the lifer wing. It had been after the prisoners were locked up, so while probably not appropriate for professionals charged with keeping some of the highest-risk men in the country safely detained, this wasn't anything particularly concerning. However, officer Louise had been passing by at the time, seen the mess generated and rightly called the officers out on it, threatening to report them to the senior officer. Most of the officers had taken this in good humor and stopped, but one, perhaps someone who disliked Louise or being told what to do by women, couldn't help firing back: "Piss off, Lou, we know about you and Paul."

What had he meant? Perhaps nothing would have come of it had Louise not decided to press the issue, which she did probably because she realized that she could not continue to work in the prison if she could not command the respect of her colleagues. However, what came out of it was devastating. When the young male officer was questioned about his comment by the prison management, he—perhaps out of naivety, perhaps because he wanted to do the right thing—broke the code of silence that exists between staff in any big institution about mistakes their colleagues may have made. Louise, he said, was engaged in a relationship with Paul.

I was astonished as more details emerged, contradicting everything I thought I knew about the prison and Louise. The relationship was sexual and had been going on for about two months. It had started some months before that when Louise had agreed to bring Paul a men's magazine—nothing graphically pornographic, just a "lad's mag." The next thing had been a compact disc; I thought of the guitar tabs on my car seat, and my blood ran cold and hot with shame and relief that it wasn't me who'd fallen into this spider's web. Then came the real pornography, then cigarettes (all technically permitted but also potentially powerful things for a prisoner to have for trading), incrementally building up to a tiny bit of cannabis. At the same time, Paul dangled little compliments for Louise to pick up, crumbs from the master's table; even though he was a prisoner, there was no doubt that the other cons were terrified of him and his word carried weight and influence, even with some of the staff who reckoned that keeping Paul sweet meant a quiet life on the ward.

Paul was a genuine manipulator, a Machiavellian who consciously and deliberately used other people to achieve his personal goals. One of the reasons Hannibal Lecter is such a compelling depiction of a psychopath is his ability to manipulate seemingly every situation to his advantage; to extract his "quid pro quo" from every conversation or interaction. To do this, however, requires a high degree of both intelligence and life experience, and, from what I've seen, most men and women in the criminal justice system lack either of these to even the level of the average person in the street.

Most psychopaths lie, cheat, and manipulate in large part because their brains are wired from infancy to reach for these tactics in the way that we would reach for basic manners, compliments, or humor to get what we need (or think we need). But many of them also do this simply because they have never been shown another way, and the poverty of learning and socialization in some psychopaths' lives is truly disheartening. While I was working with Paul, I remember an officer telling a prisoner, "Stop pressing your cell button. Christ, you're like the boy who cried wolf." The prisoner became furious: he was a grown man in his thirties, not a boy, and, "What did wolves have to do with anything?" One of the senior officers calmed the prisoner down and told him the fable of the shepherd boy crying wolf. The prisoner was dumbfounded: nobody had ever taken the time to teach him one of the fundamental moral stories of our society.

Paul shows us, however, that there is a darker shade of manipulation than the one that is done simply as a survival tactic. He may not have been Hannibal Lecter but at the same time it certainly seemed that his every word, every act, every shared piece of gossip, was a gift that could be redeemed later to his advantage: everyone was a means to an end. Unfortunately, that very much included Louise.

Gradually, Louise had found herself spending more time with Paul. I thought of the guitar club and therapy sessions and wondered if these were even her genuine interests. I don't know when Paul first made a pass at her or if he even needed to; often it is not the brilliance of the manipulator that makes the difference between falling for their schemes or not, but rather the fact that most people have vulnerabilities that a good manipulator knows how to exploit. I had been naive and eager to please. Louise was too compassionate, too keen to help, which sounds like a bizarre weakness to have, and at the same time too invested in the role of "rule enforcer" at the prison. Once Paul had persuaded her to bend the rules even once, he knew she could potentially do anything for him because her mind would find a way of "undoing" the act of rule-breaking by being tougher with the rules; of rationalizing that since *she* was the one doing it, and she was making sure all these other rules were being followed, it must have been all right. Of course, this was also her own undoing: she had tried too hard to enforce the rules with her colleagues and they had called her bluff.

At some point, Paul and Louise's relationship had become intimate, which is no small feat in a prison bristling with security cameras and watchful staff with excellent lines of sight. When Louise had a night shift, they had met regularly in the laundry room after lockup to have sex and—worse yet— she brought in a steady stream of illicit items that Paul could trade with other prisoners, in absolute contravention of prison regulations and her job as a prison officer. But perhaps the worst part was that the two of them had used their relationship to ensure Paul was unchallenged in his dominance over the other prisoners on the wing. He would threaten them with violent repercussions if they found out about the relationship while simultaneously using the threat of staff sanctions through Louise to ensure he benefitted from any trading of luxuries or contraband. It was a racket, with stark similarities to the one Paul had run before being sent to prison, and one of the most respected and apparently upright officers was right at the heart of it.

The consequences of this were devastating for Louise. She lost her job, of course, and was charged with misconduct in public office, which was in a respect quite lucky: had she been a nurse in a secure hospital rather than a prison she could have been charged with a sexual relationship with a vulnerable adult. This would have landed her with a jail term and resulted in her being placed on the sex offenders register; a horrible end to a promising professional career. Paul had been transferred to another prison. The officers who had been involved in the ill-fated food fight had not escaped unscathed either: a couple of them had been found to have concealed information pertinent to security relating to the affair and were suspended from their positions without pay. I think the rest probably knew about it too, but prison management couldn't risk suspending many otherwise competent and respected officers.

The impact on morale within the prison had also been tough: everyone was confused that such a respected and apparently upstanding officer could have fallen prey to a psychopath in such a way. No wonder nobody was particularly pleased to see me that day: they were still trying to process all the loss and betrayal they felt. I wondered if anyone was also feeling what I was feeling. I had come very close to giving in to one of Paul's requests to bring material into a prison that—while maybe not against the strict word of the rules— might well have been the "gateway" into further or more frequent requests. I had made the first step down the dark path of wanting to make a psychopath like me, even though they had shown themselves quite capable of treating me like someone beneath their contempt, and only luck, or perhaps some kind of primal paranoia, had kept me from falling all the way down the rabbit hole of colluding with a prisoner and losing my job. For an arch-Machiavellian like Paul, it had been far too easy to identify my pressure points; I think that his skill was probably most evident in the way he humiliated me in front of other staff and prisoners before offering me a way to "redeem myself" in his eyes, to become someone he could confide his desires in again.

I wish I could say what happened to Louise was a one-off issue, but during the next three years there were three similar incidents at prisons and hospitals across the UK where nurses or prison officers had started a relationship with men in their care. A separate study by the U.S. Bureau of Justice Statistics in 2014[2] showed that inappropriate relationships between prison staff and inmates were on the rise in the United States. In every case, the patient or prisoner at the center of the case was a psychopath, and in every case the staff member was found to be the perpetrator of sexual abuse, not a victim, and lost jobs, careers, and livelihoods when they were discovered. These incidents still happen, perhaps less frequently, but there was one case reported by the media from Scotland as recently as 2019.[3] These very unfortunate tales remind us of two things: firstly, that while psychopaths can be incredibly charming, underlying that charm is always an unreservedly self-serving agenda; and secondly, that anywhere there are psychopaths, someone who becomes isolated from their peers, no matter how respected or experienced that person might be, is at risk of being compromised.

Many years later, my supervisor in a secure hospital, a very respected psychoanalyst, would describe this as "perversion": the psychopath's ability to set up a "system within a system" that is in direct contradiction to the standards the original system holds. In the case of the prison, this meant to compromise the "sealed container" of the institution by bringing in contraband and introducing a black economy running beneath the surface; and to find a way to corrupt every person and every standard. Of course, there is also a second, psychoanalytic meaning to "perversion," which is to take a sexual satisfaction from socially unacceptable desires and behaviors. In all my experience, nobody has bettered Paul in making perversion a reality.

CHAPTER THREE

Tony, the Con Man

I first met Tony on the admissions ward of a secure psychiatric hospital on my first day as an NHS employee, working on a project to understand how modern secure psychiatric wards function. Following two months of inductions and training on everything from spotting every form of marijuana currently in production to incapacitating an attacker without leaving a mark, I was permitted to step onto the ward. For me, as for everyone else starting that day, the one thought repeating endlessly in my mind was "please, *please* let me not cock up and cause a security breach," because, we were told, that would mean our jobs and our careers would be irrevocably over. Not to mention the fact that a dangerous killer or rapist might then escape to victimize the surrounding area as, we were again told, had happened many times before. The single worst security breach, of course, was to allow yourself to be manipulated by a psychopathic patient and compromise the entire hospital.

The ward was a brand-new building, still going through some teething pains: the main window in the living space faced west, meaning that even in spring it became uncomfortably hot on a sunny day, which didn't strike me as a good idea in a space for fifteen violent psychopaths. The month before I arrived one of the patients had found a way into the crawl space above and caused significant amounts of damage to the electrical work and piping, as well as huge embarrassment to the hospital management. He had made his way up there using a piece of wood that had been glued to the top of the doorframe to make it safe as a ligature point: that is, so that nobody could use the doorframe to hang themselves. The NHS Trust had promptly moved the patient to another secure hospital where, we were told, he had done almost exactly the same thing, so he'd probably be on his way back fairly soon.

In the middle of this anxious hothouse, where leisurewear-clad patients flopped listlessly around the ward, there sat a man in a well-fitted charcoal suit, looking the very picture of calm and reading a newspaper. This would be my first time meeting one, or so I thought, as I had only seen them as talking heads on TV, and heard reverent descriptions by security staff, but I knew this man had to be a consultant psychiatrist. The de facto leaders and lynchpins of any psychiatric inpatient service, psychiatrists make the big decisions about who leaves and who stays, who in their minds is "cured," and who needs to spend more of a potentially un-limited amount of time detained in the hospital. Consultants—the highest grade of psychiatrist— were paid quite considerable sums in those days and could afford such luxuries as tailored suits, undoubtedly looking down on my sociologist's uni-form of cotton-and-corduroy. Feeling ill-prepared and insecure, but mindful of my mission to talk to everyone, I reverently approached this reclining figure and introduced myself.

"Hello," said the psychiatrist, gracing me with

a small smile. "I'm Tony." Honored to be acknowl-edged by such an authority, it was at that point that I noticed Tony wasn't wearing the regulation-issue NHS Trust ID badge that we had all been told was the hospital equivalent of a liver. He must have been terribly important.

"I expect you know who I am," continued the psychiatrist, "everyone else around here does." My anxious stomach did somersaults: evidently that did not include me, which made me worry that I might have already committed a dreaded cock-up already by not knowing this man's name. What rattled me more, however, was the realization that Tony was not even wearing his key belt. *No keys!* Did he have a security *escort*? Had he been sent by the Department of Health to perform an unan-nounced inspection of the hospital? Could I possi-bly be more ignorant?

A nurse appeared at my shoulder. "Come on, Tony, you know you're not supposed to be wearing that suit after ward round has finished. Anyway, it's bang-up time now, so off you fuck." Tony glanced at the nurse momentarily, and I thought I saw the mildest trace of anger flash across his face, but then he wearily complied and—with a dramatic sigh—fucked off as requested in the direction of the patients' rooms.

My overworked brain labored through this new information before assembling the conclusion that Tony was not, in fact, a psychiatrist. Not only was he not a psychiatrist, he was a patient with an extensive history of conning and manipulating others, who was apparently also very effective at looking just like a psychiatrist. I began to think that even my elevated concerns about cocking up were not even close to high enough.

Tony was a relative exception to most of the psychopaths I've met because his early life didn't, on the face of it, sound destitute or abusive. Unlike Paul, he hadn't been born into the kind of criminal life where violence was a necessary part of growing up; and unlike a depressingly large proportion of the other patients I worked with, he hadn't wanted for food or been physically or sexually abused as a child. Instead, Tony's upbringing featured many far more insidious forms of abuse or perversion that it took me a long time to really understand, and I didn't really get it until I had a chance to talk about him with a senior clinician in another service who happened to have worked with him before. So although Tony could be a pompous ass, so much so that occasionally his care team took a kind of vicarious pleasure in watching him squirm under the predatory gaze of the other criminal psychopaths on the ward, I couldn't help sometimes but feel sorry for him. When I learned more about his family life in the following years, this feeling intensified and I often found myself relieved when he did something utterly shitty to one of the patients or reduced a nurse to tears: it helped to remind me that I was dealing with someone who was capable of absolutely terrible behavior and the most astonishing sexism.

Just as Paul's father had taught him almost everything he knew about violence, crime and aggression, Tony's dad had been an archetypal con man: a Frank Abagnale from *Catch Me If You Can,* drinking and philandering his way around the world, selling incredible things (the Pyramids! London Bridge!) to credulous people at literally unbelievable prices (yours for only £100,000!). His relationship with Tony's mother had been tense and quite insubstantial—after all, what use are a wife and child when you are a metropolitan salesman and playboy—and after a few years, when Tony was eight, he had simply disappeared. There was some suggestion that Tony's mother did not even know her sometime husband's real name, so talented was he at passing himself off as someone else. Time and Tony's inconsistent recall make it hard to be certain but nevertheless: glibness and superficial charm, multiple "marital-type" relationships and a propensity for conning others are classic hallmarks of a primary psychopath, the most genetically heritable variant. In other words, Tony's genes certainly had form.

After her husband's disappearance, Tony's bereft and lonely mother invested all her hopes and love into her son, making him in many respects a substitute for her lost husband. In what psychoanalysts would consider a classic case of narcissistic enmeshment,[1] Tony's mother became besotted with him and refused to give him punishment or sanctions, however obnoxious or extreme his behavior. I always wince inwardly when I read the *Viz* cartoon "Spoiled Bastard," as the titular character's mother endlessly permits all kinds of awful, self-centered behavior by her offspring on the basis that as a single mother this is what she has to do to show her love. But this is what Tony experienced, and the result was that he was completely unable to emotionally separate himself from his mother, both in terms of his love for her—I think that is what it was, although often this was indistinguishable from a kind of infinitely jealous indulgence—and in terms of his tendency to simply disregard any kind of boundary any other woman ever asserted for him. This made for a special kind of tension whenever he was allocated a female primary nurse, which was often given that more than 80 percent of nurses are women.

In hospital, Tony's behavior was a kind of extreme parody of a narcissistic and histrionic personality: both infuriating and yet oddly genial with a great talent for looking crestfallen, which is a lost art these days. Superficially, he was always charming and engaging; wishing everyone a good day, even—particularly—when we obviously weren't having one, and signing up for every optional activity that didn't involve physical exercise. Even when not hamming up the psychiatrist look, Tony was, relatively speaking, very well dressed, eschewing the lazy sportswear worn by the rest of the patient group in favor of a range of patterned shirts and corduroy trousers; he persisted in dressing in this fashion despite the objections of some staff and the ridicule of other patients, which took some gall when your peers included multiple murderers, drug kingpins, and serial killers.

When people mocked his posh clothes, Tony tended to respond with almost total indifference, when he even appeared to listen at all. With a deep sigh, he would respond, "Sticks and stones ..." or some other glib brush-off that was oddly effective at sending a clear message to the other patients: "I'm sure you think that's very funny, but I simply don't care what you think." Tony also had withering put-downs for staff members. One of his favorites being the evergreen, "I'll take that on board," which, at least the first time you heard it, communicated the chance he might actually be listening to what you were saying, and a superficial openness to change. The problem was, for anyone living or working with Tony, that the charm rapidly wore off at the second and third times you heard one of his glib responses or hollow compliments. "You're the only person here who ever listens to me," he once told me, "I feel I can be honest with you, but I just can't trust the other staff." Powerful stuff, perhaps, until I learned he had said the exact same thing to at least three other staff in the hospital.

Tony also stood out because he had a wide vocabulary and could give a good impression of listening, but you quickly noticed that this "listening" was actually the ability to wait patiently for you to stop speaking so that he could speak more, apparently not having paid the slightest bit of attention to what you had said. Rather, he would pick up some key words from the conversation and dangle these in front of you to give the impression of being deeply interested, while actually serving his own agenda. I remember a conversation that went something like this:

"Good morning, Tony."

"Good morning to you, Mark. You know I was thinking about something you said yesterday about social anthropology?"

"Oh, really? I—"

"Yes, I was thinking about how superior that way of thinking is to the way the psychologists think around here. You know, we really are products of our social environments, aren't we?"

In this exchange, Tony was using something I had mentioned to him about culturally contextual ways of understanding mental illness and used it to leverage his long-standing beef about the way he had been, in his view, misunderstood and mistreated by psychologists and psychiatrists. Anything I said was only of interest to him insofar as it directly served his own interests and worldview. Now you might be thinking, "Oh well, that reminds me of my friend/father/uncle/myself," and I know that all of us tend to select information that supports our worldview. Imagine, though, if you did this without ever spending a moment to listen to someone else's opinions just out of courtesy. Imagine if you didn't even feel the need to acknowledge that they might be more interesting than you. This is the blessing and the curse of the psychopath: other people and their opinions aren't even worth investing courtesy into.

Another bizarre habit Tony had was describing situations of a wildly implausible nature and making continual reference to his family's considerable wealth and to his scholarship in the areas of genetics and ancestry, specifically of British monarchs. In one exchange that really did my head in, Tony once told me, quite soon after we met, that he had written a thirteen-volume set of biographies of kings of England from William the Conqueror to Richard II. I asked him if it had been published and he said that the manuscript was "with his publisher" and they were "waiting for the right time to release it."

What made this exchange so bizarre was that Tony was clearly lying. I knew he was lying, he presumably knew that I knew that he was lying, but I couldn't bring myself to challenge the lie. This was not because I was worried about Tony's response—I've found that primary psychopaths are remarkably hard to anger—but because there wasn't any point. If I'd challenged him on it, Tony would simply have amended his lie to keep up with my questioning. The conversation played out in my head:

"Can I read it?"

"No, as I've told you, unfortunately the manu-script is with the publisher, and they won't let me have a computer in here."

"Umm . . . but, how did you write an 800,000-word book if you didn't have a computer?"

"Well, I was allowed one in prison." (Unlikely but impossible for me to check.)

"How did you deal with the controversy about the accession of Queen Matilda in 1141?"

"Oh, such a minor character—I simply elected to write her out of existence."

Lies explained by technicalities of regulations and simple bad scholarship make for a tiresome and unsatisfying conversation that I just didn't want to have. So I never did get to the bottom of the history of British kings . . . but then I still haven't seen it available for sale in any bookshop. At the time, it was like we both accepted the lie of the book for the fiction it was but pretended that it was true just because, for me, challenging it was too much hard work. Again, there's something quite perverse about this and it reminds me in hindsight of the way that a well-known business in the United States refused to pay small invoices to suppliers by simply pretending that they weren't there: daring the supplier to launch a lawsuit, knowing that the cost of such an action would likely exceed the reward.

Hopefully you have got the impression of Tony as someone who was very frustrating to work with, but also that interactions with him could be thought-provoking and that it was very possible to learn something about yourself. Whether this was the limits of your patience with fellow humans, your energy to either challenge or live with obvious lies, or your ability to feel sympathy when the person you are speaking with is so terribly unsympathetic. However, a lot of these feelings changed when I learned how and why Tony had come into the criminal justice system in the first place.

It seemed that Tony had made it his objective in life to become a more effective version of his father, the international playboy con man. Fueled by emotional and financial support from his mother, Tony stylized himself just as his father had, establishing a network of companies selling fraudulent products and Ponzi schemes, and even established his own credit union for moving money around. It was difficult to establish from Tony exactly how successful these schemes were, but certainly by the time he was first imprisoned he had staff on his payroll and enough cash to finance a lavish lifestyle. Often, while at large in the community he would introduce himself as a South African businessman, the son of a diamond mining family, and given his curiously unplaceable accent and expensive clothing this would have seemed plausible.

However, in one part of his lifestyle Tony differed considerably from most psychopaths. Psychopathic men tend to inveigle themselves into highly unequal, "marital-type" relationships, usually taken to mean relationships lasting six months or more, where they are parasitic upon their would-be spouse for money and emotional support. Of course, most of these men are also serially unfaithful, but they will generally stick around as long as they can under the pretense of commitment. But Tony was different: perhaps because of his absolute commitment to his mother, he never spoke about ever having had a "real" relationship; instead, he had preferred casual sex with male sex workers. With his conspicuous apparent wealth, he would cruise the bars and gay red-light districts of UK cities and approach male sex workers he'd taken a liking to and offer them extra money for an overnight stay. Knowing the power imbalances present in any sex worker encounter, this must have been a difficult offer to resist: I almost think of Jack the Ripper offering grapes—almost an unimaginable luxury to nineteenth-century sex workers—to his victims to entice them in.

On the day of his index offense (that is, the crime for which he would go to prison), Tony picked up a young, male sex worker and brought him back to a hotel room. He offered him additional money for what he presented as "light BDSM," to which he agreed: but what Tony had in mind was a series of brutal, sadistic punishments not mentioned in the agreement, ranging from whipping to brutal sexual abuse. When the ordeal was finished, his victim bleeding, bruised, and unconscious, Tony left, dropping a check for the agreed amount—using his own credit union's checkbook—on the ground in the hotel room.

What happened next is the subject of some dispute but the version I heard from Tony's social worker is that the sex worker, after being released from the hospital the next day, went to cash the check only to find that it then bounced. Not, it turns out, because it was fraudulent—although that would not have surprised anyone involved—but rather because Tony had simply forgotten to pay money into the relevant account. Complacency, apathy, callousness, disinterest, or just a mistake: all possible interpretations and ones that Tony was never willing to shed any light on. The victim went to the police and was able to give a very detailed description of

Tony and his clothes, which were highly visible in the small Midlands town where Tony had chosen to commit his crime: he was arrested and charged within two weeks. The whole offense was so blatant, so flagrant in its abuse of the law and absolute contempt for sex workers, the police, and a society that would accept his crooked checks, that it often crossed my mind that maybe some part of Tony's unconscious wanted him to be caught. But perhaps his narcissistic fantasy had overtaken him to the point where he genuinely thought he was untouchable.

Tony was a one-off even among psychopaths. He had no history of violent convictions before his index offense, although of course the possibility remains open that he had many other victims who never went to the police or who simply fell into the 95 percent of sexual assault cases (or in 2018, 98 percent)[2] that never make it to prosecution. One of the other men in the hospital once referred to him as a "cellophane psychopath," a phrase that I have pondered for a long time since, but have taken to mean that Tony was all "primary" psychopath:

he wasn't really antisocial and he had no "street cred" or aggression to him. Rather, Tony's personality was like cellophane: a tissue thin, reflective mask that he could rip, change, or just dispose of depending on the situation. Getting to know "the true Tony" often felt impossible, as though a cellophane wrapping insulated him, making him slippery to the touch, and I think the other patients understood this.

Sometimes I wondered if Tony was even a psychopath at all, or just a very extreme version of a narcissist, someone with narcissistic personality disorder like Brian Blackwell. Blackwell was convicted in 2005 of murdering his parents after they discovered he was using their identities to build up tens of thousands in credit card debt in order to pass himself off as an international playboy. However, Blackwell's crime was far more simplistic in many ways: he was narcissistically wounded by his parents' uncovering of his fraud and destroyed them to remove the source of the wound. Something about Tony's offending felt more sadistic; as if it was reliving a much deeper, more perverse sense of injustice that was somehow re-creating his relationship with his parents: a mother who was submissive just as a sex worker could be paid to be, and a father who represented the endless wealth and potency Tony pretended to have. So when the cellophane was ripped, what truly lay underneath was not the suave cosmopolitan he presented, but something far darker; something that I don't think any of us, except his victims, were ever allowed to see.

CHAPTER FOUR

Jason, the Liar

My wife likes to keep Radio 6 Music on in the kitchen: it keeps us company in the morning when the kids wake us up before 7 and when we're cooking dinner later in the day, the playlist is sometimes even acceptable. It was a Sunday afternoon in 2014 and I was cleaning up after lunch. Some insipid indie track had wound to its conclusion and the BBC newscaster's reassuringly stentorian tones came on with the day's stories.

"A British man has been found guilty in Italy of murder and attempted murder following a three-week crime spree in early 2013."

For some reason this tragic but not exceptional piece of news piqued my interest. "Jason Marshall," intoned the newsreader, "was sentenced to fourteen years by an Italian court for the murder of a sixty-seven-year-old Italian man . . ."

Wait a moment, I thought: *Jason Marshall?* I know that name . . . yes, he was the guy that absconded from the hospital I worked in a few years back. Wasn't he supposed to be low risk? How could this have happened?

I am going to take a different approach in this chapter and talk about Jason Marshall's case from outside my own experience; one where the information is freely available in the public domain for anyone to review. In this respect, this puts me in the reader's shoes in following the trail of evidence to think about whether a story widely reported in the media might represent a case of psychopathic disorder. As you will see, often there are contradictory details and pieces of information that suggest different possible explanations for someone's behavior, and some pieces of information don't seem to make sense in any context. This is entirely normal, even—or perhaps especially—for a forensic psychiatrist or psychologist. Very often these pro-

fessionals draw conclusions on a "balance of probabilities" rather than outright certainties.

I want to describe this case specifically because
it makes an interesting counterpoint to Paul's
and Tony's stories. These were two men who personified key aspects of the criminal psychopath: a
violent, manipulative bully who used the threat
of violence to intimidate and control others, and
a superficially charming and well-presented yet
deeply sadistic fraudster who believed everyone
was a plaything for the realization of his infan-
tile fantasies. This chapter brings to light an aspect of psychopathy that is key but has so far been
discussed only tangentially: pathological lying. The
case of Jason Marshall demonstrates how this trait
makes psychopaths so difficult to work with and
estimating their dangerousness such a challenge.
Sometimes they appear to wear so many masks—so
many identities, so many lies, so many primitive
desires. Marshall used lies to construct an identity that justified and excused his behavior; reject-
ing and revising them when convenient to the point
where the reality was impossible to discern.

Jason Marshall was born in 1989 in East Ham, an area of east London that at the time was one of the most deprived areas in all of Europe. His story sounds depressingly familiar to me, having met a lot of men in prisons and secure hospitals: his parents were heroin addicts and when Marshall was aged ten they were convicted of drug-related crimes and sent to prison. There is not a lot of reliable information about his next few years, although Marshall has given accounts that suggest he moved to Southend, the coastal Essex town, and as a teenager worked as a male escort, usually for older men. Around this time, bereft of clear role models and in and out of contact with the care system, he has also said he started to use fancy dress costumes to pose as people in positions of authority: police officers, air cadets, park attendants, and, perhaps most worryingly, a nurse.

Impersonation and fraud, such as we saw Tony engage in during the previous chapter, are aspects of "primary" psychopathy. Usually this impersonation serves a clear material purpose for the psychopath, whether that is to obtain money or favors. In Marshall's case it is not immediately clear why he assumed these multiple identities. Sometimes he would board trains posing as a member of the British Transport Police and issue bogus fines to people without tickets, and once he stole police radios from a station when in costume, but there is no indication that he ever collected the fake fines or obtained any material benefit from his actions. Perhaps he simply liked the sense of control that came from playing these socially powerful roles, intimidating other people from a position of strength.

In 2006, Jason's behavior became known to the police. He had brought a "sniffer dog" with him while checking fines on the Tube, and London Underground officials had become suspicious because the dog was a Yorkshire terrier—a small and somewhat delicate breed never used in professional work. Marshall was arrested and convicted of robbery, impersonating a police officer, and possession of an air rifle in a public place. He did not do well in prison, deliberately harming himself, and in 2008 he was transferred to a medium-security hospital—that is, a psychiatric hospital with only one gate from which unauthorized entry or departure is nearly impossible—for treatment for personality disorder. After two years he was given unescorted leave, which is usually a positive sign that treatment is progressing. However, a few weeks into the privilege he failed to return from an unescorted trip. Medium-security regulations meant that the police had to be informed, and Marshall was returned to prison within a few weeks to serve out the remainder of his sentence.

The *Hackney Gazette*, the secure unit's local paper, had something of a "20/20 hindsight epiphany" after one of his subsequent, serious convictions, in 2017. They alleged failings in management, claiming that the service treating him had been ineffective. Why, they said, wasn't this case of a convicted man absconding from a secure hospital service for psychopaths taken more seriously? Or, more directly: why did nobody see what was coming after this?

The answer to this is a complicated one and it goes beyond the issue of psychopathy into how we understand the "risk" of reoffending in criminology and forensic psychology. Essentially, reoffending risk is all about rehabilitation: about seeing how effectively someone's past crimes can be rehabilitated to prevent future crimes. At high levels of risk, where crimes are more serious or rehabilitation has failed previously, more precaution is taken because the stakes are higher: but at low levels of risk, especially where a convict has a short offending history, all the models and algorithms suggest the likelihood of reconviction is low. Since around 24 percent of mental health service users have a criminal record,[1] and nearly a fifth of people in the United States have a mental disorder,[2] the implications of trying to simply treat everyone with a conviction as high risk are massive: over 2.5 million beds would be needed. This means that distinctions need to be made, and in Marshall's case, the judgment of the Ministry of Justice was that the number and severity of his offenses would classify him as low risk by just about any standard, meaning he could serve out his sentence in prison and there would be no justification for a further expensive intervention such as hospitalization.

The problem was that—as one former nurse working for the service speaking to the *Gazette* put it, again with the glorious clarity of hindsight— "[i]t was the return to prison that caused [Marshall] to disappear into the system, and his risk to the public to be lost." Marshall was picked up by the police and was back in prison within three weeks, where he finished his sentence and was released to the community. Of course, what nobody up to this point had realized was how deep and dark his fantasy life truly was, and how the impersonations and elaborate costumes were just that: a dress rehearsal for what was to come.

After his release from prison in 2010, Marshall did not cope well with life in the community. He started drinking and using drugs heavily: a risky combination especially mixed with the psychiatric medication he was already taking. There was a brief period of stability around the London Olympics of 2012, where he was given a regular job as a street cleaner by Newham Council; but after the Olympic hubbub subsided and the cleanup was done, Marshall was made redundant and apparently began to abuse substances even more heavily than before. However, there were no more convictions, so nobody—police, professionals, nor the press—had any inkling of what was about to happen.

It was in early February 2013 when the neighbors of Umberto Gismondi heard loud thumps and screams coming from his flat in Rome. They rushed over to find the fifty-five-year-old man severely bruised and covered in blood, only repeating the name "Jason Marshall" over and over. When the ambulance arrived, the medics found he had been tied up, gagged, beaten, sprayed with pepper spray, and partially suffocated with a pillow. It was possibly a robbery or could have been—since the attacker had been interrupted—something more insidious. The police attending the scene were confused: why would an Italian victim be giving a British-sounding name? And if indeed the attacker was British, how could someone capable of such a serious assault not have been identified by the British police and highlighted as a risk when he came into Italy?

Italian police checking Gismondi's phone found that he had been exchanging messages with someone named "Gabriel" over the Badoo social networking app, which was a popular dating site, particularly for gay men, before Grindr and Tinder colonized the market. The police reasoned that "Gabriel" and "Jason Marshall" must be related, so used the signal from "Gabriel's" mobile phone through the Badoo app to track him to a bus in central Rome.

Once Marshall was in custody, police realized that an unsolved murder case from January 26, just four weeks prior to his arrest, had some remarkable similarities to the attack on Gismondi.

Vincenzo Iale, a sixty-seven-year-old Italian man living in Torvaianica, just south of Rome, had been found dead in his apartment having been strangled with electrical cord, stabbed dozens of times, then left to die, naked, in his own blood. The attacker had then taken Iale's cash card and used it to withdraw €2,000 from a cash machine;

the police believed he had been tortured to divulge the PIN. When police checked Iale's phone, they found details of an arranged meeting with "Gabriel" over the Badoo dating app. The police thought they might have found the hallmarks of a modus operandi (MO), that is, a "signature" method of committing crime, associated with a would-be serial killer. Marshall was charged with murder and attempted murder.

Details of the trial available in English are quite scant, but they sound chaotic. Marshall complained that the process was taking too long, breaching his human rights, and repeatedly interrupted proceedings to claim he was "the Archangel Gabriel, messenger of God" and "here to deliver a prophecy." He claimed a third party, a male prostitute called "Michael"—a congruently biblical choice of scapegoat—had murdered Iale in front of him. No evidence of this was offered to the court, however.

Marshall probably knew that delusional thinking about biblical characters can be characteristic of people with a psychotic illness, rather than psychopathy, and may also have known that Italian

law states that people with a mental illness are eligible for shorter sentences than those without. In
the case of murder, a life sentence can be imposed
without eligibility for parole for twenty-six years.
A psychiatrist appointed by the court suggested a
long list of diagnoses for Marshall: psychotic disorder, delusions, Asperger's syndrome, and borderline
personality disorder. In the end the judge partly
upheld the mental illness narrative and sentenced
Marshall to sixteen years in an Italian prison—
considerably below the maximum he could have imposed.

All of this is certainly strange and disturbing
enough. However, it wasn't until a year after Marshall's conviction for murder in Italy that the story
became darker yet. Peter Fasoli, a computer repair-
man living in Northolt, northwest London, had
been found dead by British police in his burned-
out apartment in January 2013. The fire brigade
had investigated at the time and concluded that
the fire had started on the bed, which was made of
highly flammable material. Likely it was started

due to a faulty light and was nothing beyond a tragic accident. As part of procedure, they referred the case to the Crown Prosecution Service, who also ruled the death as not suspicious and took no further action. It wasn't until after the conclusion of the inquiry, when his remaining possessions including his burned but functional laptop had been returned to his family, that his nephew, Christopher, discovered footage of a number of sexual encounters that Fasoli had recorded. Most of them were innocuous if somewhat surprising to his family, who had described him as a loner, but the final video, recorded on the night of the fire, must have been at once horrific and devastating to watch.

In the eight-hour video, images of which are now well-distributed on the internet, Jason Marshall is seen entering Fasoli's flat posing as an "undercover policeman," but actually wearing a T-shirt and a fake police badge and gun holster, and again calling himself Gabriel. The two chat for a while, with Marshall demanding cake, coffee, and classical music and describing his "dirty work" for

MI5. The two play this out as if it were a sexual fantasy, and it does seem to be that, until Marshall asks Fasoli to undress for his massage, at which point, perhaps mercifully, the laptop camera is deactivated. The audio continued to record. Marshall then mock "arrests" Fasoli, tying him up by the hands and feet and—with what now seems like terrible inevitability—gagging him. The recording suggests that this starts out as part of the game but rapidly turns dark, with Fasoli asking how he would know for sure whether this was "for real"; after that there are sounds of him choking, then of someone searching the apartment, spreading around what sounds like a liquid and finally the horrifying "click" of a lighter. Marshall had apparently murdered Fasoli in cold blood under the pretense of sex, then robbed him and set fire to the apartment to destroy the evidence; and he had gotten away with it for nearly two years, partly by fleeing to Italy using his victim's stolen money.

Presented with this new evidence the CPS reopened the inquiry, but because Marshall had no further UK record it wasn't until January 2017 that the link with the Iale and Gismondi attacks was made and a European arrest warrant was issued for Marshall's return to the UK to be tried for Peter Fasoli's murder. Again, when this case came to trial in July 2017, there was little to help us understand Marshall's motives. Contradicting evidence given in Rome, Marshall said that he had been so far under the influence of drink and drugs that he did not remember any of the attack. When the prosecutor asked him why he could remember the Iale murder, he responded that his Italian lawyer had told him not to use this defense as it was a poor one and he should come up with something better. Eventually in Italy he had chosen to rely on "as if" dream diaries from his court-ordered psychiatry sessions, where he had told a court psychiatrist, in an O. J. Simpson–like way, how he would have committed a murder. Under oath in the British court, Marshall claimed that "I wasn't under oath in the Italian court, and when I swear an oath to God I will never lie, I would rather die," which to me achieves the remarkable feat of mocking both the British and Italian legal systems at the same time.

At sentencing, the judge was predictably excoriating of the police and CPS decision not to thoroughly investigate the fire in Fasoli's flat and also to follow due diligence in checking the dead person's social media accounts, which would of course have revealed his planned visitor that evening. Recognizing that he was dealing with a serial killer, the judge imposed upon Marshall a sentence of thirty-nine years to be served in a UK prison. As a British citizen, his time would be served consecutively with his Italian sentence, but would last much, much longer.

I have read a lot of disturbing accounts of assaults, stabbings, murders, and rapes in the course of my work, but there is something uniquely distasteful about Marshall's offending against vulnerable older men. Part of this, I think, is that he was so callous about his responsibility: he claimed to have forgotten the crimes under the influence of drugs. This can happen when people commit crimes so terrible that they have "traumatized" themselves into amnesia, but Marshall's were not random acts of rage: they were carefully planned and effectively executed murders and attempted murders. The final attack ended only when Marshall apparently selected a victim who was too powerful for him to overcome. People who are truly psychotic, those suffering from paranoid schizophrenia for example, are seldom so instrumental in their attacks and certainly not capable of the level of planning and theater (costumes, fake identities, sex games) inherent in Marshall's crimes. Since we are dealing with someone for whom fantasy and reality are unusually connected realms, and for whom telling the truth is not something necessary or even helpful, he probably views the rest of us as unworthy or unable of judging him, meaning any explanation he gives us will have to suffice. "I'll tell them what they deserve to hear."

Because we don't have access to Marshall's psychiatric files or a copy of his sentencing records, we should be cautious in describing him as a psychopath. Court reports described him as having a "psychopathic disorder" but this is sometimes used as an old British legal technical term for any disorder involving "abnormally aggressive or seriously irresponsible conduct,"[3] and we don't have a PCL-R or any other piece of firm evidence to substantiate him being a psychopath. Several psychiatric reports commissioned by the court at his UK trial have suggested he may have had a diagnosis of Asperger's syndrome: a term, no longer used, for a high-functioning form of autistic spectrum disorder, which has no links to criminal behavior. However, since Marshall was detained in a "severe personality disorder" unit rather than a specialist hospital for offenders with autism, it is likely that psychiatrists believed that a personality disorder, such as psychopathy or antisocial personality disorder, was the most plausible explanation for his offending behavior. The nature of Marshall's lying—consistent and apparently without shame, perspective, or remorse—has been shown to be incompatible with a diagnosis of autism. Children with autism show a high degree of what is called "semantic leakage"—that is to say, they may be able to tell a simple lie initially, but their subsequent defense of the lie will show obvious inconsistencies.[4] Pathological lying, on the other hand, of the type present in psychopaths, is very much about the ability to blend lies seamlessly into one another.

Just as Marshall was able to move from identity to identity, whether as a powerful MI5 operative, then a sex worker, then a serial killer, then someone who lost his memory, pathological lying conveys that the psychopath is simply unable to tell the truth for lying, to the point where the liar forgets what the actual truth is. Why might this be? The research evidence is still fairly threadbare, but neuroscientists think that lying is essentially a skill; one that you need to practice to become good at. Psychopaths find it easier to lie generally and "learn" how to lie more quickly;[5] we think this is because of the differences to the amygdala region of their brain, which is strongly related to "lying skill." An active amygdala in a non-psychopath goes into overdrive, sending out a lot of emotion-related signals, possibly shame. In a psychopath, however, the amygdala is underactive from the start and more quickly "learns" to give a more muted response to lying over time.[6] So, in Marshall's case, his early deception in presenting himself as someone he was not—a ticket inspector, policeman, or park attendant—eventually meant that he was able to assert any identity he wished with confidence, including spies and biblical figures.

For me, what sticks out about Jason Marshall's case is not his diagnosis, or his possible psychopathy, but rather what he did: that he used people's reliance on truth and honesty—something that, I hope, is still our default expectation of people— against them in such a ruthless way. For our societies to function, we must trust people in uniform to use their power fairly, we must trust medics to be appropriately qualified, and when we allow people to become intimate with us, we trust them not to abuse that intimacy or our vulnerability that comes with it. In the same way, any psychiatrist treating a patient will sooner or later have to trust them to make good decisions for themselves; and any court expects the accused—under oath or not—to tell their truth.

Whatever his motives, Jason Marshall exploited all this trust, whether his victims (and not just the men he killed), his psychiatrists, the police, or the courts, in a way that displayed nothing but absolute contempt for their gullibility. It is chilling to think about how any person could be so absolutely alienated from this fundamental social understanding; for me, it shows how people's absolute refusal to be accountable for their actions beckons the end of our civilization.

CHAPTER FIVE
Arthur, the Parasite

When I was a young boy, my dad, up to that point an academic with a respectable but not exceptional role at a redbrick university, was offered a position in the West Indies through the Commonwealth Secretariat, a government body that supports former British colonies with, among other things, expert policy input. My father thought this was the chance of a lifetime for his family as well as his career, so we all upped sticks and moved to the West Indies. If this sounds to you like an idyllic childhood full of sun, sea, and sand then you'd be right: it was paradise. Except for one thing: the place was full of bugs and spiders, a fair proportion of which have no problem biting humans. And I *hated* bugs and spiders even before we moved out there, a situation that the foot-long poisonous centipede trapped, still wriggling, in our kitchen window on the day we arrived did not much ameliorate. Still, I survived all of these hardships and after moving back to the UK, do still pluck up the courage to visit my parents out there occasionally.

Now I'm sure that my dislike of bugs is irrational, but every time I think I'm over it the Universe gives me just enough of a reminder not to give up on the bug-hate just yet. Case in point being just last year, when a family friend in the West Indies was cleaning his house and was bitten on the face by a brown recluse spider. This is a rare occurrence: recluse spiders are not indigenous to the Caribbean and are—as per the name—very reclusive by nature, but the wound had made him terribly sick and left a very nasty (if glamorous) scar on his face. I had never heard of anything like this happening before, so as a serious and committed arachnophobe immediately went about researching recluse bites on the internet. Of course, I was trying to ensure nothing like that could ever happen to me, right?

What I found out really surprised me as it went against some of my worst fears and preconceptions about spiders: recluses, like most spiders, are not capable of simply walking up and biting you, as their fangs can't break human skin. Rather, you must somehow apply counter-pressure to them that forces their fangs into your skin, say by stepping on them, or, in our friend's case, by slapping them as they are crawling away across your face, probably as fast as possible in order to get away from you. It occurred to me that, for every offender I have worked with like Paul (in chapter two), who seeks out trouble and seems to relish it, there is another one for whom the offense seems to be a sort of "perfect storm" of difficult circumstances combined with very, very bad luck: like a kind of social counter-pressure.

My memory has no better illustration of this than Arthur. In many respects I believe that Arthur sought to avoid trouble wherever he could. In fact, I think that perennially avoiding everything— responsibility, accountability, maturity—that would normally be expected to keep him out of trouble seemed to have the opposite effect in his case. Nature abhors a vacuum, perhaps.

I first met Arthur in prison very shortly after starting my first job there, while I was still wondering if Paul was out to help me or destroy me. Unlike with Paul, however, I can scarcely recall my early interactions with Arthur; I just know I must have met him because I have the notes from a case meeting where both our names are clearly listed. Although I can remember the meeting and the attending staff, I don't remember Arthur being there at all. I don't think he can have said much, if anything. If he did, I can't remember his voice, whether it was high or low, fast or slow, baritone or alto. He was the essence of non-remarkability.

Perhaps because of that, the prospect of writing about Arthur did not initially fill me with much enthusiasm. When I decided that I wanted to write this chapter, I realized I had completely forgotten his real name and had to search through my notes to find it. In some respects, that should make writing about him straightforward: after all, Arthur is not someone whose (real) name or the details of his crime received much attention in the press. In fact, it's unlikely that anyone outside Arthur's family and the police and prison officers who dealt with his case has any idea who he is. Even in person, he is almost like a shadow personified: short, stick-thin and a shade of crepuscular gray that it doesn't quite look possible for a human being to be. If I saw him again today on the street, I don't think there is any chance I would recognize him, whereas I could pick out Paul or Tony in an instant. In other words, Arthur is barely there; and perhaps that is a very important thing to know in order to under-stand why he was so dangerous.

The Psychopathy Checklist contains a number of odd items, but at least one seems to feature a strong value judgment: "Parasitic Lifestyle," which is defined as: "An intentional, manipulative, selfish, and exploitative financial dependence on others as reflected in a lack of motivation, low self-discipline, and inability to begin or complete responsibilities." People who meet the criteria for this trait tend to be in relationships where they have carefully cho-sen friends or partners who can either be charmed or bullied into supporting all the patient's material needs, whether for money, food, drugs, booze, or even (in one case) designer clothes. The parasitic psychopath never feels any shame or remorse for this dependency, although they might fake it and promise to change just to keep the status quo, so it will continue indefinitely until they become bored, find a better mark for their parasitism or get themselves arrested.

Arthur was one of three children, having an older brother and sister. His parents had a troubled relationship and were heavy drug users, and although perhaps nothing in Arthur's history stated that he was abused, there is a suggestion that his siblings had a much worse time of it. Either way, when Arthur was ten his father left, permanently, and his brother and sister followed his cue, moving out of the family home and creating their own families and lives. This left Arthur alone with his mother, an arrangement that he found quite cozy; in fact a little too cozy, because after leaving school at sixteen Arthur showed no real interest in anything besides sitting around watching TV and prevailing on his mother to cook and clean for him. He wasn't a troublesome youth: he never got into any scrapes as far as I was aware, but neither did he really accomplish much in the way of life. He told me he had some friends that he would hang out with at the park, smoking cigarettes and occasionally playing football. But surely the point of friends is that we speak fondly of them? Arthur never even offered me a single name or adjective about any one of his friends.

Then, when Arthur was just seventeen, the unthinkable happened: his mother died very unexpectedly of a brain aneurysm. He had been completely dependent on her and was suddenly, completely, on his own. He had no job, few qualifications, and very little interest in anything. His brother offered to take him in on a short-term basis, so Arthur moved into a spare room in the house he shared with his girlfriend and tried to get a job so that he could contribute to the rent. For a while, this was successful: he got a job in a kitchen as a dishwasher and started paying some rent and occasionally buying some groceries. When

I spoke to Arthur about this, he said that he had lost the job after three months for showing up late to work too often, but he couldn't understand why this frustrated his brother so much. After all, he'd contributed to the rent already, hadn't he? The idea that rent is a constant expense didn't seem to occur to him, and neither did he seem much to care about the cost of shopping and cooking.

Signed on to unemployment benefits and sitting around the flat all day watching TV and drinking beer, it is not surprising that tensions between Arthur, his brother and—in particular—his brother's girlfriend started to escalate. Matters were made worse by the fact that the girlfriend had now become a fiancée, and they understandably wanted some space of their own. Again, Arthur was completely perplexed by this when I spoke to him about it. "I didn't cause no trouble around the place," he asserted, "just minded my own business." I don't know many couples in a position to be married who appreciate a family member colonizing their living space at all, let alone one who does not cook, go out, pay rent, or even shop with any regularity.

Eventually tensions boiled over and Arthur was given his marching orders: aged eighteen, he had to move out of his brother's house and find somewhere to live on his own. So, he packed a bag and left, but lacking any "real world" skills he wasn't able to navigate the process of getting himself into a public housing scheme, and he had no friends he knew well enough to put him up. Almost by default, Arthur became street homeless and started using drugs and drinking heavily. He also began to get in trouble with the police, racking up charges for petty crimes: drunk and disorderly, possession of drugs, and burglary. Eventually he got into a fight with someone over a drug debt and the police charged him with a more serious offense of actual bodily harm (ABH) and contacted his brother to bail him out. He reluctantly complied, but was upset by the ragged, shambling mess Arthur had become after six months on the street and brought him back into his flat to live with him and his now-wife.

However, none of the difficulties present in Arthur's previous stay had gone away, and now he

was drinking much more heavily and using cannabis and heroin whenever he could get them. This
made him unpredictable and quick to anger. Later,
working with Arthur in prison, I never quite knew
what was going to make him agitated and hostile,
and what he was just going to take in his stride.
He didn't flinch when I talked about his high score
on the psychopath test, but when I started talking
about the possibility of a schizoid personality disorder, a disorder that is mostly about someone's
disinterest in relationships and dislike of socializ-
ing, he became very agitated and we had to end
the session. I can only imagine what it was like
having Arthur live in your flat, with him malodor-
ous, grumpy, and frequently intoxicated.

Of course, this situation could not stand, and Arthur's new sister-in-law put her foot down: Arthur
had to go. The couple confronted him together and
offered to help him find public housing, but Arthur
was absolutely incandescent about being forced
out of a home he seemed to think he was entitled
to live in, although he had absolutely no financial

interest in it and contributed the bare minimum to the living environment. When he point-blank refused to leave, the argument became physical: a fight broke out between Arthur and his sister-in-law. Losing badly, Arthur ran to the kitchen and grabbed a kitchen knife, then made for his sister-in-law, whom he blamed entirely for trying to evict him and poisoning his brother against him. Then, as Arthur pulled back for a swing, he accidentally stabbed his brother in the thigh, nicking the femoral artery. Blood spurted out of the wound and his brother lost consciousness, and Arthur was literally a hair's breadth away from murdering his own kin. The ambulance crew arrived just in time to seal the wound and keep his brother from bleeding out. They were followed shortly by the police, and Arthur was jailed and charged with felony assault. The judge who tried the case noted the existing charge for ABH and recent convictions for petty crime in addition to the wounding, and for whatever reason saw someone whose risk seemed to be escalating rapidly. He imposed the new sentence of indefinite imprisonment for public protection, meaning Arthur could spend his life in prison.

For most people, this would be a life-destroying moment, but in Arthur's case I sometimes wondered if it was, in fact, the best thing that had ever happened to him. Arthur seemed to flourish in prison: he needed a great deal of structure to keep him out of trouble and needed catering to. He loved repetitive activities and wanted to stay out of everyone's way as much as possible. Unlike most of the prisoners I worked with, I don't think Arthur was an addict as such; he used drugs and drank because that was what the people around him did when he was homeless. He just wasn't creative enough to think up another pastime so went along with it. In prison, he never seemed to particularly miss drugs or his life on the outside, and he sometimes seemed to find the idea of release terrifying.

Once, later on in Arthur's sentence, I set up a meeting to discuss a risk assessment with him relating to his plans following discharge. This was a bit hopeful given that he had an indefinite sentence but is standard practice; what I didn't know was how brutalizing the whole experience was going to be for both of us.

It hadn't started well: there had been a miscommunication in the morning's timetable that had meant that Arthur had gone to the gym instead of his assessment meeting with me. Arthur loved the gym more than any other activity in prison and I knew he wasn't going to want to leave the session. However, Josie (who you may remember as the resolute psychologist from chapter two) had been absolutely clear that we were to notify the officers of any timetabling errors involving assessment sessions and have them corrected immediately. All the prison officers had a lot of respect for Josie, who had started out as an officer herself, so dropping her name tended to get things sorted out fairly quickly.

Arthur arrived ten minutes late for the session and understandably not in the best of moods, having been ripped away from his precious gym session to attend a meeting even I knew wasn't exactly the definition of urgency. When he walked in the room he was frowning so hard that the effect was like a villain from a child's cartoon when their secret plot has been foiled by a bungling hero. When combined with Arthur's regrettable tendency to keep a very narrow trimmed mustache with echoes of a German dictator, the overall effect was not of smoldering anger but camp comedy, which I doubt was his intention. He flopped into the chair opposite me and sulked. The officer accompanying him shrugged and nodded toward him as if to say, "Sorry, guv, this isn't my fault."

I sighed and opened my notepad.

"Hello, Arthur, thank you for coming here from the gym—"

"Yeah, well, I should be allowed to stay there, not fair to send someone to take me out once you've let me in there, is it? You're all the same, you lot, I—"

I interrupted. "Now, Arthur: the regulations say that these sessions take priority over everything else. You have a copy of the timetable too and you can clearly see this is what you had in for this morning. Now, I wonder why you didn't let the officers know that the gym session was a mistake."

(That wasn't really a question, I knew perfectly well why.)

"Hmph," responded Arthur, also apparently aware this was not a question.

"So, we're here today to talk about the future section of your risk assessment. Like I said last week, this is all about plans you have made for after your release. Let's start with—"

"You WHAT?!" Arthur's eyes were wide open, his pupils dilated. He looked absolutely terrified.

"Plans you have made for . . . after your release?" I ventured.

"I'm not fucking being released! Nobody told me about that, what the fuck do you mean?" His voice was about a full octave higher than usual.

"No, you're not being released, this is just about the fut—"

"You can't fucking release me! You don't have the right!" (He was definitely right on that count.)

"I'm sorry Arthur, I don't understand why you're upset. You're not going to be released soon, this is just forward-planning for when you are."

But Arthur wasn't listening to me anymore.

His "head was gone": a prison expression for when an offender gets overcome with emotion and isn't thinking anymore, just following the anger.

"You can't fucking do this to me! I knew it, I never should have trusted you all here. You're all trying to get me sent away, away back to Belmarsh where they wouldn't even let me have gym. You're all working for *him,* aren't you?"

The officer was staring at Arthur wide-eyed. Like most staff, I don't think he'd ever seen Arthur do anything more emotional than drink a cup of tea, and it was taking him a while to process this almost Jekyll-and-Hyde-like transformation. He wasn't going to be much help if Arthur decided to go for me, so I decided I had to calm things down.

"Working for who, Arthur?"

"Prince Philip of course: you all are. All of you cunts!"

I thought better of pointing out that he was technically correct as this was Her Majesty's Prison Service. I dimly remembered that Arthur had a deeply held paranoid belief that Prince Philip had personally recommended he be sent to prison even though he had done nothing wrong. As far as he was concerned, at least.

"Look, Arthur, we just need to discuss this assessment. This isn't about whether you get released or not, it's just about what you plan to do when you're back in the community on your own."

Every word of this was true, accurate and honest, and had Arthur's best interests in mind. It was also completely the wrong thing to say. Arthur got out of his chair, apparently with the intention of moving toward me, and at that moment the officer snapped out of his trance and his training kicked in. He sprang silently out of his chair and stood directly in front of Arthur, placing a large hand firmly on his shoulder.

"Come on now, Arthur, let's take a deep breath and sit back down, shall we?"

Arthur stared at him furiously for a second, then the realization this was a fight he did not want to pick dawned and he complied, sullenly. Completely confused by how a conversation about release could have nearly ended in an incident, I decided that we would end the session there. I asked the officer to take Arthur back to gym and figured Josie would be so interested to hear about Arthur's hidden emotional depths she wouldn't see this as a cop out.

I've no idea whether Arthur was standing up to gesticulate, shout more loudly, or to attack me; I feel very fortunate that the officer was so experienced as to know when to intervene, and with just the right level of assertion, so that we never had to find out. Looking back, I think that Arthur was so terrified of any discussion about release from prison that he just wanted to shut it down. However, I also think that I'd inadvertently put myself in a situation where I was re-creating the circumstances of Arthur's offense four years previously, which is never a good place to be.

Arthur's index offense, the reason he was in prison at the time, wasn't particularly unique in that the actual victim was not the original intended target of his anger, although that did add a tragic twist to his story. Rather, what was unique about Arthur was that, despite being a model prisoner in just about every respect, he was incapable of dealing with any complex emotion. He was at once absolutely dependent on the prison system and also completely unable to grasp that its purpose was not to provide him with a never-ending B&B stay with occasional waiter service (the prison was locked down once a month for training so staff would bring prisoners their meals to their cells), but rather to try to rehabilitate him.

I must confess that on this latter point we were rather lost. Working with Arthur over the next month, I could not find a single thing about life outside prison that would not be worse for him than the life he lived in prison: he was in every respect parasitic upon the prison system, just as he had been on his brother before and his mother before that. He was sad that his brother had been hurt but showed absolutely no remorse for attacking his sister-in-law, or empathy with their side of the situation that had led to the fight in the first place. Arthur also seemed to have changed the story of his offense around in his head so that it was the sister-in-law who had been holding the knife and stabbed his brother, contrary to the police report that had completely ruled out this version of events based on the location and angle of the stab wound.

After I had been working with Arthur for a couple of weeks, one of the prison physical education officers asked me if I would like to come along to the gym the next Friday. Arthur was going to be given an award, he said: apparently, he had completed a million miles on the "ergo," the rowing machine. At the time, he was one of only five people to have achieved this feat (another prisoner, John MacAvoy, made news headlines in 2016 when he set a world record for the longest distance rowed on an ergo in 24 hours—163 miles).[1] I was dumbstruck: I had thought of Arthur as a parasitic psychopath who lacked the capacity for remorse, but what psychopath has the patience to put in enough hours to end up in an elite human endurance club? Psychopaths are supposed to be impulsive, explosive: they wouldn't have the patience to apply themselves to such a target and nor should they be able to go through the long learning process of pain, punishment, and emotional reward.[2]

I thought about Arthur's case a lot, particularly about the incident with the risk assessment where he'd been unable to understand the idea of release being a hypothetical situation and thought I was trying to send him away from the prison. Over time, it occurred to me there might be another explanation for Arthur's behavior. Poor socialization, a very narrow range of interests, a literal mindset, inability to describe emotion, lack of empathy: these are all traits of high-functioning autistic spectrum disorder. The more time I spent with Arthur, and the more I read about this condition, I slowly became convinced that we had him all wrong; he was not a parasitic psychopath at all, rather he suffered from a disorder that was most likely genetic, and caused him to fundamentally lack interest in other people and socialization. His lack of empathy made him pretty much the opposite of a psychopath: someone who was almost permanently at risk of being manipulated. A prison full of psychopaths was no place for such a vulnerable man. However, the only way to definitively diagnose someone with high-functioning autism is to interview someone who would have known him as a child, since this is when autistic behavior is most prominent. Alternatively, we could find an expert in making these diagnoses in adults, but we were in a prison with only a team of mental health nurses to support prisoners' mental health.

Now as fate would have it, there was another prisoner on the wing who was behaving in a very rigid way. Derick (as he will be known) was engaged in a very odd, slightly perverse game with the prison officers where every morning, before he set off to work on the other side of the prison, he set up a row of chocolates in an apparently random order on the windowsill inside his cell. At that time there were concerns about prisoners getting access to mobile phones—BMW had just invented a phone that was about the size of a credit card, so room searches had increased in frequency, and of course the best time to search a prisoner's room is when they aren't there. So at least twice a week Derick would come back from his work to find that his chocolates had been moved from the meticulous arrangement he had placed them in, and he would

not be happy. Initially this was probably just clum-
siness on the behalf of the staff performing the
search, who didn't realize how apparently critical
the chocolates were to Derick's well-being; however, Derick started to bring this issue to the staff–
prisoner business meetings that I had the pleasure
of facilitating.

"I would just like to say that I have found that
my possessions have been tampered with again,"
Derick would say, voice faltering with high emotion.

To which another prisoner would reply, "Fuck
me ragged, not this shit again. Derick can't you just
put the fucking things away."

"No! These items are very important to me, they
make me feel safe and secure in this madhouse.
Why can't you understand that?"

One time, a senior officer, mustering every ounce
of his considerable patience, said, "Derick, we have
made every effort to ensure that property is not disturbed in the searches. But this is a prison, and
we don't determine the frequency of searches:
that's set by the governor on the basis of," the

senior officer's eyes scanned the room, seeking out Paul, our old friend from chapter two, "the presence of contraband in the prison."

Paul's Machiavellian schemes were still very much on the down-low at this point and he was entertaining himself by provoking prison staff with the fact of his simple existence and an array of dismissive facial expressions. True to form, Paul smirked at the assembled staff and prisoners.

Immune to the senior officer's reasonable explanation, and perhaps inflamed by Paul's provocative expression, Derick became even more agitated.

"I don't understand why you need to search the windowsills. I mean, sweets aren't banned and a windowsill is very easy to see, and empty apart from my very specific pattern. WHY IS IT SO HARD FOR YOU TO JUST LEAVE THEM ALONE?" Emotion spread quickly around the room.

"I can't fucking believe I'm sitting in a room arguing about chocolates," reflected another prisoner, previously silent in the meetings.

Then came the retort from another prisoner

again. "You can shut up, Staffy: we all know it's you who's been shitting in the showers every morning."

"That's fucking it, come here you c—" and at that point Staffy and his interlocuter were helped out of the room by the prison officers. The meeting was abandoned. Derick seemed oddly pleased.

Now Derick probably comes across as very sincerely wronged in this exchange, and perhaps he was, but something about it didn't quite gel with me. Derick and Arthur were about the same age but that was about the only way they were alike: Derick was a regular at the horticulture group and often tried out other groups too, "for fun." He loved engaging with the psychologists and got very bored and impatient whenever he had to give sustained attention to something. Worse still, there was something about the idea of arranging five very light sugary sweets, which the wind was probably as likely to disturb as a prison officer, that seemed to be asking for trouble, but with the absolute minimum of effort attached to it. I felt that this was a concerted attempt to provoke confrontation with the staff; one from which Derick would always come out looking like the wronged party. Nor could I understand how or why chocolates could have such emotional significance for anyone: where I'd seen obsessional "hoarding" behavior like this in the past, the hoarded objects had at least had some intrinsic value. A patient in a hospital I'd worked at before coming to the prison had hoarded pairs of Nike sneakers; another had kept vintage fountain pens: all things where the value was clear. Chocolates were easily replaced, had no specific value and were, as Derick said, absolutely legal in the prison, meaning that—conveniently perhaps—there could be no resolution to the situation if the staff were to "lose" the chocolates as Derick could just get more. For me, Derick was no Arthur, trapped in a world that was supposed to punish him. In fact, a lot of what I thought he was doing looked distinctly manipulative and perhaps even psychopathic.

My suspicion was that Derick was malingering, feigning his obsessive symptoms so that he had a righteous stick to beat the staff with and try to get transferred to a hospital, where he would have an easier time of it. However, one prisoner, especially Arthur, needing help was something that could be downplayed by the prison management, but if I could suggest that a psychiatrist also assess a menace like Derick, and perhaps arrange for him to be transferred alongside poor Arthur; well, that would be a result everyone could get behind.

Bringing the nurses onside with a heartfelt appeal on Arthur's behalf, we appealed to the governor about getting in an expert in autism to assess Derick and Arthur. A consultant psychiatrist and expert on autism was located and invited to the wing to review our men. Arthur could finally get the help he needed to find the life he never had and get out of prison, and Derick would be shown up as the shallow, psychopathic fraud he was and live out his jail time tormented by the chocolate removal group. That seemed to me like a just outcome.

It's rare that I get official documents from the Prison Service that I am enthusiastic about reading, and it was even rarer when I was in my late twenties. But on this occasion, I set aside time to read through the psychiatrist's report carefully, word for word. Derick's case was discussed first, and the psychiatrist had given a long narrative about his disturbed family life, inability to relate to other people, and need for routine and ritual. In the conclusion, to my great surprise, he concluded that Derick was "terribly ill-suited to a prison environment where his condition will only worsen" and "must be transferred at the earliest convenience to my clinic where he can be given the specialist care he needs." *Huh*, I thought. *There's one born every minute.* Quickly though, my mind started to picture wing business meetings without a discussion of damnable chocolates, and I reasoned that I probably knew nothing about autism after all, and the psychiatrist expert probably had excellent judgment on such matters.

Then I read the section on Arthur, which I was a lot more invested in. It was meticulous, paraphrasing everything I had written in my assessment, including a beautiful section where the psychiatrist had measured the frequency of the nervous tic that Arthur developed when talking about his offending: 0.5 Hz, or one tic every two seconds. There was even a compliment on the thoroughness of my own assessment that made my cheeks prickle. However, it was the conclusion that really made my jaw drop. With it, the psychiatrist had fixed Arthur's fate: in his opinion, Arthur was a dangerous psychopath, who could not be helped by mental health services and should remain in prison for the rest of his sentence.

I couldn't have been more wrong.

I still have copies of these psychiatric reports and even with the benefit of over ten years of hindsight and multiple readings, I don't understand how the psychiatrist put together the same information into such a different picture to that which I had. For a long time, I thought that I must have been naive or ignorant in my understandings. Now, experience suggests that sometimes professionals working in mental health are just going to disagree about how they interpret what seem like solid facts. This is especially the case when they know that a lot is at stake in terms of protecting the public or controlling access to an expensive and precious resource like a forensic mental health clinic bed. However, I still get uncomfortable when I think about Arthur, on his rowing machine, totally dependent on the system for the rest of his life. The only consolation I have is that Arthur probably thinks this is all just fine, so long as interfering busybodies like me stay away from his case.

CHAPTER SIX

Danny, the Borderline

It was my first day on the brand-new assessment ward at the hospital, in a specialized unit for men with severe personality disorder. I was being escorted by Jack, the modern matron who was also a veteran of some thirty years of psychiatric inpatient nursing. He was a sort of intimidating cross between Antonio Banderas and *Monday Night Football* announcer Howard Cosell: good-looking but gruff and jaded, who said what he liked "and liked what he bloody well said." The ward was silent and a bit tense, as they tend to be when patients and staff are new and still trying to work things out, particularly how to avoid each other as effectively as possible. Jack was unfazed by this, presumably experiencing it every day, and being too large a personality not to overcome any silence with bravado and banter.

We approached a young man, who can't have been much past eighteen but had the pale, sallow complexion and red-raw eyes of someone who has already spent a lot of time in institutional care. He looked as though he might fall over from the breeze at any given moment, and it was at this moment that Jack adopted a boxer's stance and appeared to level a punch directly at the young man's head. For a split second all my paranoid fears reached a terrifying pitch, and I thought about how I would have to blow the whistle on a man and an institution I was just starting to developing some affection for; but the punch pulled up at the last moment and the young man collapsed in a fit of conspiratorial giggles. "What's up, Jack?" he said to my companion. I wasn't sure who was the butt of the joke, if there was a joke.

This was my first introduction to Danny. Later that day I heard that he'd been left unsupervised in a medical examination room for a moment, giving him just enough time to insert a glass catheter into his penis and smash it in half. A colleague described him as "a real heart-sink patient" and I wondered what this meant, although my heart was already breaking from this awful punishment he had chosen to inflict on himself.

In a sense, every patient who comes into a secure hospital is demoralizing. They have usually had very rough lives, surrounded by varying degrees of neglect, abuse, criminality, drug abuse and mental illness, and over time this has ground them down to the point where they have committed a crime serious enough for a judge or jury to doubt the sanity of the person responsible. In other words, the crime will be serious, and the story will be traumatic and depressing in an existential kind of way. However, when we work with men and women who have been both victims and perpetrators of violence and abuse there are two things that particularly invoke feelings of despair; these are innocence and hope.

When we see innocence in a serious offender, we also know that a huge chunk of that person's life and freedom has been lost over a moment of insanity. However, we also want to feel hope because it is far harder to give up on a young person in their early twenties than it is an "old lag" in their late fifties serving out their fifth, sixth, or tenth prison sentence. Put these two together and you have a heart-sink patient: you meet them and your heart sinks at their innocence; you read the case files about their offense and it sinks even further; and finally you watch them foil and sabotage every chance they have at rehabilitation, wasting all of their life away in institutions, and your heart is broken.

Danny came into the system young. His father had been highly abusive toward his mother and older brother before leaving the family for good when Danny was a small boy. His mother, who seemed like someone trying to make the absolute best of being dealt a terrible hand in life, had struggled with poor mental health, probably exacerbated by the physical abuse from her ex-husband

and later partners. On a visit to the hospital, Danny's brother revealed that, when Danny was a baby, their mother had stored him in a drawer in the desk in the house to hide him from his father's wrath (although when Danny confronted her over this later she flatly denied it). When Danny was eight his mother was judged unable to care for him and Danny was taken into foster care.

Foster care is a difficult place for a young child, irrespective of the hardships they may have faced at home. Foster parents are very varied in their approaches to raising the children they take in, but the better ones will recognize their own limits and quickly return truly disruptive kids into social care. Danny had a safe initial placement but with a very large family, who had two of their own children and four other foster kids. Clearly the parents were very good at raising healthy children, but what they did not do was closely monitor what the kids got up to. Danny and his siblings would frequently go out around the town, searching for old buildings to play in, and sometimes steal or set fires. Once the kids, together with some friends, found a warehouse on the edge of town and went clambering around it. Danny was small and spry and found a way to climb up into the rafters of the building. Someone, Danny doesn't remember who, set a fire in the ground floor and the old, dry timbers quickly caught fire, trapping him upstairs. Fortunately, someone in the group noticed Danny was unaccounted for and called the fire brigade before running away. The firefighters rescued him with nothing more than some minor smoke inhalation, but that was the end of his first relatively stable foster placement and he was taken into a care home. From that point on it was a chaotic series of foster placements, care homes, and increasing involvement with gangs, who provided him a place to make some semi-stable friendships. Eventually he was discharged from the care system at sixteen with some minor offenses already on his police record, mainly low-level involvement in gang-related drug-dealing.

Trying to predict what this kind of diffuse, disrupted life will do to a young adult's personality is an alchemical art, but in Danny's case it played out

with a kind of sick logic. Without a clear father figure, without his mother, and being passed around
foster parents and the care system, Danny never
really had a chance to figure out who he was. Confused about how to be a man and angry with his
missing mother for deserting him, even though she
was virtually helpless (young men always seem
to blame their mothers for the difficulties in their
lives so they can remain strong like their awful,
abusive fathers, identifying with the aggressors in
their life),[1] Danny found the transition to adulthood extremely difficult. He tended to turn his
rage and confusion inward, harming himself with
razors and knives and leaving terrifying scars—
some of them on his face—that intimidated others
and pushed them even further away. From what
I could work out, even the gang leaders began to
avoid him, presumably finding him too unstable
and unpredictable for any serious work.

Identity confusion, emotional dysregulation,
impulsive unpredictability, and inwardly directed
anger are often considered to be the core traits of a

psychiatric condition called borderline personality disorder. Unlike psychopathy, it is formally recognized in the American Psychiatric Association's DSM. Also unlike psychopathy, borderline personality is generally found to be more common in women than in men,[2] and there are many aspects of the disorder that seem incompatible with most of the key traits of psychopathic disorder. How can someone who does not care about others' perceptions of them be agonized by a lack of identity? How can a psychopath's callous unemotionality be compatible with emotional dysregulation? The short answer, of course, is that it can't, and the reason that someone like Danny can be a "borderline psychopath" is more about the psychopath test, the PCL-R, than any real, separate disorder. Because more than half of the items in the test are about impulsivity and antisociality, some traits of psychopathy can coexist with borderline personality disorder to a high enough degree to give someone the diagnosis of "psychopath," although they won't have some of the most core traits of the disorder. So, while the idea of a narcissistic borderline makes little sense, Danny's rage, fragility, and absorption with his self-loathing did make him curiously dispassionate to, even callous about, the pain he inflicted on others.

Into this confused, angry young man's life came the Church of England, when a local vicar took a special interest in Danny. The church offered Danny some stability in a life otherwise dominated by chaos, and something approaching stability, rather like a gang. The vicar seemed unperturbed by Danny's extreme appearance, and they spoke regularly about faith and religion—even a life as a clergyman. I believe that Danny found something fundamentally important in these conversations: he sought to re-create this with many of the other religious leaders who worked at the hospital, deciding at various times to convert to Islam, Wicca, and Satanism.

The fact that none of these stuck in hospital, however, might clue you in to the fact that it was in the community church that Danny's internalized chaos claimed its first serious victim. One of the

most difficult and persistent problems of working
with people with a diagnosis of borderline personality disorder is their hunger for identity, for something tangible to affix themselves to, so that they
can look in the mirror and finally recognize themselves. As professionals, we often fall into the trap
of trying to feed this bottomless hunger, of trying
to "fix" things, as if it is possible to find an identity on someone's behalf and fit it to them. In most
cases we fail. We cannot fill the void, and instead of
becoming heroes we are identified as failures and
ultimately rejected. This rejection can take many
forms, but perhaps there is something to the idea
that the stronger the hunger, the more ferocious the
response.

So it was with Danny: after some months attending church, helping out at events and having
long discussions with the vicar, something was
said that caused Danny to perceive a rejection. I
have no way of knowing exactly what this was, as
Danny didn't discuss his offense with anyone and
the details in his case files were scant. However,
from his interactions with the chaplain in the hos-

pital, as they gamely and bravely tried to support his transitions between different belief systems, I came to understand the story.

Matters of faith and spirituality are necessarily loaded with emotion and feeling. Rejection from a faith is a terrible blow to the ego; likely why excommunication used to be considered such an awful punishment before the Enlightenment. My suspicion is that Danny wanted unconsciously to "test" the vicar's commitment to him, to see if he was really another absent, untrustworthy father, and said something to try to provoke a rejection. Whether this was voicing curiosity about another religion, or—given Danny's taste for extreme actions and statements—possibly about Satanism, I don't know, but whatever it was, it was too much for the vicar and he angrily dismissed Danny. As the vicar turned to walk away, Danny produced a knife that he always carried with him and stabbed him in the back, puncturing a lung. Terrified of what he had done, Danny ran.

The vicar, although terribly injured, survived, called the police and Danny, who did not have either friends or trust from the criminal under-world to protect him, was quickly picked up and charged with attempted murder, later reduced to wounding with intent. This lesser offense still carries a potentially hefty sentence, and when Danny was convicted the judge took into account the nature of the attack—unprovoked, cold-blooded, attacking from behind—and sentenced him to ten years in prison.

Prison was not a good place for Danny, it is both boring and involves a lot of unsupervised alone time. He began to experiment with extreme ways of hurting himself, in particular searching for any means to emasculate himself, seemingly blaming his manhood for the terrible thing he had done. British prisons are tough places but prison staff know when they have met their match and applied for a hospital transfer, which meant that Danny would serve out his sentence in a secure hospital and would have to remain there until a psychiatrist deemed him safe enough to release. From the notes around his transfer, the psychiatrists assessing Danny had unusually few reservations about accepting him.

When I met Danny, the problem of self-harm was serious. He was not allowed anything that could be used to tie small ligatures as he would wrap these around his genitals to starve them of blood, so they'd drop off. As well as facial scarring, he had a persistent wound in his leg that he obsessively worried so it never fully healed, and that he could open up with a fingernail, producing large amounts of blood and pain virtually on demand. Most of the time his hospital room was an unusually sparse place as Danny proved able to turn the most mundane objects—compact discs, shoelaces, pens and pencils—against his body.

I found Danny easy to get on with at first, but the more time I spent with him the more difficult our interactions became. One period of seven days was particularly difficult: one Friday I was happily playing table football with him on the ward, but by Wednesday my notes say that I found myself experiencing him as "incredibly annoying" and as "having a negative effect on my interactions with other staff and patients"—he insisted on following me around and telling me repetitively about his semi-delusional religious beliefs. The following Friday his mental state had become so unstable that he had been placed in seclusion by the nursing staff.

Having never seen a secluded patient prior to that point, I felt compelled—perhaps partly voyeuristically, partly out of a grim sense of scientific duty—to investigate. Danny was sitting naked on the bed, with no mattress (he had apparently found a way to remove the threads from the plastic to use as tourniquets around his penis) and his genitals firmly clenched between his legs—whether this was to hide his dignity or to attempt to disguise his own masculinity from himself or others was not clear. He heard me talking to the duty nurse observing him from the corridor and, smiling, tried to look for me, but I couldn't bring myself to meet his gaze or let him know I had seen him like this. Inside the seclusion area I saw a cold, alien image, like David Bowie in Nicolas Roeg's *The Man Who Fell to Earth*. The walls were covered with blood, and Danny had daubed a series of largely meaningless words together with a collection of what looked like pagan symbols in a pentagrammic shape. This blood had been taken from the wound on the inside of his leg. There were splashes of blood all over the floor and the bed, but nothing else in the room whatsoever but a steady flow of staff coming to look at the patient, almost as if this was a piece of extreme performance art. This felt voyeuristic and inappropriate, but the duty nurse justified it to me, saying that they were all involved in the patient's care and therefore needed to understand what they were dealing with better. As someone watching the watchers, I almost felt doubly guilty for being involved in this; I also hadn't been working in institutions long enough to have built a thick skin.

The scene had been harrowing and the incident left its mark. I had recurring nightmares about blood and alien environments for some weeks afterward. My own interactions with Danny became very difficult following this experience, too; perhaps the hardest part being that Danny himself seemed completely unaffected by and dissociated from his behavior that day: he wanted to talk to me as if nothing had happened, and I couldn't bring myself to reciprocate, to separate the man from the blood painter in his lonely cell.

In many ways I learned more from Danny than any other patient: his actions had reordered the way I thought about psychopaths and patients in general. He had reminded me that I had to find a way to limit the empathy I felt with them: not because they were undeserving of it, but because the potential damage to my own state of mind was too great. I wondered if this was why I was warned about heart-sink patients; it wasn't that they were dangerous to us physically, but rather to our own mental states. After working with Danny I was forced at once to create stronger boundaries about myself, and to approach my interactions with patients and prisoners in a much more clinical, and I worried also less authentic, way.

Danny's case showed me how paper-thin the

line between psychopathy and insanity sometimes is. The distinction is a difficult and confusing one that comes very much from the unclear separation of disciplines between between psychiatry and psychology. It is not helped by the fact that "psychopathy" sounds similar to "psychosis," which is a term referring to severe and usually acute forms of mental illness that impair someone's ability to understand reality; and it is nearly indistinguishable from "psychopathology," which is a general term for any kind of disorder of the mind or brain. However, psychopathy is neither a mental illness nor a description of any kind of "general" state of mind. Rather it refers to a condition that we believe is partly genetically based and partly about the kind of environment we encounter as we grow up, that results in some areas of the brain underdeveloping, usually those that control our ability to recognize emotions such as fear or sadness in others, and our ability to make effective calculations about risk.

This means that psychopaths are not like people with psychosis, who have "too much" going on in their minds and lose contact with reality; nor are they suffering from a common or "neurotic" kind of mental disorder such as depression or anxiety. Instead, they have failed to develop important parts of their personality, including the abilities to form lasting relationships or to show the warmth toward others that we all rely on to navigate us through life. There's a particularly resonant moment in series two of *Killing Eve* where narcissistic magnate Aaron Peel describes Villanelle as "a void": it's an excellent characterization because it draws attention to the idea that a psychopath is missing very important abilities that we all take for granted. Without them they have to function on "best guesses" about people's reactions and how to mimic things like warmth and intimacy.

Danny hung on the most precarious of ledges between reality—albeit a warped kind of reality where emotions were always too hot, too intense, and overpowering—and psychosis, a condition where he didn't seem to be in contact with himself at all, and this would let him do unspeakable things to himself and other people. Literally, he was almost constantly on this borderline, which is where the term comes from.

I'm almost done with Danny's story but there is something of an epilogue to it. When I was finishing up my time at the hospital, Danny had seemed much more stable and almost at peace. He had expressed to one of his psychologists that his quest to emasculate himself came from a place of wanting to change his gender as he was uncomfortable being a man. I thought this made sense: it explained where his disgust with his genitalia came from, and perhaps his dissatisfaction with his life choices so far. Better still, a medical doctor specializing in gender reassignment surgery had met with Danny and thought him an "excellent candidate" for the surgery. On my last day, I found out that an appointment had been booked for a month's time where Danny would become a woman; a huge step for a young man and perhaps a braver one in the mid-2000s than it is today. All his clinical team were very supportive of the step.

Months later, I heard from a colleague that, just a week before the reassignment surgery, Danny had pulled out of the operation, saying he had been pushed into it by the consultant and it was all a "misunderstanding." I wasn't quite sure what to think about this: I had hoped that this surgery might have been the answer to Danny's problems, but I was wrong. I wondered how many more years of confusion he would suffer; whether he would ever find an identity he could stick with; and even if he did, whether this would be enough to get him re-leased before he was no longer a young man.

CHAPTER SEVEN

Angela, the Remorseless

When I had my first placement at one of Britain's three high-security mental hospitals, at the age of twenty-six, the personality disorder unit where I was based was a kind of "hospital within a hospital," to get to which you had to walk all the way through the main hospital, along the corridor off which all the specialist wards branched, including the intellectual disability wards and the women's service. I had been on the placement for only about three weeks and was walking past the women's wards when the door slammed open, a good deal harder than anyone's blood pressure in a high-security hospital, especially mine, would ideally have liked. The group of people I was walking with immediately flattened against the wall (which had a thick padded section in the middle) to maximize the thoroughfare and minimize our chances of being hit by flailing limbs. Out through the door backed a nurse, moving jerkily as if trying to catch a ball being thrown to him. He was shortly followed by a large, nearly naked woman, with smears of blood (her own? Another patient's? Someone else's?) on her skin, screaming incomprehensibly and lashing out in virtually every direction, with a clump of about six staff of all sexes, shapes, sizes, and grades (nursing uniforms were banned in 1992[1] so everyone wore plain clothes), desperately trying to get a hold of her. The flailing limbs and screeching noises made the restraint scenes in Nicolas Winding Refn's *Bronson* look like a Tom and Jerry caper: this was a matter of life and death.

"Shower time," muttered one of the nurses gnomically as the clump, having got a firm grip on the still-screaming, still-struggling, and still-bloody woman, marched past us toward the recreation area in the center of the hospital. I wasn't sure if this was an explanation or a destination.

I turned to give my best "What the fuck?" glance

to the person next to me: it was Johnny, a recently qualified clinical psychologist who I had met on induction a few weeks before.

"That's going to be my ward," he said, in a voice that made me think of a British Tommy about to go over the top.

I was shocked at what I had witnessed. Over time I came to think that prisons and secure hospitals are structured and operated in a way that seems to torment and antagonize female patients in the same way as it provides an odd kind of containment for men like Arthur. Where men become aggressive and "difficult" when they find institutions hard to cope with, this closed existence seems to cause female prisoners and patients to attack themselves; to injure and destroy their own bodies.[2] I have always found this much harder to deal with emotionally than the consequences of interpersonal violence; I think because with a case of "typical" physical violence the divide between victim and perpetrator is clear, but with self-harm the patient is at once perpetrator and victim, and it can be very difficult to reconcile your anger at the perpetrator part with your empathy with the victim part.

Perhaps the fact that women struggle to cope with incarceration isn't too surprising. Prisons and asylums are institutions designed by men, for men, and can seem dehumanizing enough even toward men. No thought has been paid to women's places in them, and it wasn't until 2003 that the U.S. Serious and Violent Offender Reentry Initiative (SVORI) for adult female offenders was introduced at a federal level.

The idea of a female psychopath seems to capture the imagination of writers and artists in a unique way. If the government estimated that there were only forty female criminal psychopaths in 2002 and two thousand male, then the literature looks a little skewed. The portrayal of Aileen Wuornos in *Monster, Killing Eve*'s Villanelle, or *Dangerous Liaisons'* Marquise de Merteuil are all enduring characters, with countless parallels in less well-known films, books, and TV shows: the female psychopath exists more concretely in our media than she does in reality. As I said in chapter one, we know so very little about real female psychopaths that it seems somewhat bizarre that so many writers should decide to take them on as characters.

There seem to be two ways to write a female psychopath in fiction. The most common approach is to keep the same emotional and interpersonal features of psychopathy that are present in men, but subtract the "messy" antisocial and lifestyle aspects (impulsivity, parasitism, general criminality) and replace them with a propensity to seek control of others through seduction and manipulation. The other approach, which I think is harder to nail because it goes against the grain of what we think women are, is to just write a woman as you would a male psychopath—a messy, brutal, remorseless criminal—and see how far you can get away with it. When Phoebe Waller-Bridge said that she'd used a murderer from Arizona, Angela Simpson, as part inspiration for the character of Villanelle, I was intrigued. The rarity of female psychopaths is one of the reasons I don't have much experience of working with them; but, frankly, the second reason is that I find them terrifying, much more so than men. Often that which we fear most also intrigues us, and so here I am.

I can see why Angela Simpson is a good case for an examination of a real-life female psychopath. Her crime was needlessly brutal and relentless, and for a while she gave a vast number of TV interviews where she almost seemed to revel in unveiling her callous lack of empathy and remorse for her crime to reporters. In many ways she comes across as a monster: the kind of killer that serial-killer obsessives would have collected books over had she not been caught so early in her spree.

Angela Simpson was already acquainted with a forty-six-year-old man named Terry Neely, a former convict who appeared to have taken a shine to her, perhaps a sexual attraction or perhaps, as one documentary speculated, because she was a strong woman who had strong negative beliefs about the police and their persecution of minorities.[3] Apparently to impress Simpson, Neely told her that while in prison he had snitched on a man he shared a cell with, and implied (seemingly without any basis) that he was also an informant for the police. This was the wrong thing to say, however, as Simpson had decided that snitches were absolutely at the top of her hit list, even ahead of sex offenders and the police.

Some days later, in August 2009, Neely ran into Simpson again, and she offered him drugs and sex if he came back to her apartment. Neely, a wheelchair user, complied, and Simpson persuaded him to leave his wheelchair outside the apartment, which as we shall see becomes significant later. Upon entering, though, he was tied to a chair in front of a mirror and then subjected to a horrifying two days of torture. Simpson repeatedly beat him unconscious with a tire iron and stabbed him more than fifty times with a variety of knives. She then extracted his teeth with pliers, and drove a three-inch nail into his skull using a hammer. Waking up the next morning, Simpson finally killed Neely by strangling him with a TV cable and then dismembered his body. She called her accomplice—a skinhead named Edward McFarland—and the two of them borrowed a neighbor's van to dump

Neely's remains in a garbage can outside a local church and set fire to it. Apparently, Simpson actually told the van owner—who was later called as a witness—that she had killed Neely and needed the van to dispose of the body.

Because this case is so much in the public domain, and because of the very "classical" way she presents as a psychopath, there are a few things about Angela's case that illustrate some very important points about psychopathy and human development. The questions I am really trying to answer here are: what makes a psychopath? And, what might be different about a real female psychopath?

Simpson's crime is not a particularly complex one, although it is on the more brutal side of killings as far as my experience goes. What is more complex is Simpson's forensic and developmental history: the details are sketchy and Simpson herself tells multiple, contradictory stories to different interviewers about her history, motivations, details about her offense, and even the number of her victims.

What we do know is that Simpson was born in 1975 in Phoenix, Arizona. Her childhood has been reported as being "chaotic," and she was repeatedly placed into foster care as a result of physical and sexual abuse within the family as a child;[4] Simpson describes being "hospitalized" from the age of ten for psychiatric issues. Perhaps as a result, she developed a drug habit[5] in her early adulthood. She had four children before her early thirties, but considering her drug problems, a court determined that they should live with their grandmother. To fund her drug addiction, Simpson turned to sex work, and as far as we know this was her primary source of income.

Why Simpson suddenly decided to turn from a drug-using sex worker, someone who was likely victimized by drug dealers and abusive clients, into a self-righteous "avenging angel" is not clear. What we do know is that in June 2009, aged thirty-three, she looked up a known sex offender in the area and, together with Edward McFarland, broke into the man's house, tied him up, beat him, and robbed his property, warning him that they would be back. The police did not initially connect Simpson to the crime.

In August 2009, three days after Neely last left his house, a local pastor was "awakened to the smell of burning flesh" outside his church. The fire brigade were called, and when they found human remains they notified the police. Although they could identify the victim, the police could find no evidence of who might have done this to him, and nor could they find Neely's wheelchair.

Shortly after this, Simpson was arrested and jailed for an armed robbery she had committed two months earlier, where she had tied up the victim—a convicted sex offender—and threatened him repeatedly. Figuring that the modus operandi in the two cases was similar and having spoken to the neighbor who had lent Simpson the van, the police checked Simpson's apartment. Sure enough, the missing wheelchair was outside, and inside they found enough evidence of Neely's blood to be sure that they had their killer. They charged Simpson with murder in the first degree (the most serious murder charge in the United States) and McFarland with aiding and abetting. Simpson "proudly" confessed to killing Neely to the police in an interview but pled not guilty in court, presumably to avoid the death penalty.

In the months between Simpson's arrest and her court case, she gave several interviews to local reporters, who visited her in jail, where she suggested that she did commit the crime and that she was glad she did it. I can't imagine her defense attorney's face on seeing some of this footage on national television as one of the primary conditions of the charge is that the killing is both "willful" and "premeditated," arguably both things that Simpson strongly evidenced in her appearances. It's these interviews that I think became the main basis of Simpson's celebrity, and the material that Phoebe Waller-Bridge described as "gold dust" when looking for inspiration as to how to characterize Villanelle.

One of the most revealing pieces of footage

relating to the case is a short section from an interview Simpson gave to a 3TV reporter in 2012—it's
the most popular hit for her name on Google. Right
toward the start of the interview, the reporter asks,
"Why did this man deserve to die? You claimed he
was a snitch, but . . ."

Simpson responds immediately, almost inter-
rupting: "Well, he told me he was a snitch, on many
occasions, but that doesn't matter. Why did you
guys want to kill me?"

"What?"

"[The city of] Phoenix wanted to kill me. What's
the difference? Everybody has a reason to kill. My
reason might not be good to you, but your reason
wasn't any good to me."

"Umm . . ." stumbles the reporter.

Although he is pursuing a deeply stupid line
of questioning—asking a psychopath for moral
reasoning about her victim—Simpson pounds the
reporter's argument into dust through a ferocious
pseudo-logic that plays on the moral equivalence
of murder and capital punishment. Surely the
reporter is there to interview a murderer who has

already shown her absolute lack of remorse in previous appearances: why go digging here? Is he surprised to find a woman who effectively stares him down like a man would, rather than give him "soft" answers that might placate the audience and make her appear more sympathetic? When the reporter continues with a prurient line of questioning about the offense ("What exactly happened over those three days?"), he gets a withering stare and, "What do you mean?" Simpson is mocking him, pushing the interviewer to describe the crime when it clearly makes him uncomfortable. However, in this respect Angela reminds me a lot of Paul: they both seem to want, consciously or otherwise, to see people squirm as they assume as much control as they can in the interview.

There are a few aspects of Simpson herself, if not her case, that I think are particularly interesting. For a variety of reasons, I think there is a high probability that Simpson is a psychopath. First, the court ordered two psychiatric evaluations during her pretrial hearings: had they found any evidence of severe mental illness, such as schizophrenia, she would have been referred to a specialist mental health court, but this did not happen. Psychopathy, as it is not listed as a mental disorder in the main diagnostic systems (although its common partner, antisocial personality disorder, is), is not usually recognized as a basis for an insanity defense, so the most likely outcome of the psych evaluation was either no disorder or psychopathy.

Second, Simpson has most of the features of primary psychopathy: she has no remorse for her crime and has a callous and unemotional attitude toward her victim; she is glib and superficial in her interviews, citing a poorly defined criminal code as the explanation for her offending ("snitches get stitches") when she has no extended criminal record that suggests she knows about policing or prison; she feels she is in some way "entitled" to take life, which displays considerable grandiosity in her worldview; and she is clearly given to antisocial behavior, breaking rules, taking illegal drugs, and being sexually promiscuous.

Notably lacking in this list is any indication that

she shares the characteristics of the most common fictitious female psychopaths I noted at the start of the chapter: she isn't particularly given to conning or manipulative behavior. McFarland, who helped her dispose of the body, quickly turned against her in court, suggesting no allegiance to, or belief in, Simpson and her crusade. In her interviews she made little attempt to charm and seemed to have little time for presenting herself in a positive light. She arguably manipulated Neely into coming to her apartment, but perhaps it would not be a difficult task to attract a loner with mobility issues and a criminal history into the flat of a woman known to engage in sex work.

What is most interesting, though, is how the perception of Simpson as a psychopath relates to what we perceive as "male" and "female" characteristics in society and how these translate into our mythology and cultural understandings of psychopathy and killers in general. The way Simpson acts challenges the idea of the "feminine" psychopath: rather, she presents herself in the same way as a male psychopath does. There are, for example, clear similarities with Ted Bundy's notorious "confession" videos from the late 1980s. Extensive and intense eye contact, an evident disinterest in emotionally engaging with the reporter's highly charged questions. Both Simpson and Bundy also have a simple, clear defense or rationalization for what they have done: Simpson thinks informants need to die and views her conviction as an unfortunate but unavoidable consequence of her righteous crusade; Bundy views himself as a victim of pornography use and sees this as a "plague" affecting young men in the United States. In both cases, two people in prison for life, Bundy awaiting his imminent execution, wrestle absolute control of the interview away from their interlocutor: they dictate their appearance in the eyes of the viewer, they use the interview to advance their view of the world and they never get emotional or distracted by the line of questioning or obvious appeals to emotion. The reporter asked Simpson about her children and she responded, simply, "I don't want to talk about my children."

In short, Angela Simpson presents with virtually the same spread of traits as a male psychopath: she is not a "gendered" psychopath. Nor can it be coincidence that Aileen Wuornos, the female killer probably most associated with psychopathy in women, presents in much the same way: an aggressive predator without conscience,[6] not a manipulator of others. Some research studies have found some differential patterns in the presentation of male and female psychopaths, where women are more deceitful and less antisocial overall,[7] but these also don't match up with the literary or popular stereotypes of the femme fatale. Both Wuornos and Simpson used their sexuality to some extent in their offending, but sexuality—or rather, the use of sexual desire and intimacy to control and manipulate—was central to Paul's case, as it was to Ted Bundy's.

In the interview for 3TV, Simpson is invited to dwell on the idea of whether her gender affects the way she is perceived. The interviewer asks:

"You're sort of an interesting character because, first of all . . . women don't commit crimes this heinous."

"Right."

"Usually this kind of crime is more the domain of men."

[Smiling] "That's unfortunate."

"You think more women should . . . ?"

"Oh yeah, equal opportunities, definitely." [Smirks]

Simpson is playing with the interviewer here, of course, but the "equal opportunities" comment is interesting. She seems to be saying that these kinds of stereotypes about women as incapable of remorseless, psychopathic crimes are invalid, almost as though she is making a case for more female serial killers. It's very likely that this is why Phoebe Waller-Bridge drew on these interviews in fleshing out the character of Villanelle in the *Killing Eve* series: to ask the question "what would a female psychopath be like if they were thrown into a male role." I think this juxtaposition is so powerful because it reminds us exactly how we expect women to behave onscreen: to be weak or contrite when they are violent, or to be a cynical "manipulator" psychopath, like the Marquise de

Merteuil, rather than an enforcer like Villanelle or any number of male hit man characters. Villanelle gets a license for callous, remorseless, even evil behavior that we accept and even applaud in male psychopaths such as Dexter, but one we haven't seen before in female characters.

There is another interesting question here about what a psychopath is "supposed" to be in society's eyes. Simpson's case seems to inspire, more than any of the other stories in this book, use of the word "evil" to describe her and her actions. Of course, the liberal use of this term may have something to do with the fact that she was a black woman from a poor neighborhood, whereas Jason Marshall, who was also "almost" a serial killer, is often depicted as confused and failed by the system. But can anyone be inherently "evil" and what would this mean?

The idea of "evil" is a major contributor to some of the more draconian ideas about how psychopaths are managed in criminal justice systems across the world, from near-permanent isolation in the U.S. supermax system to the indefinite confinement of the "long-stay" program in the Netherlands, where there is no maximum sentence and offenders can remain in custody for the rest of their lives. It's also wrongheaded as it confuses "amorality"—that is, being without a moral compass in the way a psychopath is—with "immorality," or being fundamentally wicked. Sure, it may be true that there are "evil" people in the world, and it may be that some of them are psychopaths; however it is not the case that all psychopaths are "evil," or even that they have learned very basic distinctions between "good" and "bad" that you and I take for granted. This is in part because their brains are not wired to learn in a similar way to a non-psychopath:[8] they are focused on satisfying their basic needs and whichever primitive (in the sense of almost childlike) desires they have developed during their infancy.

When considering Angela Simpson's case, my impression is that, feeling a failure as a mother and a provider, she was driven to find something within her life that she could view as "good." By terrorizing and taking the lives of men she then believed to be evil, who contributed to the bad things in her life by committing sexual abuse or informing on "good" criminals, she found a way to show herself that she was not a bad person. I think she probably saw herself as the opposite of a bad person: a kind of avenging angel. Perhaps this audacity—in a woman, of all things—was why the judge chose to sentence her to natural life in prison, plus an additional fourteen years: a unicorn sentence for a unicorn offender.

About six minutes into Simpson's famous 3TV interview, the reporter asks an interesting question, or at least one that has bothered me somewhat about the case given the police's flat denial of any involvement with her victim. He asks:

"That's what did it [for] him . . . the bragging about putting people in prison, people you knew?"

Simpson responds, "No, I didn't know any of them, no."

"Do you believe him? Do you think he was a snitch?"

"Well . . . 'oops' if he wasn't!"

CHAPTER EIGHT

Eddie, the Redeemed

It doesn't get much further away from the stereotypes than this. I've come to meet a psychopath, not in the safety of a hospital or a prison surrounded by burly guards, but in a house in a very normal north London street. Two small dogs caper around our feet while we drink very decent espresso from Eddie's espresso machine and eat cakes. Eddie tells stories, I tell stories: we laugh. We have an in-joke about why he is called "Sid." Eddie tells me about his past, about growing up in a dysfunctional and sometimes abusive family, about the people who have died because of his actions. I try to listen and be perceptive but fair in my questions. Sometimes I think Eddie perceives me to be a bit of a "right one"; sometimes, despite my best efforts, I think I am judging him for what he did many years ago. Still, it feels we both have a job to do here, and that is to understand how Eddie went from taking someone's life when in his twenties and spending time in a secure mental hospital to sipping espresso in domestic bliss. It's a complex story, full of anger, despair, and violence, but also in many ways the most powerful case in this book.

Working in services for severe personality disorder, it's an unfortunate fact of life that you will get used to having your heart broken by your clients, just as Danny did to me when I was very new to it all. A few years after working with him I did a very short piece of work with a charity that catered to men and women with severe psychotic disorders, such as schizophrenia. I was there for only a couple of weeks, but after I left I got a couple of lovely letters from clients thanking me for giving up my time to help them. I was absolutely taken aback: in fifteen years of work with personality-disordered offenders I had never had a single letter of thanks.

It's entirely possible I'm a dreadful person and an inept clinician, but I also think that, in the eyes of the people I've worked with who have become success stories, I am the last thing they want to think of.

Perhaps more important, though, I've seen how the system and the clients can fail each other terribly: men I've worked with have been sent back to prison because they aren't willing to change anything about themselves in therapy; others who make it all the way to the hospital gate (literally) only to sabotage their progress with a stupid decision and remain inside for another year or more. I've also worked with men who progressed through the system and were successfully discharged, but then reentered the system, usually by breaching the terms of their release, only for me to meet them again going the wrong way into more secure care as I moved down from high-security to medium-security work. Heart-sink, indeed.

I have been aware of Eddie's case for a long time, and we met once in person at a conference a few years back, but I'd never spent much time with him before today. I decided to approach him about being interviewed for this book because his former doctor, a brilliant forensic psychotherapist who supervised me for five years, always viewed Eddie as one of her greatest success stories. Eddie, she would say, just seemed to get the idea that changing yourself was not something anyone else could do for you: you had to take responsibility for what you had done and for the process of change before you could even begin. This sounds so easy, but it was this very step that over half of the men I worked with never seemed to "get": they always wanted to blame someone else for them ending up in prison or a secure hospital. Now Eddie isn't the only man I know to set his life straight, but he certainly had the highest hill to climb in order to achieve this, because when he was a younger man he did some terrible, scary things.

Eddie is quite an intimidating presence, even though he's in his fifties now and sometimes uses a cane to get around. He is a big man: tall and well-built, and his hands seem enormous, like a northern warrior from *Game of Thrones*. He is polite and extremely generous to me both with his time and his energy, but he has a directness to his speech and movement that makes you wonder what it's like to get on the wrong side of him. Sometimes he talks about feeling his temper rise when someone behaves badly in a queue on the street, but Eddie has made his mind up that losing control of his emotions is just not something that interests him anymore: he has moved on.

The story he has to tell of how he got to this place is a very instructive one, because it helps us to understand what can go so badly wrong in someone's life for them to end up being called a psychopath.

Eddie was born near the Docklands area of London in the 1960s. This wasn't a good time for the London docks: following the Blitz, when they were almost completely destroyed, they had a golden period of rebuilding and success, but eventually they were unable to support the massive container ships that now dominate international naval trade.

As a result, between 1960 and 1981 the docks were slowly demobilized and demolished, leaving behind local communities that had relied on them for jobs, social investment, and economic development.

Eddie's childhood and young adulthood was intimately connected to the docks, both through the work that went on there and the less salubrious aspects of dock life, including illegal goods, drugs, smuggling, and other petty crime. His biological father died when Eddie was very young, and his mother started another relationship soon after, which produced a younger half brother, Charlie, to go with Eddie and his older brother, Dan. Life around this time sounds fairly normal for Eddie and his brothers: his stepfather, Martin, was a bit of a wheeler-dealer and a ladies' man, but both parents were working and the kids were minded by their maternal grandmother. From the age of six or seven, Eddie described doing things with his friends and brothers that we might describe as "rascally"—playing "Knock down Ginger" (knocking on a house door and running away); sneaking a £20 note from Martin's wallet and going on spending sprees in London, leaving his mother to take the rap; stealing goodies like cream, cheese, and yogurt from the milk van when the milkman stopped to make deliveries in a high-rise block. Sometimes he'd get shouted at by his stepfather, but his behavior was nothing very unusual.

Things started to go awry for Eddie when he was ten. Sick of Martin's womanizing, Eddie's mum left him and found a new boyfriend. Initially charming to the whole family, once he had "got his feet under the table," as Eddie put it, he started to become far more domineering with his wife and stepchildren, physically abusing them and enforcing a tyrannical system of discipline that meant he was completely in control of family life. Eddie describes him being like a "sergeant major," constantly shouting and giving disciplinary beatings.

One time, Eddie came up the stairs in the house to find his new stepfather dragging his mother into the bedroom by the hair, something that upset him enough to pick up a knife from downstairs and come back to "do him." When he went into the bedroom, however, he saw them having sex, which confused and disgusted him. He was unsure whether this meant that everything was OK, but with the hindsight of an adult he is certain that his stepfather was raping his mother. He said that he always lived with the guilt of not doing anything, but at the same time felt betrayed that his mother allowed it to happen, even though she was probably just trying to survive.

Eddie's stepfather started to play mind games with the boys: Eddie recalled a particularly unnerving episode when he was thirteen where he woke up in the morning to find that the room he shared with Charlie was on fire. As he told me the story:

"The fire was all over the place, little fires here and there. My hands were all burned up and swollen from trying to get out of the room. All of a sudden, my stepfather comes running up the stairs, trying to get us out, like, 'Come on, come on!' My little brother was blamed for starting the fire, but he was only four or five at the time and I truly believe in my heart that it was my mother's husband—*that fucking thing*—who did it, just so he could be the hero."

I asked Eddie whether he thought that his stepfather intended to hurt them: he said no, but we kicked it around for a while, and Eddie said he thought perhaps this was a way of taking the children out of the picture: by setting a fire and ensuring the children would be blamed, he then had the ability to get the kids sent away so he could monopolize their mother. Whether this is true or not, that was exactly what happened: Dan was sent to his aunt's house and Eddie and Charlie were sent to live with Martin, where he stayed for a couple of years. Now fifteen, Eddie had decided to leave school, and Martin gave him a job working for his construction company. However, he was paid only £8 a day, less than a third the wage of the older workers, who made £25, which made Eddie feel exploited. Eddie's behavior began to worsen during this period—hardly surprising as his family was being broken apart—and he started to hang out with older boys, stealing cars and pinching goods from the containers in the docks that were often left unattended.

One day Eddie simply refused to go to work, with what sounds like steadfast teenage obstinacy. Martin's new wife shot him a look of contempt, and in response Eddie picked up the keys to Martin's car and drove off down the road. The police eventually caught up with him, so Eddie ditched the car in a supermarket car park and hid between two freezer units. However, in what was to become something of a recurring theme in Eddie's criminal life, there was a stroke of serious misfortune: an off-duty senior policeman happened to be doing his shopping, caught sight of him, and directed the uniformed bobbies to Eddie's hiding place. He was taken to the police station and the arresting officers found a gold bracelet, without any packing or receipt, in the glove compartment. The bracelet actually belonged to Martin, and although it was not completely legal—as no tax had been paid on it—it was not stolen. However the police assumed it was, and worked Eddie over about where it had been nicked from—Eddie observed dryly that the story concocted by the arresting officer, where Eddie's nonexistent girlfriend, who worked in a nonexistent jewelry shop, was handing him stolen gold bracelets to fence, would make a "decent book, maybe better than yours, Mark"—but after getting nothing out of him the police went to arrest Martin and put him in the cell next to Eddie.

Eventually one of them made a phone call to Eddie's uncle, who actually was a gold dealer, and he managed to concoct a plausible enough story to get both of them released. However, although Martin did not press charges over the car, he was not pleased with Eddie: "I'm too old for this shit. You'll have to go back to your mum's."

Back with his mum, Eddie returned to school briefly, but he was very affected by the breakup of his family and continued to engage in what he calls "skullduggery": hanging out at the docks, causing trouble, breaking into cars, and occasionally fencing stolen goods in a local pub that seemed to be a hive of black market sales. He had also started seeing a woman in her early twenties called Mary, who lived near the docks and who, according to

Eddie, had a reputation for "entertaining" school-boys in their late teens with sex and drugs. Eddie met Mary after making a prurient trip to her place with a friend, which from the way he put it sounds like something of a rite of passage for Docklands boys, but their relationship became closer than most.

This all changed quickly, however. One lunch-time Eddie and a group of six kids from his school went over to the high school next door and started causing mischief, tipping tables and drawing on the walls. As soon as a teacher from the school spotted them, they ran back to their own school, but the teacher followed them. The boys were made to do a lineup, and the teacher pointed out just Eddie as one of the trespassers: again, unlucky as he was one of the six trespassers. This was the 1970s, so it is possible that Eddie might have faced a caning for this (corporal punishment was outlawed in the UK in 1986), but Eddie told me that wasn't the reason for what happened next. Perhaps reminded of his abusive stepfather waggling his finger, Eddie lost his temper, "went a bit psycho" as he put it, and attacked the teacher, punching him and punching him, until two of his own teachers pulled him off. The teacher was unharmed; he seemed to know how to defend himself (perhaps this was a necessary qualification for working in an east London school at that time), but the police were called and arrested Eddie again. He was suspended from school and charged with actual bodily harm.

Eddie was sentenced to three months in a detention center (what would now be a young offenders' institution), which was difficult: he felt bullied by the staff, although no more than anyone else—"they were shitbags to everyone and we were treated like dogs," Eddie put it punchily—and got into several fights with the other inmates. However, he did make one friend, and they happened to be released on the same day.

On the day of his release, Eddie's mother made the train journey across the country to collect him. It was quite cold, so she had brought along his favorite coat, something he now recognizes as a lovely gesture. At the time, however, he was embarrassed to be seen to be a "mummy's boy" in front of his friend. After they made the journey back to London, rather than coming home with his mother, Eddie left her at the station and went straight to see Mary, the older woman by the dockside, leaving his mother distraught. "I was just thinking with my other fella," he put it.

He started smoking cannabis with Mary and taking diethylpropion, a weight-loss tablet similar to amphetamines that she had a regular supply of from the dockworkers. "I knew she was very promiscuous, but I was very needy . . . I needed to be attached to someone," Eddie told me. "I don't know if I maybe needed a family because mine was split up; there was a lot of confusion in my mind. I became infatuated with her and extremely jealous and extremely insecure: I was controlling, but I expected her to be faithful to me while I was out with other ladies. I was always terrible to her: I'd slap and punch and kick her, it was horrendous."

Eddie also started to take more to drinking, hanging out in the pub with his friends. Despite being only fifteen or sixteen at the time, the landlords took little notice: "We were cash-paying customers and could probably pass for eighteen most of the time."

If this sounds like a volatile situation—drugs, alcohol, jealousy, infidelity, domestic abuse—then it certainly ended dramatically, with Mary holding a large knife to Eddie during an argument in the kitchen. "Go on then, stick it in me," he remembered mocking her, not believing she would do it, but Eddie had miscalculated the seriousness of the situation, or perhaps Mary's instability, and she stabbed him in the abdomen. He had to be rushed to hospital for stitches, and although there was no lasting damage, that was the end of Eddie's first real relationship with a woman.

Often psychologists talk in quite general terms about "adverse childhood experiences" (ACEs) that can have consequences on a child's emotional and intellectual development as well as increasing their chances of being both victims and perpetrators of violent crime.[1] In Eddie's case, we have the detail we need to understand the impact of the abusive, controlling behavior his family suffered at the hands of his second stepfather. Murderously angry with his stepfather for abusing him and his brothers, and sexually dominating his mother, Eddie came to look for signs of this behavior in all the male authority figures he met, from Martin to the schoolteacher, while at the same time blaming his mother for bringing the abuser into his home and submitting to him. If this logic sounds flawed— after all, how could Eddie's mum have defended herself, let alone her sons, from a larger, aggressive man—this may be because of a psychological process called "identification with the aggressor" that I identified with Danny in chapter six. Eddie did not want to see himself as abused, and therefore weak by the standards of masculinity at the time, so despite hating him he came to act more like his stepfather—violent and controlling in relationships—and saw his mother as weak and culpable. He unconsciously edited out emotions and memories that suggested she was not complicit but helpless: being controlled, raped, and beaten by her partner. In Eddie's mind this was how women had to be: weak victims who were complicit in every beating they received.

His first relationship and heartbreak behind him, Eddie was back at his mum's house, still smoking cannabis and financing his habit by stealing from containers being stored at the docks. It wasn't long before he met another girl, Jeanne, and began another very intense relationship with her. After about nine months, when they were both seventeen, they discovered Jeanne was pregnant. Eddie's docks income wasn't stable or high, and he needed money to finance a family. His first port of call was to go back to Martin, who really seemed to have a soft spot for Eddie. Martin asked him, "Can you get out of bed in the morning?" and when Eddie promised him "yes" Martin offered to take him back on, forgiving the theft of his car. When Eddie asked about the pay, however, Martin's response was "£8 a day," the same rate he had always paid him and still a third of the rate of the older workers. Eddie took this extremely personally, as if he wasn't worth any more in Martin's eyes than he had been two years ago. As he described it to me, Eddie "lost the plot," punching Martin in the jaw and storming out. Perhaps to teach Eddie a lesson, Martin thought that it was a good idea to press civil charges against him, but he insisted on conducting his own prosecution, which rather backfired. When the judge asked Eddie why he'd hit the plaintiff, Eddie responded:

"Well he was only paying me eight pounds an hour."

"That's a reasonable rate for someone his age, your honor," responded Martin.

The judge nodded approval and looked at Eddie. Eddie searched his head for something to say.

"Yeah, well . . . what about the tax?" he said. "The tax you're meant to pay on the other guys?"

The judge looked at Martin, cocking his head. What about the tax, indeed?

Martin went rather pale and silent. The judge frowned.

"Case dismissed," he said.

With the child's birth coming ever closer, Eddie became desperate: with Jeanne he planned a confidence heist on a local jewelers. Eddie would walk in and ask to see some bracelets, then Jeanne would come in off the street and open the door long enough for Eddie to pick up the tray of bracelets and run out with them, making it appear like an opportunistic theft with no involvement from Jeanne. Unfortunately, this was not something out of *Ocean's Eleven*: a woman overheard what the two of them were planning outside the shop and secretly notified the staff. When Jeanne came in, the staff locked the door after her and called the police, who arrested both of them. Eddie pleaded guilty, which meant the police didn't press charges against Jeanne, but also meant that Eddie went back to prison, this time to a borstal—a kind of detention center with an emphasis on training and rehabilitation.

Eddie says he didn't mind the borstal so much, although he bullied the other inmates and kept getting involved in fights, but he remembers how he became obsessed with phoning his girlfriend, although the prison didn't have any official phone lines for prisoners:

"As I said to you, Mark, I was always needy, always clingy . . . and I was always on the phone to her. I used to go to the office and beg them to let me call her, because the separation was so intense, I needed to talk to her. They usually let me do that, but I used to tear the arse out of it, making phone call after phone call. After one visit, I came up to the office and asked to use the phone, but the officer just got out the phone log and showed me: call after call after call, in my name, to Jeanne. He said, 'No you can't.'

"So I picked a pen up off the desk and put it to my throat, and said, 'I'm going to do myself': I basically took myself hostage, you know, let me have a phone call or I'll do the loony thing."

Eddie chuckles about this, perhaps at the idea

of anyone threatening themselves with a pen, but although he got his phone call, the staff were not amused: they transferred him to a young offenders' institution with special provision for young men with psychiatric problems. He says there wasn't much in the way of support for mental illness, it wasn't a hospital and he saw a psychologist only once or twice, but it was one of the happier times in his life as the institution was well-stocked with amenities, including a pool table.

However, Jeanne wrote to Eddie when he was about two months from release saying that she was breaking up with him. Eddie says that he didn't make a big deal of this, that the staff took it far more seriously than he did, calling him into a meeting with two senior officers and the matron to solemnly disclose the news that he had been dumped. "I thought someone had died!" Eddie says to me.

He was duly released back to his mum's house and Jeanne brought the baby around to see him, but Eddie remembers, "I just didn't feel any connection

to her . . . like she wasn't really my baby or something. Jeanne said, 'Are you going to help me raise
this baby?' and I just said, 'No.'"

Jeanne had another boyfriend, one of the neighborhood boys, who Eddie really seems to like—
"I just respected him, you know? He was a lovely
guy."—which I think made him something of a
rarity as far as the men in Eddie's life went, and
they all agreed amicably that it was best if Jeanne
and her new partner raised the baby without Eddie's input. If this sounds a bit like a non-story, I
think that's the point: Eddie had really seemed to
respond well to the time on his own in the YOI,
and when he was clean and sober he was capable
of being the better man and making life decisions
that considered other people's feelings and the
greater good, rather than just his own satisfaction. I think this is what makes Eddie likable
despite all the bad choices he has made, and the
harm he has caused: I get the sense that he has
a moral compass, and that he would rather find
solutions that work out well for everyone. Unfortu-

nately, as a young man he was rarely sober enough for this moral reasoning to have a chance.

Nothing in Eddie's early life tended to last. Now aged nineteen he started another relationship with a woman his own age. Again, he started using drugs and drinking, again his girlfriend became pregnant, and again she ended up giving birth while Eddie was in prison. Eddie had gone out to a party with his male friends and taken a bunch of pills—he didn't know what they were, he'd just taken everything he'd been offered—and sexually assaulted a woman. He had been walking behind her on the way home, caught up and started a conversation with her. They'd approached a park and Eddie had suggested a "kiss and a cuddle" but she refused. Eddie had put his hand down her top and grabbed her breast. Eddie describes being furious with himself about this, and rightly so: it was a stupid, self-serving crime full of callous entitlement. Not only were convictions for sexual crimes in the 1980s around six times what they are today, but the girl he had attacked was part of the local community. When Eddie was drinking in the pub a few weeks later, her brothers and a group of their friends spotted him, attacked him, and then called the police. There had also been a witness: someone had seen Eddie assault the woman and seen her struggle and protest.

Now anyone who has been to prison themselves will attest that there is a very different life for those convicted of sex offenses from those with "normal" (that is to say, violent) offenses. There is an implicit hierarchy of crime, with robbers—in my experience, some of the most psychopathic offenders—at the top, followed by violent offenders, then sexual offenders against adults, then snitches or informers, and sexual offenders against children are at the very bottom. Modern jails in Britain usually operate a quasi-segregation system whereby "vulnerable prisoners" or "VPs," typically sex offenders plus those who are at risk of harm from other prisoners, are kept in separate wings where the risk against them can be managed. Eddie's previous visits to jail had been as a young offender serving time for theft or violence: an offender at the top of the heap. Now he was a young man in an adult jail for a sexual offense, right down at the bottom. He describes how, on his first reception to the adult prison, the orderlies were serving prisoners: when they asked him to state his index offense and sentence, he refused and they had assumed (correctly) that he was a sex offender and rushed him: five against one.

Scared and deeply ashamed of himself, Eddie took the option of a VP wing for a few weeks, where he began to try to make sense of it all. His solution, not the easiest one but probably the only way to keep himself as the "good guy" in his life story, was simply to start forcing himself to believe he simply hadn't done it:

"I was saying to myself every night, 'I never done it, I never done it.' Then when I went to sleep I'd keep hearing it, too: 'I never done it.' And I ended up believing it, to a certain extent. I decided to go back on the regular wing and told the governor; at the time they couldn't legally keep me on VP so off I went."

Of course, infected with this combination of toxic masculinity, self-delusion, and a regular supply of cannabis sourced from his brothers, who had set themselves up as dealers, Eddie's first order of business was to get revenge on the inmates who had attacked him at reception. He bided his time until he caught one of them alone in his cell with the door open, then charged in. Here's Eddie's account:

"We started having a punch-up, and I just bit onto his ear. The bell went off—someone must have heard the commotion—and the screws came in, lifted me up, and I'm there with my teeth still on his earhole. They said, 'You're gonna have to let go or we'll hit you with the truncheons,' so I let go and they carried me down the block. I got a week down the block, lost earnings, but then I got back on the wing and all the fellas [that attacked me] were coming up to me saying, 'Oh, it was nothing to do with me.' I'm not trying to give the impression I was really dangerous. I was scared, scared of talking to people, scared of interacting . . . but I *was* up for it, and they knew I was up for it; so they just got themselves shipped out."

I didn't get the impression here that Eddie was trying to puff himself up: I think he was a bit incredulous at the way his plan, namely "convince yourself you didn't assault that woman, and go after the guys that think you did so they can't tell anyone else," had worked out. It was almost like a perfect reinforcement of every violent, aggressive, guilt-denying, victim-blaming impulse Eddie had had inside. Having established himself as a top dog, Eddie went on to make good in the adult prison: he developed a good relationship with the officers, started a job in the kitchen (a coveted role, as food is perhaps the most important commodity in prison after contraband) and the attacks stopped. For a while. Of course, this being Eddie, it was only temporary: after a few months of relative peace, he tipped a tea urn over another prisoner who had taken umbrage at the way Eddie poured his cuppa, and off went Eddie to another prison.

I have met a lot of men like the young Eddie:

men for whom prison is not a quiet place to "do your bird and keep your head down" in the words of one lifer (who, ironically, was terrible at keeping his own advice and was constantly in segregation), but rather something between a Roman gladiatorial ring and an opportunity to get your own back against "the system." I do understand why Eddie himself was so angry with men in positions of power—from his biological father to his mother's third husband to the prison officers who allowed him to be shamed and assaulted in reception, they had let him down again and again. However, this grievance attitude to prison has a real danger that the prisoner becomes like Charles Salvador, a.k.a. Charles Bronson, the British robber who was originally sentenced to seven years in 1974 but has spent his entire life behind bars. Bronson is now serving a life sentence because of his repeated attacks on prison officers and prison property.

Prison is a hard place, no doubt: but it can get inside some angry young men's heads and become a far worse place than it is intended to be: an internal prison that they are forever trying to break out of while losing sight of what it means to be free. I was horrified to find out recently that a young man I worked with in the early 2000s, who had been given a five-year sentence for grievous bodily harm, was still in institutions: he had been transferred to a secure hospital and there caused so much damage and disturbance that the psychiatrists felt he was unsafe to release. Now in his fifties, he had recently had a stroke—although the hospital was moving to release him, he was quite frail and there are concerns that he might not be able to manage living in society again.

Fortunately, despite his transgressive behavior, Eddie managed to escape any further sanctions or prison time. When he was released after sixteen months inside, Eddie's life followed a pretty similar pattern to the previous time. Again, he met his new child, a boy, and made up with his girlfriend, but once again they agreed to go their separate ways and Eddie moved on to a new woman. Part of me wonders if maybe taking on the responsibilities of a father might have settled Eddie down a bit and got him away from drink, drugs, and crime, but then I think about how worryingly close the younger Eddie's controlling, aggressive behavior sometimes came to that of his stepfather. That part of me starts to worry for any child to be around such unpredictability, and perhaps this was just the way things had to be, as Eddie crashed from bad situation to worse situation.

To make money, Eddie had settled into a very lucrative job acting as a "hoister"—a professional shoplifter—of designer clothes from big department stores. He was, for once, making good money and was well-dressed. Then, Eddie and his girlfriend went out drinking and smoking, and on the way back from the pub they had a disagreement with a group of girls also walking down the street. Words were exchanged, and one of the girls ran off and returned with her father, a man Eddie knew from his days of boosting goods at the docks, together with his stepson, Jimmy, who was packing a knife, and started threatening Eddie.

Someone—he doesn't remember who—passed

Eddie a knife of his own, and he set off after the men down the street back to their house. The men closed the door in his face, to which Eddie responded by throwing a garden gnome through the window. The father and Jimmy came running out at Eddie, armed with a knife and a baseball bat respectively, and chased him back down the street. Then the unthinkable happened: Jimmy took a swing at Eddie, who ducked the blow and tripped, sending the hand holding his own knife flying out backward. Jimmy overbalanced, having missed, and fell chest-first onto the knife, which penetrated his heart. Suddenly, Eddie was responsible for the death of one of his childhood friends.

I don't know whether anyone would have been hurt that evening if Eddie had not tripped. The way he told it, it sounded like most of the evening was just regular bravado and posturing, and once again it was that extra bit of bad luck in a risky situation that turned Eddie into a killer. Although the prosecution initially argued for murder, there was no evidence to support that charge and the jury found Eddie guilty of manslaughter. He was given a five-year sentence.

I know from reading many newspaper articles about killers that the general public dislike feeling empathy for the perpetrator. In Eddie's case, though, it sounds as though the knowledge of what he had done—taken a life after a pointless argument—affected him terribly. He battled with it internally, trying to keep up the facade of a tough guy, of a psychopath who didn't care about what he'd done:

"There were times within my prison sentence when I felt quite happy to be in that category, 'I've taken someone's life,' like a chest-out thing. But when I let it come to me and thought about it and thought about it, it devastated me."

This sentence was not a good one for Eddie. He had started to develop psychotic symptoms consistent with post-traumatic stress disorder, probably worsened by the high-grade cannabis his brothers were still sending him. The combination of drugs and trauma led him to start experiencing delusional parasitosis: a condition where someone believes they are infested with insects or bugs, spiders in Eddie's case, which caused him to scratch his head and pull out his hair. Also, because of the drugs, he became known as a troublemaker within the prison and he was frequently in conflict with the officers. Eddie explains one incident:

"I was on one wing that was full of psychos, the nut-nut [psychiatric] wing. It's supposed to be a medical wing, but if you fuck up on the normal wing, they'd put you there, because it was horrific. One morning I was having a shave, and it was back in the day when you had to share the razors—they stored them in some solution, but it was still dangerous [for catching bloodborne infections].

"Anyway, I did half my face, and then I started getting all cut. So I went to the screw: 'Here, can I have a new blade, it's cutting me to bits, look,' and he just says, 'No you can't, you have to use that one.' I said, 'Come on, be fair; I've got a visit this afternoon,' but he just said, 'No.' So I said, 'All right, I'll just finish up with this one then,' and he said, 'No you won't; shaving's finished now.' So I walk out and I've only got half a beard. So they're pushing me down the landing, jostling me, and I just turn around and flobbed [spat] in one of their faces.

"That was it: I was dragged down the metal stairs, put in a solitary cell and had a pot of piss thrown over me, because it was back in the days when we still slopped out [until the 1990s, prisoners had to use buckets for urine and feces] and I was in there for three or four days."

At the end of this he was offered the chance to go to HMP Grendon, a therapeutic community that is a place where prisoners who want to change their lives can receive psychological treatment for their offending, but unfortunately Eddie had only a few months left to serve on his sentence and the community decided this wasn't long enough for him to do the work he needed. Perhaps they were right, but this meant that Eddie received only short-term, medical treatment for his symptoms: clunky and only partly effective antipsychotic medication. Then he was released without any further support.

"When you take a life, it has a huge effect on you. It hurt me. Obviously, it hurt the boy's family more, but still, it damaged me. When I came out I was twenty-five and an angry young man. I started drinking again, puffing and thieving . . . I came back to Docklands, but I felt in danger over all the things I'd done."

Scared of the consequences of his crimes against members of the Docklands community, Eddie moved around the country, eventually settling in Southend. Fundamentally, he was without help and unable to get out of repeating the same cycles: drinking, smoking, stealing, and getting into relationships with women whose own instability and promiscuity was like a red rag to a bull for Eddie. The relationships would turn violent, with Eddie nearly always having the last word and sometimes badly hurting his partners in the process.

One of his only stable points in this was perhaps Janine, a woman from Docklands who had taken a shine to Eddie since they were teenagers and with whom he'd had an on-and-off relationship for many years. Unlike a lot of the other women he had been involved with, Janine seemed to be a calming and stable influence on Eddie: he had met her parents, who liked him, and he'd never en-gaged with her in the fights and abuse that had plagued his other relationships.

When Eddie was about thirty, things were go-ing particularly badly for him in Southend, and he came back to his mum's in Docklands to try to regroup. A letter from Janine was there waiting for him and he gave her a call. They spent some time together, and after a few days she suggested he come over to her parents' house for dinner, saying, "I've got something to show you." Curious, Eddie came over to her place and she took him upstairs and told him, "I've become a prison officer; look, here's the uniform."

Eddie was taken aback. Not only had the two of them shared more than just the occasional spliff, but Eddie was a convicted criminal. His relation-ship with prison officers in general was difficult, to say the least: for every reasonable officer he had worked with, there was another "screw" who he felt had messed with him or abused their power over him in some way.

I don't fully understand Janine's motives for telling Eddie this about herself; perhaps she thought that he would inevitably be back in prison and was preparing for the worst, but even then I don't think she could have ever imagined how bad things would get. To start with, things between Janine and Eddie cooled a bit and she stopped returning his calls. Shortly afterward, Janine moved into a flat with another female officer, Sonia, to save money.

Christmas Eve came around and Eddie, feeling lonely, went around to Janine's place to find her. Sonia answered the door and said that Janine was out, so Eddie suggested that they go for a Christmas drink together. Sonia agreed, so they had three or four drinks in the pub, chatting happily, and then he walked Sonia back to the flat. When they got back, Eddie asked, "Listen, can I come up and use the phone to call Janine at her parents'?" Sonia said she wasn't sure, but in the days before mobile phones she perhaps thought it would be unfair to make Eddie walk home just to make a call, so she agreed, perhaps reluctantly, and they went upstairs together to the bedroom where the phone was.

When they got upstairs, though, Eddie told me he went from wanting to make the call to a very different set of thoughts. He remembers feeling angry at Janine for freezing him out, scared of women he couldn't ever seem to make a proper relationship with, and angry with prison officers for the way he'd been treated in his last sentence. He grabbed at Sonia and told her he wanted to have sex. Sonia said no, and Eddie said that he remembered being overwhelmed by pure hatred.

"You cunts fucked me right about, and I always said I'd get my revenge, so this is it."

Eddie forced a petrified Sonia down on the bed and raped her.

Eddie ran off to Southend and drank himself into a haze. When he was arrested a few days later for robbing a man in the street—for £4, he recalls—the police identified him as wanted for the rape. He intended to plead not guilty, but Sonia's statement was persuasive—bold, detailed, and plausible—so Eddie went for guilty and was given a nine-year sentence. Suddenly he was in the care of prison officers again, one of whose best friend he had raped.

To the credit of prison officers everywhere, however, aside from being moved around a lot, Eddie was never victimized. "They were professional, and they stuck to it," he said. Eddie still had a very wayward approach to prison life: he continued to deal cannabis and extort other prisoners who wouldn't pay, and was placed in solitary confinement for thirteen months in a single stretch. He doesn't hold a grudge though: this was the game he had chosen to play during his sentence.

There's a long pause on the tape after Eddie tells me the story of the rape, as I try to make sense of it. My first thought was, why did he not just wait for Janine to come back if he wanted sex? But I was wrong here. Most rape isn't about sex, it's about something else: about revenge and control. Eddie told me that when he said "you cunts" to Sonia he meant prison officers, but I think that it could

equally have meant women; or anyone in authority throughout his life. None of this excuses what
he did, and Eddie is the first person to admit
this, but understanding and forgiving are different things. I also felt angry and frustrated at the
younger Eddie, making the same mistakes over
and over and over, and never learning. At the same
time, though, I thought: *Did nobody ever think to
offer him some help?* One of the great difficulties of
personality disorders is that they tend to be "ego
syntonic," a fancy way of saying that people with a
diagnosis of these disorders don't often think that
there's anything wrong at all.

Eddie had come within a hair's breadth of being admitted to a treatment program at Grendon
for his offending but had missed out because of a
technicality. Instead he had gone on to repeat his
destructive cycle of minor crime, drug and alcohol
abuse, meeting a partner who was poorly matched
for him, starting a relationship that was too intense
to last, then finally committing a serious crime that
sent him to prison, where he continued taking and
dealing drugs. I believe that there is evidence from

Eddie's past that this is a surprisingly fragile cycle of events: take away one aspect, be it alcohol, drugs in prison, or the relationship, and the whole chain is preventable. Nobody in a position of authority seemed to realize this, however, and combined with Eddie's natural distrust of anyone in authority—the controlling "sergeant majors"—he was never offered the help he needed.

As it happened, help for Eddie did finally come. He was thirty-seven when he left prison after being found guilty of rape; it was twenty years after his first prison sentence. He told me he remembered walking around south London one day feeling "murderous," like he was "in a lot of trouble" and might seriously hurt someone. He noticed that as he walked around train stations, people recoiled to get out of his way, as though he looked like he might lash out at any moment. He felt like he had become so many things that he hated—he had nothing, had lost so many relationships, and now he had the knowledge that he had it in him to rape another person—and he booked himself an appointment at the local mental health clinic and asked for help. He was referred to the forensic psychotherapy service in Hackney to work with Dr. C., a noted consultant psychotherapist who worked in a psychoanalytic way.

Hearing Eddie describe this now, I am struck by how easy it was for him to get help the moment he asked for it. I'm also reminded of the many young men I have worked with who have asked for this same kind of help in the last ten to fifteen years but been rebuffed by mental health trusts because there are so few forensic outpatient services remaining.

Very quickly after starting weekly sessions with Dr. C., things started to change for Eddie. He stopped getting routinely involved with crime, started to avoid violent situations, and finally started to think through his interactions with other people. He met another woman, Tina, and managed to sustain his longest-ever relationship. Finally, it looked as though the cycle had been broken for Eddie, but then fate intervened again. His mother became very unwell, and after a yearlong illness, during which Eddie had moved back to be with her, she died in her home in Docklands.

One of the most interesting phenomena of classical behavioral psychology is something called the "extinction burst";[2] this is something that happens as an organism (a human or any other animal) is on the verge of giving up on a learned behavior. For a brief period, the frequency of the behavior that is going "extinct"[3] shows a "burst" of frequency, almost as if it is raging against its inevitable loss, as the organism tries one last time to get the reward it used to with the behavior. In Eddie's case, this meant that after his mother's death his antisocial tendencies suddenly made a ferocious comeback. He started "hoisting" again and doing drugs with his partner. Worse yet, he tried to hide this behavior from Dr. C. because he felt ashamed, promising instead that everything was fine.

His relationship with Tina became unstable, full of dramatic (if not violent) arguments, and they started to get into the on-and-off cycle that had characterized his relationship with Janine. One night,

Eddie went out and got steaming drunk, and when he returned to the flat they shared, Tina—perhaps not unreasonably—refused to let him in. He started shouting, and she shouted back, and since this was getting nowhere, he asked Tina to at least throw him the car keys so he could go somewhere else for the night. She did, but not before calling the police: although we'll never know if this was out of a protective instinct for herself or for Eddie, who was about to drive his car while blind drunk.

Sure enough, the moment Eddie got in his car, the police showed up and started to pursue him. In almost a reflex, Eddie went faster and faster to escape, but then lost control while doing 120 mph and hit a sloped crash barrier in the middle of the road that flipped his car up and over a roundabout into a wall on the opposite side. The impact smashed Eddie's pelvis in five places and put him in intensive care for three months. Tina dumped him while he was still confined to his bed, although they did agree to remain friends.

Recovery from the accident was slow and difficult, and one of the side effects was that Eddie had several complex hernias from where intestinal tissue had pushed through the weakened area around his pelvis. He had to have another operation to treat this, and while he was recovering, he met Sara—a recent divorcee—who was an outpatient. They got on very well, and Sara invited him to visit her on her farm in Dorset. Eddie—showing remarkably persistent dedication to the cause of doomed intimate relationships—hitchhiked all the way from Docklands to Dorset with a barely healed pelvis.

We know the plot of this movie, though. Sara was wealthy, independent, and enjoying her life, and had no intentions of being monogamous with a man who lived more than a hundred miles away. She was seeing other men and wasn't making much of an effort to hide it, so Eddie found out and, inevitably, "hit the roof." At least he managed to refrain from physically hurting Sara, but instead humiliated her by pouring a bucket of ice-cold water over her. Sara didn't take kindly to this and told the police, who pressed a common assault charge against Eddie. Common assault, unlike assault occasioning actual bodily harm, is not usually punished with prison time in the UK, but Eddie was classed as a "dangerous offender" as a result of his previous convictions, meaning it was treated as seriously as possible and he was given a two-year prison sentence.

When he told me this story, I noticed that Eddie's face was contorted into an expression of complete contempt; he was furious with himself. I told him this, and he said:

"I was devastated, you know. At the time I felt I was living the dream: my own house, drinking and smoking when I wanted. The money I had, the freedom I had . . . and I'd just thrown it all away. All of a sudden I was going to lose my house, my freedom, my self-respect . . . I was just disgusted with myself. I just thought, 'My fucking life's finished.' So I did the only thing I could, I wrote to Dr. C. from prison."

As it happens, I know Dr. C. very well; she was the lead therapist on a couple of the cases I have described already. She does not suffer fools gladly and usually takes colossal fuckups of the scale that Eddie had just committed very seriously. So she must have really seen something in Eddie worth persevering with, because she came to see him in prison and recommend a transfer to a secure hospital where she worked under the Mental Health Act. This hospital offered a therapeutic community model, like Grendon prison, where Eddie would be forced to work on his offending behavior, as well as his anger and violent, controlling behavior. Unlike Dr. C.'s outpatient clinic, he wouldn't be able to leave the secure hospital to hoist goods, meet women, or make up stories about what he was up to the night before. He would still have to serve out his sentence, but while he did that he would have to face up to his problems or be sent back to prison. Eddie made a good decision: he agreed to Dr. C.'s offer to move to the hospital. He confessed to me:

"I was sort of in two minds, I wanted to change, I was disgusted with myself, but at the same time I sort of wanted an easy ride. It was only when I got there that I realized it wasn't, it wasn't at all. It's changed my life, and I'm constantly surprised I'm not doing a life sentence, and it's mostly because of Dr. C. and the unit."

I asked Eddie what he thought made the therapeutic community approach work for him.

"I would walk around the unit and hear all these
people shouting and moaning, kicking off, and I
thought: *That's exactly how I was*. But I also saw
people change from that place, and I wanted to do
that too. I think I came to see that I was in pain, all
the time, and Dr. C. and the others showed me empathy, compassion, but also were straight up with
me: why did I always have to have all these drugs
inside me to speak to other people? And why did it
always have to be me sitting inside the prison cell?
I would want to go on the rampage and she'd just
ask me: 'Well, why does it have to be you who's the
one who does that?' And that just made me think,
you know, 'Why should it be me? Why not someone
else for once?'"

All this took place nearly twenty years ago now.
Eddie finished his sentence, was discharged from
the secure unit and even his sessions with Dr. C.
have come to an end. He has been in the same relationship for the last nine years, and says his life

is both happy and normal. As he and I finished our second round of cakes after our final interview session, I was inclined to agree, and at the same time I thought we were both a bit relieved and amazed to have made it through his history. I asked Eddie what the word "psychopath" meant to him:

"Dr. C. explained to me that a psychopath is someone who does things off the social norm. But I would say a psychopath is someone who's a raving lunatic, who goes around stabbing people or hurting people, and I have done that, but someone who has no feelings about it. Some of the thoughts and feelings I did get, I still get, but I push them away: I just think it's not worth it. I used to let the thoughts build but now I have to close them off. I don't know if you can develop empathy, but I believe I have. I mean, there have been times when I just didn't give a fuck; I had no empathy for anyone."

Is Eddie really a psychopath? Officially he is: he has the Psychopathy Test results to prove it and has spent time in a service specially designed for men with that diagnosis, which in the end transformed his life for the better. He has spent sixteen years of his life in prison, including time for manslaughter, actual bodily harm, and rape: very serious crimes that it is hard to believe anyone with a shred of empathy would ever have committed. As I explained to Eddie, though, I think that he developed a psychopathic persona, a defense, in response to the brutality of his childhood with his mother's third husband. I think that, for Eddie, coming to believe that everyone else was undeserving of love or respect, and everything had to be about getting what he wanted, was the only way to protect himself and make sense of his family's victimization at the hands of a man who sounds manipulative, aggressive and controlling: the traits of a psychopath. Had his mother stayed with Martin, for example, I am sure that Eddie would still have got into trouble a lot when he was younger, but I think that over time this would have faded away and he could have led a fulfilling life outside of prison.

So for me, Eddie's psychopathy is only surface-deep. He has shown a lack of remorse and empathy, he has broken the law, been aggressive, a juvenile delinquent, a serial monogamist, occasionally leeching off his partners, and someone who has been unable to control his behavior. What he isn't, though, is any kind of Machiavellian like Paul or Tony. He is not a pathological liar, although he has certainly told some whoppers, and he's not grandiose or superficially charming. In fact, he comes across as a bit prickly at first, and it takes a while to warm up to him; almost the exact opposite of Tony's oozy charm. Sometimes I struggled to match Eddie's current empathy with his terrible past, but unlike a lot of offenders I have worked with, he doesn't just tell me he has changed: he shows me. He talks about his particular shame for raping Sonia when, "she was lovely to me, she never did me any harm." When we got to the equally difficult subject of his relationship with his mother after the abuse from her third husband, Eddie told me: "I've sat here with my mum and talked about it. She thought I hated her for it, and I told her no, no . . .

now I'm older I understand that she was living in fear."

What also strikes me about Eddie is that he jumped at the first real offer of help he received, and it changed his life. Yes, he nearly fucked it up along the way, but every psychologist knows about the Stages of Change theory[4]—that even after we start to change our fundamental behaviors there will be lapses on the way to maintaining them permanently, and that is normal. It's just that Eddie's behavior was so extreme, and he was so locked into this destructive downward spiral of relationships with his partners, that perhaps we should be relieved that—while unacceptable—his last aggressive act was to inflict humiliation and discomfort with the water bucket rather than physical injury.

I'm not sure that Eddie's pathway to happiness, a crime-free life, and the ability to have civilized conversation with a former prison psychologist over coffee and cakes would work for every case in this book, let alone all psychopaths, although I wish that was the case. But it does remind me that there is always hope, and that sometimes it is just the offer of real help, help that means talking about the difficult stuff and not just dishing out platitudes and medication, that is the most important thing. It is so easy to write off an angry, violent young man as a lost cause, as an untreatable psychopath, as so many people did throughout Eddie's life, and forget that nobody is defined entirely by being a psychopath: there is always an individual human being with a history, wants, and needs underneath that callous exterior. If we forget that, we forget how and why to have hope.

and extensive offending history, and a history severe mental illness as well as psychopathy, he could change the direction of his life while he still had time to live it. I learned a lot from interviewing him for this book, but while he gave me a lot of hope, he puts cases like Danny and Tony, where I couldn't see a happy ending, into sharp contrast.

I said in the introduction that I wanted to write a book about how diverse and complex psychopaths are, how ineffective we are at understanding and rehabilitating them, and perhaps also start the process of trying to rehumanize people's perceptions of psychopaths and their stories. Whatever the endless spew of articles in popular magazines might say, psychopaths are not something you should routinely worry about. I get it: nobody wants to inadvertently start a relationship with a psychopath. But, as we have seen, psychopaths are not people whom it is easy to be in a relationship with. It very quickly becomes clear when a potential partner is not interested in your emotional fulfillment, or much else about you at all. This is a good sign—not restricted to dating psychopaths—

CHAPTER NINE

Psychopathy Is Bad for Your Health

Looking back, I'm struck by how dark some of these stories are; far darker than they exist in my working memory where I tend to "edit out" some of the nastier bits, probably to make the recollections easier to live with. The hardest part of some of the stories is the sense of tragedy: if only this small thing had been different, none of this might have happened. I chose to finish the case studies with Eddie, not because it was one of the few positive stories—fortunately there have been many positive endings in my experience—but because Eddie's criminal history was relatively serious, and in general it is those men with the most serious histories who find it hardest to make changes. What is also unique about Eddie is that despite his complex

that you should probably leave that relationship and take your chances elsewhere, and if you do not then there are probably things in your own mind that should be a higher priority for you to address than your partner's mental health issues.

Psychopaths don't have a monopoly on manipulation and bullying, nor do people with narcissistic or borderline personality disorder. Nor is it easy even for someone very experienced and skilled at making these kind of distinctions always to tell whether someone is a "vulnerable narcissist" or an "aggressive borderline"—so you should be very wary when reading an article that tells you that these are the kind of people you should avoid on the dating scene. If you start to learn how to tell them apart, call my boss and you can have my job.

There are many creative attempts by academics and some clinicians to move the discussion about psychopathy away from criminality and the Psychopathy Test and into community psychology and psychiatry. This is helpful, because there are a fair number of people in the community who would not meet the criteria for criminal psychopathy on the PCL-R, but do have a lot of the emotional (or "affective") and interpersonal features that make up a major part of psychopathy: lack of remorse, pathological lying, glib and superficial charm, conning and manipulative; but none of the anti-social elements. These are often called "successful psychopaths"—successful in the dual sense of both "succeeding at life" but also perhaps in "not having been caught doing anything criminal"—and may make up 3.5 percent of people in the business world.[1] How concerned should you be about a "psychopath" who is no more likely than a non-psychopath to commit violence? Certainly, "successful" psychopaths are often experts in relational aggression—bullying, controlling behavior designed to damage people's social status[2]—but there is also some evidence that these people are different from criminal psychopaths in fundamental aspects of their brain function. As well as a higher IQ, in some studies higher than the population average,[3] and less impairment in the areas of their brain typically associated with criminal psychopathy, they often have high levels of "cognitive empathy," that is, the ability to recognize emotion in others without feeling it.[4]

I have two problems with this argument. First, my clinical experience says that some "successful" psychopaths do indeed make it into the criminal justice system: this is why I picked Tony as a case study. Anyone who can set up a fraudulent business empire, including a credit union, and also survive in high-security conditions surrounded by murderers and so-called "unsuccessful" psychopaths, must have an abnormally high level of cunning, at least. So "successful" psychopaths are not necessarily defined by evading capture, and don't take my word for it: watch Fyre Festival organizer Billy McFarland's continuing to sell counterfeit event tickets, while out on bail over charges over the huge fraud of his own event. Defining the adaptability of someone's disorder in relation to the highly complex social question of whether they are detected and punished for it seems a bit arbitrary, to say the least.

But my second problem with the idea that psychopaths are broadly "successful" or "unsuccessful" is more logical than experiential: I don't know if two people who are different in terms of their neurophysiology, executive function, and emotional reasoning are really the same type of person, or whether they can both meaningfully be given the same label, whether that's "psychopath" or something else altogether. Sure, I wouldn't particularly want to work for a so-called "successful" psychopath, but I'd take that over working for someone like Paul on any day of the week, month, year, or century. In fact, I think I'd really like to work with James Fallon at Stanford (Hi, Jim!), but we'll come back to him later.

Part of the reason we're so preoccupied with psychopaths is that the media are always leading the way on it for us. Frustratingly, discussions of psychopathy in the press are almost always inaccurate; it's pointless giving out the list of twenty items on the Psychopathy Test *yet again* to fill up space on a newspaper page when anyone who uses the test needs to have either a PhD or extensive clinical training, go on a three-day course explicitly accredited by Robert Hare himself, and complete a set of case studies to within an acceptable level of accuracy. Having the list of psychopathic traits on their own without the highly copyrighted rubric describing them is like having a list of the component parts of the *Discovery* shuttle—well, at least a Volkswagen Beetle—you can try to put them together without expert help but what comes out is most likely going to be a confusing mess.

Even when the press feature interviews with experts, the articles can end up being misleading. Different theoretical perspectives—psychoanalytic, neurocognitive, genetic—are presented as the same thing, but they have a surprisingly large number of disagreements about where psychopathy comes from and the best way to address it. One of the biggest issues, which isn't by any means unique to psychopathy—I've moaned about it applying to narcissism just as much[5]—is that lots of researchers will give out semi-validated (meaning that they showed some base-level agreement with the Psychopathy Test in one study) self-report questionnaires to a sample of college students and use this to deduce fundamental truths about psychopaths.

Universities issue a press release with the word "psychopath" and the media get excited.

But we wouldn't confuse "people who feel tired" (or parents, as we are usually known) with "chronic fatigue syndrome" because, if we did, the diagnosis wouldn't have any meaning. Why are we so keen to accept this with psychopathy? It makes sense that psychopathy should be a continuum, sure, but there is some convincing evidence that actually asking psychopaths—who, let us not forget, are supposed to be pathological liars—about their psychopathy is very different to measuring it using a checklist based on professional judgment.[6] Perhaps the take-home message is that our understanding of psychopathy has developed tremendously.

Some of the most useful, well-conducted research on psychopaths comes from geneticists and genetic epidemiologists such as Essi Viding, who found that children with high levels of callous and unemotional traits that can predict adult psychopathy often have a similar genetic profile.[7] But I don't think that criminal psychopaths ever come from stable, safe "good enough" homes and families. Genetic heritage, or "character," is an important factor, but it is the environment the child grows up in that makes the difference. James Fallon has the genes and the brain of a psychopath, sure, but he isn't a risk to anyone and his contribution to society is far more valuable than the fact he's a bit distant with his kids and wishes annoying dinner guests would "fuck off." So although I think that an overhaul of the terminology, diagnostic process, and treatment of psychopathy is long, long overdue, I also think that in some ways it's helpful that psychopathy is mostly shackled to criminal behavior by the PCL-R. I can accept this is scientifically problematic, but morally it is far more palatable than landing a quasi-clinical and highly stigmatizing diagnosis on people like Jim.

None of this means that criminal psychopaths are not culpable for what they do. Part of the journey into change is the acceptance and understanding that what you did was wrong and ultimately you are accountable for it, just as it was for Eddie.

However, I believe forensic psychology and psychiatry are often insufficiently attentive to social context, particularly in the English-speaking countries that offer rehabilitative services to psychopaths. We tend to think of psychopathy, and other mental disorders, in very biomedical terms that suggest that if we just have the right magic pill (or psychotherapy or managed clinical team) we can solve the problem. Other countries are a lot less grandiose about this, and a lot more pragmatic. In the Netherlands, for example, offenders with a diagnosis of personality disorder are assigned to a single clinic, usually close to their home, that provides care and rehabilitation for them throughout their entire sentence.

I have visited a few of these clinics but I particularly remember going to the Van der Hoeven Kliniek in Utrecht in 2005. Although it was originally set up by a psychiatrist, since the 1990s the Van der Hoeven has been run not by a psychiatrist, psychologist, or sociologist, but by an economist. Although it provides a public service of rehabilitating mentally disordered offenders underwritten by the

Dutch Ministry of Justice, everything it does seeks to be completely cost-neutral to the public. This means that, when I visited, the café, restaurant, and reception desk were all run by patients with criminal histories. The center of the clinic housed a massive workshop where patients worked on real, private manufacturing contracts producing, among other things, electric forklifts, circuit boards, and stitched leather goods, for which they were paid a real wage. When patients reduced their risk enough to move on from being inpatients confined to the hospital, they were given a flat in a building near to the clinic so that they could continue to attend the workshop and any therapy sessions they still needed.

To demonstrate the strength of this model, the staff of the clinic played a very Dutch trick on me. Or at least, I think it was a trick; perhaps they just didn't realize there was anything weird about it at all. While I was visiting one of the wards, or living blocks, I attended what I thought was a meeting of patients—all with a diagnosis of personality disorder or psychopathy plus a serious offending history—together with a couple of staff members. Throughout the meeting a couple of patients got up and left, but this happens in my clinical sessions all the time, so I didn't think too much of it. It was only when the meeting finished and everyone got up to leave that I realized that there were absolutely no staff members in the group at all: they had been the ones who had left earlier, probably because they realized everything was fine and they weren't really needed. One of the women I had thought was a staff member had in fact burned both her parents to death in their own bed when she was a teenager.

As if to ram the message home, there was even a small incident on the (mixed) ward later that day where a couple of male patients had a disagreement, and one of them started to become aggressive. In a British hospital the alarm would have sounded, and a team of specially trained nurses would have sailed in to restrain the patient and take him to a seclusion ward away from the others. In the Van der Hoeven, it was a team of patients who calmly asked the man to accompany them to the de-escalation room. Which he did. At the evening handover one of the staff nonchalantly described the aggressive patient as a "violent psychopath," as if it was no big thing.

On my last day in Utrecht I had a brief meeting with the lead psychiatrist and psychologist while walking around the park that made up the central area of the main clinic. I told them that their clinic was amazing—which from their reaction they already seemed to be well aware of—and I asked them where the inspiration for the model came from. I wished I hadn't asked: the psychiatrist chuckled and said to me, "Well, we visited the Henderson Hospital in the 1950s and we borrowed a lot of the ideas from that." The Henderson, of course, was a psychiatric unit that catered to men and women with personality disorders that was opened in 1947[8] and then closed in 2008 when the NHS reorganization meant that primary care trusts could no longer fund out-of-area care for their patients. The British invented this model—what we would call a therapeutic community, the same placement that helped Eddie so much, where the hierarchy between staff and

patients is radically diminished—and now seem
to have all but forgotten it.

Why is this story about the Dutch clinic so important? I think this about "normal" or "good enough"
human development and how few, if any, psychopaths have experienced anything like it in their
lifetimes. Although they may not have any frame
of reference for fundamental ideas such as love,
compassion, and empathy, we cannot infantilize
and re-parent psychopathic patients. Instead we
must offer a place where they have the opportunity to discover the worth and meaning of these
concepts for themselves.

There is strong emerging evidence that if you
can intervene early enough, even children with
the most appalling histories of neglect, abuse and
trauma can experience normal neurodevelopment
and "prevent" psychopathy.[9] For some men and
women, such as Eddie, the experience of even a
limited kind of care can be transformative; for others, the Pauls and Jasons of this world, perhaps
the best we can hope for is that they are able to offer a more developed kind of cognitive empathy so

they can at least identify emotions in others, if not share them.

Although the evidence is still confused and there is a lot of pessimism, and I think that a lot of this is because we are dead set on finding a single "magic pill" for psychopathy, whether that be a literal pill as we have for schizophrenia, or a psychological therapy, as we now have with cognitive behavioral therapy (CBT) for depression. Because psychopathy has a complex causality, involving genes, environment, and neuropsychology, it's likely that only a complex treatment will be effective. So, this means focusing on creating an environment that allows for healthy development to take place and avoids re-traumatization of the kind men like Danny and women in most secure settings seem to experience daily.

Psychopaths need help. Throwing away the key or, worse yet, executing psychopaths as some U.S. states do because their brain doesn't work like it "should," is pretty monstrous if we consider ourselves a society where psychopaths are supposed to be different precisely because they lack empathy with other humans. Churchill once said that a society's attitude to its prisoners was a measure of its "stored-up strength," its resolve to provide leeway for people to fail and return, like Eddie, and not be simply cast aside because of their transgressions.

As world-leading psychopath expert James Blair put it in 2013, they "deserve to be helped,"[10] and we are failing both offenders with psychopathic disorder and their victims if we continue to lack an effective framework for helping them. It *is* possible to support them to make better decisions and become better, functioning members of society.

A corollary of this is that work with psychopaths is not nearly recognized enough. Some of the experiences I have told you about, particularly my work with the young man known in this book as Danny, affected me quite profoundly, and not always in a good way. This work has, at times, given me nightmares, physical symptoms, and terrible anxiety disorder. And yet hundreds of forensic psychiatrists and psychologists, nurses, prison officers, probation officers, and social workers go to work with psychopaths every day of the year.

Most of the time they are expected just to get on with it, without proper training or a working clinical model, let alone fuss or recognition. They need proper supervision and support and a better understanding of the long-term effects of the work. Firing and criminalizing workers who were manipulated by psychopaths does nobody any favors: this is a failure of the systems that are supposed to support workers to do their jobs effectively and keep them safe.

Psychoanalysts call the staff team working around severely disordered men and women a "container":[11] a space that "contains" the disordered behavior and in doing so allows for change and understanding by their patients, and in the case of those who have committed crimes, a space that protects society too. Yet this container is not effective or safe without proper design and maintenance. In short, without the recognition that staff working in prisons and mental hospitals need a great deal of specific relational support and training, everyone is at risk.

I left clinical work with offenders with a diagnosis of psychopathy in 2015. Since then, my research has moved into questions about how we can understand and prevent violence by understanding its causes. In this bigger picture, psychopathy is not that big a deal. My colleagues and I constructed a machine-learning algorithm that modeled the causes of violence. After major risk factors such as untreated severe mental illness, male gender, anger, previous violence, and violent ideation, psychopathy did not even make the top ten most important factors related to whether someone was going to be violent.

Psychopathy is a one-size-fits-all template that provides just one contributory factor for why some people do terrible things and by its nature doesn't get close to explaining the who, when, and why of violent crime. Psychopathy isn't a disorder like erotomania where the victim and the motivation are always the same. (The erotomaniac falls in love with their victim and forms a delusional belief that the victim loves them back, despite any evidence to the contrary. Anyone who threatens this belief—the victims' real partners, usually—is at risk of anything from abuse to murder.) Psychopathy doesn't deal with motivations: in many respects it is unsatisfying as an explanation for anything, but that's because it wasn't designed that way: Cleckley thought it was a way of diagnosing why some of his clients were particularly difficult to work with, and Bob Hare thought it was a way of understanding why some prisoners are so difficult to rehabilitate. Layers of academic research, mythology, and media conjecture have buried these relatively humble origins.

All the psychopaths I have worked with have, I believe, been "made" by an early experience of life that was deeply and profoundly wrong in some important way: parents who were not "good enough" for their children because they were too focused on their own lives; abusers who were allowed into the family network; and/or a care system that simply couldn't contain the disordered behavior of these young men and, in some cases, women. Yet it is increasingly being found that the right kind of support offered to young people with antisocial and disordered behavior can be transformative: multi-systemic therapy, that works on the boundaries between families, schools, and the police to keep children and young adults out of prison;[12] intensive interventions targeted at specific patterns of abuse.[13] The problem is not that we have no way of helping people, it is that when someone does not know that they should seek help, as Eddie didn't until it was almost too late, we are very bad at seeing past the denials and minimizations of pain to make that first bold offer. It's bold because we might well know, or at least suspect, that it will be thrown back in our faces when we do.

Psychopathy as a concept and a diagnosis is at once complex and reductive: it describes a lack, an absence of something—a belief that other people have value in their own right—that a healthy individual draws great richness and satisfaction from every day of their lives. At the same time, though, it is a description that can be applied to a hugely diverse range of individuals from chaotic, self-hating young men such as Danny to high-functioning manipulators like Tony or remorseless killers like Angela. Intelligent and dedicated men such as James Fallon seem to share their brain structure with criminal psychopaths, but to no more ill effect than a bit of social gruffness. How useful a concept is it that tries to lump all of these individuals together, and how concerning that in some parts of the world such an elastic concept can determine whether you live or die?

The reasons that someone commits a serious crime are unique, complex, and difficult to unearth. That's why the best crime thrillers are almost always like archaeologies of the perpetrator's mind, peeling back layers of experiences and emotion that only make sense in relation to each other. This is what makes a psychopath, truly: not a diagnosis made by a test.

NOTES

Preface

1. Although the Barlinnie Special Unit in Glasgow (Cooke, 1989) and HMP Grendon (Shuker and Sullivan, 2010) are isolated examples of success in rehabilitating very violent criminals with a likely diagnosis of psychopathy.

Introduction

1. I am going to use the term "psychopath" in this book over the fairer description "people with a diagnosis of psychopathic disorder" simply for reasons of brevity and the reader's patience. I apologize to anyone who is offended by this, but I hope the reader will also see that I understand there is an important distinction.
2. In fact this accusation is also applied, unfortunately, to a lot of people with a diagnosis of personality disorder: see NIHME, 2003, or Center for Mental Health, 2018.
3. Rice and Harris, 1997.

Chapter One: The Masks of Psychopathy

1. Hare, 1991.

2.   Ronson, 2011.
3.   Huchzermeier, et al., 2008.
4.   Viding, et al., 2005.
5.   Blonigen, et al., 2006.
6.   Cleckley, 1941.
7.   Hare, 1980.
8.   Ratiu, et al., 2004.
9.   Macmillan, 2000.
10. Gale, et al., 2018.
11. Hagberg H, David Edwards A, Groenendaal F. Perinatal brain damage: The term infant. *Neurobiol Dis.* 2016;92(Pt A):102–112. doi:10.1016/j.nbd.2015.09.011
12. Blair, 2007.
13. Igoumenou, et al., 2017.
14. Ibid.
15. Fallon, 2013.
16. I use this word in the specific sense of John Bowlby's attachment theory (Bowlby, 1969), which is increasingly popular knowledge, especially among parents, but has its own relevance to psychopathy (e.g., Bowlby, 1946).
17. Nelson, 1994.
18. Rule, 1980.
19. Greenacre, 1945.
20. Frick and White, 2008.
21. Logan, 2011.
22. Forouzan and Cooke, 2005.
23. Quinsey, 2002.
24. Klein Tuente, et al., 2014.
25. Myers, et al., 2005.
26. Douglas, et al., 2006, Camp, Schmitt, et al., 2013.
27. Coid, et al., 2012.
28. Harris and Rice, 2006.

Chapter Two: Paul, the Hit Man

1. Coid, et al., 2009.
2. Beck, A., Rantala, R.R. & Rexroat, J. (2014) Special Report: Sexual Victimization Reported by Adult Correctional Authorities, 2009–11, Published January 2014. U.S. Department of Justice.
3. Jackson, Craig, "Nurse suspended over claims of inappropriate relationships with patients at secure Scots hospital," *The Scottish Sun*, 19 October 2019, https://www.thescottishsun.co.uk/news/4856692/rowanbank-clinic-glasgow-nurse-nhs/.

Chapter Three: Tony, the Con Man

1. For more on this sub-type see Heaver, 1944.
2. Office for National Statistics, 2018.

Chapter Four: Jason, the Liar

1. Cuellar, et al., 2007.
2. Substance Abuse and Mental Health Services Administration. (2020). Key substance use and mental health indicators in the United States: Results from the 2019 National Survey on Drug Use and Health (HHS Publication No. PEP20-07-01-001, NSDUH Series H-55). Rockville, MD: Center for Behavioral Health Statistics and Quality, Substance Abuse and Mental Health Services Administration. Retrieved from https://www.samhsa.gov/data/
3. Mental Health Act (UK), 1983.
4. Li, et al., 2011.
5. Shao and Lee, 2017.
6. Garrett, et al., 2016.

Chapter Five: Arthur, the Parasite

1. Jolly, Jasper, "Breaking Out: A man's redemption through rowing," *Row 360*, 29 January 2016.
2. MacAvoy and Turley, 2016.

Chapter Six: Danny, the Borderline

1. This idea was first suggested by Anna Freud (1936).
2. Coid, et al., 2006.

Chapter Seven: Angela, the Remorseless

1. The Blom-Cooper inquiry into high-security mental health care of 1992 (see Blom-Cooper, et al., 1992) strongly criticized the "prison-like" culture of the high-security hospitals at the expense of therapeutic input, and the influence of the Prison Officers' Association (POA) union on the delivery of nursing care. The traditional white uniforms were abolished and staff after that wore casual clothes.
2. A belief that may have had some merit as the sheriff's office was under investigation for racism, see Markon and McCrummen, 2010.
3. Knight, et al., 2017.
4. Maverty, 2014.
5. Boyd, 1993.
6. Arrigo and Griffin, 2004.
7. Strand and Belfrage, 2005.
8. For discussions of the way that psychopaths learn differently see Blair, et al., 2004, or Ling and Raine, 2018.

Chapter Eight: Eddie, the Redeemed

1. Felitti, et al., 1998.
2. Lerman and Iwata, 1995.
3. "Extinction" is a Pavlovian concept that refers to the dying out of a particular conditioned reaction (such as Pavlov's dog salivating when it hears the bell, expecting food)—if the reward is not present for long enough, the reaction will eventually become extinct. See VanElzakker, et al., 2014.
4. Prochaska and DiClemente, 1992.

Chapter Nine: Psychopathy Is Bad for Your Health

1. Babiak and Hare, 2006.
2. Crick and Grotpeter, 1995.
3. Ishikawa, et al., 2001.
4. Gao and Raine, 2010.
5. Freestone, et al., 2020.
6. Brinkley, et al., 2001.
7. Viding, et al., 2005.
8. For a good history of the Henderson and its clinical model, see Manning, 1989.
9. Perry and Szalavitz, 2017.
10. Sutton, 2012.
11. Rosenbaum and Garfield, 1996.
12. Johnides, et al., 2017.
13. Perry, 2006.

BIBLIOGRAPHY

Arrigo, B. A. and Griffin, A. (2004). Serial murder and the case of Aileen Wuornos: attachment theory, psychopathy, and predatory aggression. *Behav Sci Law*, 22(3): 375–393.

Babiak, P. and Hare, R. D. (2006). *Snakes in Suits: When Psychopaths Go to Work*. New York: Regan.

Bateman, A. and Fonagy, P. (2010). *Mentalization-based Treatment for Borderline Personality Disorders*. Oxford: Oxford University Press.

Blair, J. (2007). Dysfunctions of medial and lateral orbitofrontal cortex in psychopathy. *Ann N Y Acad Sci*, 1121: 461–479.

Blair, J., Mitchell, D. and Blair, K. (2005). *The Psychopath: Emotion and the Brain*. London: Wiley-Blackwell.

Blair, J., et al., (2004). Passive avoidance learning

in individuals with psychopathy: modulation by reward but not by punishment. *Personality and Individual Differences,* 37: 1179–1192.

Blom-Cooper, L., Brown, M., Dolan, R. and Murphy, E. (1992). *Report of the Committee of Inquiry into Complaints About Ashworth Hospital,* Cmnd 2028, vols 1 and 2. London: HMSO.

Blonigen, D. M., et al. (2006). Continuity and change in psychopathic traits as measured via normal-range personality: A longitudinal-biometric study. *J Abnorm Psychol,* 115(1): 85–95.

Bowlby, J. (1969). *Attachment and Loss, Vol. 1: Attachment* (2nd edn). New York: Basic Books.

Bowlby, J. (1946). *Forty-four Juvenile Thieves: Their Characters and Home-life* (2nd edn). London: Baillière, Tindall and Cox.

Boyd, C. J. (1993). The antecedents of women's crack cocaine abuse: Family substance abuse, sexual abuse, depression and illicit drug use. *J of Subst Abuse Treat,* 10(5): 433–438.

Brinkley, C. A., Schmitt, W. A., Smith, S. S. and Newman, J. P. (2001). Construct validation of a self-report psychopathy scale: Does Levenson's self-report psychopathy scale measure the same constructs as Hare's psychopathy checklist-revised? *Pers*, 31(7): 1021–1038.

Camp, J. P., et al. (2013). Psychopathic predators? Getting specific about the relation between psychopathy and violence. *J Consult Clin Psychol*, 81(3): 467–480.

Campbell-Meiklejohn, D. K., et al. (2012). Structure of orbitofrontal cortex predicts social influence. *Current Biology*, 22: 123–124.

Center for Mental Health, Royal College of Nursing, British Association of Social Workers, Royal College of General Practitioners, The British Psychological Society, Anna Freud National Center for Children and Families, MIND and Barnet, Enfield and Haringey NHS Trust (2018). *'Shining light in the dark corners of people's lives': The consensus statement for people with complex mental health difficulties who are diagnosed with a personality disorder.* London: MIND.

Cleckley, H. M. (1941). *The Mask of Sanity*. St. Louis: C. V. Mosby.

Coid, J., et al. (2006). Prevalence and correlates of personality disorder in Great Britain. *Br J Psychiatry*, 188(5): 423–431.

Coid, J., et al. (2009). Psychopathy among prisoners in England and Wales. *International Journal of Law and Psychiatry*, 32(3): 134–141.

Coid, J. and Yang, M. (2008). The distribution of psychopathy among a household population: categorical or dimensional? *Soc Psychiatry Psychiatr Epidemiol*, 43(10): 773–781.

Coid, J., Freestone, M. and Ullrich, S. (2012). Subtypes of psychopathy in the British household population: Findings from the national household survey of psychiatric morbidity. *Soc Psychiatry Psychiatr Epidemiol*, 47(6): 879–91.

Cooke, (1989). Containing Violent Prisoners: An Analysis of the Barlinnie Special Unit. *The British Journal of Criminology*, 29(2): 129–143.

Crick, N. R. and Grotpeter, J. K. (1995). Relational aggression, gender, and social-psychological adjustment. *Child Dev*, 66(3): 710–722.

Cuellar, A. E., Snowden, L. M. and Ewing, T. (2007). Criminal records of persons served in the public mental health system. *Psychiatr Serv*, 58(1): 114–120.

Douglas, K. S., Vincent, G. M. and Edens, J. F. (2006). Risk for criminal recidivism: The role of psychopathy. In Patrick, C. J. (ed.), *Handbook of Psychopathy*. Guilford: The Guilford Press, 533–554.

Fallon, J. (2013). *The Psychopath Inside: A Neuroscientist's Personal Journey Into the Dark Side of the Brain*. London: Penguin.

Felitti, Vincent J., et al. (1998). Relationship of childhood abuse and household dysfunction to many of the leading causes of death in adults. *Am J Prev Med*, 14(4): 245–258.

Forouzan, E. and Cooke, D. J. (2005). Figuring out la femme fatale: Conceptual and assessment issues concerning psychopathy in females. *Behav Sci Law*, 23(6): 765–778.

Freestone, M., Osman, M. and Ibrahim, Y. (2020). On the uses and abuses of narcissism for public health. *Br J Psychiatry*.

Freud, A. (1936). *The Ego and Mechanisms of Defense.* London: Routledge.

Frick, P. J. and White, S. F. (2008). Research review: The importance of callous-unemotional traits for developmental models of aggressive and antisocial behavior. *J Child Psychol Psychiatry*, 49(4): 359–375.

Gale, C., et al. (2018). Neonatal brain injuries in England: Population-based incidence derived from routinely recorded clinical data held in the National Neonatal Research Database. *Arch Dis Child Fetal Neonatal Ed*, 103(4): F301–F306.

Gao, Y. and Raine, A. (2010). Successful and unsuccessful psychopaths: A neurobiological model. *Behav Sci Law*. 28(2): 194–210.

Garrett, N., et al. (2016). The brain adapts to dishonesty. *Nat Neurosci*, 19: 1727–1732.

Greenacre, P. (1945). Conscience in the psychopath. *Am J Orthopsychiat*, 15(3): 495–509.

Hare, R. D. (1980). A research scale for the assessment of psychopathy in criminal populations. *Personality and Individual Differences*, 1(2): 111–119.

Hare, R. D. (1998). The Hare PCL-R: Some issues concerning its use and misuse. *Leg Criminol Psychol*, 3(Pt 1): 99–119.

Hare, R. D. (1991). *The Psychopathy Checklist: Revised*. Toronto: Multi-Health Systems.

Harris, G. T. and Rice, M. E. (2006). Treatment of psychopathy: A review of empirical findings. In Patrick, C. J. (ed.), *Handbook of Psychopathy*. Guilford: The Guilford Press, 555–572.

Heaver, W. L. (1944). A study of forty male psychopathic personalities before, during and after hospitalization. *Amer J Psychiat*, 100(3): 342–346.

Huchzermeier C., et al. (2008). Are there age-related effects in antisocial personality disorders and psychopathy? *J of Forensic Leg Med*, 15(4): 213–8.

Igoumenou, A., et al. (2017). Faces and facets: The variability of emotion recognition in psychopathy reflects its affective and antisocial features. *J Abnorm Psychol*, 126(8): 1066–1076.

Ishikawa, S. S., et al. (2001). Autonomic stress reactivity and executive functions in successful and unsuccessful criminal psychopaths from the community. *J Abnorm Psychol*, 110(3): 423–432.

Johnides, B. D., Borduin, C. M., Wagner, D. V. and Dopp, A. R. (2017). Effects of multisystemic therapy on caregivers of serious juvenile offenders: A 20-year follow-up to a randomized clinical trial. *J Consult Clin Psychol*, 85(4): 323–334.

Klein Tuente, S., de Vogel, V. and Stam, J. (2014). Exploring the criminal behavior of women with psychopathy: Results from a multicenter study into psychopathy and violent offending in female forensic psychiatric patients. *Int J Forensic Ment Health*, 13(4): 311–322.

Knight, B., Coid, J. W. and Ullrich, S. (2017). Non-suicidal self-injury in UK prisoners. *Int J Forensic Ment Health*, 16(2): 172–182.

Lerman, D. C. and Iwata, B. A. (1995). Prevalence of the extinction burst and its attenuation during treatment. *J Appl Behav Anal*, 28(1): 93–94.

Levin, J. and Wiest, J. B. (2018). *The Allure of Premeditated Murder: Why Some People Plan to Kill*. Lanham, MD: Rowman and Littlefield.

Li, A. S., Kelley, E. A., Evans, A. D. and Lee, K. (2011). Exploring the ability to deceive in children with autism spectrum disorders. *J Autism Dev Disord*, 41(2): 185–195.

Ling, S. and Raine, A. (2018). The neuroscience of psychopathy and forensic implications, *Psychology, Crime & Law,* 24:3: 296–312.

Logan, C. (2011). La femme fatale: The female psychopath in fiction and clinical practice. *MHRJ*, 16(3): 118–127.

MacAvoy, J. and Turley, M. (2016). *Redemption: From Iron Bars to Ironman*. Worthing: Pitch Perfect.

Macmillan, M. (2000). *An Odd Kind of Fame: Stories of Phineas Gage.* Boston: MIT Press.

Manning, N. (1989). *The Therapeutic Community Movement: Charisma and Routinisation*. London: Routledge.

Markon, J., and McCrummen, S. (2010). Judge blocks some sections of Arizona Law. Washington: *The Washington Post*.

Maverty, J. (director). (2014). *Deadly Women:*

Heartless, season 7, episode 9. Sydney, Austra-
lia: Beyond International.

Meloy, J. R. (2001). *The Mark of Cain: Psychoanalytic Insight and the Psychopath* (Kindle edn).
London: Routledge.

Mental Health Act (UK) (1983). Section 1. Retrieved
from http://www.legislation.gov.uk/ukpga/1983
/20/contents.

Myers, W. C., Gooch, E. and Meloy, J. R. (2005). The
role of psychopathy and sexuality in a female serial killer. *J Forensic Sci*, 50(3): 652–657.

National Institute for Mental Health in England
(NIHME), (2003). *Personality Disorder: No Longer a Diagnosis of Exclusion*. London: Department of Health.

Nelson, P. (1994). *Defending the Devil: My story as
Ted Bundy's Last Lawyer*. New York: William
Morrow.

Office for National Statistics, UK (2018). *Sexual offending: Victimization and the path through the
criminal justice system*. London: Office for National Statistics.

Perry, B. D. (2006). Applying principles of neuro-development to clinical work with maltreated and traumatized children: The neurosequential model of therapeutics. In Webb, N. B. (ed.), *Social Work Practice with Children and Families: Working with traumatized youth in child welfare*. Guilford: Guilford Press, 27–52.

Perry, B. D. and Szalavitz, M. (2017). *The Boy Who Was Raised as a Dog, and Other Stories from a Child Psychiatrist's Notebook* (3rd edn). London: Basic Books.

Prochaska, J. O. and DiClemente, C. C. (1992). Stages of change in the modification of problem behaviors. *Prog Behav Modif*, 28: 183–218.

Quinsey, V. L. (2002). Evolutionary theory and criminal behavior. *Leg Criminol Psychol*, 7(1): 1–13.

Ratiu, P., et al. (2004). The tale of Phineas Gage, digitally remastered. *J Neurotrauma*, 21(5): 637–43.

Rice, M. E. and Harris, G. T. (1997). Cross-validation and extension of the violent risk-appraisal guide for child molesters and rapists. *Law and Hum Behav*, 21(2): 231–38.

Ronson, J. (2011). *The Psychopath Test*. London: Picador.

Rosenbaum, B. and Garfield, D. (1996). Containers, mental space and psychodynamics. *Br J Med Psychol*, 69(Pt 4): 281–297.

Rule, A. (1980). *The Stranger Beside Me: The Shocking Inside Story of Serial Killer Ted Bundy*. London: Sphere.

Shao, R. and Lee, T. M. C. (2017). Are individuals with higher psychopathic traits better learners at lying? Behavioral and neural evidence. *Transl Psychiatry*, 7(7): e1175.

Shuker, R. and Sullivan, E. (2010). *Grendon and the Emergence of Forensic Therapeutic Communities*. London: John Wiley & Sons, Ltd.

Strand, S. and Belfrage, H. (2005). Gender differences in psychopathy in a Swedish offender sample. *Behav Sci Law*. 23(6): 837–850.

Sutton, J. (2012). "Patients with the disorder deserve to be helped." *The Psychologist*. 25: 212–213.

VanElzakker, M. B., et al. (2014). From Pavlov to PTSD: The extinction of conditioned fear in rodents, humans, and anxiety disorders. *Neurobiol Learn Mem*, 113: 3–18.

Viding, E., Blair, R. J., Moffitt, T. E. and Plomin, R. (2005). Evidence for substantial genetic risk for psychopathy in 7-year-olds. *J Child Psychol Psychiatry*, 46(6): 592–597.

ACKNOWLEDGMENTS

This book is really a product of a few of my more interesting interactions with people over the years and I am extremely grateful for all of them.

First of all, I am greatly indebted to my editor, Emma Smith at Ebury, who showed so much curiosity about the work behind *Killing Eve* and an oddly unshakeable faith in me despite my repeated deadline panics, ignorance of how to write popular science books, and constant need to apologize for everything. In writing. Her comments and guidance improved this book considerably. I should also thank Charlotte Cole, the copy editor, for making sense of large sections of the book that seemed, in hindsight, like nonsense.

Helen Czerski is a far better friend to me than I am to her, although she is pretty incredible at it so I don't feel at all bad acknowledging her superiority. She both inspired and motivated me throughout this process, including introducing me to Will Francis at Janklow and Nesbit, who has been an irreplaceable source of encouragement, pragmatism, and behind-the-scenes negotiation that helped this book to happen.

Early in the writing process my great friend Jessica Gregson gave me the best possible advice anyone could receive in writing a book, which boiled down to "just fucking write it, then worry about it," and which was exactly what I needed at the time when I only had 8,000 words written and a deadline barely months away. Hannah Jones, Georgina Mathlin, and Landon Kuester at Queen Mary showed a quiet, encouraging interest in the book from the early days of me drunkenly unveiling it (under the working title of "Killing Steve") and I hope this doesn't disappoint them.

A whole host of other people contributed to this book in various ways: firstly, the man known only as Eddie on these pages was not just a subject of the chapter he starred in but an inspiration both in terms of his story and in his generosity of spirit and sense of humor. Lara Griffiths very generously gave her time to nudge me in some directions on some stories, and Dr. Celia Taylor was greatly supportive of me, as she has been in the eleven years we have now worked together.

Cleo Van Velsen influenced my thinking about psychopathy and personality disorder more than anyone else and she is very present in these pages as an intellectual voice and a source of thought and compassion for those everyone else rejects. Jeremy Coid also influenced my thinking in complex ways, although sometimes I'm not sure whether he believes in psychopaths at all.

All the *Killing Eve* team at Sid Gentle treated me with great warmth and respect, which I hope I earned, but especially thank you Henrietta Colvin, Phoebe Waller-Bridge, Emerald Fennell, Elinor Day, Lee Morris, Chrissie Broadway, and Sally Woodward Gentle. Vicky Jones is secretly responsible for the whole thing anyway, so she should probably go at the top of this section. Dan Crinnion—a formerly unsung but now Emmy-nominated editor—gave me shelter and firm, dad-based conversation at cast parties. Adeel Akhtar was terrific to work with on the Martin character, although people now think Martin's based on me. What's that about?

I would also like to thank Amandeep Singh at Ebury, Luna Centifanti, Alice Vincent, Rebecca Nicholson, Sophia Milsom, Claire Jones (née Moore), Sarah Linton, Nicola & Victoria Larder, and Rob Williams for helpful conversations that provoked me to think deeper about this work.

My wife, Lotte, has shown fathomless patience and understanding for this project as well as tirelessly and brilliantly parenting two young children often without my (admittedly inept) assistance on evenings and weekends. I love her greatly and without her this book would not have been a possibility.

GHOSTS OF THE TSUNAMI

GHOSTS
OF THE
TSUNAMI

DEATH AND LIFE
IN JAPAN'S
DISASTER ZONE

RICHARD LLOYD PARRY

MCD ⊜ FARRAR, STRAUS AND GIROUX NEW YORK

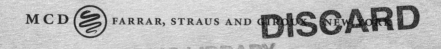

952.05
P265

MCD
Farrar, Straus and Giroux
18 West 18th Street, New York 10011

Grateful acknowledgment is made for permission to reprint the
following material:
Excerpt from "Shock" from *Collected Poems* by Anthony Thwaite, published by
Enitharmon in 2007, reprinted by permission of Anthony Thwaite.
Excerpt from *Invisible Cities* by Italo Calvino, translated by William
Weaver. Copyright © 1972 by Giulio Einaudi editore, s.p.a. Torino,
English translation copyright © 1983, 1984 by Houghton Mifflin
Harcourt Publishing Company. Reprinted by permission of Houghton
Mifflin Harcourt Publishing Company. All rights reserved.
The maps on pages xi–xv were created by Darren Bennett. The image on page 2 is
reproduced with the permission of the Tectonics Observatory at the California
Institute of Technology. The photographs on page 52 have been provided by the
Tohoku Regional Development Association. The photograph on page 126 was
taken by a survivor of the tsunami who wishes to remain anonymous.

Library of Congress Cataloging-in-Publication Data
Names: Parry, Richard Lloyd, author.
Title: Ghosts of the tsunami : death and life in Japan's disaster zone /
Richard Lloyd Parry.
Description: First American Edition. | New York : Farrar, Straus and Giroux/
MCD, [2017] | Includes bibliographical references and index.
Identifiers: LCCN 2017021678 | ISBN 9780374253974 (hardcover) |
ISBN 9780374710934 (e-book)
Subjects: LCSH: Tohoku Earthquake and Tsunami, Japan, 2011. | Tsunamis—
Japan—History—21st century. | Japan—History—Heisei period, 1989–
Classification: LCC HV600 2011.T64 P37 2017 | DDC 952.05/12—dc23
LC record available at https://lccn.loc.gov/2017021678

Designed by Abby Kagan

www.fsgbooks.com • www.mcdbooks.com
www.twitter.com/mcdbooks • www.facebook.com/mcdbooks

1   3   5   7   9   10   8   6   4   2

114256800

For Stella and Kit

What is this flesh I purchased with my pains,
This fallen star my milk sustains,
This love that makes my heart's blood stop
Or strikes a Sudden chill into my bones
And bids my hair stand up?

—W. B. YEATS

CONTENTS

CONTENTS

Japan

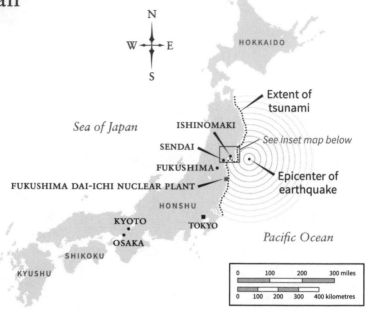

N
W E
S

HOKKAIDO

Sea of Japan

ISHINOMAKI

SENDAI

FUKUSHIMA

FUKUSHIMA DAI-ICHI NUCLEAR PLANT

HONSHU

KYOTO

OSAKA

SHIKOKU

KYUSHU

Extent of tsunami

See inset map below

Epicenter of earthquake

Pacific Ocean

TOKYO

| 0 | 100 | 200 | 300 miles |
| 0 | 100 | 200 | 300 | 400 kilometres |

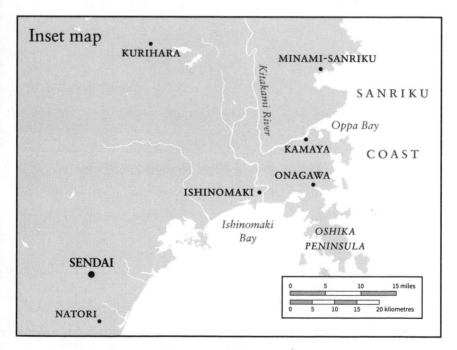

Inset map

KURIHARA

MINAMI-SANRIKU

SANRIKU

Kitakami River

Oppa Bay

KAMAYA

COAST

ONAGAWA

ISHINOMAKI

Ishinomaki Bay

OSHIKA PENINSULA

SENDAI

NATORI

| 0 | 5 | 10 | 15 miles |
| 0 | 5 | 10 | 15 | 20 kilometres |

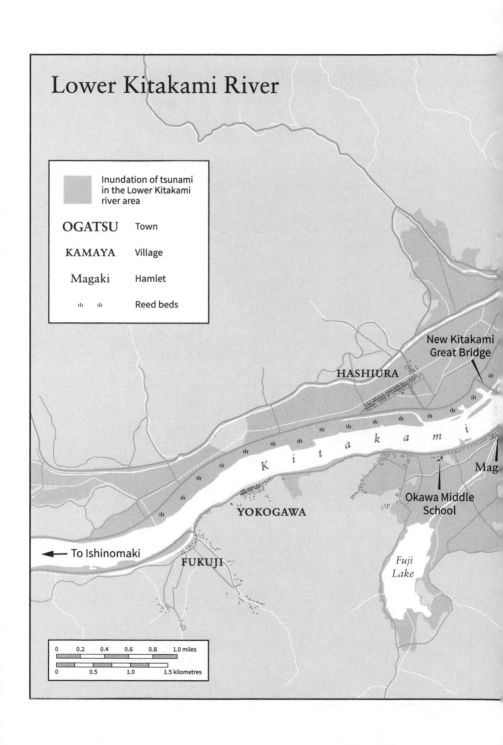

Lower Kitakami River

Inundation of tsunami in the Lower Kitakami river area

OGATSU Town

KAMAYA Village

Magaki Hamlet

⼮ ⼮ Reed beds

New Kitakami
Great Bridge

HASHIURA

Kitakami

Mag

Okawa Middle
School

YOKOGAWA

← To Ishinomaki

FUKUJI

Fuji
Lake

| 0 | 0.2 | 0.4 | 0.6 | 0.8 | 1.0 miles |

| 0 | 0.5 | 1.0 | 1.5 kilometres |

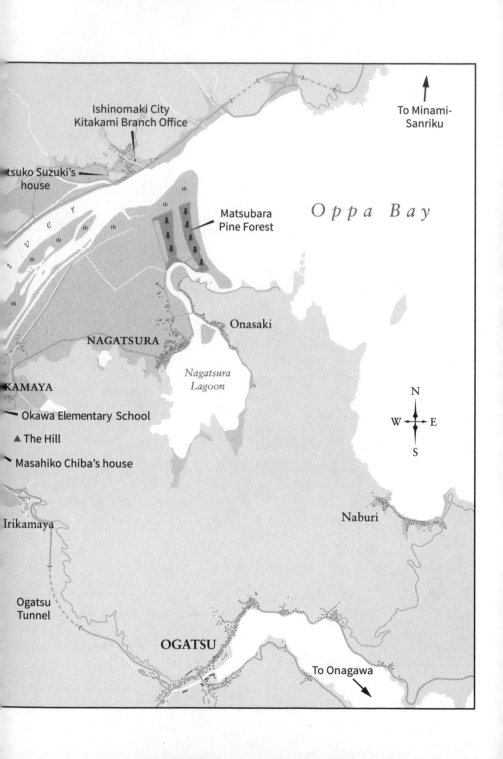

Ishinomaki City
Kitakami Branch Office

tsuko Suzuki's
house

Matsubara
Pine Forest

Oppa Bay

To Minami-
Sanriku

Onasaki

NAGATSURA

*Nagatsura
Lagoon*

KAMAYA

Okawa Elementary School

▲ The Hill

Masahiko Chiba's house

N

W ← → E

S

Irikamaya

Naburi

Ogatsu
Tunnel

OGATSU

To Onagawa

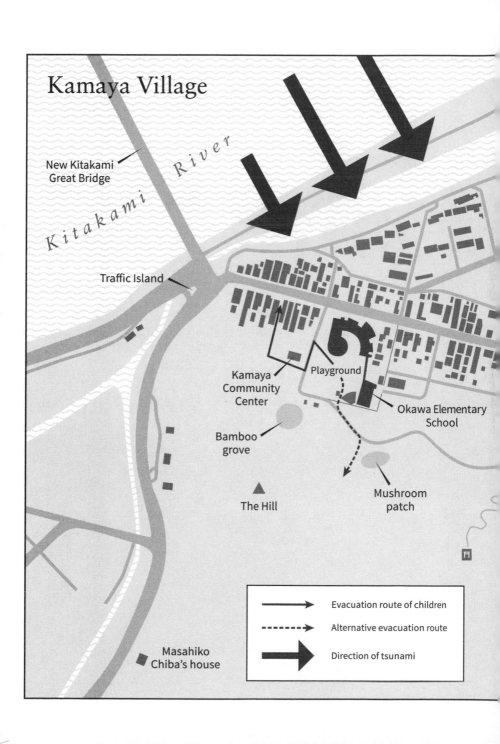

Kamaya Village

New Kitakami Great Bridge

Kitakami River

Traffic Island

Kamaya Community Center

Playground

Okawa Elementary School

Bamboo grove

The Hill

Mushroom patch

Masahiko Chiba's house

→ Evacuation route of children

----▶ Alternative evacuation route

➡ Direction of tsunami

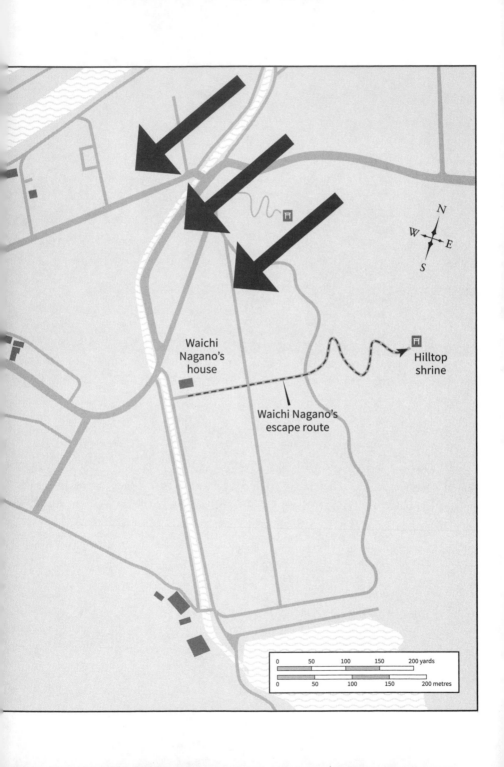

Waichi
Nagano's
house

Hilltop
shrine

Waichi Nagano's
escape route

N
W   E
S

| 0 | 50 | 100 | 150 | 200 yards |
| 0 | 50 | 100 | 150 | 200 metres |

On March 11, 2011, two catastrophes struck northeast Japan. The second began in the evening, when reactors at the Fukushima Dai-ichi nuclear power plant melted down, following the failure of their cooling systems. Explosions in three of the reactors scattered radioactive fallout across the countryside. More than 200,000 people fled their homes. But, thanks to a swift evacuation and a good deal of luck, nobody died as a result of the radiation. It is too soon to be sure about the long-term consequences of Fukushima—but it may turn out that nobody ever will.

The earthquake and tsunami that set off the nuclear disaster had a more immediate effect on human life. By the time the sea retreated, 18,500 people had been crushed, burned to death, or drowned. It was the greatest single loss of life in Japan since the atomic bombing of Nagasaki in 1945.

This book is about the first disaster: the tsunami.

GHOSTS OF THE TSUNAMI

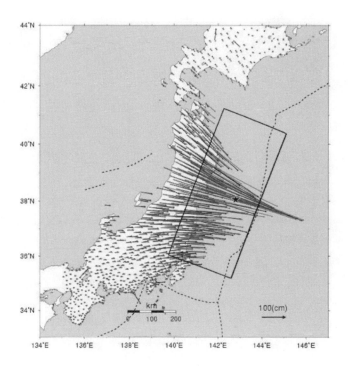

PROLOGUE: SOLID VAPOR

The eleventh of March 2011 was a cold, sunny Friday, and it was the day I saw the face of my son for the first time. I was in a clinic in central Tokyo, peering at the images on a small screen. Beside me, F—— lay, exposed, on the examination bed. Her oval belly was smeared with transparent gel; against it, the doctor pressed a glowing wand of plastic. As the wand moved, the images on the screen shifted and jumped.

We knew what to look for, but it was still astonishing to see so much of the small creature: the familiar top-heavy outline; the heart, with its flickering chambers; brain, spine, individual fingers, and so much movement—paddling arms, bucking legs, and nodding head. The angle of vision altered and revealed at once a well-formed, unearthly face, which gave a charming and very human yawn. Our second child—our boy, although we did not know this yet—was still in there, still patiently alive.

Outside the clinic it was chilly, gusty, and bright, and the wide avenue was filling with midday shoppers and workers coming out of the offices for lunch. We pushed our toddler daughter

to a café and showed her the murky photograph of her sibling-to-be, printed out from the scanner's screen.

Two hours later, I was sitting at my desk in a tenth-floor office. What exactly was I doing at the moment it began? Writing an e-mail? Reading the newspaper? Looking out the window? All that I remember of the hours before are those moments in front of the screen, which had already made the day unforgettable, and the sensation of looking into the face of my son at the halfway point between his conception and his birth.

I had lived in Japan for sixteen years, and I knew, or believed that I knew, a good deal about earthquakes. I had certainly experienced enough of them—since 1995, when I settled in Tokyo, 17,257 tremors had been felt in the capital alone. A spate of them had occurred two days earlier. I had sat out the shaking, monitored the measurements of magnitude and intensity, and reported them online with a jauntiness that now makes me ashamed:

> @dicklp
> Wed Mar 09 2011 11:51:51
> Earthquake!
>
> Wed Mar 09 2011 11:53:14
> Epicenter, Miyagi Prefecture. Tsunami warning in
> place on northern Pacific coast. In Tokyo, we are
> shaken, but not stirred.
>
> Wed Mar 09 2011 12:01:04
> More tremors . . .

Wed Mar 09 2011 12:16:56
@LiverpolitanNYC All fine here, thanks. Its wobble
was worse than its bite.

Wed Mar 09 2011 16:09:39
Latest on today's Japan earthquake horror: 10cm
tsunami reported in Iwate Prefecture. That's almost
as deep as my washing-up water.

The following day, there had been another strong tremor in the
same zone of the Pacific Ocean off northeast Japan. This one,
too, could be felt as far away as Tokyo, but even close to the epicenter it caused no injury or significant damage. "The Thursday
morning quake brought the number of quakes felt in Japan since
Wednesday to more than thirty," Kyodo news agency reported;
and plenty of them were strong tremors, not the subterranean
shivers detectable only by scientific instruments. The seismologists
warned of the potential for a "powerful aftershock" in the next
week or so, although "crustal activities" were expected to subside.

Clusters of proximate earthquakes are known as "swarms,"
and they can be the precursor to larger tremors and even volcanic
eruptions. But although many seismic disasters are preceded by
such omens, the converse is not true; most swarms buzz past
without any destructive crescendo. I had reported on this phe-
nomenon a few years earlier, when a swarm of earthquakes hinted
at a potential eruption of Mount Fuji. Nothing of the kind had
happened then; clusters of lesser earthquakes continued to come
and go; and there was no reason for particular attention or alarm
this week.

Not that there was much else happening in Japan that day,
certainly not of international interest. The prime minister was

resisting halfhearted demands that he resign over a political funding scandal. The governor of Tokyo was expected to announce whether he would stand for another term. *Ibaraki Airport Marks First Anniversary*, noted one of the news agency's headlines. *Snack Maker Debuts on Tokyo Stock Exchange*, mumbled another. Then, at 2:48 p.m., came an urgent single-line bulletin: *BREAKING NEWS: Powerful Quake Rocks Japan*.

I had felt it about a minute earlier. It began mildly and familiarly enough with gentle but unmistakable vibrations transmitted upwards through the floor of the office, followed by a side-to-side swaying. With the motion came a distinctive sound—the glassy tinkling of the window blinds as their vinyl ends buffeted against one another. The same thing had happened two days earlier and passed within moments. So even when the glass in the windows began to rattle, I stayed in my chair.

> @dicklp
> Fri Mar 11 2011 14:47:52
> Another earthquake in Tokyo . . .

> Fri Mar 11 2011 14:47:59
> Strong one . . .

> Fri Mar 11 2011 14:48:51
> strongest I've ever known in 16 yers . . .

By the time the sliding drawers of the filing cabinets gaped open, my sangfroid, as well as my typing, was beginning to fail me. From the tenth-floor window, I could see a striped red-and-white telecommunications mast on the roof of a building a hundred yards away. I told myself: "When that mast starts to wobble, I'll move." As the thought took form in my mind, I no-

ticed that a much closer structure, an arm of the same building in which I was sitting, was flexing visibly. Very quickly indeed I bent myself into the narrow space beneath my desk.

Later, I read that the vibrations had lasted for six minutes. But while they continued, time passed in an unfamiliar way. The chinking of the blinds, the buzzing of the glass, and the deep rocking motion generated an atmosphere of dreamlike unreality; by the time I emerged from my funk hole, I had little sense of how long I had been there. It was not the shaking itself that was frightening, but the way it continued to become stronger, with no way of knowing when it would end. Now books were slumping on the shelves. Now a marker board fell off a partition. The building, a nondescript twelve-story structure that had never seemed particularly old or new, sturdy or frail, was generating low groans from deep within its innards. It was a sound such as one never usually hears, a heart-sickening noise suggesting deep and mortal distress, like the death sound of a dying monster. It went on long enough for me to form distinct images about what would happen in the next stage of the earthquake's intensification: the toppling of shelves and cabinets, the exploding of glass, the collapse of the ceiling onto the floor, the floor itself giving way, and the sensation both of falling and of being crushed.

At a point difficult to define, the tremors began to ease. The building's moans faded to muttering. My heartbeat slowed. My balance, I found, had been mildly upset, and like a passenger stepping off a boat, it was hard to tell whether motion had ceased completely. Five minutes later, the cords hanging from the blinds were still wagging feebly.

Over the internal loudspeakers, an announcement from the Disaster Counter-Measures Room—every big building in Tokyo has one—assured us that the structure was safe and that we should stay inside.

@dicklp
Fri Mar 11 14:59:44
I'm fine. A frighteningly strong quake. Aftershocks.
Fires round Tokyo bay.

In Japan, there is no excuse for not being prepared for earth-quakes, and in my small office we had taken the recommended precautions. There were no heavy picture frames; the shelves and cabinets were bolted to the walls. Apart from a few fallen books and a general shifting of its contents, the room was in good order. Even the television, the most top-heavy object in the room, remained undisplaced. My Japanese colleague turned it on. Al-ready all channels were showing the same image: the map of Japan, its Pacific coastline banded with colors, red indicating an imminent danger of tsunami. The epicenter, marked by a cross, was upper right, northeast of the main island of Honshu. It was the same area that had been swarming these past days, the region of Japan known as Tohoku.*

I was dialing and redialing F——'s number, without success. The problem was not that the infrastructure was damaged, but that everyone in eastern Japan was simultaneously using his or her mobile phone. I got through by landline to the lady who looked after our nineteen-month-old daughter; the two of them were wobbly but unhurt, and still sheltering beneath the dining-room table. F——, when I finally connected to her, was in her own office, brushing up the glass from a fallen picture frame. Our conversation was punctuated by pauses, as each of us in our distinct districts of the city experienced separately the after-shocks that had begun minutes after the mother quake.

The elevators were suspended, so I walked down nine flights

---

* Pronounced "Tour-Hock-oo," with the last syllable short and abrupt.

of stairs to inspect the district of shops and offices immediately around the building. There was almost no visible damage. The stripy pole in front of an old-fashioned barber's shop lolled at an angle. I saw one crack in a window of plate glass, and a perforated gash in a wall of plaster. The streets were crowded with evacuated office workers, many of them wearing the white plastic helmets that Japanese companies provide for just such an occasion. Above the density of city buildings, a distant line of black smoke was visible in the east, where an oil refinery had caught fire. Later, some accounts gave the impression that the earthquake had been a moment of hysteria in Tokyo, in which large numbers of people experienced the sensation of a close brush with death. They were exaggerations. Modern engineering and strict building laws, evolved out of centuries of seismic destruction, had passed the test set by the earthquake. A spasm of alarm passed quickly, followed by hours of disruption, inconvenience, and boredom. But the prevailing emotion was bemused resignation rather than panic.

A man in an old-fashioned ceramics shop, where a vase sold for £5,000, had not lost a single plate. We talked to a group of elderly ladies in kimonos who had been watching a play in the nearby kabuki theater when the earthquake struck. "They'd just started the last act, and people cried out," one of them said. "But the actors kept going—they didn't hesitate at all. I thought it would subside, but it went on and on, and everyone stood up and started flooding out of the door." The star performers, the famous kabuki actors Kikugoro Onoe and Kichiemon Nakamura, bowed deeply to the audience as they fled, apologizing for the interruption.

Fri Mar 11 16:26:4
Central Tokyo calm and undamaged. In 30 mins

stroll in Ginza I saw one cracked window and a few walls.

Fri Mar 11 16:28:56
Seems to be just one fire in an oil facility in Chiba Prefecture.

Fri Mar 11 16:40:31
Eleven nuke power plants shut down in Japan. No problems reported after quakes.

Fri Mar 11 17:47:25
I've lost count of aftershocks. 15 or more. Latest one was from a different epicenter to 1st big quake, accdng to Jpn TV.

Fri Mar 11 18:20:10
To anyone struggling to get through to Tokyo—use Skype. Internet in Tokyo seems fine.

Back in the office, we turned to the television again. Already Japan's richly resourced broadcasters were mobilizing airplanes, helicopters, and manpower. The foreign channels, too, had given over their programming to rolling coverage of the situation, with that thinly disguised lust that appalling news excites in cable-news producers. I began to file reports for my newspaper's website, attempting to make sense of the packets of information that were arriving in the form of images, sounds, and text, through cable, satellite, Internet, fax, and telephone. But the facts were still frustratingly vague. An earthquake had come and gone, and the human response to it was obvious enough: a disaster unit established at the prime minister's office; airports, railways, and high-

ways shut down. Yet what actual damage had been done so far? There were patchy reports of fires, like the one at the oil refinery. But for the first few hours the seismologists could not even agree on the magnitude of the earthquake; and from the Tohoku coast itself came only silence.

Casualty figures were especially elusive. At 6:30 p.m., the television news was reporting twenty-three killed. By nine o'clock, the figure had risen to sixty-one, and after midnight, the news agencies were still speaking of sixty-four deaths. Clearly, these numbers were going to increase as communications were restored. But it also seemed obvious that in a situation such as this there was a bias towards pessimism and a tendency to entertain the very worst imaginable possibility; and that probably, in the end, it wouldn't be so bad as all that.

> @dicklp
> Fri Mar 11 17:58:43
> No reports of deaths in Tokyo so far. My hunch is that
> there will be scores, perhaps low hundreds in NE
> Japan, but no more. Not megadeath.

There are several aerial films of the incoming tsunami, but the one that plays and replays in my imagination was shot above the town of Natori, south of the city of Sendai. It begins over land rather than sea, with a view of dun winter paddy fields. Something is moving across the landscape as if it is alive, a brown-snouted animal hungrily bounding over the earth. Its head is a scum of splintered debris; entire cars bob along on its back. It seems to steam and smoke as it moves; its body looks less like water or mud than a kind of solid vapor. And then a large boat can be seen riding it inland, hundreds of yards from the sea,

and—unbelievably—blue-tiled houses, still structurally intact, spinning across the inundated fields with orange flames dancing on their roofs. The creature turns a road into a river, then swallows it whole, and then it is raging over more fields and roads towards a village and a highway thick with cars. One driver is accelerating ahead of it, racing to escape—before the car and its occupants are gobbled up by the wave.

It was the biggest earthquake ever known to have struck Japan, and the fourth most powerful in the history of seismology. It knocked the Earth ten inches off its axis; it moved Japan four feet closer to America. In the tsunami that followed, 18,500 people were drowned, burned, or crushed to death. At its peak, the water was 120 feet high. Half a million people were driven out of their homes. Three reactors in the Fukushima Dai-ichi power station melted down, spilling their radioactivity across the countryside, the world's worst nuclear accident since Chernobyl. The earthquake and tsunami caused more than $210 billion of damage, making it the most costly natural disaster ever.

It was Japan's greatest crisis since the Second World War. It ended the career of one prime minister and contributed to the demise of another. The damage caused by the tsunami disrupted manufacturing by some of the world's biggest corporations. The nuclear disaster caused weeks of power cuts, affecting 2.5 million people. As a result, Japan's remaining nuclear reactors—all fifty of them—were shut down. Hundreds of thousands of people took to the streets in anti-nuclear demonstrations; as a consequence of what happened in Fukushima, the governments of Germany, Italy, and Switzerland abandoned nuclear power altogether.

The earth around the nuclear plant will be contaminated for decades. The villages and towns destroyed by the tsunami may never be rebuilt. Pain and anxiety proliferated in ways that are still difficult to measure, among people remote from the destruc-

tive events. Farmers, suddenly unable to sell their crops, committed suicide. Blameless workers in electricity companies found themselves the object of abuse and discrimination. A generalized dread took hold, the fear of an invisible poison spread through air, through water—even, it was said, through a mother's milk. Among expatriates, it manifested itself as outright panic. Families, companies, embassies abandoned even Tokyo, 140 miles away.

Few of these facts were clear on that evening, as I sat in my office on the tenth floor. But they were becoming obvious the following morning. By then, I was driving from Tokyo towards the ruined coast. I would spend weeks in Tohoku, traveling up and down the strip of land, three miles deep in some places, which had been consumed by the water. I visited a hospital where the wards at night were lit by candles; a hundred yards away, to add to the atmosphere of apocalypse, burning industrial oil tanks sent columns of flame high into the air. I saw towns that had been first flooded, then incinerated; cars that had been lifted up and dropped onto the roofs of high buildings; and iron ocean-going ships deposited in city streets.

Cautiously I entered the ghostly exclusion zone around the nuclear plant, where cows were dying of thirst in the fields, and the abandoned villages were inhabited by packs of pet dogs, gradually turning wild; masked, gloved, and hooded in a protective suit, I entered the broken plant myself. I interviewed survivors, evacuees, politicians, and nuclear experts, and reported day by day on the feckless squirming of the Japanese authorities. I wrote scores of newspaper articles, as well as hundreds of fizzy tweets, and was interviewed on radio and television. And yet the experience felt like a disordered dream.

Those who work in zones of war and disaster acquire after a time the knack of detachment. This is professional necessity: no doctor, aid worker, or reporter can do his job if he is crushed by

the spectacle of death and suffering. The trick is to preserve compassion, without bearing each individual tragedy as your own; and I had mastered this technique. I knew the facts of what had happened, and I knew they were appalling. But at my core, I was not appalled.

"All at once . . . something we could only have imagined was upon us—and we could still only imagine it," wrote Philip Gourevitch. "That is what fascinates me most in existence: the peculiar necessity of imagining what is, in fact, real." The events that constituted the disaster were so diverse, and so vast in their implications, that I never felt that I was doing the story justice. It was like a huge and awkwardly shaped package without corners or handles: however many different ways I tried, it was impossible to hoist it off the ground. In the weeks afterward, I felt wonder, pity, and sadness. But for much of the time I experienced a numb detachment and the troubling sense of having completely missed the point.

It was quite late on, the summer after the tsunami, when I heard about a small community on the coast that had suffered an exceptional tragedy. Its name was Okawa; it lay in a forgotten fold of Japan, below hills and among rice fields, close to the mouth of a great river. I traveled to this obscure place, and spent days and weeks there. In the years that followed, I encountered many survivors and stories of the tsunami, but it was to Okawa that I returned time and again. And it was there, at the school, that I eventually became able to imagine.

PART I

THE SCHOOL BENEATH

THE WAVE

HAVING GONE, I WILL COME

The first time I met her, in the big wooden house at the foot of the hills, Sayomi Shito recalled the night when her youngest daughter, Chisato, sat suddenly up in bed and cried out, "The school has gone."

"She was asleep," her mother told me. "And then she woke up in tears. I asked her, 'Why? What do you mean, "gone"?' She said, 'A big earthquake.' She was really shouting. She used to sleep-walk occasionally, and she used to mutter odd things now and then. Sometimes she'd get up and walk around, not knowing what she was doing, and I had to guide her back to bed. But she had never had a fright like that before."

It wasn't that Chisato, who was eleven, was particularly afraid of earthquakes. A few weeks after her nightmare, on March 9, 2011, there was a strong tremor, which shook the concrete walls of Okawa Elementary School, where she was a pupil—the onset of the swarm that I also experienced two hundred miles away in Tokyo. Chisato and the other children had crawled under their desks while the shaking continued, then put on their plastic helmets, followed their teachers out to the playground, and stood in

neat lines while their names were called out and ticked off. But rumbles large and small were common all over Japan, and at home that evening she had not even mentioned it.

Sayomi Shito was curly-haired, round-faced, and bespectacled, an unabashed, confiding woman in her mid-forties. Japanese conventions of restraint and politesse sometimes made hard work of interviews, but Sayomi was an effusive talker, with a droll and gossipy sense of humor. I spent long mornings at her home, in a tide of jokes, cakes, biscuits, and cups of tea. She could talk unprompted for an hour at a stretch, frowning, smiling, and shaking her head as if taken aback by her own recollection. Some people are cast adrift by loss, and when Sayomi spoke of her grief, the pain was as intense as anyone's. But anger and indignation had kept her tethered, and bred in her a scathing self-confidence.

The Shitos (their name was pronounced "Sh'tore," like a cross between "shore" and "store") were a very close family. Sayomi's older son and daughter, Kenya and Tomoka, were fifteen and thirteen, but the children all still slept on mattresses alongside their parents in the big room on the upper floor. That Friday, March 11, Sayomi had risen as usual at a quarter past six. It was the day of her son's graduation ceremony from middle school, and her thoughts were filled with mundane, practical matters. "I used to wake Chisato after everyone else had got up," she said. "I'd sit her on my knee and pat her back, and hug her like a koala bear, and she'd lean into me. It was something I liked to do every morning. I'd hug her, and say, 'Wakey, wakey' and we'd start the day. It was our secret moment. But that day she got up on her own."

Chisato had been out of sorts that morning. It came out later that she had quarreled, in trivial, childish fashion, with her older brother and sister. In the kitchen she prepared breakfast for herself; Sayomi still remembered hearing the *ting* of the grill when the toast was ready. The school bus reached the stop around the

corner at 6:56, and Chisato always left the house exactly three minutes before. "She walked past me with her bag on her shoulder, and I realized that I hadn't talked to her yet," Sayomi remembered. "So I said, 'Chi, my love, wait a moment. What's up? Not so happy today?' She said, 'It's nothing,' but rather gloomily. Some days, I used to give her a hug before she went out. That morning, to cheer her up, I gave her a high five. But she was looking at the ground when she walked away."

In Japanese, domestic leave-taking follows an unvarying formula. The person departing says *itte kimasu*, which means literally, "Having gone, I will come back." Those who remain behind respond with *itte rasshai*, which means "Having gone, be back." *Sayonara*, the word that foreigners are taught is the Japanese for "goodbye," is too final for most occasions, implying a prolonged or indefinite separation. *Itte kimasu* contains a different emotional charge: the promise of an intended return.

All along the lowest reach of the Kitakami River, from the lagoon in the east to the hills in the west, with varying degrees of alacrity and reluctance, young pupils of Okawa Elementary School and their parents were conducting the same exchange.

—*Itte kimasu.*
—*Itte rasshai!*

Even before it began, Sayomi told me, Chisato's life had had about it something fated and magical. She had been conceived on Sayomi's thirty-third birthday; she was born on Christmas Eve 1999, a sentimental day even in Japan, where practicing Christians are few. Sayomi went into labor in the afternoon; within an hour, she was back in her bed, eating Christmas cake. The following day, on Christmas morning, the ground was covered in immaculate snow; and a week later, the world celebrated the

beginning of the third millennium. The infant Chisato was as undemanding in the world as she had been entering it. "She was always with me," Sayomi said. "In the sling on my front. On my back, when I was cooking. Beside me, in the child seat in the car, or in my lap when I was sitting down. It was as if she was attached to my skin. And she always slept beside me, in the same room, at my right hand, up until that day."

Fukuji was a gathering of hamlets around a triangular expanse of paddy fields. On two sides were low hills, forested densely with pine; the Shito family house stood on their lowest slope. On the third, northern side was the great Kitakami River, the longest and widest in northern Japan, flowing east towards the Pacific, six miles away. Within a few minutes of the Shitos' home, depending on the season, you could hike, toboggan, skate, hunt, fish, and swim in fresh or salt water. Chisato played with dolls and drew pictures with her sister, but what she liked most was to run at large with her friends Mizuho and Aika, and the dog and cat that belonged to the old lady next door.

She had what her mother identified as a sixth sense. "She used to do things for you before you said you wanted them," Sayomi said. "She had that gift of anticipation. For example, my husband is a joiner. The first time Chisato saw him do his carpentry at home, she was standing watching him. And she'd know what tool or material he needed next. She'd say, 'Here you are, Dad,' and pass it to him. He'd say, 'How much she understands! She's a remarkable girl.'"

Her friends used to tease Chisato by calling her "the security camera," because she was aware of things to which other eleven-year-olds were oblivious. She noticed, before the other girls, when a gang of boys in the class went into a sniggering cluster, plotting some prank. She knew who had a crush on whom, and whether the feeling was reciprocated. Okawa Elementary School was a small

place, with barely a hundred children; in Chisato's fifth-grade class there were just fifteen. It was a warm, close, oppressively intimate arrangement, unforgiving of anyone who stood apart. Chisato hated it.

"There was no doubt about it," said Sayomi. "She hated the teachers. She used to say that school is where teachers tell you lies. But she never refused to go. She said, 'If I miss school, it's you who'll get into trouble.' She knew that she had to do something she didn't want to do."

Sayomi said, "I feel very bad now about letting her go to school with such a feeling. But I didn't want to be the mother who stops her child's education. It wasn't that she was bullied, or anything like that. But perhaps there are children who are better off staying at home, who love their mum more than being with their friends. Everyone you talk to says, 'At least when it happened my child was at the school she loved, with the friends she loved, and the teachers she loved.' Of course, parents want to believe that. But if they asked their kids, 'Do you really like that school? Do you really love those teachers?' then not all of them would say yes."

Many people spoke of it as just another day, but Sayomi Shito remembered a strangeness about that Friday.

After breakfast, she had driven to the local middle school for her son Kenya's graduation ceremony. She took the narrow road across the fields, turned right onto the highway along the river, and passed through the larger village of Yokogawa. Just beyond the village shrine, a small hill bulged out, forcing the road hard up against the water and blocking the view of its lower reaches. Beyond it a wide and magnificent vista opened up, of the broad river with its deep reed beds and stubbled brown paddies on both

sides, and huge blue skies above green hills. In the distance was the low line of the New Kitakami Great Bridge, six hundred yards across, connecting Okawa in the south with the Kitakami district on the northern bank.

After the ceremony, Sayomi and Kenya drove farther down the river to the next village, where a modest celebration was being held for the middle-school graduates. This was Kamaya, where Okawa Elementary School was also situated. Twenty or thirty teenagers and their mothers were gathering in a hall, virtually across the road from Chisato's classroom. Friends who might not see one another again said their goodbyes and exchanged gifts; there was a table of comforting home-cooked foods. Sayomi expected the event to go on until the mid-afternoon, but soon after two o'clock people began to drift away. Kenya wanted to go home. But first there was the question of what to do about Chisato.

Lessons at Okawa Elementary School finished at 2:30, but it was always another ten or fifteen minutes before anyone began to leave, as the children gathered up their things, and the teachers handed out notices or made announcements. Should they linger in wait for Chisato, for what might be another half hour? Or should they go home now, and leave her to take the bus as usual? Sayomi stood by her car in front of the school, considering this small dilemma. And, as she remembered it later, a powerful sense of the uncanny overcame her, in this, the last hour of the old world. "It had been a clear, fine day until noon," she said. "By the time the party came to an end, it was already becoming cloudy, but there was no wind. Not a single leaf was moving on the trees. I couldn't sense any life at all. It was as if a film had stopped, as if time had stopped. It was an uncomfortable atmosphere, not the atmosphere of an ordinary day. I didn't like the fact that I couldn't hear the children in the school—even when they were in their lessons, you could always hear the voices of the little ones. Normally, I might

have walked in and said, 'I popped in to pick up my daughter.' But the school felt . . . isolated."

I asked Sayomi what explained this curious atmosphere. She said, "Living here in this countryside, people coexist with nature. With animals, with plants, with all of this environment. When the wind blows, I hear the sound of the trees, and I know from that sound the condition of the wind. When it's about to snow, I sense the snow in the air. I feel by instinct the character of the atmosphere surrounding me. That air and that atmosphere are important, almost more important than people. I think Chisato was a girl who also had those instincts.

"But then Kenya said, 'Shall we go?' And I thought that it was time to go home. Perhaps it was some kind of intuition that I had to leave. Perhaps that was it. But what I said to myself was: 'If we go home now, he will have more time to see his friends.' So we went home."

Sayomi was upstairs changing when the shock struck. Her older daughter, Tomoka, had been at home when they returned and had had no lunch. Sayomi set a pan of noodles on the flame, and went to her room. As soon as the shaking began, at 2:46 p.m., she shouted down to the children to turn off the stove and to get outside. Her keenest anxiety was not for them, but for her elderly parents, who lived with the family on the ground floor. Sayomi's mother was frail and slow; her father was both mildly confused and very stubborn. She ran downstairs to find him attempting to gather up the polished black funeral tablets of the family's dead ancestors, which were tumbling from the household Buddhist altar. Sayomi gave up trying to reason with him and stumbled outside, to the big tree where the rest of the family had gathered.

"The shaking was so strong, I couldn't stand up," she said.

"Even outside, crouching down, we were almost falling over. I looked at the metal shutters on the garage—they had ripples going through them. The electricity lines and poles were swaying. It was as if the whole world was collapsing—it was like the special effects in a film about the end of the world. I was amazed that the house didn't fall down. I tried to get the kids into the car, but I couldn't even get the door open. Even holding on to the car, I was afraid that it was going to roll over. So I told the children, 'Stay away from the car,' and then all that we could do was crouch on the ground."

She remembered being conscious of sounds, and of their absence. Despite the proximity of the forest, there was no birdsong, or any sign of birds on the wing. But the next-door neighbor's dog, a placid animal and a favorite of Chisato's, was barking raucously, while the cat pelted into the hills and out of sight. "It felt as if it continued for a long time, perhaps five minutes," Sayomi said. "And the feeling of being shaken carried on, even after the shaking had stopped. The electricity poles and wires were still wobbling, so it was difficult to know whether the earth was still moving or whether it was the trembling in myself. The children were upset. Kenya was looking around and shouting, 'Grandpa! What happened to Grandpa?'"

The old man finally tottered from the house, without his ancestors.

But now the poles and wires and shutters were vibrating again, in the first of a long succession of aftershocks. Sayomi herded her parents and the children into the car, and drove down the lane to a spot in the rice fields where much of the population of Fukuji was already converging. Chairs and mattresses were being laid out for children and old people, and neighbors were exclaiming to one another over what had happened. But from this vantage point, it was clear that any physical damage had been

remarkably slight. Apart from the displacement of a few roof tiles, none of the houses in the area, as far as Sayomi could tell, had collapsed or suffered serious damage. There was wonder, and a residue of alarm, but no one was panicking or hysterical. Like a reflection in water after ripples, normality seemed steadily to be reasserting itself.

Sayomi sent a text message to her husband, reporting on the family's situation, and received one in return. The building site where Takahiro was working had been thrown into disarray by the shaking, but he was unhurt. She looked around, at friends and neighbors performing acts of kindness, a community spontaneously organizing itself to help the old, young, and weak. It occurred to her then that the returning bus, which would bring Chisato home from school, was due at any moment. After settling her parents and children among their neighbors, she drove the few hundred yards to the river to meet it.

Half a dozen cars had pulled up on the main road along the river; their drivers stood beside them, discussing the situation. Wood from a timber yard was said to have spilled onto the road up ahead, making the way hazardous. None of the drivers had seen the obstruction for himself. But none made any move to investigate. People were calm; none gave any sign of impatience or trepidation. But in the inertness of the scene, Sayomi intuited anxiety and strain. She tried to text her husband again. Immediately after the earthquake, messages had gone through without difficulty, although voice calls were impossible. But now the network had shut down.

Over the next hour, Sayomi drove back and forth between the road, where she waited for the appearance of the school bus, and the rice field, where she checked on the well-being of her family.

As she shuttled to and fro, the soothing sense of normality winning out over disaster drained rapidly away.

Sayomi's attention was drawn to one of the channels that connected with the great river, part of a network of slack creeks that irrigated the paddies. Its level rose and fell with the cycles of the rice crop, but it was never completely dry. Now, though, the water in it had almost entirely disappeared; the muddy bottom was visible, glistening grayly. The next time she looked, the situation had reversed: the stream was engorged with surging water from the river, and pieces of dark unidentifiable debris were racing along its churning surface. Soon the adjoining fields were flooded with water. The spectacle was remarkable enough for Sayomi to make a film of it on her mobile phone. The brief clip recorded the time, 3:58 p.m., and a snatch of news from the car radio: ". . . as a result of the tsunami which hit Onagawa, houses are reported to have been inundated up to their roofs and vehicles have been washed away. Maintain strict vigilance . . ."

The word "tsunami" was well known to Sayomi, of course; stronger earthquakes, if they occurred under the sea, were commonly followed by a tsunami warning. The size of the waves would be reported on the television as they came in: thirty inches, fifteen inches, four inches—phenomena scarcely visible to the untrained eye, often measurable only by harbor gauges. But the radio was speaking of Ō-tsunami—a "super-tsunami," twenty feet high—and all of this in Onagawa, a fishing port just an hour's drive to the south. "I knew that twenty feet was big, although knowing it is different from feeling it," Sayomi said. "But to hear that it was capable of washing away cars, that brought it home. I tried to stay calm. There was nothing else I could do."

Sayomi went back to the main road and waited for her daughter, as dusk swallowed up the day.

She had been standing in front of Okawa Elementary School an hour and a half ago; it should have been the most natural thing in the world to drive back down the road along the river to collect Chisato. It was only four miles downstream, but there were no cars at all coming from that direction. The drivers loitering at the lock said that the way was dangerous, although no one seemed willing to explain exactly why. Wet, sleety snow had begun to fall. The river was behaving as if it was possessed. The surface of the water was bulging and flexing like the muscles beneath the skin of an athlete; large, irregularly shaped objects were dimly visible on its surface. Sayomi lingered by the river, watching the road, until after it was dark.

At home, she found her house intact, but littered with fallen and broken objects, and without electricity, gas, or water. She improvised a meal out of leftovers, and forced herself not to worry about Chisato. Plenty of families in Fukuji were waiting for children who had not come back from the elementary school, and none showed excessive concern. Chisato's teachers were trained to deal with emergencies. The concrete school was built more strongly than the wooden houses of Fukuji, all of which had ridden out the earthquake. Most reassuring to Sayomi, who had attended the school herself, was its position immediately in front of a seven-hundred-foot hill. A track, rising from the back of the playground, ascended quickly to a point beyond the reach of even a "super-tsunami." Without electricity, people in Fukuji had no access to television or the Internet; none had yet seen the images of the devouring wave, which were being played over and over again across the world. Instead, they listened to the local radio station, which was retailing the cautious, official casualty figures: scores confirmed dead, hundreds more likely. Then came an unambiguous

report, which everyone waiting up that evening remembered: two hundred people, locals and children, were sheltering in Okawa Elementary School, cut off and awaiting rescue.

Sayomi's relief at hearing this was a measure of the anxiety that she had been reluctant to admit even to herself. "One of the other mums was saying that they were probably staying in the upper gallery of the gym, and enjoying a pajama party," Sayomi remembered. "We said to one another, 'Poor old Chisato. She's going to be hungry and cold.' We were no more worried than that."

But when Takahiro finally reached home that night, after an exhausting journey along cracked and congested roads, the first thing Sayomi said to him was "Chisato's not back."

The family spent the night in the car, as a precaution against aftershocks. Squeezed side by side in the upright seats, no one slept much. Sayomi was kept awake by a single phrase, which sounded over and over in her head: "Chisato's not here, Chisato's not here, Chisato's not here."

It was bitterly cold, and the darkness was overwhelming. Everyone who lived through that night was amazed by the intense clarity of the sky overhead and the brightness of the stars. They found themselves in a land without power, television, telephones, a place suddenly plucked up and folded into a pocket of time, disconnected from the twenty-first century. Sayomi got up at dawn, stiff and cold. Gas and water had been restored, so she could at least make tea and cook. Then came news that spread excitedly among the mothers of Okawa Elementary School. A helicopter was flying there to pick up the trapped children and to lift them out. Takahiro and the other men of the village were preparing a place for it to land. Chisato was coming home at last.

WHERE ARE THE CHILDREN?

Daisuke Konno was a stalwart of the judo team and captain of the sixth-grade class, but he was a gentle, softhearted boy and that day he didn't want to go to school, either. There was barely a week to go until graduation; his mother, Hitomi, pushed him out of the door. It was a cold morning in the unreliable period between winter and spring. But there was nothing ominous about it, and neither mother nor son was the kind to be troubled by supernatural intimations of disaster. Photographs of Daisuke show a cheery round face with a self-deprecating smile. "He loved judo," Hitomi said. "And to his friends he put on a tough face. But to me, back at home, he used to complain about the pain of being thrown. And at school it seems that a group of the boys had been told off by the teacher. That was the only reason he didn't want to go."

—*Itte kimasu*, said the reluctant Daisuke.

—*Itte rasshai*, Hitomi responded.

The Konno family lived in the village of Magaki, three miles downstream of Sayomi's home in Fukuji. The bus passed through here, but Okawa Elementary School was close enough that the

children of Magaki made the journey by foot. Daisuke (his name was pronounced "Dice-keh") walked along the river's edge with a slouching gang of classmates. The riverbank at this point was hardly elevated at all; the breadth of the road was all that separated the houses from the lapping water.

Hitomi's husband had already gone to work. She followed soon after her son, leaving behind her parents-in-law and two teenage daughters. She drove south, away from the river and up a road that ascended into the hills through hairpin bends and entered a mile-long tunnel, to emerge above the fishing port of Ogatsu. By eight o'clock, she was seated at her keyboard in the small doctor's surgery where she worked as a receptionist, awaiting the arrival of the first patient of the day.

It was an unexceptional morning. Hitomi ate a packed lunch at her desk. She was a warm, calm woman of forty, with a core of firm-minded common sense beneath an exterior of kindly humility, well suited to dealing with the clinic's mostly elderly, and frequently confused, patients. Apart from handling appointments, processing payments, and keeping the accounts, she supervised the operation of an elaborate apparatus that used an electrical current to massage the muscles. She had just plugged two old ladies into the current when the earthquake began its violent shaking.

She tried to rise, but couldn't. The patients in the waiting room were crying out in alarm. Behind Hitomi were tall flasks in which metal instruments were being sterilized. The boiling water inside them was slopping noisily over the sides, to form steaming pools on the floor.

When the motion had subsided, Hitomi removed the electrodes from the old ladies and handed back the insurance cards as the patients hurried out.

She sent a text message to her oldest daughter, Mari, who was

at home in Magaki. The reply quickly came back: *We're all fine. Don't worry.*

Hitomi mopped up the water from the sterilizing flasks and discussed with the doctor what to do. Ogatsu was on the sea, at the head of a narrow bay. After the strong, but lesser, earthquake two days ago, many people had evacuated the town; but no tsunami had come. As they were recalling this, a man entered the clinic, a sales rep for a pharmaceutical company, with the news that an evacuation warning had been issued and that everyone should retreat to higher ground. Hitomi picked up her jacket and bag and walked to her car. "I remember that the whole town was incredibly quiet," she said. "I could hear a tap dripping at the back of the clinic, the kind of sound that you would never normally notice." Later, she realized this was that ghostly moment in the advent of a tsunami when the water withdraws, exposing seabed and harbor floor, before surging back in with full force. It was the absence of the familiar shush and slap of the sea that made tiny, domestic noises unnaturally noticeable.

She drove back up the hill; even inside the moving car, she could feel the aftershocks. Without thinking, she entered the tunnel, and then immediately began to worry about the solidity of its ceiling, and the unimaginable volumes of stone and earth above it. On the far side, she pulled into a rest stop where other evacuees were waiting, and sat for a while, considering what to do next. She started off down the road again and passed a local man she knew, who waved her to a stop.

"I wouldn't go down there, if I were you," the man said, pointing in the direction of Hitomi's home in Magaki.

"Why not?" Hitomi asked. But the man just mumbled something she couldn't hear.

It had begun snowing. "It wasn't late, still not yet four o'clock," Hitomi remembered. "I was sending text messages and trying to

phone home, but now nothing connected. It was very dark, unusually dark overhead. I started driving down again, but someone else I knew stopped me and said, 'Don't go on.'"

A few hundred yards down the road was a vantage point from which Magaki and the country around it could be seen clearly. The man gave no explanation for his warning, and Hitomi did not press him for one. Instead, she retreated to the rest stop and spent a cold and uncomfortable night in the car.

She drove down the road again as it started to become light, and soon reached the point where the hills fell away on the left, revealing the broad Kitakami River valley below, the view Hitomi saw every afternoon when she drove back from work. On both of its banks, a wide margin of level fields rose suddenly into forested hills. On the near side was Hitomi's home village of Magaki, and then an expanse of paddies stretching to the Fuji lake; the polished blue and red roofs of other hamlets glittered at the edges of the hills. It was an archetypal view of the Japanese countryside: abundant nature, tamed and cultivated by man. But now she struggled to make sense of what she saw.

Everything up to and in between the hills was water. There was only water: buildings and fields had gone. The water was black in the early light; floating on it were continents and trailing archipelagos of dark scummy rubble, brown in color and composed of broken tree trunks. Every patch of land that was not elevated had been absorbed by the river, which had been annexed in turn by the sea. In this new geography, the Fuji lake was no longer a lake, but the inner reach of an openmouthed bay; the river was not a river, but a wide maritime inlet. Okawa Elementary School was invisible, hidden from view by the great shoulder of hills from which Hitomi looked down. But the road, the houses, and Magaki, where Hitomi's home and family had been, were washed from the earth.

Upstream in Fukuji, the news about the helicopter set off a clatter of collective activity. Sayomi's husband, Takahiro, spent the early morning helping to mark off a space where the rescued children could land safely. Sayomi and the other mothers made heaps of rice balls and brought them to the local community center, where the evacuees were to be taken to recover from their ordeal. She kept two of the rice balls back and put them in her pocket so that, even if she was one of the last to arrive, Chisato would not go hungry.

The helicopter was expected at 11:00 a.m. Families converged on Fukuji from along the river: brothers, sisters, parents, and grandparents, dressed against the cold in fleeces and puffer jackets, and carrying bags and rucksacks with hot drinks and bars of chocolate, and more warm clothes for their returning sons and daughters.

They stood looking up at the sky. There was almost no conversation among them. Helicopters came and went all morning. The blue ones were from the police. One or two might have been military aircraft of the Japan Self-Defense Forces. None of them landed at Fukuji.

"We waited for four hours," Sayomi said. "There weren't just a few helicopters, there were a lot. We waited and waited. None of them even came close to us. A very desperate feeling was growing in me."

The men of the village conferred once again, and decided to send a team downriver to go to the school and find out for themselves what was going on.

They drove past the spilled planks from the timber yard and through the village of Yokogawa, where everything appeared normal: a Shinto shrine, a Buddhist temple, and two rows of

houses facing one another across the road, none of them visibly damaged. Then they reached the rise that jutted out and concealed the view of the last stretch of the great river. It became obvious only as they crossed it that this unremarkable barrier marked the threshold dividing life from death.

Physically, Yokogawa had been untouched by the disaster. A high embankment and the bend in the river had shielded it from the water. But beyond the hill, the tsunami had surged upstream, overwhelmed the embankment, and risen with deadly force. The men looked out to see what Hitomi, from her opposite vantage point, also saw: the highway and embankment overwhelmed, the bridge broken, and the land turned to sea.

Hitomi drove down in the dawn light, through perfect stillness and hush. Hers was the only car on the road; it was as if the world was newly formed and she was the first to enter it. The surface of the great expanse of water flashed black and silver with the changing angle of the sun. But at the foot of the hill, Hitomi discovered that not all of the land had been overwhelmed.

In the innermost reaches of the valley, a hamlet called Irikamaya had been spared. The village hall had become a refugee center. Hitomi could see human figures milling around it. The roofs were covered in snow. The people were wrapped in coats and fleeces against the morning chill. She stumbled out of her car, calling out her children's names and reeling from face to face in search of one that she knew. But everyone seemed to be looking for somebody, and none was from Magaki. Then, with a jolt of recognition and relief, she saw a boy whom she knew from Okawa Elementary School—Tetsuya Tadano, a younger member of Daisuke's judo team. His clothes were filthy. His right eye was bruised and swollen shut.

"Tetsuya! Oh, Tetsuya, are you okay? What happened, Tetsuya? What happened to Daisuke?"

"We were running away," said Tetsuya. "When we were running, Dai fell over. I tried to pull him up by his collar, but he couldn't get up."

"So what happened to him? What happened to him, Tetsuya?"

The boy shook his head.

Then Hitomi noticed another fifth-grade boy, Kohei Takahashi, similarly ragged and begrimed.

"Kohei, where's Daisuke?"

"Dai was with me," he said. "He was behind me, running. We were in the water together. He was just behind me."

"So what happened to him, Kohei?"

"He was floating."

Outside she found a third face from the elementary school: a teacher named Junji Endo, a man who surely could provide some answers.

"Mr. Endo! Mr. Endo, it's Hitomi Konno, Daisuke's mother. What happened? What happened at the school?"

The teacher was sitting alone, hugging his knees with both hands. Hitomi leaned down to him and repeated herself. He hardly looked up.

"Mr. Endo? What happened at the school, Mr. Endo?"

He appeared to be in a state of deep abstraction. To Hitomi, it was as if his emotions had drained out of him.

"No idea," he mumbled eventually. "No idea what's going on."

Hitomi struggled to assemble these fragments of information. The elementary school was on the other side of the hill from where she now stood. The two boys must have climbed up and over it in just the last few hours. If they had escaped, then others, including Daisuke, must have done the same; he might be up there still, on that hill. Hitomi walked away from the community

center and back down the road, wading in places, and began to climb the hill herself, calling her son's name.

"Dai! Daisuke! Has anyone seen Daisuke Konno?"

But there was no one there. The area was so large, and paths branched in all directions, separated from one another by a density of pines. She descended the hill and stopped. Then she turned towards the river and waded farther up the road to the place where her home had been.

"It was just a lake," Hitomi remembered. "I couldn't even see the foundations of the houses. I was walking all around and getting very wet, calling the names of each member of my family. I wasn't really conscious of what I was doing. I thought that if I kept calling their names, someone would reply. People tried to stop me. They were looking at me as if I was mad. But I couldn't think what else to do."

Sayomi's husband, Takahiro, did not accompany his neighbors on their mission downriver. For reasons that were not discussed, it had been decided that men with children at Okawa Elementary School should be excluded from the party. But Takahiro heard from them on their return. They had eventually got a lift by boat to a spot on the embankment close to Magaki. One group of men had gone to Irikamaya. The rest had picked their way through the rubble to the school itself.

Going about the village, Sayomi crossed paths with the wife of one of the men in the party. "The woman was weeping," she remembered. "She refused to look me in the eye." But Sayomi insisted that she didn't feel hopeless. She said, "I strongly believed that, although they might not be coming back by helicopter, the children were fine. There were no phones or electricity. They

might have been taken to the big sports center in town, and just not been able to get in touch with us."

She was at home when Takahiro came back from the briefing by the search party. Japanese parents address one another as *otō-san* and *okaa-san*—Father and Mother—particularly when family matters are being discussed, and this was how Takahiro began.

"He came in and called to me, 'Mother . . .'" Sayomi remembered. "And I thought it might be good news."

"Mother, there's no hope," Takahiro said. "There's no hope."

"What?" said Sayomi. "No hope for what?"

"The school is done for," he said. "There is no hope."

"I just seized his shirt," Sayomi told me. "I grabbed his chest. 'I don't understand,' I said. Then I couldn't stand up anymore."

Takahiro recounted what he had been told: that the bodies of two children from the school had been recovered so far, with many more certain to be found, and that only a handful had survived, including two pupils from the fifth grade.

"One of them must be Chisato," Sayomi said.

"They are both boys," said Takahiro.

"Who?"

"One of them is Kohei."

To Sayomi, leaning backward over the brink, this name was like a harness buckled around her waist; a smile came to her mouth as she recalled the moment. For in the fifth-grade class Chisato and Kohei were the keenest rivals, and had been since they were small. "After sports day, Chisato would say, 'I was faster than Kohei' or 'I easily beat Kohei,'" Sayomi told me. If Kohei had survived, then it was impossible that Chisato was not alive too.

JIGOKU

Hitomi Konno finally reached the school early the following morning. It was March 13, 2011, the Sunday.

In a different time, the walk from Irikamaya would have taken twenty minutes, but Hitomi spent more than an hour picking her way along the road beneath the hill, over an obstacle course of water and debris. The rubble included large sections of houses that had been picked up and then dropped by the wave, cars and vans, upended and crushed, and the smallest household items: shoes, sodden garments, cooking pots, teapots, spoons. Broken pine trees made up an inexplicably large volume of the mess; their resinous scent competed with the corrupt stink of the black mud, which coated everything that was not submerged in water. Of the houses that had once been here, not one in twenty survived even as a ruin.

Finally Hitomi reached the point where the inland road met the highway along the river, beside the New Kitakami Great Bridge. The northernmost third of the bridge, a span of two hundred yards, had collapsed and disappeared into the water, exposing bare concrete piles. From here, the road had angled down into

Kamaya, a typically jumbled Japanese village of low concrete build-ings alongside traditional wooden houses with tiled roofs. Until two days ago, all but the top of Okawa Elementary School had been obscured by them, and by the cherry trees planted around it.

Today, though, the school was the first thing Hitomi saw, or its outline. It was cocooned in a spiky, angular mesh of interlock-ing fragments, large and small—tree trunks, the joists of houses, boats, beds, bicycles, sheds, and refrigerators. A buckled car protruded from the window of one of the upper classrooms. A hundred yards beyond, a single concrete structure—the village clinic—was still standing, and in the middle distance a filament-thin steel communications mast. But the buildings in the main street of houses, the lanes that led off it and the houses and shops arrayed along them—all had ceased to exist.

Beyond Kamaya had been a succession of hamlets, and be-yond them fields, low hills, the swaying curve of the river, and finally the Pacific Ocean. At the river's distant mouth there was a beach, popular with surfers and swimmers, and a dense forest of pines, which had been planted as a windbreak and a place of rec-reation. It was those pine trunks, twenty thousand of them, that had been ripped out and transported three miles inland, distrib-uting their distinctive smell. The village, the hamlets, the fields, and everything else between here and the sea had gone.

No photograph could describe the spectacle. Even television images failed to encompass the panoramic quality of the disas-ter, the sense within the plane of destruction of being surrounded by it on all sides, sometimes as far as the eye could see. "It was hell," Hitomi said. "Everything had disappeared. It was as if an atomic bomb had fallen." This comparison, for which many people reached, was not an exaggeration. Only two forces can inflict greater damage than a tsunami: collision with an asteroid or nu-clear explosion. The scenes along four hundred miles of coast that

morning resembled those of Hiroshima and Nagasaki in August 1945, but with water substituted for fire, mud for ash, the stink of fish and ooze for scorched wood and smoke.

Even the most intense aerial bombing leaves the walls and foundations of burned-out buildings, as well as parks and woods, roads and tracks, fields and cemeteries. The tsunami spared nothing, and achieved feats of surreal juxtaposition that no explosion could match. It plucked forests up by their roots and scattered them miles inland. It peeled the macadam off the roads, and cast it hither and thither in buckled ribbons. It stripped houses to their foundations, and lifted cars, lorries, ships, and corpses onto the tops of tall buildings.

A man named Ryosuke Abe reached Kamaya at about the same time as Hitomi. His house, his wife, his daughter, his son-in-law, and his two grandchildren had been in the village at the time of the tsunami. Abe himself worked on a building site in the city, and his way home had been blocked by the flooded road and broken bridge. By the time he got to the village, two policemen had taken up positions in front of it. To his amazement and indignation, they diffidently tried to bar his way. He began to argue, then gave up and simply walked straight past them.

Abe, Hitomi, and everyone describing the scene in the first days after the tsunami used the same word. *Jigoku*: hell. The image they had in mind was not the conventional landscape of lurid demons and extravagant, fiery tortures. There are other hells in Japanese iconography—hells of ice and water, mud and excrement, in which naked figures, stripped of all dignity, lie scattered across a broken plain.

"What stays in my memory," Abe said, "is pine trees, and the

legs and arms of children sticking out from under the mud and the rubbish."

Abe was a village leader, a construction boss, an active, practical-minded man in his early sixties. He began to pull bodies out and to lay them on the roadside. At first he used his bare hands. Then he waded back to his car and returned with his tools. In some places a shovel was useless, because the bodies of the children were so thickly heaped on top of one another, where they had been laid by the retreating wave.

By the afternoon, a handful of people had gathered to join the effort. It was dangerous, precarious work, because there was so little solid ground. Even where the waters had receded, they had left layered decks of rubble that slid or collapsed underfoot, all of it broken, much of it razor-sharp and covered with foul, squelching mud. Stepping uncertainly among the jutting spines and raw edges, the men in the group hauled up tree trunks and broken spars of wood, bent back sheets of corrugated aluminum, and pried open the doors of crushed cars. When they found bodies, they carried them to a traffic island opposite the bridge where the women, among them Hitomi Konno, laid them out and washed them in murky water hauled by bucket from the river. "Of course there was nothing to cover the bodies with," Hitomi said. "We pulled mattresses out of the rubble and laid them out on those, and covered them up with sheets, clothes, anything we could find." Almost as carefully as the bodies, they retrieved and set aside the distinctive square rucksacks, carefully labeled with name and class, that all Japanese elementary schoolchildren carry.

There was no panic, or even much sense of urgency. Without anyone saying as much, it was understood that there was no question of finding anyone alive. "No one was just looking for his own friends or grandchildren," Mr. Abe said. "We were pulling

everyone out, whoever they were. Every man was weeping as he worked."

Friends, rivals, neighbors, schoolmates, nodding acquaintances, blood relatives, old sweethearts—all came out of the undiscriminating muck.

By the end of the first day, Abe had dug out ten children. Most of them had lost their clothes and their name badges. But he recognized many of the faces.

That afternoon, someone told Abe that they had seen his wife, Fumiko. He hurried to Irikamaya and there she was, with his daughter, both of them uninjured. "It was more than a matter of being relieved," he said. "I couldn't believe that they were alive." But his son-in-law and two granddaughters were still missing.

He would spend three months in the village, picking through mud in the search for bodies. One day, the women called him over to the place where the bodies were laid out for washing. Among them was his own ten-year-old granddaughter, Nao. Abe had lifted her out himself. She had been so covered with mud that he had not recognized her.

Nao's nine-year-old sister, Mai, was found a week later, and their father a week after that. "The older girl was just the way she had always been," Abe told me. "She was perfect. It was just as if she was asleep. But a week later—well, seven days in those conditions makes a big difference." And he wept.

Nine miles inland, beyond the reach of the wave, was an indoor sports center, which had become a center for emergency relief. Entire families were sleeping on the basketball court on borrowed blankets and squares of folded cardboard. Sayomi Shito's eldest sister, Takami, a brisk and formidable woman whose own family lived safely inland, took upon herself the job of going there to

find her niece and bring her home. The confusion caused by the disaster was extreme, but people did not simply disappear. How difficult could it be?

Okawa Elementary School.

Fifth Grade.

Chisato Shito.

But after joining the throng inside the sports center, Takami felt her confidence fall away. She found herself one among hundreds, moving anxiously from one desk and dormitory and notice board to another.

After several fruitless hours, someone suggested a different kind of place where such a girl might be. Takami's heart quailed at the thought; she didn't have the strength to go alone. She picked up her other sister and drove with her to the place, where they consulted a much shorter list of names. But only immediate family members were allowed inside.

She went to Chisato's father, Takahiro, and told him what she had found.

Soon after, Takahiro came to Sayomi. She was in the kitchen again, preparing the latest batch of rice balls. Takahiro said, "Mother, it's time to prepare yourself. We've found Chisato."

Sayomi told me, "When I heard that, I started to leave at once. But then I realized that I'd need food for her to eat, and clothes for her to wear, and all kinds of things, so I went about getting them all together."

Takahiro said, "You don't need any of that. Just come."

It was two years later when Sayomi told me the story. As she remembered it, she got into the car without knowing where she was being taken, but in the calm belief that she was about to be reunited with her daughter.

To Sayomi's surprise, they drove past the sports center where the refugees were sheltering and up the hill to a place she knew

intimately—the high school where Sayomi and her sisters had all been pupils, and where Chisato would eventually go. "There was a kind of reception desk that they'd set up there," she said. "Takahiro and my brother-in-law stood by it, going through some sort of documents. They told me to stay in the car."

Sayomi slipped out and ran into the school. She found herself inside its gymnasium.

"It was the first time I'd been there in thirty years," she said. "There were tables and chairs. They'd divided off part of the gym with plastic sheets. So I looked in, and there were blue tarpaulins on the floor and shapes laid out on them, covered with blankets."

A man was approaching Sayomi, holding out a pair of shoes. "He was saying, 'Is there any mistake?' There wasn't a mistake. They were Chisato's shoes. I saw her name inside them, in my handwriting."

Now Takahiro was in the gymnasium. He was gathering one of the shapes up in his arms and lifting the blanket.

"Don't come yet," he said to Sayomi.

"But I could see," she told me.

She went on: "He lifted up one of the blankets. And then he was nodding, and saying something to the man who was in charge there. When I saw that, I thought, 'What are you nodding for? Don't nod. Don't nod.' They were telling me not to come in, but I rushed in. Chisato was there. She was covered in mud. She was naked. She looked very calm, just as if she was asleep. I held her and lifted her up, and called her name over and over, but she didn't answer. I tried to massage her, to restore her breathing. But it had no effect. I rubbed the mud from her cheeks, and wiped it out of her mouth. It was in her nose too, and it was in her ears. But we had only two small towels. I wiped and wiped the mud, and soon the towels were black. I had nothing else, so I used my clothes to wipe off the mud. Her eyes were half-open—and that was the way

she used to sleep, the way she was when she was in a very deep sleep. But there was muck in her eyes, and there were no towels and no water, and so I licked Chisato's eyes with my tongue to wash off the muck, but I couldn't get them clean, and the muck kept coming out."

Hitomi Konno and her husband, Hiroyuki, found each other the following week. It was at that moment that she gave up hope. She had been spending mornings at the school, where she washed and identified bodies, and the afternoons in Irikamaya village hall, where she cooked and cleaned for her fellow refugees. It was difficult to know what else to do, for she was still looking for her children, Mari, Rika, and Daisuke, and her mother- and father-in-law. Hitomi had no illusions about what had happened; she understood what the worst was, for it was all around her. But she was sustained, like many in her situation, by the simple instinct that, whatever was happening to other people, it was impossible—in fact, it would be ridiculous—for her own family to be extinct. Insupportable, soul-crushing, unfathomable—but also just silly. *We're all fine. Don't worry*, Mari had written in those first moments after the earthquake. "I thought, 'They must be alive. They must be alive,'" Hitomi said. "I couldn't give up. When the phones came back on, I sent text messages, I tried calling over and over again."

Hitomi took a boat to the big sports center, and found Hiroyuki there.

It is conventional to picture such reunions as joyful moments of emotional release. But the emotions are too big and too mixed with despair. Over the past few days, Hiroyuki had arrived at the belief that he had lost his parents, two daughters, son, and wife. When he saw Hitomi, he adjusted his understanding: as it turned

45

out, he had lost his mother, father, and three children. "Of course we were glad to see each other," Hitomi said. "But we were so preoccupied with thoughts of the children. Until I found them, I couldn't feel any relief."

Hitomi's head-shaking refusal to take death seriously was not shared by her husband. Hiroyuki joined the search for bodies, in Kamaya, and in the area of the Fuji lake, where many of the component parts of their home village, Magaki, had fetched up. One day they found the top part of their house—the upper floor and roof, virtually intact, tossed by the wave onto a shore of the lake. A team was grimly assembled to break through the tiles. The Konnos expected the fulfillment of all their fears, the trapped corpses of their family. Inside, the tatami mats were still in place, but there was little else there. They found Rika's pink Hello Kitty purse and what came to be very precious: an old album filled with photographs of the children when they were small.

Daisuke was the first to be recovered, a week after the wave, followed by Hiroyuki's father. Rika, who had died four days before her seventeenth birthday, was found at the end of the month. Old Mrs. Konno and eighteen-year-old Mari were found in early April.

Daisuke was at the bottom of the hill behind the school, not far from the traffic island, in one of several small heaps of children. The girls and their grandparents lay in different places, but there were clues that suggested what had happened to them. Old Mr. Konno had his car keys in his pocket. His wife was carrying bags of clothes, and the girls had snacks and charger cables for their mobile phones. They were preparing a departure; they might have been about to get into the car when the tsunami struck. Perhaps they were worried about Daisuke, or about Hitomi. Perhaps they were waiting for one or both of them to return before making their escape.

Hitomi went to see Daisuke at the high-school gymnasium, and found him uninjured. "He looked as if he was sleeping," she said. "He looked as if he would wake up if I called his name. I still remember his face as it was then." But when she came back the next day, a jolting change had taken place. Drops of blood had issued from Daisuke's eyes, like tears. She wiped them away, but overnight, and every night after that, Daisuke shed more tears of blood. Hitomi understood that this was because of changes that were taking place inside the container of her son's body. But she couldn't help also seeing it as a symbol of the pain of his hovering spirit, and of how desperately he had wanted to live.

It had been difficult even to find coffins. Every crematorium within reach of the coast was backed up for several days. People were driving for hundreds of miles to hold a funeral. What Hitomi and Hiroyuki most urgently needed now was a supply of dry ice, first for one, then for two, and eventually for five sets of remains. An undertaker explained that each body needed four pieces of ice—two to go under the arms and two under the legs. As the spring warmth came on, each piece lasted only a few days. Hiroyuki would drive around for hours and finally locate ice in a neighboring town—but the next time he went there, its supply would be gone. In the month it took for all five bodies to be recovered and cremated, Hitomi's and Hiroyuki's lives were dominated by the daily struggle to protect their children and parents from decay.

Apart from their family, the Konnos had also lost their home and everything in it. While they were organizing ice and funerals, Hitomi and Hiroyuki stayed first with his elderly grandmother, and then moved to a vacant house owned by an aunt and uncle. For them, as for many of the parents from the school, those early

weeks were a time of numb frenzy rather than supine grief, a losing struggle to remain on top of a hundred pressing practical matters.

It was about a month after the disaster that Hitomi had a phone call from Kazutaka Sato, a man she knew as Yuki's dad.

Yuki Sato was Daisuke's best friend and confrere in mischief. The two boys walked to school together, practiced judo together, and fished together in the Kitakami River. Yuki had also died on March 11.

By this stage, the scale of the tragedy at Okawa Elementary School had become clear. The school had 108 children. Of the seventy-eight who were there at the moment of the tsunami, seventy-four, and ten out of eleven teachers, had died. But a handful of parents had gone to the school after the earthquake, picked up their children, and taken them to safety. One of the girls who had been saved in this way, Amane Ukitsu, had been in the sixth-grade class with Daisuke and Yuki. Mr. Sato had recently talked to Amane, and now he was telephoning, full of emotion, to share with Hitomi the story that he had heard from their sons' surviving classmate.

Sato had asked Amane about the moments before her mother took her away from the school, the period after the earthquake and before the tsunami. His beloved son had died at the age of twelve; now he wanted to know everything that it was possible to know about Yuki in the last minutes of his life. How had he appeared? What had he spoken of? Had he been afraid?

Amane described how the building shook violently, but suffered no serious damage, and how the children and teachers evacuated the building, just as they had for the lesser tremor two days earlier. The pupils had lined up by class. Amane stood with Yuki, Daisuke, and the rest of the sixth grade.

The names were quickly checked off, and the children were

told to remain where they stood. Soon sirens and announcements could be heard, urging evacuation to higher ground. It was cold in the playground. But there was no move to go back inside, or anywhere else. Chilled by the wind, the children became restless. And now there was a loudspeaker van driving around, warning of a "super-tsunami" coming in from the sea.

Amane recounted how Daisuke, the class captain, and Yuki, his sidekick, addressed their class teacher, a man named Takashi Sasaki.

Sir, let's go up the hill.

We should climb the hill, sir.

If we stay here, the ground might split open and swallow us up.

We'll die if we stay here!

The teacher shushed them and told them to remain where they were.

Soon after, Amane's mother arrived and hurriedly drove her away. The family lost their house, but she was one of only five children left alive from the sixth-grade class.

Mr. Sato's telephone call left Hitomi trembling. She had had no time or energy left over to contemplate them before—but this story lit up like a floodlight questions that had been flickering dimly in her grief-darkened mind. What, after all, had been going on at the school in the period between the earthquake and the wave? Why had everyone not evacuated to the hill behind it, as her own son had apparently suggested? If he had been able to see the sense of this, why had not his teachers? Why had they, and Daisuke, and everyone else, had to die?

PART II

AREA OF SEARCH

ABUNDANT NATURE

The territory of the Okawa Elementary School appears on globes and atlases as an unlabeled blank. The two great plains surrounding Tokyo and Osaka, the megacities at Japan's core, are a density of roads, railways, and place names, which dwindle and fade to the north of the main island of Honshu. Even before disaster struck its coast, nowhere in Japan was closer to the world of the dead.

In ancient times, the region known as Tohoku was a notorious frontier realm of barbarians, goblins, and bitter cold. Even today, it remains a remote, marginal, faintly melancholy place, the symbol of a rural tradition that, for city dwellers, is no more than a folk memory.

The seventeenth-century haiku poet Bashō wrote about Tohoku in his famous travel sketch *The Narrow Road to the Deep North*, in which it figures as an emblem of loneliness and isolation. Even after Japan's rapid modernization in the late nineteenth century, Tohoku was poorer, hungrier, and more backward than anywhere else. Northern men, tough and uncomplaining, filled the imperial armies. The fields were rich in grain and fruit, but

their produce was consumed in the richer south, and a bad harvest often left Tohoku in famine. There were three commodities, it used to be said, that the north supplied to Tokyo: rice, fighting men, and whores.

Today, Tohoku makes up one-third of the area of Honshu, but one-tenth of its population. It is associated with an impenetrable regional dialect, a quality of eeriness, and an archaic spirituality that are exotic even to modern Japanese. In the north, there are secret Buddhist cults, and old temples where the corpses of former priests are displayed as leering mummies. There is a sisterhood of blind shamanesses who gather once a year at a volcano called Mount Fear, the legendary entrance to the underworld. Tohoku has bullet trains and Wi-Fi, and the rest of the twenty-first-century conveniences. But the mobile network gives out in the remoter hills and bays, and beneath the glaze of affluence, something lingers of the old stereotype of Tohoku people as brooding, incomprehensible, and a little spooky.

I knew the region's largest city, Sendai, which was as blandly pleasant as most of Japan's prefectural capitals. But the other names reeled off by the television news on the night of March 11—Otsuchi, Ofunato, Rikuzen-Takata, Kesennuma—were as obscure to many Japanese as they were to foreigners. And between Kesennuma and the fishing port of Ishinomaki, an intricately spiky coastline, indented with deep and narrow bays, the atlas displayed no place names at all.

A larger-scale map revealed the name of this obscure zone: the Sanriku Coast. Three physical features distinguished it: two obvious and spectacular, the other stealthy and invisible. The first was the Kitakami, Tohoku's greatest river, which rose in the mountains and flowed south to empty itself through two distinct mouths, one in Ishinomaki, one at a thinly populated place called Oppa Bay. The second was those sharp, fjord-like bays, called rias,

formed by river valleys that over the millennia had been drowned by the rising sea. The third was the meeting point, deep beneath the ocean, of the Pacific and North American tectonic plates, titanic segments of the Earth's crust, from whose grating friction earthquakes and tsunamis are born.

On this jagged coast, close to Oppa Bay, was Okawa Elementary School. I traveled there for the first time in September 2011. Half a year had passed since the disaster, and in that time I had made repeated journeys to the tsunami zone. At first it had been accessible only by car, along roads strewn with rubble, after hours of lining up for a single jerry can of rationed fuel. In time, gasoline supplies resumed, and after anxious checks on the safety of its tracks, the *shinkansen*, or bullet train, restarted its northbound service. Early September is high summer in Japan; the air was hot and full, and the sky was a cloudless, fine-grained blue. The *shinkansen* raced smoothly and effortlessly north, slurping up the distance so quickly that the ninety-minute journey felt closer to commuting than to travel. But to come to Tohoku was always to experience a transformation. In spring, the snow in the northeast lingered longer and deeper on the ground. Plum and cherry blossoms flowered and fell later; summer here was less harsh, less sticky, and gave way sooner to the chill of autumn. Arrival from Tokyo brought a palpable shift in the air and its qualities, a sense of transition experienced on the skin and in the back of the throat.

Sendai station, where my companions and I alighted, displayed no visible signs of the disaster. Our hired car maneuvered north, through a city center of silver office buildings and department stores, and mounted the overhead expressway, also recently reopened after months of structural checks. After an hour, the city of Ishinomaki came into view on the coastal plain ahead:

hangar-like factories and shopping malls, and billows of white smoke out of aluminum chimneys.

No city suffered more in the tsunami than Ishinomaki. Most of its center had been inundated; one-fifth of those who died in the disaster died here, in a town of 160,000 people. The fishing port had been entirely destroyed by the wave, along with the shipyard and an immense paper mill. But three-quarters of the Ishinomaki municipality was another world altogether, a hinterland of steep hills and forests, penetrated by the broad agricultural plain of the Kitakami River; and fishing villages at the head of the deep ria bays, separated from one another by elaborately ramifying peninsulas, which extended talon-like fingers into the ocean.

Beyond the town, we descended from the expressway and entered a realm of bright fields bordered by dark hills. Some of them contained heavy-stalked rice, ripe for harvest; others held greenhouses of tomatoes and fruit. The houses along the road were built of wood with stately tiled roofs. The sky, which was already huge overhead, gaped wider as the hills fell away and we turned east along the bank of the Kitakami.

Most Japanese rivers are a wretched sight, even outside the big cities. Upstream dams drain them of power and volume. Towns and factories suck off their waters and pump back effluent, human and chemical. The Kitakami, by contrast, is wide, full, clean, and alive. Its single dam is in the upper northern reaches, leaving the salmon free to swarm every autumn to their spawning grounds. Its breadth—hundreds of yards across, even deep inland—opens up vistas of sky and mountains in the built-up towns through which it passes. Herons, swans, and teal live among the dense beds of reeds that grow along its banks; every year the reeds are harvested to furnish thatch for temples and shrines. The river's southern outlet, where it meets the sea at Ishinomaki, is a tumult

of wharves, cranes, and containers. But its other mouth, at Oppa Bay, is that rare thing in a populous industrialized country—a great river estuary left to sand, eagles, rocks, and currents.

This was the prospect revealed to us as we drove along the Kitakami into Okawa that morning: the arching sky; the green hills divided from one another by valleys packed with rice; villages at the edge of the fields; and, in the hazy distance, lagoon and sea. It was an ideal, an archetypal scene: farm and forest, fresh and salt water, nature and humanity in balance. Trees covered the mountains, and the sea dashed the rocks, but both were welcoming to the hunter and fisherman. The river was wide and powerful, but tamed by bridge and embankment. The tiled houses were small and few, but the fields, hills, and water paid tribute to them. Human civilization was the pivot about which the natural world turned.

On the Sanriku Coast you experienced the sensation of entering an altered world. It was a subtle change—for all the jokes about spooky Tohoku yokels, there was nothing unsophisticated about northerners. But there was a shagginess about them, compared to the lacquered neatness of Tokyo people—a robust, tousled quality suggestive of bracing weather, and an indifference to indulgences such as indoor heating. Everyone had strong boots and thick socks; in the colder months, they all wore nylon fleeces, often two, even inside. The hair of both men and women stuck up in tufts, as if it had just been tugged through several layers of thick sweaters and incompletely patted down. Certain surnames— Konno, Sato, Sasaki—cropped up again and again, as if there was a limited supply of them, as in a society composed of clans. People in Sanriku had clear, pale complexions, and the transition from bitter wind to warm interior flushed their cheeks rosy and bright.

Everyone talked about the beauty of nature, and his or her relationship with it. Everyone seemed to have deep family roots in the area, reaching decades and centuries into the past.

I met an old man named Sadayoshi Kumagai, whose memory went back before the Second World War. His ancestors had been samurai riflemen; the family had lived in the area for three hundred years. Old Mr. Kumagai was a master thatcher, who had traveled the country constructing temple roofs out of the fine Kitakami reeds. "It was a while before I understood," he said. "But there's no doubting it. I've been everywhere in this country, from Hokkaido to Okinawa. And nowhere else has the abundance of nature we have here: mountains, river, marsh, sea. People who never leave the area don't understand how lucky they are. There's no place like this."

He grew up in Hashiura, a village opposite Okawa Elementary School on the north bank of the river. It was an isolated, even backward community of horse-drawn carts and unmade roads. But for a young boy it was a place of wonder and adventure. In the summer, the village children swam in the river and the sea. In autumn, they followed the trails into the hills and gathered nuts and chocolate vine. A little way off the road was the site of a Neolithic village: classmates of Kumagai used to come to school bearing fragments of four-thousand-year-old pots. Kumagai's grandfather taught him to shoot—there were duck and pheasant in the hills above the river and, in Oshika to the south, wild deer. "We didn't hunt for fun, but for a living," he said. "When we took game, we sold it." Once, in a moment of opportunistic mischief, the young Kumagai shot and slayed a swan. "I was so proud of myself, and I told everyone what I'd done. Well, the police heard about it, and they came around and gave me a good telling off."

On their hunting expeditions, Kumagai's grandfather told the boy about the wonder and horror of the tsunami. The old

man had lived through two of them in his own lifetime, and the historical record went back much farther than that. "The province of Mutsu"—eastern Tohoku—"trembled and greatly shook," recorded a chronicle of A.D. 869, the eleventh year of the Jogan Era:

> People cried and screamed, and could not stand. Some died beneath the weight of their fallen houses; some were buried alive in earth and sand when the ground sheared open beneath them . . . Great walls, gates, warehouses and embankments were destroyed. The mouth of the sea roared like thunder, and violent waves rose up, surging through the rivers, until, in the blink of an eye, they reached the wall of Taga Castle. The flood extended for so many *ri* that you could not tell where the sea ended and the land began. Fields and roads were transformed into ocean. There was no time to board boats or to climb the hills; a thousand people drowned.

Geologists found layers of fine sand across the sedimentary layers of the Sendai plane—the wash of immense tsunamis that had recurred at intervals of eight hundred to a thousand years. Lesser waves were many times more frequent. Among many other years, they struck the Sanriku Coast in 1585, 1611, 1677, 1687, 1689, 1716, 1793, 1868, and 1894. Their effects were especially devastating when they encountered the long, narrow ria bays, which concentrated the waves and channeled them like funnels onto the fishing villages within. The most destructive of modern times was the Meiji Sanriku Tsunami of 1896, when twenty-two thousand died after what had felt—because it occurred far out at sea—like a mild and inconsequential earthquake. In 1933, the year before Sadayoshi Kumagai was born, another moderate tremor generated waves as high as a hundred feet, which killed three thousand people. "My grandfather lived through both of those,

and he talked about them," he said. "I was always told that when an earthquake strikes we must be prepared for a tsunami." There were even "tsunami stones" marking the extent of previous inundations, engraved by earlier generations with solemn warnings not to build dwellings below them. The fishermen on the Pacific coast to the east, whose homes faced directly onto the ocean, were brought up to know instinctively what to do after the earth shook: ascend without hesitation to high ground, and stay there. But the people of Kitakami lived on a river, not the sea. And what if there was no shaking at all?

On May 22, 1960, a 9.5-magnitude earthquake, still the most powerful ever recorded, struck the seabed off the west coast of Chile. Waves eighty feet high inundated the city of Valdivia, killing a thousand people along the coast. Twenty-two hours after the earthquake, the tsunami struck Japan, having traversed 10,500 miles of sea. It was the morning of May 24; none but a handful of seismologists in Tokyo knew what had happened in Chile, and even they never imagined the effect it would have twenty-two hours later on the far side of the Pacific. The Sanriku Coast saw the worst of it; in places, the water was more than twenty feet high. One hundred and forty-two people were killed that day, because of an occurrence in the depths of the ocean bed literally half a world away.

In Hashiura, Sadayoshi Kumagai saw the tsunami from Chile surging up the Kitakami River. "It was this mass of black," he said. "Huge stones were rolling over and over upstream. It wasn't just one wave, but one after another. The water rose so high—it came halfway up the bank. I had never seen that happen before. I thought at the time what a strange and powerful thing it was. But I never imagined that it could ever come up *over* the bank."

When the earthquake struck on March 11, 2011, Kumagai recognized immediately that a tsunami could follow, and what a

menace it would be to anyone on the river. With a prickling of alarm, he remembered that eight of his employees were gathering reeds on an island close to the mouth of the Kitakami. He rushed down to the bank and supervised their evacuation by boat. Filled with relief that his people had been brought to safety, he drove back to Hashiura.

He was in the open when the tsunami arrived. He watched the black shape breach the bank and tumble towards him. He leaped into his car and reached the road into the hills seconds ahead of the water. From there, he looked down as the second tsunami of his life destroyed Okawa and Hashiura, including his own house and office. "It was like a black mountain coming over," he said. "It was incredible that the mountain was moving. I saw a car with its taillights on going under the water. There must have been somebody inside. Another few seconds and I would have been in the water too."

Much of the beauty of Okawa derived from the many things that were not there—those everyday uglinesses unthinkingly accepted by city dwellers. Even as we drove in on that September afternoon, I was conscious of their absence. Between the outskirts of Ishinomaki and the sea, there were few traffic lights, road signs, vending machines, or telegraph poles. There were no strip-lit restaurants or twenty-four-hour convenience stores, no billboards or cash machines. Most transforming of all was the character of local sound: the song of birds and cicadas in the trees, the low noise of the river, the slap of waves, and a subtle, pervasive, barely audible susurration, which took me days to identify—that of air passing through the reeds.

Ryosuke Abe, who spent those weeks searching through its remains after the disaster, was the headman of Kamaya; no one I

61

met talked more passionately about the life of the village. The home he described, and the childhood he remembered, was that of the archetypal *furusato*, the Japanese Arcadia, the village of the imagination, with its forested hills, paddies cut by a meandering river, a small local school, and family-run shops.

There was Aizawa the tobacconist and, across the road, Mogami the sake-seller, with its distinctive green-and-orange awning. Suzuki the tofu-seller was farther down the road, next to the Takahashi Beauty Parlor. Kamaya had its own *koban*, or police box, manned by a single officer, and the Kamaya Clinic, run by the well-regarded Dr. Suzuki. And dominating the center of the village, fronted by a row of cherry trees, was the school.

"Kamaya was a place of abundant nature," Abe said. "The natural world was so rich. These days, when kids go for a picnic, they get on a bus. They don't really know their way around their own area. But we roamed far and wide—Nagatsuura, Onosaki, Fukuji. We'd play baseball on the beach—each hamlet had a little team. We played in the river—you could swim anywhere. We spent the whole summer outside."

Most families had more than one source of income: a job, or at least part-time work, in Ishinomaki, supplemented by a small household farm and gleanings from the forest and river. The hills produced their own harvest of mushrooms, berries, and chestnuts. The local rice variety was called Love-at-First-Sight. The briny mingling of the freshwater and the salt had intriguing effects on natural life. It made the reeds thin, but very strong. It nurtured unlikely fish, such as the spiky-finned, bull-headed sculpions, and *shijimi* clams, which were sold across Japan as a delicious ingredient for soup. "We had so much from the river," Ryosuke Abe said. "We used to make a trap out of an oak branch and its leaves. You put it on the riverbed, and when you pulled it up onto the boat with a landing net, it was full of eels—big fat eels."

Three hundred and ninety-three people lived in Kamaya at the time of the tsunami. More than half of them—197 people—died, and every one of their houses was destroyed. Virtually all who survived did so because they were away from the village at the time, at work or running errands. Of those who were present in Kamaya that afternoon, only about twenty had not drowned by the time the sun went down. And these numbers did not include the teachers and children who died at the school. It was easy, often too easy, to reach for superlatives in describing the tragedy of the tsunami. But in all the disaster zone, I reflected as I drove in that September afternoon, I knew of no single community that had lost so much of itself.

The road, which had been fully repaired, at first gave no clues about what had happened six months earlier. The vegetation along the riverside had begun to grow back, and the rubble had been tidied away. But the fields, which a mile back had the glow of ripe rice, were muddy and unplanted, and here and there were discreet relics of destruction: a buckled pickup truck among long grass; a windowless, roofless building alone in the mud. My eye was drawn to the screen of our car's satellite navigation system. Kamaya was visible upon it as a mesh of lines and rectangles, with each block of houses distinct, the school, the police station, and the community center individually marked. We reached the turning to the New Kitakami Great Bridge, which was teeming with repair workers in yellow vests. On the satnav screen, the moving dot representing our car paused on the threshold of the glowing village. But in the real world there was nothing there.

I knew what had happened at Okawa. Everyone knew. It was the worst of the tsunami, the story hardest among all the stories to hear. I was always conscious, on reaching the school, of a faint

dizziness, a quailing of the heart at the idea of the place. And yet the site itself possessed an air of quiet, even tranquillity: a two-story block beneath an angled red roof, with concrete arms enclosing what would once have been the playground. The buildings were windowless and battered, their surfaces abraded by impacts, with walls warped and toppled in places, but still, for the most part, sound on their steel frame. Above was a steep and thickly wooded hill, buttressed at its foot by a concrete wall.

At the front was a weather-beaten table bearing a jumble of objects that identified it as a makeshift shrine. There were vases of flowers, incense holders, and wooden funeral tablets bearing characters brushed in ink. There were bottles of juice and sweets, soft toys, and a framed photograph of the village in sunshine, with the river, hills, and summer sky magnificent in the background.

Standing in front of the shrine, tidying a vase of flowers, was a figure in boots and a heavy coat, her hair tied up in a ponytail. Her name was Naomi Hiratsuka. She lived upriver; her daughter, Koharu, had been a pupil at the school. She was the woman I had come here to find.

THE MUD

Naomi lived in a big house in the village of Yokogawa, with four generations of her husband's family. Its oldest occupant, his grandmother, was in her late nineties; Naomi's younger daughter, Sae, was two and a half. Naomi had been in her bedroom at the moment of the earthquake, lulling the small girl to sleep. The fast, vertical motion was "like being inside a cocktail shaker." By the time the shocks had dissipated, the house was an obstacle course of books, furniture, and broken glass. Her six-year-old son Toma was trapped in another room, its door blocked by fallen objects. It took Naomi half an hour to free him, as the walls and floor flexed and wobbled in the aftershocks.

Nobody in the family had been physically hurt, but downstairs the house was in even greater disarray. Naomi's mother-in-law was tending to the distraught great-grandmother; her father-in-law, who held high office in the local neighborhood association, was taking stock of the situation outside.

He was an uncommunicative man; "traditional" would have been the polite way of describing his conception of family and the appropriate behavior of its members. When he returned

from his reconnoitering, Naomi was preparing to go to Okawa Elementary School to collect her twelve-year-old daughter, Koharu. "I had no doubt that the school was okay," she said. "But it had been such a strong quake, I thought I ought to pick her up." Mr. Hiratsuka Senior resisted this idea, for reasons that were obscure. "He said, 'This is not the moment.' I didn't know exactly what he meant." The old man had walked around the village; Naomi realized later that he must have looked over the bank and observed the condition of the river. But he was a man who rarely felt the need to explain his decisions, certainly not to a daughter-in-law. "I think that he himself was in a panic, although he didn't show it," she said. "We didn't have much conversation. He's the kind who keeps his thoughts to himself."

Naomi had sent a text message to her husband, but received no reply before the network went down. There was no electricity and therefore no television. Even the municipal loudspeakers, which broadcast information in times of emergency, were silent; and it was snowing. "I remember thinking about Koharu stuck at the school, and I thought that it must be so cold there," Naomi said. "I was glad that I'd told her to put on an extra layer of underwear. I thought that as long as they wrapped up well, they'd be okay." In the absence of any news—good or bad—about the state of the wider world, all she could think of was to stay inside and tend to those members of the family who were safe at home.

This course of action coincided exactly with her father-in-law's view of the role and duties of a young woman and mother.

Shortly before dusk, old Mr. Hiratsuka announced that he was going out again. His intention was to walk downriver and retrieve a radio from the hut at his nearby allotment. It was still light when he left. He returned in darkness an hour later, gasping and reeling, drenched in water, plastered with mud and leaves, and lucky to be alive.

Physically, Yokogawa was untouched by the disaster that was taking place. The high embankment and the bend in the river had shielded it from the water, to the extent that Naomi still had no idea there had been a tsunami. But on the far side of the jutting hill, five and a half miles from the sea, Mr. Hiratsuka found himself on a road rinsed by the ocean. As he walked along it, a new surge broke the river's edge and quickly covered the asphalt. It tugged at his feet, and then at his ankles and knees, and before he understood what was happening, he had lost his footing and was flailing in currents of black water. They were dragging him back towards the river, where he would certainly have drowned, when he became painfully but securely entangled in a tree, which held him fast while the water drained away.

He staggered back home past the bend in the river, without his radio. "He said later that he nearly died," Naomi remembered. "He was upset. He didn't say so, but perhaps that was the moment when he understood what had happened."

The following morning, Naomi persuaded her father-in-law to make an effort at reaching the school. Immediately beyond Yokogawa the water had receded, and they were able to drive to the point where the road disappeared into the water. A group of people had gathered there; some of them seemed to be crying. Mr. Hiratsuka told Naomi to stay in the car, and strode over to investigate. He came back a few minutes later; the terseness of his replies suggested that he hadn't found out very much. Naomi was not especially worried. Like everyone else, she had heard the report that two hundred children and local people were cut off by water at Okawa Elementary School, awaiting rescue. Like the other mothers, she had turned up that morning to meet the helicopter that never came. But mostly she was preoccupied with the burden

of feeding and cleaning a household in which she was expected to be the source of nurture for both young and old. "The children were scared by the aftershocks," she said. "And the old people were all in a dither. I was on maternity leave—I was supposed to be looking after my child. But for the next few days, all I can remember was cooking. When the time came to go out and find food, my mother- and father-in-law did that. I was at home taking care of the children, and cooking and cooking again, morning, noon, and night."

On Sunday morning, two of Naomi's friends, the mother and father of two children at Okawa Elementary School, came by to say that they were going to make another attempt at getting through. Would Naomi like to come? She badly wanted to go with them—but who would look after the other two children in her absence? Her father-in-law had a solution: she would stay at home, and he would go instead.

He returned at lunchtime.

"What happened?" asked Naomi.

"We got to the school," he said.

"How was it?" asked Naomi.

"I saw Arika's body there." Arika was a twelve-year-old classmate of Koharu's. "There were several other bodies of children there. But not Koharu. I could not find Koharu. I heard that a few of the children survived and went to Irikamaya. But Koharu was not there. So I think it is hopeless. You need to give up."

Naomi found herself unable to speak. "I wanted to ask so much more, I wanted to know the details," she said. "But there was something about the way he said, 'Give up.'"

Then Mr. Hiratsuka said, "We have to accept this. You need to give up hope. The important thing now is to look after the children who are still alive." With that, the conversation was over.

Naomi told me: "He had said it—and so I realized there really

was no hope. That was the moment when I knew that Koharu was not alive. But I couldn't show my grief. Mr. Hiratsuka is . . . Mr. Hiratsuka is a very strict, controlled person. He is not the kind of man who allows his natural feelings to show. He had lost his granddaughter. I know that he may have felt very sad, but he contains his feelings. Nonetheless, if he found me in a state of sadness, he should have refrained from saying words that would hurt me. But he did not refrain."

Naomi's mother-in-law had heard the exchange and stood nearby, weeping. Mr. Hiratsuka spoke scoldingly to his wife and ordered her to quell her tears.

Naomi's husband, Shinichiro, reached home the following day. Like his wife, before she took her maternity leave, he was a teacher, at a high school in Ishinomaki, which had become a refuge for a thousand people made homeless by the tsunami. His presence diluted the authority of his father and made acceptable Naomi's absence from the house. With Shinichiro, she drove down the road as far as the waters allowed. There she met the mother of another girl from Okawa Elementary School, who told them that she had just identified her own daughter at the school gymnasium upriver. She thought she might have seen Koharu's body there too.

The Hiratsukas drove inland to the gymnasium mortuary. More and more bodies were coming in, and the place was in the grip of bureaucratic confusion. There were papers to be filed, and incoming bodies had to be examined by a doctor and formally logged, a process that sometimes took days. Naomi and Shinichiro had young children and needy old people back at home; they couldn't wait. They filled out the necessary documents and left.

The following day, Shinichiro left his family and went back to

his school in the city to help with the care of the refugees there. His wife did not question the decision; no one in his family regarded it as bizarre or remarkable, any more than it was bizarre to expect a mother newly grieving for her young daughter to cook, wash, and clean. None of his colleagues would have reproached Shinichiro if he had walked away from his school to look for his child's body. But no self-respecting Japanese teacher could have done so with an easy conscience. It was just one example of the kind of dutifulness routinely expected of a public servant.

Shinichiro came home whenever he felt able. When he did, he and Naomi went to the school gymnasium. There were two hundred bodies there by the end of the week. "They were laid out on blue tarpaulins," she said. "A lot of them were people I knew. There were parents of pupils of mine. There were classmates of Koharu's. I was able to say, 'I know him, and I know him, and I know her.' But none of them was Koharu."

After ten days, they decided to go to Okawa Elementary School to see what was happening there. The water had receded to the point where they could drive and wade to Kamaya. Rough paths had been cleared by the volunteer firemen, who were using a digger to part the debris. But rubble still overwhelmed the school buildings, and on top of the clagging mud was a thin layer of snow. Next to the traffic island at the entrance to the village there were blue vinyl sheets, on which bodies were laid out to be washed before being taken to the mortuary. Half a dozen mothers lingered there, waiting for their children to be lifted out.

Naomi looked at the faces of the people on the blue sheets, hoping all the time to recognize Koharu. She was a tall girl with unruly, shoulder-length hair and a plump, humorous face. Naomi thought about the last moments they had spent together. As her mother tended to Koharu's little brother and sister, as her septuagenarian grandfather prepared breakfast for her grandmother,

and the grandmother fussed over her near-centenarian great-grandmother, Koharu had quietly dressed, eaten, and left for the school bus. She was about to enter her last week of elementary school; she and Naomi had discussed what she would wear for the graduation ceremony. Most of the other girls favored jackets and tartan skirts, in emulation of the starlets of a toothsome pop band. But Koharu had chosen a *hakama*, an elegantly formal traditional skirt of high pleats worn over a kimono. The skirt had been Naomi's, but Koharu was already almost as tall as her mother, and it required little alteration.

Naomi came back to the school whenever she could. Time, as she experienced it, was passing in an unfamiliar way. There was so much to do for the family at home, and doing it was such an effort. She would spend hours waiting on line for gasoline and food, drive home, drop off her supplies, and then drive to the mortuary, or wade through black water to the school to scrutinize the dead. One day she found one of Koharu's shoes, and later her school backpack. These finds were heartbreaking and consoling at the same time. Naomi harbored no false hopes. Bodies were still coming out of the debris at the rate of several a day. She knew it was only a matter of time before her daughter's came out too.

At the beginning of April, the nurseries and kindergartens reopened. With the two youngest children off her hands during the day, Naomi was able to devote herself to the search for Koharu.

She found herself one of a dwindling group of parents, loitering by the traffic island at the entrance to Kamaya. There was a shy, quiet man named Masaru Naganuma who was looking for his seven-year-old son, Koto; as a qualified heavy-vehicle operator, Masaru sometimes drove the digger that scooped and divided the mud. Naomi became very close to a woman named Miho Suzuki,

who had buried her twelve-year-old son, Kento, but was still searching for her nine-year-old daughter, Hana.

Masaru, in particular, was unswerving in his determination to find his son. Each morning Naomi would come to the school and watch him out in the black mud, turning it over and over with the arm of the yellow digger. As spring came on, rich color returned to the hills and the river—the dark green of the pines, the lighter shades of the deciduous trees, and the fluffy yellow of bamboo. But at the heart of the landscape of leaf and water was darkness: this pit of mud, which had sucked down everything precious and refused to give it up. How deep was that mud? It seemed bottomless. It stuck to Naomi's clothes and boots, and followed her home in her car. Liquid mud dripped off the caterpillar tracks on Masaru's digger as he rode it out every morning to look for his little boy. "Just look around this place," Naomi said. "What parent could rest, having left the body of their child under this earth and rubble, or floating out there in the sea?"

Naomi was a teacher of English. She spoke it well, when she tried, with a clear American accent. But she lacked all confidence, and in our conversations she used Japanese. Describing the events following the disaster, she talked fast and fluently, with sharp, emphatic gestures. But when I asked her about herself, she became hesitant and ill at ease.

She had grown up in Sendai, but studied at a university in Okinawa, the chain of beautiful, subtropical islands far south of the Japanese mainland, where her father had been born. She had gone there filled with excitement and aspiration, but came away disappointed. "I have Okinawan blood, but I had never lived there," she said. "I wanted to study the old Okinawan language and learn Okinawan dance. But I accomplished less than half of what I

wanted." After graduation, she left the sunny south and returned to the cold northern territory of her birth.

Of all the Okawa mothers I met, Naomi was the clearest-sighted, even in the intensity of grief. For many of those who experienced it, the tragedy of the tsunami was formless, black, and ineffable, an immense and overwhelming monster that blocked out the sun. But to Naomi, no less stricken than the others, it was glittering and sharp and appallingly bright. This harshly illuminated clarity was the opposite of consoling. It pierced, rather than smothered, and left nowhere to hide.

In all the time I spent with Naomi, I never went to her home. Her father-in-law did not care for journalists, and she didn't want to upset him unnecessarily. We would meet at the school and drive back up the road towards Ishinomaki to talk in a roadside restaurant. At the beginning, she told me, the search for the missing children had been performed by local people, who cleared away what rubble they could, and by the police, who supervised the processing of the dead. Then came soldiers of the Japan Self-Defense Forces. At first this had been a cause for optimism, as the mesh of rubble encasing the school was removed piece by piece. But the longer the search for the children went on, the more the scale of the task was exposed.

In the early days, children had been found all around, thrown up against the hollows of the hill—thirty-four of them in one soft heap. Then they began to come out in smaller groups of one or two; and then the flow diminished to a trickle. By late March, some thirty of the seventy-four missing children had still not been found; a fortnight later, there were just ten missing. At the end of April, four children were recovered in quick succession from a pond that had supplied water to the rice fields of Kamaya. Some of them were five feet below the water and mud, beyond the reach of even a bamboo pole. It had become obvious that to search it

fully, the whole area would first have to be drained. So mechanical pumps were acquired, and a generator that had to be fueled around the clock. Then bodies began to turn up in the Fuji lake, two miles away, on the far side of the hill.

Rather than comprising a single wave, the tsunami had consisted of repeated pulses of water, washing in and washing out again, weaving over, under, and across one another. Some of the objects that fell into its embrace had been lifted and deposited close to their point of origin; but many had been sucked under and thrown up, pulled back and dashed forward again, in an irretrievably complex operation of internal currents and eddies. The obvious places had all been searched; nowadays, new sets of remains were being found far from the school; and whenever this happened, the potential area of search expanded once again.

In May, a doctor took swabs from the mouths of Naomi, Shinichiro, and their children, in order to isolate Koharu's DNA. At the end of that month, parts of a small body washed up in Naburi, a fishing village on the Pacific coast, four miles from the school, across lagoon and mountains. The condition of the remains made it impossible to identify them by sight; it took three months for the laboratory to establish that they belonged not to Koharu, but to another missing girl.

The soldiers extended their search upriver to Magaki and towards the Fuji lake, and downriver to the villages around the Nagatsuura lagoon. New units rotated in and out from all over the country; Naomi met so many different commanders that, with their identical uniforms and short hair, she found it hard to tell them apart. Then, three months after the tsunami, the Self-Defense Forces withdrew.

The search operation, which formerly consisted of ten earth-

movers and hundreds of men, shrank to a single team of policemen, and Masaru Naganuma in his digger. Naomi and Miho still
came to the school every day. By this stage, there wasn't much they
could usefully do. When Masaru's steel arm uncovered something,
they would wade out and examine it. They found mattresses and
motorcycles and wardrobes, but no more remains. They tidied
the shrine in front of the school and threw away the dead flowers. Sometimes a second digger would work in tandem with the
first one. As they moved side by side, their long yellow limbs
waving and plunging, it was almost as if they were dancing.

An idea was taking form in Naomi's mind. She consulted
Masaru about it. "Why not try?" he said. In late June, she partici-
pated in a weeklong course at a training center near Sendai. All
the other participants were men. They showed no curiosity about
Naomi, and she felt no urge to explain herself. At the end of the
week, she came away with a license to operate earthmoving equipment, one of the few women in Japan to possess such a qualification. She went immediately to work, borrowing a digger of her
own and sifting the mud in search of Koharu.

Her father-in-law strongly opposed this development. He
argued that operating heavy machinery was dangerous for a
woman, and that her place was at home, looking after her children,
husband, and in-laws. Naomi listened patiently to what he had to
say and paid it no attention.

THE OLD AND THE YOUNG

When I heard the news, two weeks afterward, the surprise was not that Takashi Shimokawara was dead, but that he had lived this long. I was driving back to Tokyo late in March 2011 when a friend called and read out the small, down-page headline in a Japanese newspaper: *Noted Athlete Dies in Tsunami*. For the past fortnight, as I traveled among the ruined coastal towns of northeast Japan, I had found myself thinking about Mr. Shimokawara and the afternoon that I had spent with him two and a half years earlier.

I had never heard of Kamaishi, the town where he lived; the train that took us there was slow and trundling, and stopped at stations that were no more than platforms beside a deserted road. It was a freezing December afternoon in one of the coldest parts of the country, but Mr. Shimokawara's house was cozy and warm. His daughter-in-law served green tea and biscuits as he showed us his world-record certificates, and later we drove to the recreation ground where he trained, and photographed him as he stretched and jogged and made practice throws of his javelin and shot.

After more tea, we said our goodbyes, and took the slow train

home again. One fact alone had elevated this from an interesting to an unforgettable experience: Mr. Shimokawara was 102 years old.

Even to lift a javelin would be an achievement for most such men, but Mr. Shimokawara threw it farther than anyone his age. He competed in the class known as M-100, for athletes in their eleventh decade of life. His record throw—of 12:75 meters, at the Japan Masters Athletics championship in 2008—broke the world centenarian javelin record, formerly held by an American. Often, after our brief meeting, I would find myself thinking of Mr. Shimokawara and wondering how he was.

Far from having merely clung on to life, he had flourished. The previous year, he had turned 104. The article recording his death reported that at the Japan Masters in 2010 he had narrowly failed to beat his own world records. Eighteen thousand five hundred people died in the disaster, and each of them was a tragedy. But to have survived to such a great age triumphantly fit and alert, to have lived through two world wars, only to be felled by something as capricious and random as a tsunami, was unbearably bitter and ironic.

A month later, I went back to Kamaishi to look for traces of one of the disaster's oldest victims. I found them in the home where I had talked to him two and a half years before, a stout two-story house, still standing 400 yards from the sea. Mr. Shimokawara's middle-aged grandson, Minoru, was sorting through what remained, with a team of helpers and friends. There was his grandfather's white tracksuit, and the postcard confirming his most recent achievements—3:79 meters in the shot and 7:31 meters in the discus. And there were photograph albums, sodden but intact, the colors of the prints bulging and dissolving before our eyes.

They contained pictures of Mr. Shimokawara holding his medals, standing alongside his wife and at a school reunion. All of them showed a cheerful elderly man, not all that much fitter or healthier than the one I had met—and plenty of these photographs were more than forty years old.

This is the most dizzying, and at the same time the most banal, thing about the situation of centenarians—just how very, very old they are. Takashi Shimokawara was born eight years before the First World War, and outlived all of his contemporaries and two of his six children. The youngest of his eight great-grandchildren was younger than him by more than a century. And yet there had been nothing about Mr. Shimokawara to suggest that he would live to such an age.

Both his parents died in their fifties. He led an active life as a high-school PE teacher, but he had his share of illness, including tuberculosis and gallstones. He admitted to me that as a young man he used to drink and smoke heavily, and that he still enjoyed a glass of sake with meals.

"When did you give up smoking?" I asked.

"When I was eighty," he said.

I recounted this to his grandson, who smiled and said, "He lied. When I went drinking with him, he had much more than a glass, and he used to cadge my cigarettes."

All his life Mr. Shimokawara was active in the community, as a teacher, a local councillor, and, in later years, a local celebrity. But despite being surrounded by people, I recognized something painful: that he was intensely, unquenchably lonely. He had been a widower for thirty-five years. Many of the children he taught as a schoolmaster had long ago died of old age. "All my brothers and sisters are dead," he said. "I'm the last. My oldest friends are twenty years younger than me. My situation is fearful, in a way. So many

have died around me—I have been to so many funerals. I don't cry about it, but this is my biggest sadness, this loneliness."

The second painful thing dawned on me a little later: that, at the age of 102, Mr. Shimokawara had a lively fear of death.

Lulled by clichés about "serene" old people, I had assumed that attachment to life diminishes with age. But here was an extreme example of the opposite: an ancient man fending off death with javelin and discus. It was this—the urge to stay on his feet at all costs—that drove his athletic achievements. "The most important thing of all is to stay supple and flexible," he said. "The moment you will be most stiff is when you die—you never get stiffer than that. So you've got to sleep well, eat well, and keep moving." And all of this made the facts of his eventual death all the more pitiful.

Because Mr. Shimokawara's son and daughter-in-law died with him, his friends and family had to work out for themselves the puzzle of the family car. It was found a few days after the disaster, carefully parked on a hill, safely beyond the reach of the tsunami. This discovery immediately inspired hope—for repeated searches of the area around the family home had turned up no trace of the Shimokawaras. Then eight days later, the three bodies were recovered from a public hall a few hundred yards from the house—and it was this that unlocked the sad truth.

In Kamaishi, as elsewhere, the earthquake itself caused little serious damage, and tsunami warnings were immediately broadcast through loudspeakers across the town. Mr. Shimokawara's seventy-three-year-old son had plenty of time to help his father and wife into the car and to drive them to the single-story public hall. It was only a few hundred yards from the sea, and scarcely

more elevated than the family house. But by the time this became obvious, it would have been much too late.

The wave surged around Mr. Shimokawara's house, although its upper floor was spared. But it overwhelmed the public hall and drowned those who had retreated there. Three minutes' walking distance farther up the road, the water petered out against a steadily rising slope. "If they had stayed with the car, or walked up the road, or even just stayed at home and climbed the stairs, they would have made it," said Keizo Tada, an old friend. Instead, as a good citizen obediently following the drill, Mr. Shimokawara's son drove to safety, parked his car, and calmly and obliviously walked back down the hill to his death.

Takashi Shimokawara had lived through the 1933 tsunami, the Chile tsunami in 1960, and countless minor waves and false alarms. When his old friend Tada last spoke to him, he had talked of the forthcoming athletics championship when he would compete in the over-105 age group. Without question, he would have set new world records—he would, literally, have been in a class of his own.

The funeral of such an old man would not normally be an occasion of intense grief and tragedy, but this one was. "To be honest, I still don't feel as if they are dead," said Minoru, who buried his mother, father, and grandfather on the same day. "Of course, I have identified the bodies, signed the documents, and organized the cremation. But it's as if I'm in the middle of a nightmare, and the real pain is still coming towards me."

The tsunami was a disaster visited above all upon the old. Fifty-four percent of those who perished were age sixty-five or older, and the older you were, the worse your chances. But the converse

of this was even more striking. The younger you were, the more likely you were to survive—and the number of children who were killed was astonishingly small.

In the Indian Ocean tsunami that struck Indonesia, Sri Lanka, and Thailand in 2004, children died disproportionately because they were less physically capable of swimming and dragging themselves to safety. In Japan, the opposite was true. Out of the 18,500 dead and missing, only 351—fewer than one in fifty— were schoolchildren. Four out of five of them died somewhere other than school: because they were off sick that afternoon or had been quickly picked up by anxious parents. It was much more dangerous, in other words, to be reunited with your family than to remain with your teachers.

If you are ever exposed to a violent earthquake, the safest place you could hope to be is Japan; and the best spot of all is in-side a Japanese school.* Decades of technological experiment have bred the most resilient and strictly regulated construction in the world. Even against the immensity of the tsunami, Japan's seawalls, warning systems, and evacuation drills saved an un-countable number of lives: however great the catastrophe of 2011, the damage caused would have been many times worse if it had happened in any other country. And nowhere are precautions against natural disaster more robust than in state schools.

They are built on iron frames out of reinforced concrete. They are often situated on hills and elevations, and all of them are required to have detailed disaster plans and to practice them

---

* One of the worst places, of course, is anywhere near a nuclear reactor, such as those inside the Fukushima Dai-ichi nuclear power plant. But the fact of that man-made disaster, set off by the naturally occurring earthquake and tsu-nami, does not contradict what I have to say here about the resilience of Japa-nese construction in general.

regularly. On that afternoon, Japanese architecture and bureau-cracy did an almost perfect job of protecting the young.

No school collapsed or suffered serious physical damage in the earthquake. Nine of them were completely overwhelmed by the tsunami, and at one of them, in the town of Minami-Sanriku, a boy of thirteen was drowned as his class hurried to higher ground. But with one exception, every other school got all its children to safety.

On March 11, 2011, seventy-five children in Japan died in the care of their teachers. Seventy-four of them were at Okawa Elementary School. Later, many of their parents were tormented by self-reproach for not rushing there to collect them. But far from being neglectful or lazy, they had followed the course of action that, in every other circumstance, would have been most likely to secure their safety and survival.

"I was hardly conscious of what I was doing," said Katsura Sato. "There were so many feelings. All I could do was to deal with life one piece at a time. We had lost Mizuho, my dearest girl. But we hadn't lost anything else. My other two children were fine. Our house was untouched. People on the coast lost their families, their houses, and their community. There were people who were still looking for their loved ones. They were much worse off than us. Once water and electricity returned, we got back to some kind of ordinary life."

Katsura was an art teacher at a high school in Ishinomaki and lived with her husband, parents-in-law, and three children in Fukuji, a few hundred yards from Sayomi Shito and her family. Katsura and Sayomi's daughters, Mizuho and Chisato, were best friends at Okawa Elementary School. They were cremated on the same day. "Until then," Katsura said, "that was all I could con-

centrate on. After the cremation—well, I'm usually healthy, but I became ill. I couldn't get up. I stayed in bed for three days. And I started thinking and thinking, and I became very suspicious about the circumstances in which we lost our daughter. I knew that this was a great natural disaster, and I assumed at the beginning that there must have been many other cases like this, other schools where the same thing happened. But why did I never hear of them?"

In the villages along the river, as they began to catch their breath in the weeks following the disaster, other parents were asking the same question.

Much of their suspicion focused on the actions of two men. The first of them was Junji Endo, the only teacher to have survived the tsunami, whom Hitomi Konno had seen, stunned and almost speechless, in Irikamaya in the early morning after the disaster. The second was the principal of the school, a man named Teruyuki Kashiba. By chance, Kashiba had been off work that Friday afternoon and was attending the graduation ceremony of his own daughter at another school miles inland. Whatever had gone wrong at Okawa, the testimony of these two—the only surviving adult witness to the events at the school, and its head, the man responsible for all its safety procedures—was clearly crucial. But since that first morning of dread and confusion, no one seemed to have seen or heard from Endo; and even the principal had been strangely elusive.

The searchers picking through the mud were surprised not to see Kashiba at the ruins of the school. He eventually put in an appearance, six days after the tsunami, followed by a train of journalists and cameramen. Two weeks later, Katsura Sato was startled to see Kashiba's face on the local television news, and even more amazed by the subject of the report—a ceremony at Okawa Elementary School. The thirty surviving children were

marking the start of the new school year, which in Japan begins in April. Okawa Elementary had been reconstituted in a classroom at another school in the area. Katsura remembered clearly the words that the principal used in addressing the children: "Let's forge a common effort to rebuild a school full of smiles, for the sake of our friends who died."

"At first the children were a bit nervous," Kashiba told the television interviewer. "But when I said these words to them, they nodded firmly."

School ceremonies, even for young children, are a matter of great importance in Japan, occasions of pleasure and pride for an entire family. Fifty-four families had lost children at the school; none had received notification of a ceremony in which their dead sons and daughters should have been participants. The intention was clear enough—to make some attempt at resuming normal life, and to create a place where the survivors could pick up again the business of simply being schoolchildren. But it was experienced by many of the grieving families as a punch to the stomach.

"The invitations were sent out to the parents of the kids who survived," Katsura said. "I thought, 'Our kids are gone, but aren't we still Okawa parents?' We had had no explanation—no word from the school at all. This principal, Kashiba, turned up at the school once or twice, without even getting his hands dirty. And then we see him on television, talking about 'smiles.'"

Katsura went on, "It was as if they were abandoning us before the kids were even buried. That night I couldn't sleep for anger. I said to my husband, 'How can we let this happen?' And I wondered: Was it just me who thought like that?"

EXPLANATIONS

Four weeks after the tsunami, the Ishinomaki City Board of Education, supervisory authority of Okawa Elementary School, convened an "explanatory meeting" for families of the children who had died there. The meeting gave the impression of having been arranged hastily, in chastened response to the fusillade of anger that had been directed against the board after the mishandled opening ceremony. It was held on a Saturday evening at the inland school to which the surviving children of Okawa Elementary had been relocated. Journalists were not admitted, but one of the parents made a video recording of the proceedings. It shows Kashiba, the principal, and five representatives of the education board seated on a row of chairs in the blue overalls that are the uniform of Japanese public officials. Opposite, with only their backs visible to the video camera, sit the parents and other relatives, ninety-seven of them all told. The room was unheated; in the film, everyone is swaddled in coats, hats, and scarves.

The meeting opened conventionally enough, with introductions by a Mr. Konno, head of the secretariat of the board of education. He began with an apology: he had lost his voice, and

would therefore deliver only brief opening remarks. "Good evening to you all," he croaked. "I extend my sincerest sympathies to those who fell victim to this disaster. In particular, I offer sincere prayers for those who died. This month, the children should have welcomed spring, their breasts swelling with hope. However, on the eleventh of March, the day of that huge disaster, a great tsunami snatched away in a moment the smallest pleasures of daily life. Having lost the irreplaceable, precious lives of many children and teachers, we face an unhappy spring."

Public meetings in Japan are blandly formulaic occasions, by and large, replete with stock phrases, and characterized by an absence of confrontation or verbal fireworks. But then Mr. Konno gave the floor to Kashiba, the principal, and it quickly became clear that this was not going to be an ordinary meeting.

Grief and anger threatened the reputations of everyone connected to the school; for many people, it became impossible to look objectively on the character of Teruyuki Kashiba. He was a short, plump, gray-haired man in his late fifties, with oval spectacles and a habit of sucking in his lips at moments of stress or reflection. After a decade as deputy head in other schools, he had been appointed to Okawa the previous April. Even before the disaster, no one seemed sure quite what to make of Kashiba. After a year, not all of the parents knew who he was.

It was not his fault that he had been away from the school that afternoon; his horror and distress can only be imagined. But he made a grave error of judgment, first in taking so long to go to the site after the disaster, and then by his conduct when he did show his face. He was never forgiven for his failure to make any effort, even a token one, to help with the search for bodies. On his first visit, he answered questions from the media and took a

lot of photographs with an expensive camera. On another occasion, he was seen expending anxious effort in a hunt for the school safe.

By the time of the meeting in the school, the rage and misery of the parents had been gathering for a month. That evening they found their object in Mr. Kashiba.

"Until the afternoon of the eleventh of March," he mumbled, when his turn came to speak, "there were smiles on the faces of the children, and laughter in the voices of the children, but, truly, seventy-four children, ten teachers were lost. I apologize sincerely."

"Can't hear you!" called a voice from the audience.

"Don't you have a mike?" said someone else.

Kashiba continued. "At the school, when I stood in front of the building, I could imagine the faces of the children. It was terrible."

"When did you go to the school?" someone interrupted.

"Yeah, when did you go?" called another.

"What day did I go?" asked the ruffled principal. "It was the seventeenth of March."

"Our daughter died on the eleventh."

Kashiba bowed his head. "I apologize," he said. "The delay in responding, the failures—there were so many—I am truly sorry."

At that moment, a frisson passed through the assembled parents, as people in the room became aware of an unexpected presence—a man sitting at the far left, dressed in black. His head and shoulders were slumped forward, to the extent that it was difficult to see his face at all.

"Well, well, well," someone called out. "If it isn't Junji Endo."

Even those who later harbored the greatest distrust towards him admitted that, before the disaster, Endo had been a successful

and popular teacher. He was a self-deprecating, bespectacled man in his forties, third in the hierarchy of the school's small staff. As head of teaching, he had no classroom of his own, but moved between the different grades teaching nature and science. "The children were very close to him," Hitomi Konno told me. "Daisuke was a member of the nature club, and Mr. Endo used to show them deer horns, and how to make fishhooks, and tell them all kinds of stories about crocodiles and piranhas. They thought he was amazing."

He had previously taught in the fishing village of Aikawa, seven miles up the coast. Among his responsibilities at Aikawa Elementary School had been disaster preparedness. Plenty of teachers would have treated this as a routine matter, demanding nothing more than the organization of evacuation drills and the updating of parents' telephone numbers. But Endo went much further. The emergency manual at Aikawa stated that, in the case of a tsunami warning, pupils and staff should evacuate to the flat roof of the three-story building. Endo judged this to be inadequate. He rewrote the plan to require escape up a steep hill to the Shinto shrine behind the school.

Aikawa Elementary had been built on flat ground virtually at sea level, just two hundred yards from the water. When the tsunami struck here, it was more than fifty feet high and it overwhelmed the school completely. The roof was covered by the waves: anyone who had retreated there would have died. But, following the revised procedure, the teachers and children had quickly climbed the hill, and not a single one was hurt. At his old school, Junji Endo could rightly claim to have saved scores of lives.

In different circumstances, he might have been an object of sympathy and admiration. But since the morning after the disaster, no one seemed to have heard from him. His whereabouts,

and the story he had to tell, had become matters of intense speculation—and now here he was.

"He saved his own life," someone called from the audience. "*He*'s still alive. So let him talk to us."

A board of education official named Shigemi Kato spoke. "Mr. Endo himself has injuries—he suffered a dislocation and frostbite and had to go to the hospital. He's presently suffering from a serious psychological illness. Please keep this in mind as you listen to him."

"No fucking kidding," someone said. "Well, we parents are ill too."

With an appearance of great difficulty and distress, Endo began to speak. His head and upper body were bent almost parallel to the ground. He frequently became choked with emotion; sometimes he appeared to be on the verge of collapse.

"I'm sorry," he said. "I couldn't help. I'm so truly sorry for that."

The heckling ceased.

"Allow me to describe what happened on that day," he said. "There may be gaps in my memory. Please forgive me if there are."

"It was a Friday," Endo began, "and lessons had just finished for the day when the shaking began. It must have been the time when the children were getting ready to go home, and they were with their teachers for the class meeting. The electricity was cut off and the loudspeaker didn't work, so I ran up to the classrooms on the second floor and said to each class, 'Get under your desks, and hold on to them.' The children seemed scared, but the class teachers were telling them that it would all be okay. After the tremors

subsided, I went back to each class in turn and told them to come out and evacuate."

Endo remained behind, and checked the classrooms and toilets for stragglers. By the time he emerged, the roll had been taken and the children were sitting in the playground. "Some of them were vomiting from panic," Endo said, "and some could not stop crying. The teachers were trying to calm them down. It had begun to snow, and some of the children had escaped in bare feet. I went back in and brought sweaters and shoes, and had them put them on."

By now, local people from Kamaya were turning up at the school. They had fled their homes during the shaking, and asked to be allowed to shelter in the school gym. Endo explained that the broken glass there made it unsuitable. "While I was doing that," he said, "parents began arriving to pick up their children, and it was the deputy head, mainly, who checked off the names and handed them over."

A voice cried out from the audience of bereaved parents, "Why did you do that? If you'd just put everyone in cars and driven up a hill, they would all have been saved."

Endo continued without replying. "After that, I learned that a tsunami was on its way. Of course, one alternative was the hill. But because the shocks were so strong and it was shaking continuously, I . . ."

He trailed off, then began again. It is difficult to translate what came next: the sentences were rambling and ungrammatical; the sequence of events was confused. "So when the tsunami hit," he said, "because we never imagined such a big tsunami coming, we discussed whether we should evacuate to the safest part of the school, the upper gallery of the gym or the second floor of the school building, and I—because the damage to the school building was so bad—I went into the school building to have a

look. Various things had fallen over, but I thought that we could go back in there. I returned to the playground, but by then a move had begun to evacuate immediately."

The destination was the traffic island near the bridge, four hundred yards away and around the corner on the main road. The children formed a column, which threaded out of the back of the school and through the parking lot of the Kamaya Village Hall. Endo brought up the rear.

As he was passing through the parking lot, he became aware of a powerful rush of air.

He said, "It was a tremendous gust of wind, and a noise like I'd never heard before. I didn't know what was happening at first, but when I looked at the road in front of the school in the direction of the Kamaya high street, I could see an immense tsunami. It was coming down the road." The column of children was advancing directly into the coming wave. Endo immediately shouted, "The hill! The hill! This way!" and urged the children in the opposite direction, towards the rear of the school. "But when I reached the hill," he said, "I was slipping on the snow and couldn't climb, and there were children all around me.

"Just as I reached the hill, two cedars collapsed. They struck me on my right arm and left shoulder, and I became trapped. I felt the tsunami wash over me, and I thought that was it, but the tree was lifted off me, perhaps by the water, and when I looked up the slope, I saw a boy from the third grade calling for help. I'd lost my glasses and my shoes, but I knew I had to do everything to save this child. 'Go, go up!' I called. 'Climb for your life!' . . . The noise of the water was getting closer. 'Up, up!' I shouted as I pushed him."

By now it had begun to snow. The boy had swallowed a lot of water, and both his clothes and the teacher's were soaking wet. "I realized that it was impossible to go down," Endo said, "and that

I would have to spend the night on the hill with this child." They found a hollow at the foot of a tree, and sat shoulder-to-shoulder on a heap of pine needles. "But the noise of the water was still getting closer," Endo said. "And then—I don't know if it was just a feeling—it seemed that with every aftershock there was a crunch of trees falling down. The boy said, 'It's coming! It's still coming closer! I'm scared, I'm scared! Let's go, let's go higher.' "

At the top of the hill, the ground was covered with thickening snow. Endo found that he was unable to move his arm, the one that had been struck by the tree. Propped against his teacher's shoulder, the child nodded off, and Endo began to worry about the small sleeping body in its wet clothes. "It was getting dark and it was terribly cold," he said. "I thought if we stayed as we were, the child might freeze to death."

In the blackness, he could see little without his spectacles. But he supposed that, if they walked down the other side of the hill, they would eventually encounter cars and motorists on the Ogatsu road. "I asked the boy to be my eyes," Endo said, "and to tell me whether it was safe to go down. As we walked down step by step, I could make out headlamps on the road. We headed in that direction. We walked towards the light. And then there were people at a house, and we said, 'Please help,' and they helped us."

They ended up at Irikamaya, where Hitomi found them. The next day, Endo was helped to the hospital in Ishinomaki; and from there he went home.

Endo said, "There are moments that have slipped from my mind, but this is more or less how it was on that day."

He said, "Every single day, I dream about the children playing happily in the schoolyard. I dream about the teachers and the deputy head, who were preparing so hard for the graduation ceremony that was coming up. I'm so sorry."

With that, his head and upper body slumped; at one point, it

appeared that Endo was going to collapse onto the floor, and the members of the board of education jumped to their feet to support him. His naked distress, as raw as a wound, must have seemed to them to supply everything that they could not, with their formal politeness and their flowery clichés about swelling breasts. Who could question the abject pain of Mr. Endo, and the agony of his survival? Konno, Kashiba, and the other suited officials might have hoped that this would be the end of the meeting, perhaps the beginning of the end of the whole dreadful business. There was a silence as those present adjusted to the fact that Endo's account was over. The meeting was poised at a moment of pivot: it might have turned either way. Then a man in the audience got to his feet.

His name was Toshimitsu Sasaki. His seven-year-old boy, Tetsuma, and his nine-year-old daughter, Nagomi, had died at the school. "Teachers, principal, members of the board of education," he said—and the formality of this address must have raised the hope that matters would continue hereafter on a stable and predictable footing. Then he went on.

"Why didn't you come quickly to the school the next day?" he asked Kashiba. "Why didn't you come until the seventeenth? Do you know how many children are still missing now? Can you name them? Can you name the children who died? The families left behind—all of us have been going mad. There are ten of them still missing out there. *Do you understand?* Imagine how we feel, those parents who are still searching every day. Every day in dirty clothes. And if we don't go there to search, we go mad."

Sasaki stood up in front of the table behind which the officials sat, their eyes on the ground. He was wearing a blue windbreaker and brandishing something in his hand, which he waved in their downturned faces.

"Just this shoe," he said, his voice rising. "That's all we've

found. All ruined, like this. My daughter—is this it?" He slammed the shoe down on the table, and Konno flinched. "My daughter!" he screamed. "Is she a shoe?"

The meeting went on for two and a half hours. In all that time, Kashiba and the others spoke in total for no more than a few minutes. Now and then, a request for information would be formulated, and a faltering and incomplete answer given—about what tsunami warnings had been given and received, and what Kashiba had done and failed to do, and when. But most of the time was taken up by the parents, one after another, shouting, snarling, pleading, whispering, and crying, with an anger directed almost exclusively towards the figure of the principal. On the video, he sits with eyes downcast. The faces of his accusers are invisible; their backs tremble as they denounce him:

—Tricky old bastard.
—Fuck off, you sod!
—I will devote my whole life to this, you bastard. I will spend my whole life avenging those children. I won't let you hide anywhere.

People almost never speak like this in Japan—not in public, not to teachers and government officials. It is difficult to underestimate the violence of these interventions, and the intensity of emotion that they betrayed.

One woman said: "We believed that they would come back the next day. Everyone believed that. Everyone had faith in the school. Everyone believed they must be safe, because they were at school."

A man said: "Every day, I hear our son and daughter crying, screaming, 'Dad, help me!' They are crying out in my dreams. They never leave my dreams."

Much of the torrent of words took the form of questions. "Did you see those swollen faces?" a father asked. "They had changed so much after one month. A rotten thing. That was a human being, you know. A person. Dumped on a truck, covered with a rag. Come and talk to us after you find your own child like that, you bastard."

Another asked: "Do you know the number of missing children in each class, Principal? *Without* looking at that piece of paper. You don't, do you? You have to look at your piece of paper. Our kids—are they just a piece of paper? You don't remember any of their faces, do you?"

Their grief was unquenchable, but what they were seeking was not mysterious—and a group of more sensitive men, less oppressed by protocol and panic, could have transformed the atmosphere in the room. All the parents wanted was a reflection of their own grief, a glimmer of recognition of their loss, a sense that they were facing not a government department, but fellow human beings. As their passion rose, they abandoned the indirectness of standard Japanese and expressed themselves ever more bluntly in the slurring dialect of Tohoku. And rather than emerging to meet them, the bureaucrats retreated in the opposite direction, into ever fussier and more bloodless speech.

Asked about the search for the missing, Konno said: "At present, personnel from the Japan Self-Defense Forces, central government, and the police are making their best efforts to recover remains of those regrettably not found yet. Hereafter, we will continue the search beneath the detritus, and the like."

Pressed on a proposal to hold a joint funeral for the children,

Kashiba, the head, responded: "By consulting with members of the board of education, and talking to bereaved family members, I suppose I think that I want to decide whether we will do this or not."

"Don't patronize us, like bumpkins," someone shouted.

"Is it because we are in the country that you treat us like this?" asked another.

"If we were in the city, this wouldn't happen," said a third voice.

The words came, and kept coming:

—Principal, have you ever thought about the feelings of the children during that hour that they were waiting? How scared they must have been—have you thought about that? How cold they were, and their screaming for their mums and dads. And there was a hill, a hill right there!

—You people who came to the school after the road was cleared—you don't know anything. I was there when it was just trees, pine trees scattered all around. We didn't know where to start. Walking through the water in boots, with that sound, *squelch-squelch*. You'll never understand what it was like to walk through that water, with the squelching, and the mud getting into your boots. Even when they found their own children, mums and dads came back to look for the others. What did you look for? Fuck you. You looked for the school safe.

—Will you come to the school, Principal? Will you search?
—We'll lend you a shovel, if you don't have one.
—If you haven't got the boots, we can give you as many as you want.
—You've only got nice leather shoes, haven't you?
—And he's got a nice camera.

—It took us four years to have a child . . .

—Us too. We managed only after long years. And now he's gone.

—Can't you do something?

—Please return our child to us.

—Every night, I . . . What . . . ? What can we do?

—They were our future.

—Please, please, return him.

—Yes!

—Release him!

It was after nine o'clock by the time the meeting broke up. Kashiba looked dazed. There were plenty of people present who had not spoken, but who felt sympathy for the principal and had been mortified by the shouting. Now their minds were racing. Much remained unresolved—but they had, at least, finally heard from the wretched Endo, and received an account of the missing time in the playground, on which everyone had been so unbearably fixated. His account made it clear that there had been tsunami warnings, that they had been received by the teachers and acted on—even if much too late.

The nine-year-old boy who had been with Endo on the mountain, whom he had huddled against in an effort to save him from the cold, was called Seina Yamamoto. His mother was present at the meeting and went to the teacher to thank him. While they were talking, another mother, whose son had died, also approached. She wanted to ask Endo if he remembered anything about her own boy; like many of the parents, she was avid for a last glimpse of him, just the memory of a word or two, or the look on his face. But the education officials told her that Endo was "unwell" and prevented her from speaking to him. Quickly, it would become clear that much of what he had said was not true at all. And after that evening, he vanished from sight.

GHOSTS

I met a priest in northern Japan who exorcised the spirits of people who had drowned in the tsunami. The ghosts did not appear in large numbers until autumn of that year, but Reverend Kaneta's first case of possession came to him after less than a fortnight. He was chief priest at a Zen temple in the inland town of Kurihara. The earthquake on March 11 was the most violent that he or anyone he knew had ever experienced. The great wooden beams of the temple's halls had flexed and groaned with the strain. Power, water, and telephone lines were fractured for days; deprived of electricity, people in Kurihara, thirty miles from the coast, had a dimmer idea of what was going on there than television viewers on the other side of the world. But it became clear enough when first a handful of families, and then a mass of them, began arriving at Reverend Kaneta's temple with corpses to bury.

More than eighteen thousand people had died at a stroke. In the space of a month, Reverend Kaneta performed funeral services for two hundred of them. More appalling than the scale of death was the spectacle of the bereaved survivors. "They didn't

cry," Kaneta said. "There was no emotion at all. The loss was so profound, and death had come so suddenly. They understood the facts of their situation individually—that they had lost their homes, lost their livelihoods, and lost their families. They understood each piece, but they couldn't see it as a whole, and they couldn't understand what they should do, or sometimes even where they were. I couldn't really talk to them, to be honest. All I could do was stay with them, and read the sutras and conduct the ceremonies. That was the thing I could do."

Amid this numbness and horror, Reverend Kaneta received a visit from a man he knew, a local builder whom I will call Takeshi Ono.

Ono was ashamed of what had happened, and didn't want his real name to be published. It was difficult at first to understand the reason for this shame. He was a strong, stocky man in his late thirties, the kind of man most comfortable in blue overalls, with a head of youthfully dense and tousled hair. "He's such an innocent person," Reverend Kaneta said to me. "He takes everything at face value. You're from England, aren't you? He's like your Mr. Bean." I wouldn't have gone so far, because there was nothing ridiculous about Ono. But there was a dreamy ingenuousness about him, which made the story he told all the more believable.

He had been at work on a house when the earthquake struck. He clung to the ground for as long as it lasted; even his truck shook as if it was about to topple over. The drive home, along roads without traffic lights, was alarming, but the physical damage was remarkably slight: a few telegraph poles lolling at an angle, toppled garden walls. As the owner of a small building firm, he was perfectly equipped to deal with the practical inconveniences inflicted by the earthquake. Ono spent the next few days busying himself

with camping stoves, generators, and jerry cans, and paying little attention to the news.

But once television was restored, it was impossible to be unaware of what had happened. Ono watched the endlessly replayed image of the explosive plume above the nuclear reactor, and the mobile-phone films of the black wave crunching up ports, houses, shopping centers, cars, and human figures. These were places he had known all his life, fishing towns and beaches just over the hills, an hour's drive away. And the spectacle of their destruction produced in Ono a sensation of glassy detachment, a feeling common at that time, even among those most directly stricken by displacement and bereavement.

"My life had returned to normal," he told me. "I had gasoline, I had an electricity generator, no one I knew was dead or hurt. I hadn't seen the tsunami myself, not with my own eyes, so I felt as if I was in a kind of dream."

Ten days after the disaster, Ono, his wife, and his widowed mother drove over the mountains to see for themselves.

They left in the morning in good spirits, stopped on the way to go shopping, and reached the coast in time for lunch. For most of the way, the scene was familiar: brown rice fields, villages of wood and tile, bridges over wide, slow rivers. Once they had climbed into the hills, they passed more and more emergency vehicles, not only those of the police and fire services, but the green trucks of the Self-Defense Forces. As the road descended towards the coast, their jaunty mood began to evaporate. Suddenly, before they understood where they were, they had entered the tsunami zone.

There was no advance warning, no marginal area of incremental damage. The wave had come in with full force, spent itself, and stopped at a point as clearly defined as the reach of a high

tide. Above it, nothing had been touched; below it, everything was changed.

This was the point at which shame entered Ono's narrative, and he became reluctant to describe in detail what he did or where he went. "I saw the rubble, I saw the sea," he said. "I saw buildings damaged by the tsunami. It wasn't just the things themselves, but the atmosphere. It was a place I used to go so often. It was such a shock to see it. And all the police and soldiers there. It's difficult to describe. It felt dangerous. My first thought was that this is terrible. My next feeling was 'Is it real?'"

Ono, his wife, and his mother sat down for dinner as usual that evening. He remembered that he drank two small cans of beer with the meal. Afterward, and for no obvious reason, he began calling friends on his mobile phone. "I'd just ring and say, 'Hi, how are you?'—that kind of thing," he told me. "It wasn't that I had much to say. I don't know why, but I was starting to feel very lonely."

His wife had already left the house when he woke the next morning. Ono had no particular work of his own and passed an idle day at home. His mother bustled in and out, but she seemed mysteriously upset, even angry. When his wife returned from her office, she was similarly tense.

"Is something wrong?" Ono asked.

"I'm divorcing you!" she replied.

"Divorce? But why? Why?"

And so his wife and mother described the events of the night before, after the round of needy phone calls. How Ono had jumped down onto all fours and begun licking the tatami mats and futon, and squirmed on them like a beast. How at first they

had nervously laughed at his tomfoolery, but had been silenced when he began snarling, "You must die. You must die. Everyone must die. Everything must die and be lost." In front of the house was an unsown field, and Ono had run out into it and rolled over and over in the mud, as if he was being tumbled by a wave, shouting, "There, over there! They're all over there—look!" Then he had stood up and walked out into the field, calling, "I'm coming to you. I'm coming over to that side," before his wife physically wrestled him back into the house. The writhing and bellowing went on all night until, around five in the morning, Ono cried out, "There's something on top of me," collapsed, and fell asleep.

"My wife and my mother were so anxious and upset," he said. "Of course, I told them how sorry I was. But I had no memory of what I did or why."

It went on for three nights.

The next evening, as darkness fell, he saw figures walking past the house: parents and children, a group of young friends, a grandfather and a child. "The people were covered in mud," he said. "They were no more than twenty feet away, and they stared at me, but I wasn't afraid. I just thought, 'Why are they in those muddy things? Why don't they change their clothes? Perhaps their washing machine's broken.' They were like people I might have known once or seen before somewhere. The scene was flickering, like a film. But I felt perfectly normal, and I thought that they were just ordinary people."

The next day, Ono was lethargic and inert. At night, he would lie down, sleep heavily for ten minutes, then wake up as lively and refreshed as if eight hours had passed. He staggered when he walked, glared at his wife and mother, and even waved a knife. "Drop dead!" he would snarl. "Everyone else is dead, so die!"

After three days of pleading by his family, he went to Rever-

end Kaneta at the temple. "His eyes were dull," Kaneta said. "Like a person with depression after taking their medication. I knew at a glance that something was wrong." Ono recounted the visit to the coast, and his wife and mother described his behavior in the days since. "The Reverend was looking hard at me as I spoke," Ono said, "and in part of my mind I was saying, 'Don't look at me like that, you bastard. I hate your guts! Why are you looking at me?'"

Kaneta took Ono by the hand and led him, tottering, into the main hall of the temple. "He told me to sit down. I was not myself. I still remember that strong feeling of resistance. But part of me was also relieved—I wanted to be helped and to believe in the priest. The part of me that was still me wanted to be saved."

Kaneta beat the temple drum as he chanted the Heart Sutra:

> There are no eyes, no ears, no nose, no tongue,
> no body, mind; no color, sound, or smell;
> no taste, no touch, no thing; no realm of sight,
> no realm of thoughts; no ignorance, no end
> to ignorance; no old age and no death;
> no end to age and death; no suffering,
> nor any cause of suffering, nor end
> to suffering, no path, no wisdom
> and no fulfillment.

Ono's wife told him later how he pressed his hands together in prayer and how, as the priest's recitation continued, they rose high above his head as if being pulled from above.

> gone gone gone beyond
> gone altogether beyond
> O what an awakening
> —all hail!

The priest splashed him with holy water, and then abruptly Ono returned to his senses and found himself with wet hair and shirt, filled with a sensation of tranquillity and release. "My head was light," he said. "In a moment, the thing that had been there had gone. I felt fine physically, but my nose was blocked as if I'd come down with a heavy cold."

Kaneta spoke sternly to him; both understood what had happened. "Ono told me that he'd walked along the beach in that devastated area, eating an ice cream," the priest said. "He even put up a sign in the car against the windshield saying DISASTER RELIEF, so that no one would stop him. He went there flippantly, without giving it any thought at all. I told him, 'You fool. If you go to a place like that where many people have died, you must go with a feeling of respect. That's common sense. You have suffered a kind of punishment for what you did. Something got hold of you, perhaps the dead who cannot accept yet that they are dead. They have been trying to express their regret and their resentment through you.'" Kaneta suddenly smiled as he remembered it. "Mr. Bean!" he said indulgently. "He's so innocent and open. That's another reason why they were able to possess him."

Ono recognized all of this, and more. It was not just the spirits of men and women that had possessed him, he saw now, but also animals—cats and dogs and other beasts that had drowned with their masters.

He thanked the priest and drove home. His nose was streaming as if with catarrh, but what came out was not mucus, but a pink jelly like nothing he had seen before.

The wave penetrated no more than a few miles inland, but over the hills in Kurihara it transformed the life of Reverend Taio Kaneta. He had inherited the temple from his father, and the task

of dealing with the survivors of the tsunami tested him in ways for which he was unprepared. It had been the greatest disaster of postwar Japan. And yet the pain did not announce itself; it dug underground and burrowed deep. Once the immediate emergency had abated, once the bodies were cremated, the memorial services held, and the homeless sheltered, Reverend Kaneta set about trying to gain entry into the dungeon of silence in which he saw so many of the survivors languishing.

He began traveling around the coast with a group of fellow priests, organizing a mobile event that he called "Café de Monku"—a bilingual pun. As well as being the Japanese pronunciation of the English word "monk," *monku* means "complaint." "We think it will take a long time to get back to a calm, quiet, ordinary life," read the flyer that he distributed. "Why don't you come and join us—take a break and have a little moan? The monks will listen to your complaint—and have a *monku* of their own too."

Under this pretext—a casual cup of tea and a friendly chat—people came to the temples and community centers where Café de Monku was held. Many were living in "temporary residences," the grim prefabricated huts, freezing in winter and sweltering in summer, where those who could afford nothing better ended up. The priests listened sympathetically and made a point of not asking too many questions. "People don't like to cry," said Kaneta. "They see it as selfish. Among those who are living in the temporary homes, there's hardly anyone who has not lost a member of their family. Everyone's in the same boat, so they don't like to seem self-indulgent. But when they start talking, and when you listen to them, and sense their gritted teeth and their suffering, all the suffering they can't and won't express, in time the tears come, and they flow without end."

Haltingly, apologetically, then with increasing fluency, the survivors spoke of the terror of the wave, the pain of bereavement,

and their fears for the future. They also talked about encounters with the supernatural.

They described sightings of ghostly strangers, friends and neighbors, and dead loved ones. They reported hauntings at home, at work, in offices and public places, on the beaches and in the ruined towns. The experiences ranged from eerie dreams and feelings of vague unease to cases, like that of Takeshi Ono, of outright possession.

A young man complained of pressure on his chest at night, as if some creature was straddling him as he slept. A teenage girl spoke of a fearful figure who squatted in her house. A middle-aged man hated to go out in the rain, because of the eyes of the dead, which stared out at him from puddles.

A civil servant in Soma visited a devastated stretch of coast and saw a solitary woman in a scarlet dress far from the nearest road or house, with no means of transport in sight. When he looked for her again, she had disappeared.

A fire station in Tagajo received calls to places where all the houses had been destroyed by the tsunami. The crews went out to the ruins anyway, prayed for the spirits of those who had died—and the ghostly calls ceased.

A taxi in the city of Sendai picked up a sad-faced man who asked to be taken to an address that no longer existed. Halfway through the journey, the driver looked into his mirror to see that the rear seat was empty. He drove on anyway, stopped in front of the leveled foundations of a destroyed house, and politely opened the door to allow the invisible passenger out at his former home.

At a refugee community in Onagawa, an old neighbor would appear in the living rooms of the temporary houses and sit down for a cup of tea with their startled occupants. No one had the heart to tell her that she was dead; the cushion on which she had sat was wet with seawater.

Such stories came from all over the devastated area. Priests—Christian and Shinto, as well as Buddhist—found themselves called on repeatedly to quell unhappy spirits. A Buddhist monk wrote an article in a learned journal about "the ghost problem," and academics at Tohoku University began to catalogue the stories. In Kyoto, the matter was debated at a scholarly symposium.

"Religious people all argue about whether these are really the spirits of the dead," Kaneta told me. "I don't get into it, because what matters is that people are seeing them, and in these circumstances, after this disaster, it is perfectly natural. So many died, and all at once. At home, at work, at school—the wave came in and they were gone. The dead had no time to prepare themselves. The people left behind had no time to say goodbye. Those who lost their families, and those who died—they have strong feelings of attachment. The dead are attached to the living, and those who have lost them are attached to the dead. It's inevitable that there are ghosts."

He said: "So many people are having these experiences. It's impossible to identify who and where they all are. But there are countless such people, and their number is going to increase. And all we do is treat the symptoms."

When opinion polls put the question "How religious are you?," Japanese rank among the most ungodly people in the world. It took a catastrophe for me to understand how misleading this self-assessment is. It is true that the organized religions, Buddhism and Shinto, have little influence on private or national life. But over the centuries both have been pressed into the service of the true faith of Japan: the cult of the ancestors.

I knew about the household altars, or *butsudan*, which are still seen in most homes and on which the memorial tablets of

dead ancestors—the *ihai*—are displayed. The *butsudan* are cabinets of lacquer and gilt, with openwork carvings of flowers and trees; the *ihai* are upright tablets of black lacquered wood, vertically inscribed in gold. Offerings of flowers, incense, food, fruit, and drinks are placed before them; at the summer Festival of the Dead, families light lanterns to welcome home the ancestral spirits. I had taken these picturesque practices to be matters of symbolism and custom, attended to in the same way that people in the West will participate in a Christian funeral without any literal belief in the words of the liturgy. But in Japan spiritual beliefs are regarded less as expressions of faith than as simple common sense, so lightly and casually worn that it is easy to miss them altogether. "The dead are not as dead there as they are in our own society," wrote the religious scholar Herman Ooms. "It has always made perfect sense in Japan as far back as history goes to treat the dead as more alive than we do . . . even to the extent that death becomes a variant, not a negation of life."

At the heart of ancestor worship is a contract. The food, drink, prayers, and rituals offered by their descendants gratify the dead, who in turn bestow good fortune on the living. Families vary in how seriously they take these ceremonies, but even for the unobservant, the dead play a continuing part in domestic life. For much of the time, their status is something like that of beloved, deaf, and slightly batty old folk who cannot expect to be at the center of the family, but who are made to feel included on important occasions. Young people who have passed important entrance examinations, gotten a job, or made a good marriage kneel before the *butsudan* to report their success. Victory or defeat in an important legal case, for example, is shared with the ancestors in the same way.

When grief is raw, the presence of the deceased is overwhelming. In households that had lost children in the tsunami, it be-

came routine, after half an hour of tea and chat, to be asked if I would like to "meet" the dead sons and daughters. I would be led to a shrine covered with framed photographs, with toys, favorite drinks and snacks, letters, drawings, and school exercise books. One mother commissioned carefully Photoshopped portraits of her children, showing them as they would have been had they lived—a boy who died in elementary school smiling proudly in high-school uniform, an eighteen-year-old girl as she should have looked in kimono at her coming-of-age ceremony. Another decked the altar with makeup and acrylic fingernails that her daughter would have worn if she had lived to become a teenager. Here, every morning, they began the day by talking to their dead children, weeping love and apology, as unselfconsciously as if they were speaking over a long-distance telephone line.

The tsunami did appalling violence to the religion of the ancestors.

Along with walls, roofs, and people, the water carried away household altars, memorial tablets, and family photographs. Cemetery vaults were ripped open by the wave, and the bones of the dead scattered. Temples were destroyed, along with memorial books, listing the names of ancestors over generations. "The memorial tablets—it's difficult to exaggerate their importance," Yozo Taniyama, a priest friend of Kaneta's, told me. "When there's a fire or an earthquake, the *ihai* are the first thing that many people will save, before money or documents. I think that people died in the tsunami because they went home for the *ihai*. It's life, the life of the ancestors. It's like saving your late father's life."

When people die violently or prematurely, in anger or anguish, they are at risk of becoming *gaki*: "hungry ghosts," who wander between worlds, propagating curses and mischief. There are rituals for placating unhappy spirits, but in the aftermath of the disaster, few families were in a position to perform these.

And then there were those ancestors who lost all their living descendants to the wave. Their well-being in the afterlife depended entirely on the reverence of living families, which was permanently and irrevocably cut off: their situation was as helpless as that of orphaned children.

Tsunamis anywhere destroy property and kill the living, but in Japan they inflict a third kind of injury, unique and invisible, on the dead. At a stroke, thousands of spirits had passed from life to death; countless others were cut loose from their moorings in the afterlife. How could they all be cared for? Who was to honor the compact between the living and the dead? In such circumstances, how could there fail to be a swarm of ghosts?

It was in the summer after the tsunami that Naomi Hiratsuka began to speak to her dead daughter, Koharu. At first, and unlike most people she knew, she had hesitated. Shamanism, and varieties of mediumship, were deeply established in Tohoku, and many of the bereaved were turning to those who practiced them. Naomi had her doubts about the existence of such gifts, but above all she detested the way in which some people, especially in the media, treated the subject, in an effort to squeeze spooky entertainment out of tragedy. She had been especially sickened by an article in a Japanese magazine about teenagers daring one another to make nighttime visits to the site of Okawa Elementary School, in the hope of encountering its ghosts.

But the search for Koharu and the other missing children was going so badly, bogged down both in the literal mud and in a morass of bureaucratic complication. Naomi was in close touch with the police unit, which was carrying out its own search, and got to know its commanders. One day they made a suggestion that surprised her at the time—that if she knew of any mediums

or psychics who had advice to offer, particularly about specific places to direct the search, she should pass it on.

A friend introduced her to a young man in his twenties who was known to have the ability to see and hear the dead. Recently, people said, he had heard a voice in a dense bamboo thicket by the Fuji lake—and when it was searched, bones were indeed found, and identified as the remains of a missing woman. Naomi arranged to meet the young psychic late one evening at the ruin of the school. It was the summer festival of Tanabata, the star festival, when people hang trees with handwritten poems and prayers, and with delicate paper decorations: streamers, purses, birds, dolls. They walked side by side in the humid darkness, between the shell of the school and the hill behind it. At a small shrine on the hill, Naomi tied decorations of her own around the bamboo and prayed for Koharu's return. It was a hot, windless night, but the colored paper danced and shivered strangely in the motionless air. "It is the children who are moving the decorations," the psychic said. "They are delighted with them."

They walked past a long line of rubble, roughly heaped up into great mounds. Hundreds of people had died in this small area. It was possible that bodies were still contained within the heaps. The psychic said, "I can hear a voice. I think it is the voice of a woman, not a child." And Naomi, straining, also heard it, although too faintly for the words to be distinguishable. "It was just an ordinary voice," she said. "It sounded as if she was having an ordinary conversation. But when I looked around, there was nobody there."

Naomi said, "I didn't used to believe in such things, and I'd never had an experience like that before. But having lived through the disaster, having been through what I had, perhaps it's quite natural that I would hear such a voice."

She spent a lot of time with the young man. They walked

together for hours through the wide environs of the school—around the Fuji lake, and as far in the other direction as the Nagatsuura lagoon. He gave Naomi a crystal on a length of cord, which she would hold suspended over a large-scale map in the hope of divining Koharu's whereabouts. She told the police about the voice she had heard at the rubble mounds, and they were thoroughly sifted. But no human remains were found.

During their long walks, the young psychic would describe to Naomi the invisible scene surrounding them. One might have expected a consoling picture of life after death, but the vision he described was appalling. Naomi compared it to a famous Japanese horror film, *Ring*, which itself drew on the hell imagery of medieval art. "He said that there were pale figures like the ghosts in that film, many, many of them crawling on the ground. Some of them were stuck in the water, covered in mud, and swallowing the dirty water in terrible suffering. Some of them were trapped and trying to get out. But he couldn't tell which of them were the spirits of people who had already been found, and which of them were those like my daughter, who were still missing."

Naomi began to seek out other means of reaching the dead. The introductions were easily made—many of the Okawa mothers were consulting one psychic or another. Having started out a skeptic, she found herself holding conversations with Koharu herself.

The medium, whose name was Sumi, ran a small coffee shop in the city. Sometimes Naomi and Shinichiro went to see her in person; sometimes Koharu's utterances were conveyed over the telephone, and even by e-mail and text message. But Naomi was quickly persuaded of their authenticity. Sumi conveyed so perfectly the tone and character of the Koharu that her family remembered—the chattiness, bossiness, and sweetness of a girl

about to become a teenager. Through Sumi, Koharu dictated a detailed list of presents that were to be given in her name to members of the family—a particular kind of drawing pad and pencils for her brother, a pink bag for her little sister. She instructed Naomi to serve the family with powdered green-tea sweets, which she had always loved. But apart from the convincing childishness, there was an unexpected maturity in much of what she said, which might have been that of the medium, but which seemed at times to be the authority acquired by those, even in their young years, who have passed through death.

Koharu asked in detail about the well-being of her family, especially her siblings, and showed great concern about her mother's career. "She seemed to think that Sae, the baby, would be okay," Naomi said. "But she wanted me to give a lot more attention to Toma, who was older. And she told me to finish my maternity leave and go back to work. All of this helped, it helped us so much to carry on with an ordinary life, even after death. It was so welcome."

What neither the medium nor the spirit ever seemed able to say was the thing Naomi most wanted to know: the resting place of Koharu, or her bodily remnant. "Sumi told us that finding the remains is not everything. She said, 'You might think that the kids want their parents to find them, that they are desperate to go back home. But they are already home. They are already in a very good place. And the more you bury yourselves in the search, the more desperate you will become.'"

Naomi's friend Miho visited another medium, and drew the deepest consolation from her conversations with her missing daughter, Hana. "It was just like talking to her," Miho said. "It was just as if Hana was standing there, at my side. She said that she was in heaven, and that she was very happy. The woman knew all about our daily life, how Hana talked, the kinds of expressions

she used. If she said that she was suffering, if she'd been crying for help, and saying, 'Mum, get me out of here!' I wouldn't have been able to bear it. But the words I heard always made me feel calmer."

Sometimes the messages from the dead contradicted one another. One of the first things Hana told her mother, Miho, was that she should not harbor any blame or resentment towards the teachers at the school. "The teachers are crying in heaven, and that is hard for us," she said through the medium. "They are suffering, and watching them makes us children feel sad." But another psychic, at another time, told Miho the opposite: that the children were bitter and angry towards the teachers for letting them die so needlessly, for failing to lead them to the obvious places of safety and survival.

WHAT IT'S ALL ABOUT

The young man who had given her the crystal, the psychic who described cinematic specters writhing in the mud, said to Naomi Hiratsuka, "Your child will come to you in a dream. She will show you images of the place where she will be found. They will be like slides in your mind." But when she found what she was looking for, it didn't happen like that at all.

Naomi's thinking about the search for the children changed over time. Her faith in the supernatural began to flag; instead, she invested it in her digger and its muddy yellow arm. The conversations with her daughter were consoling, but Sumi, who could relay eerily specific messages from Koharu, became evasive when asked about the location of her body. "So many of us were consulting psychics, and people with those powers," Naomi said. "And we were all hearing different stories. When you think about it, someone must have been making a lot of money."

Naomi took to visiting Koharu's old classroom. In the weeks that they had spent there, the men of the Self-Defense Forces had restored to the school an extraordinary, and even disturbing, degree of order. The windows and doors were broken, but the

rooms had been swept, almost scoured, and the sediment of sludge deposited by the wave had dwindled to a smear of muddy dust. Warped textbooks had been carefully stacked and shelved; sodden dressing up-clothes had been restored to their box—a red wig, a fairy's wings. On Koharu's locker, the four characters of her name were still visible; Naomi left sweets and soft drinks there, to lure her daughter back. And the cleaner the classroom got, the sadder she became.

A many-fingered peninsula groped out into the sea between Ogatsu and Oppa Bay, a territory of rocks, pines, and seagulls. The village of Naburi was at the end of the road, fifty houses in a tight triangle of land hard up against the hills. A concrete pier sheltered a little harbor; rocky, unpeopled islands were visible in the bay. A hundred and eighty people lived there, most of them over seventy years old. Japan had countless isolated ancient populations such as this, places of sharp, harsh beauty and little else, which offered nothing at all for the young, and little reason for anyone else to stay, except habit, or resignation, or an overpowering love of fishing and the sea.

The water had reached a height of thirty-five meters here: 115 feet, as high as an eleven-story building, almost four times as high as the tsunami predicted on the radio. But as soon as he had felt the earthquake, an old fisherman named Yuichiro Kamiyama had moored his boat and gone about the houses, chivvying the villagers up the steep hill. From there, they watched the water withdrawing from the harbor, and returning unstoppably to overwhelm first the seawall, then the road, and then the alleys dividing the wooden houses, until it lifted them up and spun them around on its frothing surface. The water rose and rose through the pines on the hillside towards the spot where the

dumbfounded villagers were watching. A few feet below where they crouched, it slowed and withdrew.

The sight reminded Kamiyama of the summer Festival of the Dead, when illuminated paper lanterns are set adrift on the tide to guide the spirits back across to the far world. "The houses receded all together, along with the sea," he said. "They were all in a row, like the festival lanterns, floating out over the seawall. And the electricity poles too, with the wires between them. Those wires are strong—they didn't break. They were all taken back intact into the sea. Perhaps I shouldn't say so, but it was beautiful."

There was nothing left of Naburi. "It looked as if time had gone backward," said Kamiyama. "It looked like a place in an ancient era, before humans came." But in the whole village only two people had died, both of them after returning down the hill to retrieve precious items forgotten in the evacuation. "With something like a tsunami, a decision has to be made very quickly," Kamiyama said. "What's needed is immediate action by someone with initiative. You don't have time to hold a meeting. So long as someone says, 'Go to the mountain!' without any doubt or hesitation, then people will go."

By August, five months later, the fishermen were buying new nets and boats and beginning to go out to sea again. Early one morning, they noticed a commotion among the gulls, thirty feet out in the harbor. The birds were crying and circling something, with dives and pecks. One of the boats went out to have a look, and then the police were called, and three officers arrived in a patrol car and went out with the fishermen to retrieve the object in the water. "It was the calmest day of the season," Kamiyama remembered. "The water was so still and clear. They brought her onto the quay here, with all the gulls overhead. We shouldn't think ill of the birds. We shouldn't imagine them pecking her flesh. We should thank the seagulls, who showed us where she

was, so she could see her mother and father again. Though she died, she was protected by the sea."

Naomi was in Sendai at her mother's house; later, she felt a sense of failure that she had not been at the school when the news came, on duty in the cabin of her digger. It arrived in the form of a text message from the police: another set of remains had been found in Naburi. They had been provisionally identified as those of a woman aged twenty to forty years old. But the body was described as being incomplete. Naomi telephoned the head of the local police, a man she had come to know well, and asked for more information. He told her that, although most of the clothes were absent, the unidentified woman had been wearing an outer set of thick thermal underpants. They were pink, with the motif of a white heart. With this, Naomi knew in an instant that Koharu had been found. The forecast for March 11 had been for cold weather, and possibly snow. And so Naomi had put this warm undergarment out for her daughter, a few hours before the tsunami.

She went to the police station with her husband, and examined the garment with her own eyes. "I knew immediately that it was hers," she said. "And it was reasonable that they thought it was an adult, because Koharu was tall for her age. But then they were asking me, over and over, 'Are you sure? Are you sure this is hers? Is there no chance that someone else could have been wearing similar clothes?' And I lost my confidence."

Naomi asked to see the remains with her own eyes. The policemen looked uncertainly at one another. During the months she had spent in the mud, Naomi had beheld numerous dead bodies, in various states. The last one, in April, had been the twelve-year-old daughter of a friend. "She was wearing jeans,

with a belt," Naomi remembered. "Of course, she was not in a normal condition. Some of her hair had come away. But she was recognizable. So I knew the kind of thing to expect. I had a sense of how human bodies change in time, and how it becomes difficult to identify them. But I asked to see Koharu in the hope of some kind of . . . spiritual understanding, some kind of recognition that in seeing part of her body, I was looking at my daughter.

"The police kept asking me, 'Are you sure? Will you be okay?' I said that I would." They led Naomi in, and removed the sheet from the object on the table. She looked at what lay beneath it, and held that in her gaze. "But it was just a lump of something," she said. "Without arms. Without legs. Without a head. And this was my daughter, my little girl. I don't regret seeing her. But the hope that I had, the hope that I would recognize her, was not fulfilled."

This was the moment Naomi had been praying for through all these months, the moment of certainty and reunion, when death was supposed to settle for a few moments on her palm, like a squawking, flapping bird suddenly made still. But it was not to be. There was no real doubt, to the Hiratsukas or to the policemen, that this was Koharu. But without the certainty of a positive identification, they would have to wait for the results of a DNA test, which would take months.

Naomi and Shinichiro walked out to their car, dazed. As she was climbing in, Naomi experienced a sudden pain in her back. Her legs locked. She found herself unable to move. "This had never happened to me before," she said. "So I thought it had to be Koharu trying to hold me there."

She said to her husband, "I want to call Sumi." The medium picked up the phone immediately. As soon as she had heard what had happened, she said, "It is Koharu." Naomi's paralysis in the parking lot, the words of the medium—these were enough for the police, who released the body the next day.

The Hiratsukas cremated Koharu on August 11, 2011. It was 153 days since the tsunami. A week later, Naomi was back at the school at the wheel of her digger, searching for Koto Naganuma, Hana Suzuki, Yuto Suzuki, and Yui Takeyama, the four school-mates of Koharu whose bodies had still not been found.

"We used to think that we were bringing up our children," said Sayomi Shito. "But then we discovered that it was we, the parents, who were being brought up by them. We thought that the children were the weakest among us, and that we protected them. But they were the keystone. All the other pieces depended on them. When they were taken away, we realized this for the first time. We thought that we were looking after them. But it was the children who supported us."

I pictured the image that Sayomi had called to mind: an arched stone bridge collapsing; masonry crashing into a river. She went on: "Nothing is capable of changing the situation. It's not about the passing of time. It's not about kind words. It's not about psychological support. It's not about money. None of that can change anything. There's a space that is empty and that will never be filled."

For survivors of the disaster, various kinds of assistance—practical and financial—were made available by the government, but there was little in the way of formal counseling or mental-health care. Many of the institutions to which people would instinctively have turned—village, family, workplace—were themselves broken by the wave. But out of the pieces, in the frag-mented towns and temporary houses, new forms of community emerged, cemented by loneliness, grief, and practical necessity. In Fukuji, a particularly strong and well-organized group of friends formed around Sayomi and Takahiro Shito.

One evening, at Sayomi's invitation, I went to meet them. All were parents of children who had died at Okawa Elementary School. These were the hecklers of the principal and his colleagues, the violators of protocol and convention—but in person they were warm, courteous, and patient people, unmarked by visible scars of ego or aggression. At their core were the Shitos and their neighbors, the Satos—Katsura and Toshiro, whose daughter Mizuho had been Chisato's playmate. Hitomi Konno and Kazutaka Sato, whose sons, Daisuke and Yuki, had been best friends in the fifth grade, were also members of the group. Then there was a third Sato family: Tomoko and Mitsuhiro, who had lost their only child, a ten-year-old boy named Kenta. The friends met once a week or more; they communicated every day by telephone, e-mail, and text. It was through grief that they had found one another, but grief in itself was not what united them. The power of their grief, which gave it form, channeling it like the banks of a river, was rage.

I spent many days with the bereaved of the tsunami, notebook in hand, digital recorder on the table. My questions, or the answers to them, often made them cry. I used to ask myself: What am I doing here? Why should these people talk to me? Sayomi and her friends cried too. But their rage justified it. The conversation propelled itself forward and back, round and round, and on and on. I scarcely had to ask questions at all.

Hitomi Konno said, "Every day, I think about my children and how each of them would be, if they were here. Today would be a birthday, for example. Or this month one of them would have been taking an entrance examination. In my heart, the children are still growing up. But I can't see them growing up."

Mitsuhiro Sato said, "When I think, 'If he was alive, he'd be doing this and that,' it makes me despair even more. Our child was our dream, and now that dream will never come true."

Takahiro Shito said, "The child is the center of your life, and as the child matures, the parents mature too. Birth, growing up, school, finding a job, getting married—in all of that, they're the center of us."

"These feelings can't be understood by others," said Sayomi. "People say, 'Well, it's been a while now.' But we cannot say that."

Mitsuhiro's wife, Tomoko, said: "The feeling of desperately wanting to see him, but never being able to see him, is getting stronger and stronger. If we knew that they were somewhere, if we could only see them for a time, a little time, that would be enough. This need to see him, to hold him and touch him, is getting bigger and bigger."

There was a silence, marked by sighs. Then Kazutaka Sato spoke. He was a pale man in his mid-forties, with short, tufty hair and weary features. He had been sitting around the table, nodding from time to time, silently listening. Then he said, "It's the matter of how they died."

He spoke calmly, almost matter-of-factly, without obvious anger or distress. "The more we look into it," Sato said, "the more we learn. And the better we understand that these were lives that could have been saved. The tsunami was a huge disaster. But there was only one school—just one school in the country—where the children lost their lives like this: Okawa Elementary School. That is a fact, and that fact can be explained only by a failure, the failure of the school to save the children's lives. They failed. And they have made no apology and given no proper explanation. The tsunami—the damage has been huge, and we are all suffering from that. But on top of that, we have to go through the torment of losing our children in this way. That is what it's about, that's what all of this is about. It's about how they died."

———

The truth about what happened in the tsunami was itself the opposite of a tsunami. There was no grand climax, no crashing wave or rumbling of the earth. The facts came out in trickles and drips, some falling naturally, some squeezed out by wringing hands. The stray words of a surviving child, revealing an unrecognized failure. A document exposing contradictions in the official account. The official account itself, wobbling and bending. Every few months there was a new "explanatory meeting," at which the bureaucrats of the Ishinomaki Education Board submitted themselves to the anger of the parents. Reluctantly and with trepidation, people came forward to tell their stories. A freelance journalist, Masaki Ikegami, did dogged work submitting freedom-of-information requests for city documents and scrutinizing them for inconsistencies.

The account furnished by the surviving teacher, Mr. Endo, had seemed at first clear and credible enough. The pupils had evacuated their classrooms, and been lined up and counted off in the playground. A few parents had arrived to pick up their children. An orderly evacuation had begun. As it was under way, the wave had come in. Endo gave an impression of teachers acting with urgency and dispatch, professional men and women conscientiously following procedure, who were helplessly—and blamelessly—overwhelmed by an unimaginable disaster. And this might have made sense within a time span of fifteen or twenty, or even thirty, minutes. But the earthquake had struck at 2:46 p.m. The hands of the school clock were frozen at 3:37 p.m., when the building's electricity was quenched by the rising water. This was the central question of the Okawa tragedy: What exactly happened between the first event and the second? What was going on at Okawa school for the last fifty-one minutes of its existence?

PART III

WHAT HAPPENED AT OKAWA

THE LAST HOUR OF THE OLD WORLD

Tetsuya Tadano was a stocky boy of eleven, with close-cropped hair and an air of mild, amused mischief. His family's house was across the rice fields in one of the hamlets at the back of the larger village of Kamaya; every morning he made the twenty-minute walk to school with his nine-year-old sister, Mina, along the embankment of the river. The eleventh of March was the fortieth birthday of their mother, Shiroe; a small celebration was planned at home that evening. But otherwise it was an unremarkable Friday afternoon.

At lunchtime on that day, the children rode on unicycles in the courtyard and foraged in its margins for four-leafed clovers. It was cold, and a piercing wind came off the river; Tetsuya and his friends stood in a row with their hands in their pockets, and turned their backs on it to keep the chill off their faces. Across the road, the families from the middle school were holding their graduation party. Sayomi Shito emerged from it and experienced that eerie moment of stillness and unease that she would later describe. At 2:45 p.m., the Okawa school bus was waiting in the parking lot, with its engine running; a few of the smaller pupils

had already climbed in. But most of the children were still in their classrooms, finishing up the last school business of the week.

A minute later, the sixth-grade class were singing "Happy Birthday" to one of their number, a girl named Manno. It was in the middle of this song that the earthquake struck. "It was shaking very slowly from side to side," said Soma Sato, one of the sixth-grade boys. "They weren't small, fast shakes—it felt gigantic. The teachers were running up and down, saying, 'Hold on to your desks.'"

In the library, a man named Shinichi Suzuki was waiting for his son, who was in the sickroom, having been taken ill earlier in the day. He watched as the water in the school fish tank slopped over its sides in waves. In Tetsuya's class, the fifth grade were getting ready to go home for the day. "When the earthquake first hit, we all took cover under our desks," he said. "As the shaking got stronger, everyone was saying things like, 'Whoa! This is big. You okay?' When it stopped, the teacher said right away, 'Follow me outside.' So we all put on our helmets and went out."

The school building was evacuated with exemplary speed. Scarcely five minutes after they had been crouching under their desks, the children were in the playground, lined up in their classes, in the hard plastic helmets that were stored in each child's locker. Two days earlier they had gone through the same drill. Compared to Wednesday's earthquake, though, this one was several times more frightening. Much later, the city authorities would compile a minute-by-minute log of the events of that afternoon, based on interviews with surviving witnesses. It conveys something of the atmosphere after a big earthquake, of excitement and resignation, lightheartedness and dread:

Child: Everyone sat down and the roll was taken. The lower-grade girls were crying, and Miss Shirota and Miss Konno were

stroking their heads and saying, "It's fine." One of the sixth-grade boys was saying, "I wonder if my game console at home is okay."

Child: The lower grades were messing around. There were kids running about.

Child: It must have been a kind of "earthquake sickness," because there were little kids throwing up.

Child: My friend said, "I wonder if there'll be a tsunami."

The alarm of the younger children was renewed by repeated, jolting aftershocks. There were secondary earthquakes at 2:51 p.m., 2:54 p.m., 2:55 p.m., and 2:58 p.m. As early as 2:49 p.m., while the vibrations of the mother quake were still jangling outward across northern and eastern Japan, the Meteorological Agency issued a warning: a six-meter- or twenty-foot-high tsunami was expected; everyone on the coast of northeast Japan should evacuate to higher ground.

Eleven adults were present in the playground, among them the six class teachers; the special-needs teacher, Ms. Suzuki; the school nurse, Ms. Konno; Ms. Kawabata, the school secretary; and Junji Endo, the head of teaching. In the absence of the principal, Teruyuki Kashiba, the senior teacher was Toshiya Ishizaka, his fifty-four-year-old deputy. It was Ishizaka who was listening to the battery-powered radio on which the tsunami warning was being broadcast, again and again. It was on him that the fate of those waiting in the playground depended.

———

Many people found it impossible to forgive Ishizaka, even in death. But those who knew him well remembered him with love. He grew up inland; the Chile tsunami, which struck when he was three, would have been just a story to him. He was a soft, sensitive man who formed deep friendships with his young pupils, which continued long after they had grown up. "He certainly wasn't a handsome kind of guy," I heard from one woman who had been taught by Ishizaka twenty-five years earlier in another, inland school. "A bit short, not fat, but certainly chubby. He was always smiling. His smile was what struck me. He didn't drink or smoke, which was unusual for a man back then."

She described the summer night when Ishizaka took his pupils out to look up at the sky and learn the names of the constellations, and the weekend when he had invited the entire class of thirty children to his mother's home. "He put us on the train, and then drove in his car alongside the track," she said. "He was keeping parallel with the train, and waving to us. We were so excited! He attached great importance to solidarity within the class, to getting everyone to work and act together. In all my days of school life, the two years with him were the most memorable and important."

Some of the Okawa parents conveyed a different impression. They agreed about his gentleness, his warmth and affability. All remarked on the depth and frequency of his bows, and the politeness of his language. But there seemed in this to be an unvoiced suggestion that, even in a society that esteems formal courtesy, the deputy head's behavior went beyond the demands of good manners, and crossed the line between respect and obsequiousness.

There were more aftershocks at 3:03 p.m., at 3:06 p.m., and at 3:12 p.m. At 3:14 p.m., the Meteorological Agency updated its warning: the tsunami was expected to come in at a height of ten meters, or thirty-three feet.

The teachers in the playground formed a huddle beneath the cherry trees and engaged in a discussion in low voices.

Like many Japanese institutions, the operations of Okawa Elementary School were governed by a manual: among the documents that Ms. Kawabata, the school secretary, brought out from her office into the playground, there would certainly have been a copy of this. The Education Plan, as it was called, was reviewed annually and covered everything from moral and ethical principles to the protocol for sports days, parents' meetings, and graduation ceremonies. One section was devoted to emergencies, including fire, flood, and epidemic. It included a form that was to be filled out and returned by each family, listing the names, telephone numbers, and addresses of parents, guardians, and anyone authorized to pick up a child from the school. This information was supposed to be updated every year. Kashiba, the principal, had not done this, which suggests, at the least, mild laxity in disaster preparedness.

The Education Plan was based on a template adjusted according to the circumstances of each school. Even in Japan, none but a handful of schools needed to make provisions for volcanic eruptions, for example; those located inland could confidently strike out the section on tsunamis. Ishizaka, who had revised the manual under Kashiba's supervision, had chosen to retain it, but he had left unchanged the generic wording of the template:

Primary evacuation place: school grounds.
Secondary evacuation place, in case of tsunami: vacant land
near school, or park, etc.

The vagueness of this language was unhelpful. The reference to "park, etc." made little sense out here in the countryside,

where there were fields and hills, but no parks as such. As for "vacant land," there was an abundance of that—the question was: Where?

The school bus was waiting in the parking lot. It had a capacity of forty-five; at a squeeze, the whole school and its staff could have relocated to the heights of the Ogatsu Pass in two journeys. On the eastern edge of the village were two more roads that led up into the hills, one of them to a hilltop Shinto shrine in a forest clearing. But there was a still closer and more obvious place of safety.

Three features bounded the village of Kamaya in a rough triangle: the river to the northwest, the paddy fields to the east, and, to the south, an unnamed, forested hill, 725 feet at its highest point. In places, the slope presented a strenuous, even perilous climb up steep and thicketed sides. But at one point there was a gentle and accessible path, familiar to all at the school. Until a few years ago, the children had gone up there as part of their science lessons, to cultivate a patch of shiitake mushrooms. This was a climb that the smallest among the children could have easily managed. Within five minutes—the time it had taken them to evacuate their classrooms—the entire school could have ascended hundreds of feet above sea level, beyond the reach of any conceivable tsunami.

But the Education Plan, so minutely prescriptive about other elements in the life of the school, made no clear adjudication about a place of evacuation. In the villages by the sea, including Aizawa, where Junji Endo used to teach, teachers and children were ascending without hesitation up steep paths and cliff steps. In Okawa, Deputy Principal Ishizaka stood in the playground and found only those words to puzzle over: *vacant land near school, or park, etc.*

The school appeared to have suffered no important damage, but while the aftershocks continued, it was judged to be imprudent to go back inside. It was Junji Endo, as the second-ranking teacher present, who darted in and out of the school buildings on this or that errand, while the class teachers kept an eye on their pupils and discussed what they might do. The roll call revealed that a third-grade girl was missing; Endo went back in, and found her cowering in the toilet stalls. Many of the children were cold; it was Endo who retrieved their coats and gloves, and who took them to a discreet corner of the playground when they needed to relieve themselves. Occupied thus, he spent little time in active conversation with the other teachers. But it was clear what course of action Endo favored, and what would have happened if he had been in charge.

"The deputy head took the helm, and the class teachers were attached to their classes," he wrote later. "I was running around, and I had no idea what they were talking about." He recalled one brief conversation with Ishizaka, after checking for stragglers inside the school. "I asked, 'What should we do? Should we run to the hills?' I was told that it was impossible with the shaking."

But Amane Ukitsu, one of the survivors from the sixth grade, recalled a much more dramatic intervention. Endo, she said, had reemerged from the school, calling out loudly, "To the hill! The hill! Run to the hill!"

His alarm was picked up by Hitomi's son, Daisuke, and his friend, Yuki Sato, who made their own appeals to their sixth-grade teacher, Takashi Sasaki.

We should climb the hill, sir.

If we stay here, the ground might split open and swallow us up. We'll die if we stay here!

The boys began to run in the direction of the shiitake-mushroom patch, Amane remembered. But Endo was overruled, the boys were ordered to come back and shut up, and they returned obediently to their class.

Two distinct groups of people were beginning to gather at the school. The first were parents and grandparents, arriving by car and on foot to pick up children. The second were local people from the village—to complicate matters further, Okawa Elementary was itself designated an official place of evacuation for Kamaya. And a drastic difference of opinion, verging at times on open conflict, was manifesting itself in the attitudes of the two groups.

The parents, by and large, wanted to get their children out and away as soon as possible. "I kept looking at the cars arriving and wondering, 'Is Mum going to come?'" said Fuka, the twin sister of Soma Sato. "I was so worried. When she appeared I burst into tears. Mum couldn't stop crying, either." At least one teacher, Takashi Sasaki, actively discouraged families from leaving the school. "Teacher said, 'You'll be safe here,'" Soma remembered. "Mum said, 'Our house is higher up. We'll be safer there.'"

From the education board's log:

Child: My mum came to pick me up, and we told Takashi that I was going home. We were told, "It's dangerous to go home now, so better stay in the school."

Parent: I told Takashi, "The radio says that there's a ten-meter tsunami coming." I said, "Run up the hill!" and pointed to the hill. I was told, "Calm down, ma'am."

The local people also pooh-poohed the danger. The village head of Kamaya, Toshio Takahashi, appears to have been particularly outspoken on the subject. Everyone central to the discussion is dead—but from the fragmentary glimpses provided by the survivors, it is clear that there was an active effort to lobby the deputy principal to keep the children in the school playground:

> Child: There were teachers who said, "Let's escape to the mountain," but then there were teachers and local people who said, "It's safer at the school."

> Parent: The deputy head was consulting with local people, four or five of them, in their seventies or older. "Will the mountain at the back collapse? I want the children to climb it. Is it impossible?"
> Child: The deputy head said it was better to run to the mountain, but someone from Kamaya said, "We're fine just here." They seemed to be arguing.

> Child: The deputy head and the headman of Kamaya were quarreling. [The deputy head said] "Let them climb the mountain." The headman said, "It won't come this far, so let's go to the traffic island."

"The teachers were panicking," said one parent. Another described how the hair and clothes of Ishizaka were plastered to his head and body by sweat, despite the coldness of the day. But a third said that although the teachers "were not calm, they weren't panicking, I think." This atmosphere of strain and irresolution confused people who stepped into it. Tetsuya Tadano and his

sister Mina were relieved to see their mother, Shiroe. "It seemed that she actually wanted to escape with us to higher ground," said Tetsuya. "But all the parents and guardians were just standing around. She said, 'Wait a minute, I need to pick something up from home.' So I just gave her my bags and stayed where I was."

It was a weekday afternoon, and the working people of Kamaya were away at their shops, factories, and offices. Most of the parents who came to the school were full-time mothers and housewives; most of the villagers offering their opinions were retired, elderly, and male. It was another enactment of the ancient dialogue, its lines written centuries ago, between the entreating voices of women and the oblivious, overbearing dismissiveness of old men.

Toshinobu Oikawa was a white-shirted, gray-suited man in his late fifties who worked in the local branch of the Ishinomaki town government. He was in his office, across the bridge from the school on the north bank of the river, when the earthquake struck. Within five minutes, the first warning, of a twenty-foot tsunami, was received from the Meteorological Agency. The town office had a backup generator, but the failure of electricity in the rest of the district had disabled many of the loudspeakers through which the municipality broadcast important announcements. Within fifteen minutes, Oikawa and five of his colleagues were climbing into three cars mounted with rooftop speakers of their own, and setting out to deliver the warning in person.

The roads they drove along were fissured by cracks. In places, earth and stones had slid onto them from the hillsides above. They crossed the Kitakami Great Bridge and drove through

Kamaya towards the communities most at risk from a tsunami, the villages closest to the sea around the Nagatsuura lagoon. They were driving through the outer margins of Kamaya when Oikawa became aware of something extraordinary taking place two miles ahead of them, at the point where the sea met the land.

The place was Matsubara, the spit of fields and sand where a ribbon of pine forest grew alongside the beach. There were twenty thousand of the trees. They were a century old. Many of them were more than sixty feet high. And now, as Oikawa watched, the sea was overwhelming them, swallowing up their pointed green peaks and tearing up the forest in a frothing surge. "I could see the white of the wave, foaming over the top of the trees," he said. "It was coming down over them like a waterfall. I could see it with my own eyes. And there were cars coming in the other direction, and the drivers were shouting at us, 'The tsunami is coming. Get out! Get out!' So immediately we made a U-turn and went back the way we'd come."

Within seconds, they were driving through Kamaya again. More aftershocks were taking place. But it was as if the entire village had fallen under a spell.

Oikawa's colleague, Sato, was shouting through the car's loudspeaker, "A super-tsunami has reached Matsubara. Evacuate! Evacuate to higher ground!" Municipal announcements in Japan are typically delivered in tones of glazed calm; those who survived remembered the pleading, almost crazed quality of this one. "There were seven or eight people standing around the street, chatting," Oikawa remembered. "They paid us no attention. I saw the patrol car parked in front of the village police box. But the policeman wasn't passing on the warning, and he wasn't trying to escape, either. We passed the school. We were driving fast, we didn't stop, and we couldn't clearly see the playground.

But they must have heard our message too. The school bus was just standing there."

The old men of Kamaya didn't think of themselves as living by the sea.

A tsunami was a coastal hazard, an affliction of beaches, harbors, and fishing communities, places hard up against the waves. But Kamaya was a farming village, a world apart. Between Okawa Elementary School and the beach at Matsubara was a distance in a straight line of two and a quarter miles. Screened by the houses and shops of Kamaya, the sea was inaudible and invisible. One local woman described to me the surprise, among many other shocks, of looking out from what had formerly been Kamaya after its human structures had been wiped away. "It was only after the houses had gone that I noticed it," she said. "I had always thought of us as living inland, alongside a river. But now, with the houses gone, all of a sudden there was the ocean."

The Kitakami was the gate through which the tsunami gained admittance to the land. And the river channeled and concentrated it, binding it tighter and stronger, and loosed it over the fragile embankment.

In Kamaya, people were doing what they always did after an earthquake: tidying up. Among them was a farmer in his sixties named Waichi Nagano, who lived in a big house out in the fields. "I heard all the warnings," he said. "There was the loudspeaker car from the town hall going up and down, saying, 'Super-tsunami imminent: evacuate, evacuate!' There were a lot of sirens too. Everyone in the village must have heard them. But we didn't take it seriously."

Nagano was the fifth generation to have inhabited and

farmed this land. Families such as his possessed an ancestral consciousness, composed of personal memory, historical anecdote, and local lore: nowhere in that storehouse of hereditary experience was there any recollection of tsunamis. "Until then, no tsunami had ever damaged Kamaya," Nagano said. "We knew people in Ogatsu once had a tsunami, and we knew about the Chile earthquake. But they didn't have the slightest effect on this village. So people thought it could never reach here. People felt safe."

The experience of the generations, the reassurance of the ancestors—these beat louder in the blood than the voices from the loudspeaker cars, screeching, "Evacuate! Evacuate!"

Nagano was in his shed, gathering up his scattered farming tools, when his wife called to him from the front of the house. There he saw the tsunami coming over the embankment six hundred yards away and smashing into the buildings in front of it. He bolted inside and shouted to his daughter and granddaughter. The four of them jumped into two cars and began to maneuver onto the road. Nagano's wife suddenly opened the door, saying, "My bag—I forgot my handbag." "No! No!" Nagano shouted. "Please get back in the car." It was two hundred yards to the point where the road began to rise in its ascent up the hill. Seconds after they reached it, the waters rushed in behind them.

Nagano looked back from the hill to see his home in the rice fields, and Kamaya behind it, being overwhelmed by the sea. Within a few seconds, the house had broken up and disappeared. Little more than a minute had passed between the moment when he first glimpsed the tsunami and now, as he stared down, panting, over the destruction of his home, his fields, his village, the inheritance of five generations. "It was a scene of hell," Nagano said. "It was just hell. It was as if we were in a dream. We could not believe what was happening."

In the playground, the children were becoming restless. A mood of bored resignation had established itself. The tidy lines in which each class had been standing dissolved into seated circles on the ground. Local people from the village sat on mats and cushions, which they had brought from their homes. It was cold. People shared blankets and hand-warmers, and the teachers extracted from a storeroom two open-topped metal drums in which fires could be lit. There was no sense of anything much happening, or that anything was likely to happen very soon.

Children continued to leave with their parents, and said their goodbyes to friends and teachers. After-school activities were canceled; plans by her friends in the sixth grade to continue celebrations of Manno's birthday were deferred. "Manno-*chan* was right next to me," said one girl. "I had promised her a birthday present after basketball practice. I said, 'I won't be able to give it to you after all. I'm sorry.' She said, 'That's okay.'"

Not everyone in Kamaya was indifferent to the warnings. The chronological log produced by the education board refers to several local people who repeatedly urged an evacuation. In the official account, they are identified only by capital letters. It is not clear what became of them:

Parent: F (local person) ran over yelling, "Run! There's a tsunami coming." Someone, I don't know who, said, "What? That's a bit scary, isn't it?"

Parent: I was told by D, "The tsunami will come at 3:30," and he showed me his mobile phone and said, "We only have twenty minutes left."

Parent: A man next to the bicycle shed pointed to the mountain and said loudly, "There's a tsunami coming, so climb to high ground!" I don't know if the school staff heard him.

At 3:25 p.m., Oikawa and the three loudspeaker vans drove past, blaring their desperate warning. In the school playground, the teachers were preparing to burn wood in the oil drums to keep the children warm.

At 3:30 p.m., an elderly man named Kazuo Takahashi fled his home next to the river. He too had ignored the warnings until he became abruptly aware of the sea streaming over the embankment beside his house. It seemed to be coming from below the earth, as well as across it: metal manhole covers in the road were being lifted upwards by rising water; mud was oozing up between the cracks that the earthquake had opened in the road. Takahashi directed his car towards the obvious closest place of evacuation, the hill behind the school. On the main street of Kamaya he saw friends and acquaintances standing and chatting. He rolled down his window and called to them, "There's a tsunami coming. Get out!" He passed his cousin and his wife and delivered the same warning. They waved, smiled, and ignored him.

Takahashi parked his car next to the village community center, adjacent to the school. The other Mr. Takahashi, the village head who was so vigorously opposed to evacuation, was helpfully directing the cars. As he climbed out and made for the hill, Kazuo Takahashi became aware of a large number of children issuing forth from the school in a hurry.

Among them was Tetsuya Tadano. He had remained in the playground with his class; after disappearing on her vague errand, his mother, Shiroe, had not returned. Mr. Ishizaka, the deputy head, had been absent from the playground. He reappeared

suddenly, with an unexpected instruction. "A tsunami seems to be coming," he called. "Quickly. We're going to the traffic island. Get into line, and don't run." Obediently, the children stood up and filed out of the playground. They left in their classes, the oldest children first. But as some walked, some trotted, and others ran, the classes quickly began to merge and overlap.

Tetsuya and his friend Daisuke Konno were at the front of the group. The traffic island was less than four hundred yards away, just outside the village at the point where the road met the Kitakami Great Bridge. But instead of leaving through the front entrance of the school, the children were led out of the side, along the foot of the hill and then down a narrow alley that connected with the village street. It was as he approached this junction that Tetsuya saw a black mass of water rushing along the main road ahead of him.

Barely a minute had passed since he had left the playground. He was conscious of a roaring sound, and a sheet of white spray above the black. It was not emerging from straight ahead, from the direction of the sea. It was streaming in from the left, from the river, the direction in which the children had been ordered to run.

Some of those at the front of the line froze in the face of the wave. Others, including Tetsuya and Daisuke, turned at once and ran back the way they had come. The rest of the children were continuing to hurry towards the main road; the little ones towards the back were visibly puzzled by the sight of the older children pelting hectically in the opposite direction.

At the top of the alley, the two boys found themselves at the foot of the hill. This was the steepest and most thickly forested section of the slope, difficult to climb at the best of times. At some point, Tetsuya became aware that Daisuke had fallen, and he tried, and failed, to pull his friend up. Then Tetsuya was scrambling up the hill. As he did so, he looked back over his shoulder

and saw the darkness of the tsunami rising behind him. Soon it was at his feet, his calves, his buttocks, his back. "It felt like the huge force of gravity when it hit me," he said. "It was as if someone with great strength was pushing. I couldn't breathe, I was struggling for breath." He became aware of a rock and a tree, and found himself trapped between them, with the water rising about him. Then darkness overcame him.

INSIDE THE TSUNAMI

Everyone who experienced the tsunami saw, heard, and smelled something subtly different. Much depended upon where you were, and the obstacles that the water had to overcome to reach you. Some described a waterfall, cascading over seawall and embankment. For others, it was a fast-rising flood between houses, deceptively slight at first, tugging trippingly at the feet and ankles, but quickly sucking and battering at legs and chests and shoulders. In color, it was described as brown, gray, black, white. The one thing it did not resemble in the least was a conventional ocean wave, the wave from the famous woodblock print by Hokusai: blue-green and cresting elegantly in tentacles of foam. The tsunami was a thing of a different order, darker, stranger, massively more powerful and violent, without kindness or cruelty, beauty or ugliness, wholly alien. It was the sea coming onto land, the ocean itself picking up its feet and charging at you with a roar in its throat.

It stank of brine, mud, and seaweed. Most disturbing of all were the sounds it generated as it collided with, and digested, the stuff of the human world: the crunch and squeal of wood and concrete,

metal and tile. In places, a mysterious dust billowed above it, like the cloud of pulverized matter that floats above a demolished building. It was as if neighborhoods, villages, whole towns were being placed inside the jaws of a giant compressor and crushed.

From the hillside where they had narrowly escaped to safety, Waichi Nagano and his wife, Hideko, could see the whole scene spread out below them, as the water swept in pulsing surges over the embankment and across the village and the fields. "It was a huge black mountain of water that came on all at once and destroyed the houses," he said. "It was like a solid thing. And there was this strange sound, difficult to describe. It wasn't like the sound of the sea. It was more like the roaring of the earth, mixed with a kind of crumpling, groaning noise, which was the houses breaking up."

There was another, fainter noise. "It was the voices of children," said Hideko. "They were crying out—'Help! Help!'" On the hill above, where he had half climbed, half floated to safety, Kazuo Takahashi heard them too. "I heard children," he said. "But the water was swirling around, there was the crunching sound of the wave and the rubble, and their voices became weaker and weaker."

How does it feel to die in a tsunami? What are the thoughts and sensations of someone in those final moments? Everyone who contemplated the disaster asked themselves these questions; the mind fluttered about them like an insect around a flame. One day I mentioned it, hesitatingly, to a local man. "Do you really want to know the answer to that question?" he asked. "Because I have a friend who can tell you."

He arranged the meeting for the following evening. His friend's name was Teruo Konno and, like Toshinobu Oikawa, he

worked in the branch office of the Ishinomaki city hall. Oikawa was the model of the local bureaucrat: quiet, patient, dogged. But Konno was an imaginative and restless character. As a boy, he had dreamed of leaving Tohoku and traveling the world. His parents, seeking to quell this impulse, had discouraged him from going to university, and Konno had spent his life in the place where he grew up, and his career in local government. In March 2011, he had been deputy head of the local development section, responsible, among other things, for "disaster countermeasures."

Few people were more knowledgeable about the menace of earthquakes and their particular threat to the Kitakami area. "Our assumption was that there would be another big quake," Konno said. "There hadn't been a tsunami since the 1896 and 1933 quakes, so we expected that too." There was no doubt that the small village where the town office was located, situated at the mouth of the river, two and a half miles downstream of Kamaya, would be in its path. Konno and his colleagues bent their efforts to ensuring that they would ride it out.

The two-story branch office had been built on a rise fifteen feet above sea level, and its ground floor had been elevated a further ten feet above that. Essential utilities, such as electricity and communications, had been installed on the uppermost floor. On the wall was a digital readout that recorded the intensity of tremors as they occurred.* As recently as the previous August, the city government had conducted a drill in which police, fire bri-

* "Intensity" refers to the effect an earthquake has on the ground, and varies from place to place, depending on their distance from the epicenter (by contrast with magnitude, which is a single number, measuring the energy released by a tremor). The Japan Meteorological Agency measures intensity on a scale of one to seven. Intensity 1 describes hardly noticeable shaking. At intensity 7, people and objects are hurled around, landslides occur, and many buildings are damaged and destroyed.

gade, and local officials acted out their roles in case of an earthquake and tsunami.

When the moment finally arrived, Konno experienced it with the calm detachment of a disaster professional.

"It came in three stages," he told me. "When the shaking first began it was strong but slow. I looked at the monitor. It showed an intensity of upper five, and I knew that this was it." Even as the rocking continued, he was calling to his staff to make a public announcement: a tsunami warning, he knew, would soon be issued. "But the shaking went on," Konno said. "It got stronger and stronger. The PC screens and piles of documents were all falling off the desks. And then in the third stage, it became worse still."

Konno gripped his desk amid a tumult of competing sounds. Pieces of office furniture were rattling and colliding as they shunted across the room. Filing cabinets were disgorging their files. Now he looked up again at the wall-mounted readout of seismic intensity: it displayed only an error message. Then, gradually, like the slowing of a beating heart, the shaking and the panic eased, and the employees of the Ishinomaki Kitakami General Branch Office sprang to their appointed tasks.

The emergency generator rumbled into life, the toppled television was lifted off the floor and reconnected, and the tsunami warning was relayed through the municipal loudspeakers. Oikawa and his men were dispatched to those communities where the loudspeakers had failed. Just as had been planned, representatives of the police and the fire brigade relocated to the town branch office. "Everything functioned very well," Konno said. "No one was hurt, everyone was calm, and there was only slight damage to the building. We had drilled for this. Everyone knew who should do what, and what to do next."

Soon there were fifty-seven people in the branch office. Thirty-one of them were locals who had evacuated from more

vulnerable premises to the safety of the strong, modern building. They included six children from a nearby school, the counterpart of Okawa Elementary School on the north side of the river, as well as eight old people from the local day-care center. Three of them were in wheelchairs; four more were carried in on stretchers. Volunteers sprang forward to help them safely and comfortably up to the sanctuary of the second floor.

At 3:14 p.m., the estimated height of the imminent tsunami was revised from twenty feet to thirty-three feet. But at some point the backup electricity generator failed, and Konno and his colleagues never received this information. It would have made no difference anyway.

The building, mounted on its elevation, faced inland, with its back to the river and its front entrance facing the hills over the small village below. From his window, the only water Konno could see was a sluggish brown stream, little more than a drain, which trickled into the Kitakami. "That was the first thing I noticed," he said. "The water in the creek had become white. It was churning and frothing, and it was flowing the wrong way. Then it was overflowing, and there was more water coming in from the river behind, and it was surrounding the houses. I saw the post-office building, lifting up and turning over in the water. Some of the houses were being crushed, but some of them were lifting up and floating." The destruction was accompanied by that mysterious noise. "I never heard anything like it," Konno said. "It was partly the rushing of the water, but also the sound of timber, twisting and tearing." In the space of five minutes, the entire community of eighty houses had been physically uprooted and thrust, bobbing, against the barrier of the hills.

Nothing in Konno's simulations and hazard maps had prepared him for this. "People in the office were looking down on it, amazed," he said. "It was unbelievable. It was as if it was happening somewhere else. But at the time I was thinking, 'Well, this is it—a twenty-foot tsunami.' And I assumed that would be the end of it."

Through the window, he observed that the parking lot below was being washed over by black water. At the same moment, a profound shudder went through the whole building. Even without being able to see it, Konno understood what had happened: the large plate-glass windows on the ground floor had broken under the pressure of the wave, which was washing through the lower part of the building.

"It was like the bursting of a dam," he said. "Desks, chairs, documents were washing out of the other side. It felt like another earthquake. It was shaking the whole building again. The lights and the panels in the ceiling were falling down."

The town officials, the police, the firemen, the schoolchildren, and the old people and their carers looked on helplessly as the water surged. Konno, remembering the disaster drills, gave the order that everyone should move into a corner room, structurally the strongest part of the building. As he closed the door on them, there was another mighty impact. One of his subordinates ran to report to Konno what happened: the roof of the large public hall next door had lifted off and collided with the branch office.

Konno returned to his desk. The speed of events was difficult to grasp. Until moments ago, he had been leading a trained team in the execution of a well-rehearsed and rational plan. Now he, and all those around him, were facing death. The forces acting on the building were pushing it to the extremes of its resistance.

The ground floor was completely underwater; now the wave was rising through the upper floor. Konno climbed onto his desk, as black water sucked and slapped around it with violent force. Then there was another, immense percussion, and suddenly he was tumbling through open air.

The outside world was cold; Konno had the sensation of falling through it very slowly. He was able to take in the sight of the building from which he had just been propelled, with water surging out of all its windows. He was aware of another colleague, a man named Abe, falling through space alongside him: the image of Abe's surprised, bespectacled face lodged in his mind. Then Konno was in the water.

It was churning and raging with violent internal motion. Konno described it as "like being in a washing machine"; he was paralyzed by the water's grip. He was aware of having been forced down, and of touching asphalt—the surface of the parking lot, which was now the bottom of the sea. And he understood that his life was coming to its end. "It's true what people say. You see the faces of your family, of your friends. It's true—I remember it. All those faces. The last words in my mind were, 'I'm done for— I'm sorry.' It's a feeling different from fear. Just a frank feeling of sorrow, and regret."

As he was viewing the gallery of his past, Konno found himself able to move his neck, and then his arms and legs, and, kicking and thrashing, he propelled himself upwards and broke the surface.

He cast around for something to hold on to. A tree branch came into his grip, but it was too small. He exchanged it for a thicker spar of timber. On the surface, he could make out Abe, minus his glasses, gripping on to a sturdy log and being carried north, away from the river and towards the hills. But Konno was

spinning in the opposite direction, towards what had been the river and was now the sea.

Having faced death without fear, now he became afraid. "It was like being sucked into a whirlpool," he said. "I went under again, and again I thought this must be the end. And then, somehow, I was released from it, and I was in the middle of the river in a slow and quiet stream."

He caught hold of a wide wooden panel, the section of a house's outer wall, a stable support compared to the rotating tree branches. Gripping this, he drifted steadily towards the bank again and the hills that rose out of the flood. He could tell, more or less, where the submerged embankment and road must be; he imagined lowering his feet in the shallower reaches and wading to safety. But just as hope was returning, the tsunami began to withdraw, and the stampeding waters reversed direction.

Konno found himself being carried back out into the stream and towards the river's mouth. Familiar landmarks passed at racing speed. He saw the outline of his office building—it had not collapsed after all. Clinging to his raft, Konno was rushed downstream by the withdrawing tide, through the river's gaping mouth, and out towards the horizon of the Pacific Ocean.

He lost all sense of time passing. He could see or hear no other living creature. It was as if the whole world had succumbed to the flood and he was its only survivor. His Ark was that section of wooden wall, six feet by three, which he half gripped, half sprawled over. It saved his life—a smaller, less stable support would quickly have exhausted his energy and cast him off. Although he had crossed the threshold from river to sea, he remained within the broad sweep of Oppa Bay, and he never lost

sight of the land. After the first great pulse of the tsunami had pulled him back, the next one surged in and bore him back up the river again.

He was swept beyond the starting point of his journey towards the spot where a small park had formerly been, below a high section of embankment. The water was pouring over it in a black waterfall; Konno floated at the top, teetering on its brink. He was afraid that in the churn of the waterfall he would lose consciousness, and momentarily he did. When he came to, he was suspended on a crust of jammed and overlapping rubble. In it was the red-tiled roof of a house, sturdy and intact around its wooden frame. He pulled himself up onto it, and for the first time since falling from his office he was out of the water.

Then began what he described as the most frightening part of his ordeal, as he suddenly became aware of the profound cold.

"A wind began to blow," he said. "A violent snowy wind. It was so cold. I had only a wet shirt, no jacket, no shoes. I started shivering. I could see the hills. They were close, and I am a good swimmer. But I was so cold and I knew that I would not make it. My senses were failing me again. I started counting. I wanted to know how long it would take before the tsunami reversed and took me out to sea again. I got to one hundred and sixty—I remember that number. And then the roof I was lying on began to move."

As his raft spun on the water, Konno began to lose himself again. Then into his failing vision came a place that he knew well. It was the home of an elderly lady named Mitsuko Suzuki, an old friend and formerly a teacher at the local nursery school. Her house was built a little way up the slope in a protective fold of the hill. Its ground floor was flooded, but the upper story was clear of the water. From it, he heard a voice call out, "Hang on there!"

It was Mrs. Suzuki. She had seen the roof, and the prone figure clinging to it, without recognizing who it was. And now, as if guided by her voice, the floating roof was edging towards her house. It came to a stop, wedged up tight against her front door.

The face of the old lady looked down on him. "Young Teruo!" she said. "What are you doing here? Climb up. Climb up!"

"I can't, Mrs. Suzuki," Konno answered. "I have no strength."

"What are you talking about? No strength? Just come up."

Now the wave was renewing itself and pulling the roof away from the house again. It was Konno's last chance. He forced himself up and found himself in a spaghetti of fallen electrical cables. "I was tangled up in them," he said. "I held on to them. And then I was swimming into her house through the front door. It was dark. Mrs. Suzuki was upstairs. She was calling my name and shining a torch. I don't know how I managed. I lost my memory of all that. But I got upstairs."

It was after five o'clock. Konno had spent more than two and a half hours in the water. He had saved himself from drowning, but now he was dying of hypothermia. He began to display the mania associated with the condition. Mrs. Suzuki described to him later how, even at the extremity of exhaustion, he had acted like a madman, pulling open her drawers and cupboards, throwing their contents on the floor and scrabbling to find dry clothes. The old teacher soothed him, undressed him, laid him in her own bed, and rubbed warmth back into him. Konno remembered nothing of this. He was conscious only of something he called "the golden hand." "It was Mrs. Suzuki's hand," he said. "But it was also the hand of a Buddha. It was curved, soft, warm. I don't think I ever saw her physically, during that time. I couldn't

open my eyes. But I saw the soft, round Buddha with golden hands."

He woke abruptly the next morning, electrified by anxiety. From Mrs. Suzuki's window, he could see that the water had retreated; ignoring her anxious pleas, he made his way towards the town office. He wanted to find the others who had been sheltering there, the people whom he had herded into the secure room. It was no more than a few hundred yards from the old lady's house. Picking through snow and rubble in a pair of slippers, it took him an hour. He scaled a rise from which the office was visible, and immediately understood that the worst had happened.

The building itself was a gaping shell. The area all around it was littered with bodies, half submerged in muddy pools, draped over railings. Most terrifying of all was the complete silence. "It was a world without sound, without any sound at all," said Konno. "I was trembling with terror."

A single other survivor from the town office had washed up to the hill and been helped to safety. Everyone else had died— the policemen, the firemen, the children, and the old people on walking sticks and in wheelchairs. Abe, whom Konno had seen bobbing towards the hills, had reached them, alive. But there he had lost his strength and died of exposure during the night.

What was it that spared Konno when so many others died? Was it physical strength or mental determination—or just the lucky timing of a last deep breath of air before he plunged into the water? His body was black with bruises where objects in the water had collided with him, but his face was unmarked, and his worst injuries were three broken fingers. He returned immediately to work, organizing refugees, identifying bodies, consoling the families of the bereaved.

They were dreadful, crushing tasks, even for one who had not gone through such an experience. But Konno found that it had

left him with an indifference to mental hardship, and an absence of trepidation of any kind. He had no fear, of life or of death. He was like a man who had suffered a dangerous disease, to survive with complete immunity to future infection. The prospect of his own extinction—now, soon, or far in the future—was a matter to him of no concern at all.

THE RIVER OF THREE CROSSINGS

Tetsuya Tadano came to on the hill, blinded by mud and with the roar of the tsunami in his ears. His limbs were immobilized by spars of debris and by something else, something wriggling and alive, which was shifting its weight on top of him. It was Kohei Takahashi, Tetsuya's friend and fifth-grade classmate. Kohei's life had been saved by a household refrigerator. It had floated past with its door open as he thrashed in the water, and he had squirmed into it, ridden it like a boat, and been dumped by it on his schoolmate's back. "Help! I'm underneath you," Tetsuya cried. Kohei tugged him free. Standing on the steep slope, the two boys beheld the scene below.

Tetsuya's first thought was that he and his friend were already dead. He took the raging water to be the River of Three Crossings, the Japanese equivalent of the River Styx. Those who have led good lives cross the river safely by bridge; evildoers must take their chances in the dragon-ridden waters. Innocent children, being neither sinful nor virtuous, rely on a kindly Buddha to make their passage, and to protect them from the depredations of hags and demons.

"I thought I'd died," Tetsuya said. "Dead . . . the River of Three Crossings. But then there was the New Kitakami Great Bridge, and the traffic island. And so I thought this might be Kamaya after all."

The water, which had receded, began to surge up the hill again. The two boys tottered up the slope. Tetsuya's face was black and bruised. In the churn of the tsunami, the ill-fitting plastic helmet that he wore had twisted on its strap and dug brutally against his eyes. His vision was affected for weeks; he could make out only dimly what was going on in the water below.

Kohei's left wrist was broken and his skin was punctured by thorns, but his vision was unaffected. Whatever was visible of the fate of his school and his schoolmates, he saw it. He would never talk publicly about it.

Tetsuya became aware that an expression of glazed sleepiness was passing over Kohei's face. "Hang on, I thought—that's dangerous," Tetsuya said. "I can't have him saving me, then dying on me." But his friend was becoming more and more detached from the here and now. Tetsuya's mind, too, began to drift and wander. He struggled even to remember what day it was. His little sister had been in the schoolyard too; his mother, who had disappeared on her vague errand, must be out there somewhere. He thought of the soldiers of the Japan Self-Defense Forces: surely by now they must be on their way. He called out to the soldiers: *Help! Help!* "But they didn't come," Tetsuya remembered. "And while I was thinking about all these things, Kohei had fallen asleep."

With their loudspeakers blaring evacuation warnings, Toshinobu Oikawa and his colleagues from the town office had raced out of Kamaya and up to the traffic island opposite the Great

Bridge. To his dismay, cars were still coming into the village from the opposite direction, towards the oncoming tsunami. They pulled in, with the aim of setting up a checkpoint to force drivers to turn back. Hardly had they parked when the water began to pour over the embankment.

"It came down over us like a waterfall," Oikawa said. "We ran. There was no time to think." The only place of safety was a steep slope on the other side of the same hill that backed onto the school. Four of them reached it and scrambled clear, by a matter of seconds. One man, Yukinori Sato, was caught by the water, but was dragged and yanked out by his colleagues. The sixth man, Hideyuki Sugawara, was trapped in his car and tumbled away by the waters, never to be seen alive again.

From the hillside, they watched the tsunami swallow up the road and the traffic island. That was the place of evacuation chosen by the deputy principal, Ishizaka—if any of the teachers or children had ever reached it, they would have perished there under thirty feet of water. By reckoning the distance the tsunami had traveled since it broke over the pine forest and the time that had passed, Oikawa calculated its speed—more than forty miles an hour. The pines, carried by the water, added greatly to its destructive power—sixty-foot-long battering rams that clubbed and crushed whatever they encountered. Where they met the bridge, the trunks became entangled in its arches, turning it into a kind of dam and diverting the tsunami's flow over the downstream embankment—in other words, over Kamaya. "It made it much worse," said Oikawa. "There was still water going under the bridge, of course. But the barrier of trees was pushing some of it back, over the village and the school."

The construction of the embankment was of uneven quality: in places, the water washed it away like a child's sandcastle, leaving the houses behind it completely exposed. The hamlet of Magaki

suffered this fate. "Mr. Sato, who was with us, lived in Magaki," Oikawa remembered. "He watched his own house being washed away. His parents, his daughter, his grandchild were in the house. He lost all of them. He was shouting, screaming, 'My house, my house!'"

Sato had with him a video camera, and at one point he turned it on. The 118-second film is the only recording of the tsunami in full spate in the Okawa area. In the hands of the stricken cameraman, the image veers wildly back and forth between the black river, the green girders of the bridge, and Magaki, already reduced to a single house. Suddenly the camera is pointing up at trees and the sky; then it is lying on the ground amid stalks of dry grass. The voice of Sato, newly bereaved, can he heard, calling out, "Is the school okay? What about the school?"

Shivering in his sodden clothes, Sato made his way down the far side of the hill with one of his colleagues. The remaining three, led by Oikawa, climbed up it, in search of survivors. Rubbing their gloveless hands, they called aloud as they peeped between trees. Eventually their cries were answered by a strong voice, that of old Kazuo Takahashi, who had run up the hill past the fleeing schoolchildren.

Takahashi was a fierce and irascible old man. Reporters who called on him to ask about his experiences were sent packing. He had no interest in hearing it, but he was one of the heroes of that day. Half a dozen lives were saved by him at the meeting point of the land and the wave.

The tsunami had caught up with him as he climbed the hill, but he found his feet and outran it. He was aware of cries all around, and one voice close at hand. He ran to it and found a woman trying to save a young girl, who was trapped between

floating rubble. Takahashi, risking his own secure footing, reached down into the water and dragged her out. This was Nana Suzuki, from the first grade of Okawa Elementary, the youngest of the children to survive the tsunami. Striding along the margins of the hill, Takahashi pulled to safety five more people, most of them elderly.

He led the survivors to a clearing on the hill, where they settled, shivering, on the ground. A cigarette lighter was produced, and a fire kindled with twigs and fragments of bamboo. From time to time, human calls could be heard through the trees, and Takahashi marched off in pursuit of them. After uniting with Oikawa's team, they found Tetsuya and Kohei and seated them around the sputtering fire.

Fourteen people were gathered there, all told. It was by now completely dark, snowing, and profoundly cold. Most of the survivors were in wet clothes, and one old man was barefoot. No one spoke much. They fed the fire with twigs on which frost was forming. They propped up a branch close to the flames, draped with wet garments. There were no tears or hysteria; but no attempts at mutual encouragement, no songs to keep up the spirits. The minds of all those on the hill were turned to those who were not present—parents and grandparents, children and grandchildren, siblings and spouses, who must still be down there, somewhere.

Among the survivors was a married couple in their sixties, who had been thoroughly drenched by the tsunami. The woman clutched to her what Oikawa took to be a glossy black doll. Then he saw the doll moving feebly. It was a tiny dog, which had entered the water white and had come out dyed by evil-smelling mud. "It was the same with the shirts we wore," Oikawa said. "In the tsunami, everything that was white became black."

The woman's husband had no visible wounds, but it was obvi-

ous that he had suffered dreadful internal injury. He could not speak at all. From the beginning, his breathing was shallow and labored. No one present on the hill had any medical expertise, and he needed help urgently. The main road was a few hundred yards away; to the village of Irikamaya it was less than a mile. But it was pitch-black, in a forest littered with obstacles and slippery with ice. Each man and woman on the hill was completely absorbed by the personal struggle against the cold. The idea of abandoning the fire, even in pursuit of help for a gravely injured man, was insupportable. They laid him alongside the fire and tried to keep him warm. Abruptly, at around 3:00 a.m., his gasping stopped.

"No one got upset by it," Oikawa said. "Even his wife didn't display much grief. In those circumstances, after what they had all managed to survive, that thing—I mean, death—was not frightening there." It was snowing, steadily and heavily, and the earth was freezing. Tetsuya and the other two children were falling asleep on the cold ground. "Usually, you would stop that," Oikawa said. "You would stop a child from falling asleep in that kind of cold. But we let them sleep."

Around six, the sun rose. The three children, the dog, and the ten surviving men and women stirred and picked themselves up from the ground. At the high-water mark of the wave, someone found a mandarin orange and a packet of custard creams, which the children shared. None had the strength to carry the corpse, which remained behind them on the hillside. They picked their way down to the road and along it to Irikamaya, where refugees were gathering from all over the district. There they encountered another survivor—Junji Endo, the single teacher left alive, who surely must have known what had happened at the school.

PART IV

THE INVISIBLE MONSTER

巴那のこと さがし出して あげられなくて ごめんね
巴那に会いたくて毎日ここに来てるけど…
どこかに きっと いるはずなのに …巴那のいる所を
わかってあげられなくて ごめんね。
夢にも出て来てくれないから お父さんも お母さんも
おじいさんも おばあさんも みんな さみしいよ。
何もしてあげられなくて ごめんね。本当に ごめんね。
夢の中で 会えたら おもいっきり「だっこ」してあげるよ

IN THE WEB

The first place I ever lived in Tokyo was a harbor island re-claimed from the edges of the Pacific Ocean. I had been there less than two weeks when my first earthquake struck. The tremor passed while I was still asleep, leaving the faintest smudge on my conscious mind: a sudden wakefulness, fugitive unease, evasive as an exhalation of smoke. I woke up without understanding why. I felt a tugging need to switch on the light and sit up. I felt very much like a solitary foreigner in a strange city.

Over breakfast, the Japanese family with whom I was staying told me about earthquakes. Last night's tremor had been small, but unusual in that it had come and gone with a single jolt: usu-ally they rumbled on, and the abruptness of the event suggested that the stirring of the crust was incomplete and that there was more movement to come. There were earthquakes all the time, they said, every few weeks at least—some unmistakable, some difficult to distinguish from the routine rumbling of the city: construction work, passing trucks, the vibration of underground trains. The last one to cause any alarm had been six months ago: all the joints of the apartment block creaking, the ceiling lights

swinging crazily, neighbors crying out in alarm. And one day, of course, there would be a truly huge tremor, a repeat of the Great Kanto earthquake, which shook Tokyo and Yokohama before the war and started fires that killed a multitude. The Tokyo earthquake came around on a regular cycle, and the next one was already overdue.

I knew this. Everyone who comes to Japan acquires this information within a few days of arriving. The first thing you learn about Tokyo is that it won't be there for much longer.

My friends talked with gossipy animation—there was evidently a mischievous pleasure in imparting this frightening information to a new arrival. They spoke with a kind of scandalized amusement, and with no evident alarm or trepidation. Earthquakes, the mass destruction of human life, the obliteration of the city were matters of lively breakfast conversation, of no more concern than a violent rain shower or an unseasonable fall of snow.

Sometime in the next few years, it is generally assumed, Tokyo will be shaken by an earthquake powerful enough to destroy large areas of the city and set off fires and tsunamis that will kill many tens of thousands of people. The reasoning is straightforward. Every six or seven decades, for several centuries, the Kanto plain, on which Tokyo, Yokohama, and Kawasaki have merged into a single megalopolis, has been devastated by a vast tremor. The last one, which killed 140,000 people, took place in 1923. Seismologists point out that it is not, in fact, as simple as this—that past Tokyo earthquakes have originated in different faults, on separate and overlapping cycles, and that a sampling of a few hundred years is, in any case, too small to infer a pattern. But for more nuanced reasons of their own, they agree with the

conclusion: that widespread destruction is inevitable and, in geo-logical terms, imminent.

In speaking of natural disasters, large casualty figures quickly acquire an air of unreality. To put them into perspective, con-sider the victims of the two atomic bombs. In Hiroshima in August 1945, 70,000 people were killed at once, and by the end of the year 60,000 more had died of injuries and radiation sickness. The Nagasaki bomb was less destructive, with a total of about 74,000 deaths. In 2004, the Japanese government predicted that an earthquake under Tokyo could kill as many as 13,000 people—one-tenth of a Hiroshima. Six years later, it considered a scenario in which a tremor originating in one fault sets off earthquakes in two more, and concluded that across the country 24,700 people could die—one-third of a Nagasaki. Projections made after the Tohoku disaster became gloomier, or more realistic. In 2012, a new study predicted that an earthquake and tsunami originating in the Nankai Trough could take 323,000 lives along the south-central Pacific Coast and cause 623,000 injuries.

This was not the speculation of cranks or activists, but the carefully researched finding of Japan's Cabinet Office, a deeply cautious organization instinctively averse to alarmism. It took into account the many precautions and protective measures that Japan has developed—the sturdy construction, and seawalls, and regular evacuation drills. Despite all of these, its conclusion was blankly horrifying: the Nankai earthquake, which might strike at any time, could kill more people than four atomic bombs.

What is it like to live with knowledge such as this in daily life? What goes on inside the heads of those living under sentence of earthquake?

Recurring questions come to mind every few days, sometimes

every few hours, especially in a new or unfamiliar quarter of the city. Sitting in a car on an elevated expressway, or walking through an underground shopping center, you ask yourself, more in curiosity than in alarm: What if the Big One struck now? Are the pillars beneath that overpass strong enough? Would that plate-glass window hold? What would become of the large and rusty water tank on top of that old building? Finding a place to live crystallizes the situation with particular clarity. Question one: Is this apartment conveniently located, well-appointed, and reasonably priced? Question two: Will it crush me to death when the ground starts to shake?

The answer, in the case of almost all modern buildings, is no. One of the unexpected consequences of the March 2011 disaster was to diminish anxiety about earthquakes. Even in Sendai, the big city closest to the epicenter, the damage caused by the tremors alone was impressively slight. There were cracks and broken windows; the ceiling of the main hall of the station partially fell in; and on the edges of the city, older houses—especially those built on hillsides—slumped and slid on their foundations. But there were no big fires; no large modern buildings came close to collapse, and most of them suffered no significant damage at all.

In a disaster caused by an earthquake, in other words, only a tiny proportion of the victims was killed by the earthquake itself. More than 99 percent—18,400 out of 18,500—died in the water. And to survive a tsunami, it was not enough to be in a strong building; it also had to be tall. During an earthquake, open ground—an uncluttered beach, for example—is the safest place to find yourself. In a tsunami, such exposure is deadly. Mentally, a rebalancing took place as one menace receded and another loomed. There was no improvement in the overall sense of security; those who lived through March 2011 simply exchanged one

set of imaginings—of fire and blunt impact—for new mental images of death by drowning.

I live and work in strong buildings, and on elevated ground. My home, my office, and my children's schools may be badly shaken and structurally damaged, may even be rendered uninhabitable, but it is unlikely they will collapse or be inundated. Japan's wealth and advanced technology protect it from disaster better than anywhere else in the world. But the safety of any one individual depends entirely on where he or she is when the moment comes.

Over dinner one evening in Tokyo I found myself among a group of friends discussing the very worst place to be in a big earthquake. One of us suggested the Tokyo monorail, a slender ribbon of steel and concrete on which trains from the airport glide high over the chemical and oil tanks in the south of the city. Someone else imagined being trapped in the subway, amid fracturing tunnels and blackness. My own phobia was the flimsy pedestrian bridges that extend across big roads, often sandwiched between a six-lane highway below and an expressway above. But as we talked, I became aware of the restaurant in which we were sitting. It was a dark, narrow snuggery on the eighth floor of a decrepit building. Behind the counter, the chef was cheerfully pouring oil onto a pan that flared with a foot-tall plume of flame. The partitions, the doors, and the mats on which we were sitting were made of wood, paper, and rushes.

"Why does it not upset people more," the journalist Peter Popham asked, "the fact that they might any day be roasted alive, gassed to death, buried in a landslide or in the wreckage of their own homes?" People in Tokyo abandon the city from time to

time, or lose their minds, or take their own lives, for the same reasons that they do such things anywhere in the world. But no one goes mad over earthquakes. Why not? What does it do to the unconscious, even to the soul, to exist with such precariousness?

The first time I lived in Japan I was eighteen years old. I had come to Japan in search of strangeness and adventure—I had come precisely to seek out excitements such as earthquakes. But they also seemed to explain something about the city I was experiencing with such intensity. I spoke no Japanese and knew almost no one in Japan. Tokyo, with its vastness and impenetrability, answered to something in my loneliness. I left the Japanese family with whom I had been staying on the edge of the bay, and found a room in the suburbs and a job at an English conversation school. On the morning train, I stared at the ideograms in a Japanese textbook. I spent my evenings in bars with red lanterns at their doors, with new friends, most of them foreigners as transient and untethered as me. On the last train home, I exchanged smiles with Japanese girls. It was close to the height of Japan's "bubble" economy, the moment when Tokyo was briefly the richest city in history. The force of money was tearing down the old neighborhoods and throwing them up again in steel and glass. The city, as I inhabited it, was as dazzling as a filament and as thin as tissue paper. It felt, in my excitement, like a place that was physically trembling, and that could at any moment come crashing down. It seemed entirely appropriate to learn that this was literally true.

"Far from being dull to the dangers, acute awareness of them gives Tokyo people's lives tone and brio," wrote Popham, during this same period. "The satisfaction of being a cog in the most elaborate and well-oiled machine in the history of the world is given an almost erotic twist by the knowledge that the machine is poised over an abyss." Tokyo, he concluded, is "a city helpless

to save itself, and reconciled at some quite deep level to destruction and loss of life beyond all but the nuclear nightmares of other cities."

"Now I will tell how Octavia, the spider-web city, is made," says Kublai Khan, in Italo Calvino's *Invisible Cities*:

> There is a precipice between two steep mountains: the city is over the void, bound to the two crests with ropes and chains and catwalks. You walk on the little wooden ties, careful not to set your foot in the open spaces, or you cling to the hempen strands. Below there is nothing for hundreds and hundreds of feet: a few clouds glide past; farther down you can glimpse the chasm's bed.
>
> This is the foundation of the city: a net which serves as passage and as support. All the rest, instead of rising up, is hung below: rope ladders, hammocks, houses made like sacks, clothes hangers, terraces like gondolas, skins of water, gas jets, spits, baskets on strings, dumb-waiters, showers, trapezes and rings for children's games, cable cars, chandeliers, pots with trailing plants.
>
> Suspended over the abyss, the life of Octavia's inhabitants is less uncertain than in other cities. They know the net will last only so long.

Earthquakes get into your dreams. But their meaning changes as you grow older. When I was young, I was excited by the idea that Tokyo's atmosphere of impermanence was a result of its inevitable doom. But that sense of things falling apart, the conviction that the center cannot hold, is an adolescent notion: in reality, of course, the tension and insecurity came not from the city, but from within me.

The earthquake is the thing that all humans face: the banal inevitability of death. We don't know when it will come, but we know that it will. We take refuge in elaborate and ingenious precautions, but in the end they are all in vain. We think about it even when we are not thinking about it; after a while, it seems to define what we are. It comes most often for the old, but we feel it most cruelly when it also takes away the young.

"Some people can't find the words," said Naomi Hiratsuka. "They just mutter, 'Must have been terrible . . .' and that's it. It's not that they don't feel sympathy. They just don't have a way to express it. But I get sick of hearing the same phrases over and over again. And then I meet people who pretend not to know anything about it, because that's easier for them, just to ignore it and hope it'll go away. Not that I particularly want to talk to people like that."

She paused and then smiled, as if at a private joke. "The thing is that if someone doesn't mention it at all, I think, 'Why?' But if they're full of pity, I don't like that, either. I live my life day by day. I'm not always crying and feeling sorry for myself. Sometimes, even when we're out at the site, digging, we have a chat and a laugh about something. And then we feel self-conscious about people seeing us smiling. I shouldn't have to worry about things like that, should I? It's very difficult."

It is easy to imagine grief as an ennobling, purifying emotion—uncluttering the mind of what is petty and transient, and illuminating the essential. In reality, of course, grief doesn't resolve anything, any more than a blow to the head or a devastating illness. It compounds stress and complication. It multiplies anxiety and tension. It opens fissures into cracks, and cracks into gaping chasms.

From the survivors of the tsunami, I learned that everyone's

grief is different, and that it differs in small and subtle ways according to the circumstances of loss. "The first thing was this," said Naomi. "Did you lose your children, or did your children survive? That divided people immediately: the children who lived and those who died." Thirty-four of the 108 pupils at the school survived the wave—because they had been picked up in time by their parents, or crawled miraculously out of the water. The horror of survival—the destruction of their community, the deaths of so many of their friends—was not to be underestimated. But in the eyes of those whose children had perished, the families of the survivors were the beneficiaries of almost unbearably good luck.

"Some of those who lost their children find it impossible to talk to those whose children survived," Naomi said. "In some ways, it's worse for people who were close." Naomi knew one mother who had collected her children from the school and taken them to safety. Her neighbor had not done so, and her children had died. "So the neighbor says to her, 'Why? Why didn't you take my kids too?' Of course, it doesn't work like that. The school has rules—it wouldn't have been allowed. But once something like that is put into words, that friendship is over."

Even among the bereaved there were gradations of grief, a spectrum of blackness indiscernible to those on the outside. It came down to a coldhearted question: Once the water had retreated, how much did you have left? Sayomi Shito had lost her beloved daughter Chisato; it would have been unthinkably callous to point out that her two older children, her husband, her extended family, and her home were unharmed and intact. But others were acutely aware of Sayomi's circumstances, and the precise degree to which they differed from their own. Naomi, for example, had also lost one child out of three, while her home, her husband, and the rest of her family had survived. But Sayomi had been able to find and bury Chisato quickly, while Naomi had

gone through the prolonged anguish of hunting for Koharu's remains.

Then there were those worse off, who had lost some, though not all, of their children, and the entirety of their homes; and those even more wretched, who had lost their homes and their entire families. And even within this group, the most miserable division of the stricken, there were terrible distinctions. Hitomi Konno, for example, had lost her son and both her daughters, but soon recovered and cremated their bodies. In this, she was better off than Miho Suzuki, who had found her son, but five years later was still looking for her daughter, Hana.

It is true that people can be "brought together" by catastrophe, and it is human to look to this as a consolation. But the balance of disaster is never positive. New human bonds were made after the tsunami, old ones became stronger; there were countless remarkable displays of selflessness and self-sacrifice. These we remember and celebrate. We turn away from what is also commonplace: the destruction of friendship and trust; neighbors at odds; the enmity of friends and relatives. A tsunami does to human connectedness the same thing that it does to roads, bridges, and homes. And in Okawa, and everywhere in the tsunami zone, people fell to quarreling and reproaches, and felt the bitterness of injustice and envy, and fell out of love.

Naomi Hiratsuka and Sayomi Shito were scarcely more than nodding acquaintances before the disaster. After it, they grew to hate each other. Of all the Okawa mothers, they were the ones whom I came to know best, and their mutual resentment was almost palpable. Sometimes I would visit Sayomi's house after a meeting with Naomi, or vice versa. In exaggeratedly casual tones

and with a thin smile, the second woman would ask after the first, and the air in the room seemed to become colder.

Their antipathy was a function of the distinct tasks that each had set about with such energy. As Naomi sat in her digger, turning over the earth, Sayomi, her husband, and the friends whom I had met that evening were pursuing a systematic investigation into the truth about what had happened at the school. Searching letters were sent to Ishinomaki city hall. Witnesses were sought out, and their accounts compiled. The group held a press conference at which they demanded that Junji Endo come before them again, to account for the anomalies in his story; and there were consultations with lawyers.

To Sayomi, these two tasks—dredging the physical and bureaucratic mud—were complementary; Naomi's contempt was baffling to her. "By pursuing the question of what happened, by forcing the authorities to take responsibility, that will also force them to carry out the search," she said. "We talk to the media to keep up the pressure, and so that public concern won't fade away. I never interfered with her taking her digger license. I've never criticized her. So I wonder why people such as Mrs. Hiratsuka try to get us to do things their way."

But to Naomi, the campaigning of the "Fukuji group" was a practical hindrance, as well as a social embarrassment. Because they were so outspoken, Sayomi and her friends were assumed by many outsiders to be leaders among the Okawa parents, representative of the whole. But their unashamed directness, amounting, by Japanese standards, to plain aggression, irritated and mortified many. The heckling of the town officials in the public meeting was regarded as unforgivably bad manners. Their denunciations of the education board threatened the delicate architecture of relationships built up by Naomi, who depended upon the goodwill of

the city government for diggers, for fuel, and for the permissions necessary to continue her search. "I'm not in the least satisfied with the education board," Naomi told me. "But we need them, we need their cooperation, just to do what we have to do."

Something else distinguished Sayomi and the campaigning Fukuji parents, as Naomi pointed out: all had recovered the bodies of their children quickly—within a couple of weeks, at most. "From the beginning, it depended on whether you found your child or not," Naomi said. "When your child came home, when you had held a funeral, then you naturally moved on to the next question: Why did this happen? And then anger could begin. But if your child was still out there, all you could think about was her face, the only thing in your mind was the idea of finding her, finding her."

Naomi said: "The question is: What's the purpose of pursuing the truth? What do you expect to come of it? Those people"—and she meant Sayomi—"say, 'Why did it happen? Why did it happen only at Okawa, but not at other schools?' But if you knew all that, then what? They say, 'It's for the future, it's for the sake of other children. We want to draw lessons, so that our children didn't die in vain.' But is that really all it is? Or are they simply laying blame? When you know exactly what happened, are you any better off? When you've got the truth in your hand, what are you going to do with it?"

WHAT USE IS THE TRUTH?

In all their dealings with the families of the dead children, the bureaucrats of the Ishinomaki Education Board maintained an exterior of calm and fussy courtesy. In the "explanatory meetings," held several times a year, they sat in a dark-suited line, attending patiently to the distraught mothers and fathers with tilted heads. Their bows were slow and deep. In the most formal registers of language, they expressed their profound and sincere condolences. But about the city's handling of the tragedy of Okawa Elementary School there lingered an air of disreputable shabbiness, an odor of suppressed panic and cover-up. It seemed, at times, to be as much a matter of incompetence as deliberate conspiracy. But every few weeks emerged some new example of fishiness and ineptitude.

Early on, the education board had conducted an interview with the principal, Teruyuki Kashiba. The written record of this conversation contained obvious and inexplicable impossibilities. Kashiba claimed that immediately after the disaster, for example, he had traveled from his inland home to a spot on the Kitakami River in two hours, an impossibly fast journey. He described

meetings with people who had no memory of seeing him on that day, and of a visit to a place that at the time was under five feet of water.

There were interviews, too, with the surviving children. They had lived through appalling trauma; their psychological state can only be imagined. But, in some cases, there was no parent present for these interviews, or any advance warning that they were to be conducted. When young Tetsuya Tadano was questioned, his interrogators simply turned up at his new school, with no attempt to seek the permission of his father.

Parents who had been present noticed later that certain details were inexplicably omitted from the written summaries of these interviews. The most important of these were the words of Yuki Sato and Daisuke Konno, the two sixth-grade boys who had pleaded with their teacher to be allowed to escape up the hill, who had been refused, and who had both perished in the wave. A number of the surviving children had recounted this exchange. One of the officials, Shigemi Kato, had referred to it in an early meeting with the parents. This, it became clear, had been a bad and unintentional lapse on his part—ever after, when questioned about it, the members of the education board denied that any of the surviving children had ever told them such a thing. "I heard my child say during the interview that her friends were saying, 'Let's escape to the hill,'" one mother told the meeting. "But that wasn't written down at all."

The memos summarizing parts of the interviews were identically worded, as if they had been cut and pasted one into the other. No audio recordings had been made; even the name of the person conducting the interview was not indicated. When parents asked to see the written notes taken at the time, they were told that Shigemi Kato had disposed of them.

At a later meeting, Kato was pressed about the boys who had

tried to run up the hill. During this exchange, his boss, Moto Yamada, was seen looking at Kato and raising his fingers to his lips as if to silence him. The gesture could be seen on the video recording of the meeting; Yamada repeated the hushing motion three times.

And then there was the matter of the surviving teacher, Junji Endo.

Of the various untruths in Endo's testimony, the most baffling were his insistent statements about the trees. Consistently, in recounting the events after the earthquake, he described the spectacle of pines on the hillside behind the school being toppled by the earthquake and its aftershocks. He recalled being pinioned by two cedars, and how the rising tsunami had lifted them off and miraculously freed him. His account conveyed a vivid impression of panicked survivors, having narrowly escaped death by water, cowering as the hillside shook with the collapse of deadly tree trunks.

There were no fallen trees. Many people tramped up and down the hill in the weeks after the disaster, and not a single one was found. Trees, with flexible trunks and branches, efficiently dissipate the energy of earthquakes: they may shake and bend, but they rarely topple over. The landscape following the disaster was littered with pines, but these had been carried in from the beachside forest, and ripped from their roots not by the earthquake but by the tsunami.

"If it was such a big quake that so many trees fell down, all the houses would have collapsed too," said Kazutaka Sato. "Mr. Endo was a nature lover. He must have known that."

The details of Endo's testimony filtered outward from the circle of the bereaved and into the community at large. The first

person to denounce it was a car mechanic named Masahiko Chiba, whose house had been protected by its elevated position on the far side of the hill from the school. No other house so close to the river had survived the tsunami, and soon survivors—many of them wet, some of them injured—were converging on it. Among them were Junji Endo and Seina Yamamoto, the little boy who had escaped with him.

The two arrived late that afternoon. Chiba's wife was the first to see them—a man in a suit, and a young boy still wearing his white plastic helmet, stepping uncertainly down the hill. "The man in the suit said, 'I could only rescue one,'" Mrs. Chiba recalled. "Those were his first words. I think he said something about Okawa school, but I had so much to think about that I didn't listen carefully."

She remembered that the boy's shoes and socks were wet, but that Endo's clothes were dry. He still had his shoes, which he removed before stepping inside. "He wore a check suit, an indistinct brown-gray color, and a bit shabby, typical for a teacher," she said. "But it was clean and it wasn't wet. I remember this quite clearly."

One of the refugees staying in the house was an old man who could hardly walk. The following morning, Endo carried him on his back from the house to a waiting vehicle. Only a fit adult could have managed this; there was no sign at all that Endo was injured.

Later, the Chibas read about the teacher's own account of that afternoon: how he had been caught up in the tsunami and almost drowned; how he had lost his shoes and staggered down from the hillside in darkness; and how he had dislocated his shoulder. They were baffled and appalled. "The account of Endo, the teacher, is lies," Masahiko Chiba said. "Ninety percent of it is lies. But why he lied, I do not know."

In June, three months after the tsunami, Endo wrote two letters, one to Kashiba, the principal, and another addressed to the bereaved parents collectively. They were sent by fax, the day before a meeting between the families and the education board. In one more of those suspicious and inexplicable decisions taken by the board of education, it was six months before these documents were released. In them, Endo added little to the account he had given in person, but described in some detail his own agonized state of mind. "It's terrible to remember what happened then," he wrote. "I go completely pale when I think about it. My hands are trembling as I write . . . There's something wrong with my body and with my mind. I'm being selfish, I know, I'm sorry, but for the time being could you leave me alone? I'm frightened when the phone rings."

Every request from the families to meet Endo received the same response—a letter from his doctor, explaining that he was recovering from post-traumatic stress disorder and was too distressed to talk about what had happened. It was impossible to challenge such a diagnosis. But the months passed into years, and the response remained the same. "I think it's an excuse," said Kazuhiro Yoshioka, a lawyer who advised the families. "Every note from the doctor reads like a carbon copy of the last one. He always says that just three more months are needed. And the drugs he's on are no more than you'd be prescribed for insomnia.

"It may be that Mr. Endo doesn't want to appear. But the board of education twists facts to avoid responsibility. Perhaps they have gone to him and said, 'You stay in the background. Don't say anything. We'll look after this problem.'"

The men of the Ishinomaki city government were not villains. In plenty of ways they had behaved heroically. They were local bureaucrats in a small regional city. They were familiar in theory with the threat of natural disaster, but nothing in their personal or professional experience could have prepared them for an event of such magnitude and horror. They were themselves victims: many had seen their homes flooded or washed away, some had lost friends and relatives. They were reeling and in confusion, but they never abandoned their sense of public duty, and they kept the motor of administration turning over, despite crushing practical obstacles.

There were no telephones, no mains electricity, and no fuel. The city hall itself was flooded by five feet of water; its vehicles were immobilized in the parking lot. The staff abandoned the mud-slimed ground floor and worked by torchlight in the upper offices. It was not a question of merely canceling leave—city employees were required to remain on duty around the clock. Step by step, they extended themselves across the stricken municipality, first in the ruined city center, then into the outer villages, across fields and hills and forests, by bicycle, by foot, and in rubber boats. Fifteen of the city's schools, nurseries, and kindergartens were flooded, burned, or otherwise affected by the disaster; others were serving as evacuation centers for tens of thousands of displaced families. Day by day, the board of education gathered information about the state of schools, including the welfare of their children and teachers, and arranged supplies of food for the refugees.

As individuals, they were tireless and self-sacrificing; without them, a desperate situation would have been many times worse. But when confronted by their own failure, as they were at Okawa Elementary School, personal warmth and empathy were stifled by the instinct of the collective—the instinct to protect the institution against outside attack. Faced with unanswerable reproach,

it shrank back into itself, behind scales of formality and claws of bureaucratese. The faces of the kindly, hardworking local men and women who made up the education board dropped from view. Their loyalty was to a higher cause, beyond that of public duty or personal decency—that of protecting the organization from further damage to its reputation, and above all from legal attack in the courts.

The imperviousness of the city officials, their refusal to muster a human response to the grief of the families, seemed at the beginning to be a collective failure of character and of leadership. But as time passed, Sayomi and Takahiro Shito, and the other parents of the "Fukuji group," began to suspect another motivation—an obsession with avoiding anything that could be taken as an admission of liability. The metallic tang of lawyerly advice lingered around many of the bureaucrats' utterances. They were happy to express grief and condolence, and willing to abase themselves in general terms for their unworthiness. But to acknowledge specific negligence on the part of individuals, or systematic, institutional failure—that was a step that no one would take.

Then, the winter after the tsunami, they offered up a sacrifice of sorts. Teruyuki Kashiba, the principal of Okawa Elementary School, presented a signed statement of apology addressed to the parents. This "irremediable situation," he said, resulted "from my carelessness as principal." "However much I apologize," he went on, "things such as the lack of a proper emergency manual and the failure to promote crisis awareness among the staff cannot be forgiven." Two months later, he took early retirement.

It looked, on the face of it, like an important concession. But to the Fukuji parents, finely attuned to the nuances of apology, there was something about it—something in the word

"carelessness"—that smacked of evasion. They put it to the test at a meeting a few months later at which Kashiba was present.

Sayomi's husband, Takahiro Shito, addressed the now-retired principal, as he sat before the assembled parents. He pressed him on the question of the school's emergency manual, which Kashiba, in his statement of apology, had acknowledged to have been inadequate. "Reflecting on it now," Shito said, "I'd like to hear from you again what you mean by that word 'carelessness.'"

"In short," said Kashiba, "not to have checked it thoroughly was careless."

The word for carelessness in Japanese is *taiman*. Shito was fishing for another, and more potent, word: *kashitsu*—negligence.

"Do you not think," he asked, "that this carelessness amounts to negligence?"

Sitting on Kashiba's immediate left was a man named Kenetsu Shishido, deputy councillor of the board of education. Perhaps it was the temperature in the overheated room; perhaps it was the effects of a medical condition. Whatever the cause, Mr. Shishido displayed signs of intense physical discomfort during Kashiba's exchange with Takahiro Shito. He fidgeted in his chair. He wiped his face and hands repeatedly with a hand towel. At the mention of *kashitsu*, he leaned forward and back, and placed his hand on a document on the desk on which he appeared to be pointing to something. Almost imperceptibly, he muttered to Kashiba out of the corner of his mouth. Then he rubbed the towel over his hands and face again, wiped the back of his neck, and attended to an itch in his right ear.

"Principal?" said Shito, after moments of unfilled silence.

Kashiba shot a sideways glance at Deputy Councillor Shishido. "As far as that goes," he said, looking down now at the papers on the desk in front of him, "personally, I don't think so."

"You don't think so?"

"Although I might have overlooked some things, I did what I had to do, so I don't think it's negligence. I wouldn't say that myself."

Shishido was wiping his face again. This, it had become clear, was not done to quell perspiration, but to mask more muttered remarks to Kashiba.

"We can't hear what Mr. Shishido is saying to you," said Shito. At the mention of his name, Shishido looked up abruptly, with an expression of quizzical innocence.

"Move away from him," someone else called out. Sulkily, Shishido shifted his chair a few inches to the left.

Then Shito's neighbor, Katsura Sato, stood up to speak. Katsura taught art in a high school in the city of Ishinomaki; she knew from personal experience about the preparations that teachers make in anticipation of disaster. "None of them was done," she told Kashiba. "But still, as principal, you told the education board you'd done them. If we'd known, then everyone would have gone to the school to pick up their children. If everyone had gone, many more children would have been saved. Because of your 'carelessness' all those children died. It's negligence. Negligence! How long do you intend to put off admitting responsibility? Seventy-four children died, and you still don't get it."

Shishido was muttering again to Kashiba out of the corner of his mouth. "Truly," Kashiba said, after a pause, "for not being able to protect the lives of the seventy-four children and ten teachers, I feel truly sorry."

"You *feel* that," said Katsura. "But you haven't *done* anything about it. Have you? It's negligence, it's negligence!"

Shishido continued to towel his face and to mouth inaudible words.

"For the fact that I couldn't save seventy-four children and ten teachers," Kashiba said, "I apologize."

"Will you admit professional negligence?"

Shishido wiped his mouth and continued his sidelong muttering.

"I feel sorry," said Kashiba, "but ..."

Katsura Sato almost screamed, *"Will you admit negligence?"*

"I can't make that judgment."

"Who *will* make that judgment? *Answer!"*

Kashiba was looking at Shishido. Shishido was telling him something.

"I feel very sorry," Kashiba said, "but I can say only that I am truly sorry, and I apologize."

Twenty-three months after the tsunami, the Ishinomaki city government announced the establishment of something called the Okawa Elementary School Incident Verification Committee. It consisted of a panel of ten eminences, including lawyers and university professors of sociology, psychology, and behavioral science. The committee would spend a year reviewing documents and conducting interviews. Its findings were published in a two-hundred-page report in February 2014.

The committee was funded by the city at a cost of ¥57 million (£390,000, or $617,000). Its mission—"verification"—turned out to have specific and limited scope: to establish the facts and causes of what happened, but by no means to assign personal responsibility. It concluded that the deaths arose because the evacuation of the playground was delayed, and because the children and teachers eventually fled, not away from the tsunami, but towards it.

The school, the board of education, and the city government, the report said, were inadequately prepared for such a natural disaster. The municipal "hazard map," which indicated areas of

coast vulnerable to tsunami, did not include Kamaya. The possibility of a tsunami was not considered in compiling the school's disaster manual, and there were no tsunami evacuation drills. No one in the municipal government had checked on the preparations taken by the school. "Teachers at the school," the report stated, "were psychologically unable to accept that they were facing imminent danger."

If any one of these failures had not occurred, the committee concluded, the tragedy could have been avoided. "These circumstances were not unique to Okawa Elementary," said the report. "Such an accident could occur at any school." This seemed at first to be a powerful and disturbing conclusion: a warning to the country at large. But its effect was to disperse to the wind any individual blame or responsibility. A terrible thing had happened, the committee was agreeing—but it could have happened anywhere, and to anyone.

The most controversial aspects of the case—such as the silencing of the boys who wanted to run to the hill—were ignored or skated over. To the Fukuji parents, the committee's conclusions were no more than an expensive restatement of what had been obvious for more than two years. The true purpose of the exercise, they concluded, was to shut down disagreement about the tragedy by commissioning "independent" experts to produce a tepid report, which articulated mild criticisms, while sparing the careers and reputations of the guilty.

No employee of the city of Ishinomaki or its board of education was ever sacked, disciplined, or formally reproached over the deaths at Okawa Elementary School. Shigemi Kato, who destroyed the notes from the interviews with the surviving children, was promoted the following year to the role of principal at a city elementary school.

The committee's report came out in the last week of February 2014, almost three years after the tsunami. The day before the anniversary, on March 10, came a startling piece of news. The families of twenty-three children who had died at Okawa were suing the city of Ishinomaki and Miyagi Prefecture in the Sendai District Court. They were accusing them of negligence, and demanding compensation of ¥100 million—about £600,000, or $1 million— for each of the lives lost. It was two years and 364 days since the disaster, the very last moment that it was legally possible to file a case. It was the move they had secretly been planning all along.

THE TSUNAMI IS NOT WATER

The tsunami had the power of many atomic bombs, but the most impressive thing about it—more astonishing, in its way, than the spectacle of destruction—was the behavior of those who survived it. Within a matter of hours, hundreds of thousands of people were converging on schools, community halls, temples and shrines, huddling in classrooms, gymnasiums, hallways and corridors, anywhere that had space enough to unroll a quilt. They were panicked, grieving, and in shock; they included centenarians, newborn babies, and everyone in between. For the first few days, there was scant official help. Those left alive had to help themselves, which they did with unsurpassable discipline and efficiency.

Naturally, invisibly, without fuss or drama, order crystallized in the chaos of the evacuation centers. Space was allocated, bedding was improvised, and food was pooled, prepared, and distributed. Rosters, for fetching, fixing, cleaning, and cooking, were quickly established and filled. Everything was eased by the instinctive Japanese aversion to anything that could be judged messy, selfish, or otherwise antisocial. And all of it was achieved

in an atmosphere of good humor and generosity, which sometimes bordered on the ridiculous.

Among the burdens of working as a foreign journalist in Tohoku was the constant struggle to fend off gifts of food—sweets, rice balls, chocolate biscuits, fish sausage—from homeless refugees who had only enough to feed themselves for the next few days or even hours. People who had recently lost their homes apologized, with pained sincerity, for the inadequacy of their hospitality. There was no significant looting; despite the chronic shortages of everything from gas to toilet paper, no one took the opportunity of scarcity to raise their prices. I never once saw fighting or squabbling or disagreement; and, most remarkable of all, there was a complete absence of self-pity.

It was impossible not to make mental comparisons. I pictured a school gymnasium in northeast England, rather than northeast Japan, in which hundreds of people were living and sleeping literally head to toe. By this stage, they would have been murdering one another.

Every foreigner who visited the disaster zone in the early weeks was struck by it; it transformed what should have been a harrowing experience into an inspiring one. There were many terrible and fearful scenes, and bottomless pain, but the horror was offset, and almost eclipsed, by the resilience and decency of the victims. It seemed to me at the time that this was the best of Japan, the best of humanity, one of the things I loved and admired most about this country: the practical, unsensational, irrepressible strength of communities. And I found myself thinking about history, and those moments when a national shock of one kind or another had galvanized Japan and marked the beginning of a new and dynamic era.

There had been the forcible opening of the feudal country in the mid-nineteenth century by American gunships. There was

the catastrophic defeat of 1945. Both events had seemed at the time moments of irredeemable humiliation. Both had been followed by decades of resurgence and prosperity. By 2011, that atmosphere of expansive and ambitious optimism was twenty years in the past. Since the collapse of the economic bubble in the early 1990s, Japan had been adrift, becalmed between a lost prosperity and a future that was too dim and uncertain to grasp. The economy was shrinking or stagnant. Companies no longer promised the security of employment for life. The old ruling party, which had led Japan for half a century, was bankrupt of ideas and personalities; but the opposition politicians elected in its place were diffident and inept. So I was not alone in wondering whether this new disaster might turn out to be the force that jolted Japan out of the political and economic funk into which it had slithered.

A multitude of people had died at a stroke. Nuclear furnaces were venting poison into the air. In any country, surely, events such as these would be the catalyst of protest, and action, and indignant movements for change. "The Japanese people rose from the ashes of the Second World War using our fundamental strength to secure a remarkable recovery and the country's present prosperity," said Naoto Kan, the prime minister at the time. "I have not a single doubt that Japan will overcome this crisis, recover from the aftermath of the disaster, emerge stronger than ever, and establish a more vibrant and better Japan for future generations."

Nothing of the kind was to happen; the promise of rebirth glimpsed in the evacuation centers would go completely unfulfilled.

Japan changed in various ways in the years after the tsunami, but it shed energy and confidence rather than gaining them. Partly

this had to do with a gathering sense of insecurity in East Asia—the crackling belligerence of North Korea, the domineering assertiveness of China. At the core of it, though, was an ever greater disconnection between Japan's leaders and the citizenry they were supposed to represent.

Naoto Kan and the centrist politicians who were in power at the time crumpled before the tsunami. They were the first Japanese opposition party to have won an outright majority; their inexperience and poor judgment had been obvious from the day they took power. In 2009, they had won the country's biggest-ever election victory; three years later, they suffered its fourth-worst defeat. Rejuvenated by its period of opposition, the old Liberal Democratic Party was back in power, as it had been for fifty-three of the past fifty-seven years. Its victorious leader, Shinzo Abe, was the most nationalistic prime minister since the war.

He supported revision of Japan's pacifist constitution and assumed new powers to deploy its armed forces. He pooh-poohed historical accounts of atrocities committed by the Imperial Army; he was a worshipper at Yasukuni Shrine, where hanged class-A war criminals were revered as Shinto deities. Despite the nationwide anxiety about Fukushima, he was unswervingly committed to maintaining Japan's nuclear reactors. Opinion polls showed that his plans for Japan's economy were widely supported. But his views about nuclear power, about wartime history, and the anger they excited among Japan's Asian neighbors were the cause of deep unease.

At a moment when it most needed unifying leadership, Japan faced a democratic crisis. One party stood convicted of gross incompetence. The other was led by a man whose ideology was drastically at odds with the instincts of most of the population. Many of those who voted for Shinzo Abe did not like or approve of him. But he was decisive and consistent, and he had a plan,

more persuasive than any other, for restoring to Japan its economic well-being. The weakness of the opposition was so extreme that many Japanese felt they had no choice.

In government, Abe faced protests of his own—against the restart of the reactors, against his plans to allow Japanese soldiers to deploy overseas, and against a sinister new state secrecy law. I followed these demonstrations and talked to the marchers; and I was always struck by the peculiar intensity of the opposition to Abe. It was not only about his nationalist enthusiasms; something in his personality excited in the demonstrators a deep, personal loathing. He was a lackey of big business and the powerful nuclear industry, they agreed; and a militarist who could end up leading Japan back into war. Japanese do not easily reach for invective, even towards their politicians. But many of the slogans denounced him as a fascist; some of the posters depicted Abe with the mustache of Adolf Hitler.

One old marcher told me that he had lived through the war, and the devastation it had brought. He remembered the incendiary bombing of Tokyo; his cousin, a young conscript soldier, had died in the atomic bombing of Hiroshima. And now he found himself in a country in which radioactive fallout once again drifted across the land, with a prime minister who was slowly leading his people back towards militarism. "It feels to me as if history is going into reverse," he said. "Who could stand by and watch such things happen?"

A huddle had formed about us as we talked on the margins of the demonstration. People, young and old, were nodding in agreement. Behind us, slogans were being shouted through a powerful amplifier: "Against the Abe government! Against war!"

If he was against Abe, I asked the old man, then who did he prefer? Where were the wise and responsible leaders? Who should be leading Japan?

His face displayed puzzlement, then surprise, and finally em-barrassment. The protesters standing around us glanced silently at one another. A few smiled sheepishly; one man giggled. I suggested the name of Naoto Kan's successor, the feebly un-charismatic leader of the disgraced centrist party, now in opposi-tion; and people shook their heads in disgust. There must be someone, I said. But no other names were offered. I was standing among some of the most politically motivated people in Japan. Shinzo Abe was a hate figure to them, almost a bogeyman. But they could propose not a single person to take his place.

What accounts for this democratic deficit, this failure of the po-litical system to generate a dynamic politics? It is one of the mys-teries of modern Japan.

Technically, nothing is missing; all the moving parts are there. Japan has an unambiguous written constitution, an inde-pendent judiciary, and a free press. There are multiple political parties; elections are uncontaminated by coercion or corruption. And yet there is a stagnancy and lack of conviction to Japan's political life. In North America and Europe, there is no lack of odious and incompetent leaders; but there is a sense of creative friction and of evolution, of a political marketplace in which ideas and individuals less popular and effective yield, over time, to those that prove themselves fitter for purpose, and where politics—even if it has its wrong turns and dead ends—is at least in constant motion. In Japan, this is not the case; even seventy years after the war, a genuinely competitive multiparty system has still not established itself.

After the tsunami had destroyed their homes, the survivors of the wave mobilized and organized, and took control of their fate. They did this instinctively, because it appeared to them the

natural and moral thing to do. They also did so because they didn't expect official help. In any comparable disaster in the West, its victims would quickly and shrilly have been demanding to know: Where is the government? In Japan in 2011, that was a question that was rarely heard.

At the time, such low expectations were an asset, a spur to resilience and self-reliance. But low expectations are corrosive to a democratic system. It is not universally true—there are in Japan many people who are deeply and conscientiously engaged. But it is common in discussing parliamentary politics to encounter indifference, disgust, and, above all, a paralyzing resignation. Our leaders are terrible, people seem to be saying—but what can *we* do about it? It is as if politics itself is a natural disaster of which the Japanese are the helpless victims, an impersonal misfortune beyond the influence of common men, and which can only be helplessly accepted, and endured.

One-tenth of the world's active volcanoes are in Japan—the entire archipelago, in fact, consists of an immense range of volcanoes jutting out of the sea. Late every summer, typhoons churn into motion in the northwest Pacific and spend themselves on its long coast. The rain they deposit loosens the soil, which slides down the steep mountainsides in rivers of mud. In geological terms, Japan is in an appalling situation, on top of not one, but two so-called triple junctions—points at which three of the Earth's tectonic plates collide and grate against one another. Fire, wind, flood, landslide, earthquake, and tsunami: it is a country of intense, elemental violence. Harsh natural environments often breed qualities that take on the status of national characteristics—the dark fatalism of Russians, the pioneer toughness of frontier Americans. Japanese identify in themselves

the virtue of *nintai* or *gaman*, variously rendered as endurance, patience, or perseverance. Foreign journalists covering the disaster liked to refer to the "stoicism" of the survivors, but Japanese *gaman* is not a philosophical concept. The conventional translations fail to convey the passivity and abnegation that the idea contains, the extent to which *gaman* often seems indistinguishable from a collective lack of self-esteem. *Gaman* was the force that united the reeling refugees in the early days after the disaster; but it was also what neutered politics, and permitted the Japanese to feel that they had no individual power over and no responsibility for their national plight.

I happened to visit Okawa during the election campaign that brought Shinzo Abe to power. Nobody I met displayed any curiosity about the election, or even an awareness that it was taking place; it was as though it was occurring in a separate dimension, parallel with but invisible to the one through which ordinary human beings moved.

Posters along the road bore the slogans of the competing parties and photographs of their candidates. Vans mounted with loudspeakers drove through the villages, blaring out their names. It was impossible not to think of Mr. Oikawa and the men from the town office, driving along these same roads with similar equipment, broadcasting their message about the coming of the tsunami, which was similarly ignored.

"I'm not saying that they should have been rioting, and *gaman* or *nintai*—these qualities clearly had a positive role on the immediate aftermath," said Norio Akasaka, an academic specialist in the culture of Tohoku. "But people had all kinds of demands and complaints and dissatisfaction. They should have spoken out—against the national government, against the nuclear-plant operator. Their complaints were not made. They kept those things

within themselves, through endurance, through patience. And that was a bad thing."

Sometimes in Japan I wondered if it didn't come down to a simple proposition: Would you tolerate a certain amount of whining and squabbling and disorder, even a bit of looting and profiteering, if such selfishness was accompanied by a willingness on the part of ordinary people to fight a bit, to shout down authority, and to take responsibility for the people they elected?

There was another set of slogans that were ubiquitous at that time, employing a different Japanese word. *Ganbarō* is an exhortation to overcome challenges and hardships: the simplest English translations would be "persevere," "stick at it," or "do your best." *Ganbarō* is what you say to a child studying for exams, or to an athlete competing in a tournament. Banners reading *Ganbarō Tohoku!* were often to be seen in stations and public buildings. They were intended as declarations of solidarity by those—the great majority in Japan—who were personally unaffected by the disaster. But as an expression of sympathy, let alone condolence, it was a curious expression.

Was it really a source of consolation to people newly homeless and bereaved to be told, in effect, to tough it out, like a marathon runner? *Ganbarō* always seemed to me a word in which empathy with those suffering was compromised by the implication that what they were going through would be good for them in the long run.

Tohoku people were famous for their *gaman*. It was what had fortified them over the centuries against cold, poverty, and unreliable harvests. It was also, I suspected, what had made them susceptible to their historical role as Japan's exploited—inured to

selling off their daughters and sending off their sons as cannon fodder in the empire's wars. People spoke nostalgically of Tohoku as a repository of "the old Japan," by which they meant a slower, gentler, rural way of life, a "village society" unsullied by urban ugliness and the viruses of greed and commercialism. But this outward simplicity masked a deep conservatism, a repression so deeply internalized that it was experienced by its victims as common sense. The people of the old Japan shut up and got on with it—and shutting up was the crucial element. They worried deeply about what other people would think if they stood up and argued. They rejected change, and efforts at change—the idealized village was a world in which conflict, and even disharmony, were immoral, a kind of violence.

It was a hidden world, of which I only ever caught glimpses. By definition, those whose mouths have been stopped by social convention do not talk about it to an outsider. I encountered it through the stories of those who did speak out, such as Naomi Hiratsuka, whose father-in-law regarded grief as an expression of weakness; and in the accounts of the old men of Kamaya who refused to believe in the possibility of a tsunami. Most eloquent of all was Masahiko Chiba, the car mechanic into whose house Junji Endo, and dozens of other refugees, had staggered on the afternoon of the disaster.

Over the next three days, more than a hundred strangers fetched up at the Chibas' two-story house, to be fed, clothed, and sheltered. They included local people, passing motorists, local government officials, and young Tetsuya Tadano and the handful of other children who survived from Okawa Elementary School. The Chibas used up their stores of food, and gave away all their own clothes and those of their children and grandchildren. Afterward, many of those whom they had helped, including the Okawa children, returned to express their gratitude to Chiba

and his wife. Junji Endo was not one of them; nor were any of the local bureaucrats. And after he spoke publicly about the discrepancies in Endo's story, Chiba told me, he began to become aware of an invisible force of disapproval and reproach.

It came as no surprise. "In the village society, if you speak out, you will be ostracized," he said. "There's a common assumption that if you talk too much or do anything controversial, the authorities won't help you. They won't repair the road by your house. They won't give the benefit of official services. That's what people assume. We were lucky—our home and our business survived, and we didn't need their help. But plenty of people around here lost their families, their homes, their possessions. People like that are not going to speak out, or criticize the local government."

It was vanishingly subtle. No one said anything explicitly angry or reproachful—it was the Chibas' friends who cautioned them, for their own good, to remain silent. But the fact was that out of eleven car-repair businesses operating in the local area, only two, including theirs, survived the tsunami. And as the months wore on, Chiba saw official business from the local government offices and their employees consistently going to his rival.

"The children were murdered by an invisible monster," Sayomi Shito said once. "We vent our anger on it, but it doesn't react. It's like a black shadow. It has no human warmth." She went on, "The tsunami was a visible monster. But the invisible monster will last forever."

I asked, "What is the invisible monster?"

"I wonder myself what it is," said Sayomi. "Something peculiar in the Japanese, who attach importance only to the surface of things. And in the pride of people who cannot ever say sorry."

I was sitting with Sayomi and Takahiro in the Shito family's big wooden house. It was late at night; we had been sitting there since dusk. I had asked all the questions in my notebook. Now the conversation had taken on a different quality—meandering, flickering between the particular and the general, between anger and sadness; marked by shifts, jumps, silences.

Sayomi's family had lived in this village, Fukuji, for five hundred years. One of her ancestors had been a samurai who had traveled to the far northeast from distant Kyoto, Japan's most magnificent and snobbish city. As a teenager, Sayomi had come to loathe the pressure of being a member of a grand old family and to long for escape and independence. But her two older sisters quickly found husbands and left home, and there were no brothers. So when Sayomi married Takahiro, he was legally adopted by her parents as their son, a common practice among families without a male child. Thus Sayomi was pulled back to the center of the family against which she had rebelled, and became the inheritor and custodian of the line of descent.

The banks of the Kitakami were remote from the sophistication of the city, but Sayomi's forebears took a rich harvest from the sea, the river, the lagoon, the fields, and the forests. The hills cut the villages off from one another, but the water connected them. There was a sense even now of the water being older than the land, and of having a claim on it which had been only reluctantly surrendered. It was hinted at in the names of places miles inland, with no obvious connection to the sea. The land on which Okawa Elementary School had been constructed was called Nirajima—"Chive Island"; close to Fukuji was Shioden: "Salt Field." As a child, Sayomi had dug up ancient shells from paddies that had once been under the ocean. The only sites of antiquity were stone monuments and Shinto shrines; and these, almost always, were positioned upon high ground.

"Those rice fields were the sea once," Sayomi said. "Now they are the sea again. That's the thing about water—water always tells the truth. There's no argument to be had. Water goes freely where it must."

Takahiro said, "Everything made by men will be destroyed by nature in the end. Mountains and river, the creations of nature—they will remain. Everything human, that will go. We need to reconsider the respect we give to nature."

In the months and years afterward, Takahiro received invitations to give talks around the country to groups interested in the tragedy of Okawa. He accepted out of a sense of duty; he assumed that he would encounter people alert to the human component of disaster, anxious to learn how they themselves could reduce the chances of falling victim to similar catastrophe. "But I was shocked," he said, "by how low their level of awareness was." Takahiro's audiences expressed sympathy and polite horror at what had happened, but it was as if they viewed it through the wrong end of a telescope, as something small, curious, and remote from their own lives. "For them, it was someone else's problem," he said. "They didn't recognize it as the kind of thing that could happen again in the future, even happen to them. Perhaps it's the same with nuclear power. Everyone played down the dangers for all those years, and the result was this sudden, terrible situation. In Okawa school, too, the teachers played everything down, took nothing seriously."

Takahiro was a strong, healthy man in his forties. He spoke calmly; nothing in his tone suggested that he was in the grip of powerful emotions. But, as he continued, I could see that his hand was trembling.

He said, "If they don't take this opportunity, even now when so many people have died, you can't ever expect them to change the way they think or act. That's why we are pursuing the real

cause of the tragedy. If they consider this disaster but refuse to look into its core, the same tragedy could be repeated. But that's how Japan functions, which the national government can do nothing to change."

In this, and in many of the conversations I had in Okawa, it wasn't completely clear to me who "they" were. I was about to ask when Takahiro said: "As a citizen of this country, I'm ashamed of that. I think it's embarrassing. But it's something that I have to say. By telling this story, even though I am ashamed of it, perhaps we can change the situation."

The Shitos were victims; but the shame was theirs too. "They" meant "us," meant everyone. The tsunami was not the problem. Japan was the problem.

"I tell them that the tsunami is not just water," Takahiro said, in a rush. "The tsunami is a lethal weapon that can kill you in an instant. Don't think of it as water. The first thing the tsunami hit was the forest that blocked the wind from the sea. The trees are swept away, and it is those trees that break the houses, and then the rubble of the houses that hits the people. And then everything is gone. Trees, houses, rubble, people—everything. That's how the tsunami attacks. It's not water."

PREDESTINATION

Secretly, Naomi Hiratsuka sometimes used to wonder how long she could continue searching for the lost children. But she never asked herself why she did so.

After the remains of her daughter, Koharu, were recovered in August 2011, there were four who still remained missing. Yui Takeyama, who was seven years old, had died at the school alongside his sister and his mother. His surviving father, overwhelmed by grief and tied down by a full-time job, took no part in the extended search. Yuto Suzuki, a twelve-year-old boy, had been off sick and was at home in the care of his family when the wave struck—so it was arguable whether he counted as one of the victims of the tragedy at the school. Masaru Naganuma, the father of seven-year-old Koto, was the most indefatigable of all the searchers, going out alone every hour he could, in digger and boat, looking for his son in ocean, in lagoon, and in the earth. But the parent to whom Naomi became the closest was Miho, the mother of the only girl still missing, nine-year-old Hana Suzuki.

Miho had lived with her son and daughter by the Nagatsuura

lagoon, one of the communities to have been completely swept away by the tsunami. She and her husband, Yoshiaki, had both been at work inland on that afternoon. Miho's elderly parents-in-law had died in the home they all shared. Both her children died at the school; the body of her son, the older of the two, had been found after eight days. Miho and Naomi spent months together looking for Hana and Koharu; they acquired, after a time, something of the intimate ease of sisters. Naomi, the younger, was focused and determined, the well-organized teacher adept at dealing with paperwork and officialdom, who got her heavy-vehicle license and trundled her own digger out in the mud. Miho, older, gentler, and less assertive, was the one who waited supportively on the margin with towels and refreshments, ready, whenever needed, to wade out in long boots and pick through the objects turned up by the digger's claw. In 2012, police searching the lagoon had lifted out the body of an elderly couple in a submerged car; later that year, the head of a missing young woman had been recovered nearby. But, since the discovery of Koharu, no more children from Okawa school had been found. When Miho, with shaking hands, pulled bones out from the mud, they always turned out to be those of chickens and pigs.

Miho loved to draw. It was an enthusiasm that she had shared with Hana, who had spent hours creating cartoon faces in the distinctive style of Japanese *manga*, with big eyes and mouths, spangled with stars and teardrops and rainbows. One of the mediums whom Miho consulted had reported to her the consoling news that, even in the afterlife, Hana was still busily making pictures.

The shrine in front of the school was decorated with three letters, written and colored in felt-tip pen and illustrated with *manga* faces. They had been drawn and written by Miho and were addressed to her daughter. The first was faded by sun, and spattered by rain and mud. "Dear Hana," it began:

Mum and Dad moved to Grandpa's place. There are so many things there that your big brother and you used to play with, so remembering the two of you, I cry all the time. I always used to say, "Don't cry!" to your big brother and you, but now your mum cries so easily at anything at all. I'm sorry . . .

Today, Grandma and I came here again wanting to see you, just to breathe the same air with you. Even that helps. But, always I want to hear your voice, see your smile. I want to be with you.

The second was less weathered and was written on a piece of paper cut into the shape of a heart:

Dear Hana,

I'm sorry that I can't find you. I come every day, wanting to see you. You must be around here. I'm so sorry that I can't find you, Hana. You don't appear in our dreams and Dad, Mum, Grandpa, and Grandma are sad. I'm sorry I can't do anything for you. I'm so sorry. If I could see you in my dreams, I would hug you tight.

The third letter, on the day I first saw it, was so crisp that it might have been left that morning:

Dearest, dearest Hana,

Did you like your funeral?* We made a display of ♪ and ◠ in flowers. I hope that you and your big brother were glad to see them. That was the only thing that Dad and Mum could do for you.

---

* Like other families who failed to recover the remains of their loved ones, the Suzukis nonetheless conducted a funeral ceremony for their daughter at a Buddhist temple.

I wanted to prepare many dresses for you on your wedding day, even a traditional long-sleeved kimono in black like a bride in the old days . . . But Mum and Dad's dream will just be a dream now.

If you can read this letter, do come back to Mum and Dad, Hana.

After losing her home and village, her children and her parents-in-law, Miho spent four years living in a metal "temporary residence" on the outskirts of Ishinomaki. No one in the community knew her or her husband, Yoshiaki; no one asked about their circumstances; and this was how they wanted it to be.

For one in Miho's situation, even the company of other bereaved mothers was difficult to bear. The only people from whom she did not feel isolated were Naomi and their common friend Akemi, both of whom had spent long weeks searching for their own daughters. "They were the only people I could talk to," she said. "Akemi's girl was found on the forty-ninth day, and Koharu was found long after that. So they understood how I felt. And they talked to me normally—they treated me like an ordinary person. With the other families, I was always aware of the way they were looking at me and thinking about me—that they saw me as the most tragic one of them all. And that just made me feel worse."

Miho was forty-three at the time of the tsunami; Yoshiaki was six years older. Neither had brothers or sisters; each was the sole inheritor of their family line. The prospect of having another child now seemed remote, and they were stricken by the sense, peculiar to the religion of the ancestors, of having been orphaned by their own children. There was the practical fear of growing old and sick with no one to care for them; and then there was spiritual anxiety about ongoing care and reverence after death,

in the absence of descendants to pray not only for them, but for their own parents, grandparents, and generations past. "When one of us dies, who will look after the other?" Miho asked. "Who will bury us? Our closest relatives are cousins, or even more distant than that. We feel such anxiety about the future. When I think about it, it suffocates me."

Miho gave up her job as a doctor's receptionist; the search for Hana became the center of her life. She was at the school every day, to help Naomi and Masaru in their diggers. She resolved that she would look for Hana for at least two years. In the foremost part of her mind, she harbored no illusions; as the months passed, she gave up hope of finding a body, even an incomplete one—bones, a single bone, even a fragment of flesh or a strand of hair would have been enough. But in her car, Miho always kept a full set of Hana's daughter's clothes in case—just in case—they should happen upon her miraculously biding in some overlooked spot, hidden and alive.

Towards the end of 2012, though, she stopped going to the school. After careful thought about the emotional, as well as the financial, costs, she and Yoshiaki made the decision to undergo fertility treatment at the big hospital in Ishinomaki. The doctor was the same man who had delivered Hana eleven years earlier and he was optimistic: Miho, he told her, was in good health, and although she was in her mid-forties, there was no physical reason why she could not conceive again. But she would no longer be able to stand in the mud every day; the task of making a new child made it harder to look for the lost one. And at about the same time came another piece of news: Naomi Hiratsuka, who had always promised that she would continue the search for the missing children, was giving up.

The practical difficulties of searching the mud were increasing every month. The chances of finding even fragmentary remains were dwindling. For all this, though, Naomi insisted that if it had been up to her, she would have gone on looking. The decision had not been made by her, and it had not been made by her husband or father-in-law. It was her dead daughter, Koharu, who decided.

Naomi had once again become close to Sumi, the medium who had proved so adept at relaying Koharu's voice from the other world. The two women met every few weeks, spoke often by phone, and exchanged text messages and e-mails. Through Sumi, Koharu would make requests for sweets and snacks placed as offerings on the *butsudan*, and urge her mother to pay greater attention to one or the other of her surviving siblings. Naomi was still on maternity leave from her job as a high-school teacher; the moment came when she had to choose whether to return to her job or abandon it. At the time that she was contemplating this important decision, Koharu made her feelings strongly felt.

"The medium told me that Koharu wanted me to go back to work," Naomi said. "She said that she had always wanted to be a teacher when she grew up. And so she wanted me to do what she could not. The medium told me, 'The way to use your talent is not just to stay in the house and search for the missing children, but to do something active outside the home.'"

And so, in April 2013, Naomi found herself back in the classroom, at the Kanan West Junior High School in Ishinomaki. It was two years since the disaster, and three years since she had last worked. And yet the jolt she experienced came not from the strain of teaching, but from the children she taught. "My class was a ninth-grade class," she said. "In other words, they were Koharu's class." Every time she looked up from her desk, Naomi

faced children exactly the same age that her daughter would have been, if she had survived beyond the age of twelve.

She confronted a question: how to address, within the world of the school, the fact of Koharu's death? Many people knew what had happened, of course, and those who didn't only had to search for Naomi's name on the Internet to bring up the interviews she had given over the years. She did not want to be defined by her loss, but she did not want to be evasive about it, either. Sometimes the subject came up indirectly—like the occasion when one of the girls asked Naomi how many children she had. Was the answer two, or three? Naomi wondered. Neither felt correct. "They were good children, and they trusted me," she said. "I didn't want them to pity me, but I didn't want them to think that I didn't trust them, either. I sensed that they wanted me to talk about it, but I couldn't. For one thing, I couldn't be sure that I wouldn't cry."

She left it until the very last week of the school year. She brought thirty-six copies of a book about Okawa Elementary School, published by a group of the bereaved mothers, and gave one to each of her students. And she told them the story of Koharu and what had happened to her. At the end, she invited questions. The class of fifteen-year-olds sat in stupefied silence. "But I wanted them to know," Naomi said. "I don't believe that stuff, which you sometimes hear, that the children who survived must 'live their lives for those who died.' There are a lot of people around here who have feelings of guilt for surviving. We don't want children growing up that way. I told them that you have to make a life for yourself. No one should ever need to feel that they are living their life for someone else."

—————

Work, and the care of two younger children, left Naomi with little energy for anything else. It was the very best thing for her peace of mind. "Teaching was a kind of therapy for me," she said. "Very honestly, the more I work, the less I think about Koharu. I persuade myself that is a good thing."

Koharu herself confirmed that it was—or this was the message relayed by Sumi. The more time she spent with the medium, the more Naomi appreciated, and depended upon, her soothing words, and her account of the existence into which her daughter had entered in the other world. Once, Naomi made plans for a winter holiday in Okinawa, the sunny resort island where she had gone to university. She was going to catch up with old college friends—and Sumi said that she would come along too. "She said that she'd always wanted to go to Okinawa," Naomi told me. "And she said that Koharu wanted her to go, to console the spirits of those who died in the war."* It might have seemed a surprising suggestion from a twelve-year-old girl, but this, the medium explained, was part of the progression of a human spirit on the other side. Immediately after the end of her human life, Koharu had retained much of her individual character—her lovable girlishness and sense of humor. But now she was evolving into what Japanese call *hotoke-sama*—an enlightened soul, purged of the dross of human personality, the terminal stage of the soul's pilgrimage into death. "The kind of things she tells me these days, through the medium, aren't always what you'd expect from a sixth-grader," Naomi told me. "They're not just personal matters, but more general. She's becoming more . . . authentic, somehow.

---

* A quarter of a million people died in the battle of Okinawa, the bloodiest of all the battles of the Pacific War.

She's coming closer to god, or to Buddha. She's not a little child anymore."

Sumi's explanation went even further than this. Far from being a tragedy, she told Naomi, Koharu's death, and all the events that had followed on from it, had been predestined. "It is difficult to explain, and it was difficult to understand," she said. "But my husband and I both came to think that things are decided in advance."

Death, the woman explained to Naomi, is preordained at birth. More than that, the individual soul selects the time and manner of its own death. In other words, Koharu—and, by implication, the legion of others who perished in the wave—had chosen to die that day. "According to the medium, it's destiny," Naomi told me. "She says that those who die as children are elevated to a higher stage than those who die in old age. And knowing that is a comfort to me."

Naomi, who survived the disaster with two living children and an intact family home, found her daughter, buried her, returned to her career, and made an accommodation with death. Miho, childless, middle-aged, isolated in her metal hut, was unable to do so. And at some point, difficult to define, the close friendship between the two women turned to sourness and mistrust.

Both were shy of talking about it, but it seemed to have been Miho who turned away. Every spring, as the March anniversary drew near, she became intensely depressed and withdrawn. At these times, Naomi kept a respectful distance. "After I started my job again, I was busy," Naomi said. "But we would speak from time to time—for a year, it all seemed normal. Then it started to become difficult to reach her. One day, I went around to where

she was living. I didn't call in advance, just turned up. I got the impression she didn't want me there at all."

Naomi puzzled over the reason for Miho's coldness. She did not believe that it was about the search for the missing children, from which Miho was also withdrawing. It was about the hunt for something more elusive, divisive, and dangerous—the truth of what had happened at the school.

In the beginning, Naomi and Miho's solidarity had been cemented by a common isolation, a shared sense of standing alone against the world. They despised the arrogant bureaucrats of the board of education; but they also had a shared contempt for the "Fukuji group," and what they saw as the aggressive self-righteousness of people such as Sayomi Shito. The search for the children had consumed all their reserves of emotional, as well as physical, energy. But when Miho stopped going to the school, in the tense hiatus of her fertility treatment, she found herself with leisure to think through matters that she had never closely considered before: the way, as she came to think of it, that teachers had permitted the deaths of her children.

"We couldn't find Hana," she said. "So we had to find the truth. We couldn't just leave this as one more of those things that no one is to be blamed for. I can't accept that. The more time passes, the more strongly I feel this."

Naomi was torn by the contradictions of her own situation. "Seventy-four of them perished," she said, "and no one was taking responsibility. And that feeling, that outrage—of course, we have that feeling too. Someone has to take responsibility for what happened." But the only people capable of doing so were the teachers at the school and members of the education board—the colleagues and direct superiors of Naomi and her husband.

Naomi's husband, Shinichiro, was a promising and ambitious teacher who had no intention of sacrificing his career by

taking on his bosses in a campaign to heap condemnation on his own dead colleagues. "For a while, I felt that I wanted to take legal action," Naomi said. "But my husband never agreed."

A lawyer from Sendai held an open meeting for bereaved parents who wanted to learn more about the possibilities for legal action. Miho attended, and was surprised to encounter Naomi there. The atmosphere between the two women was chilly. To Miho, her former friend's presence was "insincere." It was obvious that the Hiratsukas would never join in legal action against other teachers. She half suspected them of having come to spy on the proceedings, and to report back, although to whom it was not clear.

Later that year, Shinichiro Hiratsuka was promoted to deputy principal of a big school in Ishinomaki. Miho's fertility treatment failed; mental stress and anguish, her doctor speculated, were interfering with the production of the hormones necessary for the creation of a new life.

THE ROUGH, STEEP PATH

Miho and Yoshiaki Suzuki became leading figures in the legal action against the Ishinomaki city government, which had been launched so unexpectedly and at the last possible moment. It was striking, to anyone familiar with Western modes of litigation, that it had taken so long to get under way. If a comparable tragedy had happened in Europe or the United States—scores of children dead, piercing questions about the competence of the authorities— there would have been lawyers swarming over it from the beginning. But in Japan there was an instinctive aversion to taking legal action, and a sense that those who did so were themselves breaking some profound unwritten law.

It was seen, or felt to be seen, as a failure of *gaman*, a violation of the unwritten codes of the village society. There was an assumption that unpleasant consequences—social disapproval and exclusion, even victimization—were in store for those who sued, particularly those who took on the government. People became vague and tongue-tied when pressed over this; they struggled to come up with particular examples: the nagging sense of being talked about behind your back; an obscure guilt in the hearts of

people who knew they had done nothing wrong. And the discomfort of stepping outside the snug, warm, paralyzing web of compliance that Japan weaves around its people, a fuzzy, enveloping tangle in which constraint is inseparable from the sense of being protected, and where the machinery of coercion rarely has to be applied from outside, because it is internalized so efficiently within the mind.

It takes an unusual kind of personality to be deaf to those snickering interior voices. By comparison with the West, the damages awarded by Japanese courts were low—even if they won their case, the Okawa parents would be lucky to receive half of the ¥100 million they were demanding for the life of each child. Kazuhiro Yoshioka was the lawyer who represented the Okawa parents, and even he sympathized with the reluctance of ordinary people to resort to the courts.

"It's not the kind of abuse that is obvious or explicit," he said. "But people feel themselves, in quite an insidious way, to be reproached. If a relative works at the local authority, that relative may be ill spoken of. At school, sons and daughters might be referred to as the children of someone who went to court. Cutting remarks online. It's often hard to see it clearly or to pin it down, but such people end up feeling rejected by society. Often people prefer to stay under the warm futon and endure their anger and sorrow, rather than go to court."

Japan's civil-justice system, like its democracy, appeared on the face of it to be beyond reproach. Judges were independent; bribery and intimidation were almost unknown. But at its core the system expressed a bias in favor of the status quo and the private and public institutions that upheld it. Judges, Yoshioka told me, were derisively referred to as "flounders"—flatfish who dwelled on the ocean floor, with their eyes positioned on the top of their bodies, always anxiously looking upwards. There was no

explicit conspiracy to deliver verdicts one way or another, no direct orders from on high, just an understanding, as natural as the instinct of an animal, about how the world worked and where self-interest lay. "If someone brings a lawsuit against an institution, against a big company or a bank, or a local government," said Yoshioka, "in Japan the institution will almost always win."

It was eight months after the disaster when the first of the Okawa parents, Sayomi and Takahiro Shito, came to talk to him. He gave them two pieces of advice. The first was to muster as large a group of complainants as possible, to attract the attention of the media and establish an institutional presence of their own. The second was to bide their time, and to make use of the legal resource that their opponents in the city government were unwittingly providing for them—the infuriating "explanatory meetings." "Once you've filed a case," Yoshioka said, "no one connected with it will talk anymore—they'll just say that the matter is in the courts, and use that as an excuse to say nothing. Even if you summon them to court, you get each witness in the stand for no more than an hour or two. But those explanatory meetings went on for three or four hours each. And there were ten of them." Rather than rushing to sue, it was better to draw out the city officials while their guard was down, encourage the media to report it all, and quietly accumulate as much ammunition as possible.

The families who took up the case were housewives, joiners, builders, factory workers; none had expertise in forensic inquiry. "A lot of people would assume that these ordinary blokes out in the countryside wouldn't be capable of making a cross-examination, for example, and putting sharp questions," Yoshioka said. "Well, they'd be surprised. These are pretty smart people, quite capable of following a line of inquiry and pinning down the other side."

Yoshioka made no attempt to rehearse the families for the

meetings. "I intervened as little as possible," he said, "and sometimes it got quite rough. People lost their tempers—they shouted,
'Idiot!' and 'Return my child!' Those kinds of words serve no purpose in the legal sense. But the people facing them, hearing those
words of grief, seeing the parents of dead children exposing their
hearts—I was glad for them to talk like that, because it forced
those officials to respond.

"I also tried to think about what this case was really about.
Usually it's simple—if the lawyer wins, he's done his job. But these
families were fighting for their beloved children, the children
they had lost. Even if they did win, it wouldn't end their suffering. It's not about a victory. It's about finding out what happened
to their children in the last moment of their lives, and why."

In Japanese justice, nothing happens quickly; it was not until
April 2016 that witnesses appeared to give evidence in the case
against Ishinomaki City and Miyagi Prefecture, codefendants in
the case. In the two intervening years, there had been half a dozen
hearings at which lawyers for both sides debated matters of law
and narrowed down points of contention. The plaintiffs' claim
was that the city, in the person of the teachers at Okawa Elementary School, had been guilty of negligence—*kashitsu*, the word
that Kashiba, the principal, had resisted so tenaciously—in failing
to protect the children in its care. The case centered on two questions. Could the teachers have foreseen the coming of the tsunami? And, if so, could they have saved the children from it?

The city insisted that the answer to both these questions was
no. The school was two and a half miles from the coast; even the
mightiest tsunami in living memory—the one released by the
Chile earthquake in 1960—had done no harm this far inland.
The school building, and the village around it, obscured the

teachers' view of the ocean; the spectacle of the wave overwhelming the forest of pines at the sea's edge had been invisible to them.
As soon as Deputy Principal Ishizaka had become aware of the
water coming over the riverbank, he ordered the children to
flee—but by then, tragically, but unavoidably, it was too late.

Yoshioka countered these arguments. The school may have
been a good distance from the ocean, but the tsunami had come
over the riverbank, and that was only a hundred yards away. The
village of Kamaya was scarcely above sea level at all, and had
experienced conventional flooding from the Kitakami River
in the past. Ishizaka had had the choice of several paths of
evacuation—at least three different routes up the hill behind the
school, or via the waiting school bus—all of them to places higher
and safer than the spot he chose, the traffic island on the river's
edge. And there were multiple reasons for believing that not only
should the teachers have anticipated a tsunami, but that they
did in fact do so. "If we prove that they could have foreseen the
tsunami," Yoshioka told me, "then we can win this case."

The public gallery at the Sendai District Court was full on
April 8, 2016, when the former principal, Teruyuki Kashiba, gave
his evidence; so many members of the public lined up to get in
that the available seats had to be allocated by lottery. All the familiar faces were there. The Shitos, the Konnos, the Suzukis, and
Hideaki Tadano, the father of the young survivor Tetsuya, sat
behind their lawyers. There were bureaucrats from the board of
education, and local journalists who had been covering the story
from the beginning. But the courtroom possessed a quality of
tension and formality that the explanatory meetings never had.
It was imparted by the presence of the three dark-robed judges
who swept in, as everyone in the room rose to their feet; and by
the oath that Kashiba read aloud at the witness stand.

"I swear to tell the truth according to the dictates of my con-

science," said the principal, small and plump in his charcoal-gray suit, "without omission or addition."

Kashiba was first questioned by one of the city's lawyers, who walked him through the basics of the defense case. He talked about the school's emergency manual, which set out clearly the actions to be taken in case of fire or earthquake. The school had carried out regular drills to prepare for such eventualities, and their effectiveness had been demonstrated when the strong, but lesser, earthquake had shaken the area on March 9, 2011, two days before the catastrophe. Kashiba had been at school that day; the children had evacuated calmly and quickly; the teachers had confidently discharged their designated duties. Okawa Elementary School did not bother to hold tsunami drills, for a simple reason: no one had any reason to anticipate such an event. And, whatever the plaintiffs asserted, the paths up the hill were completely unrealistic as a route of evacuation. Kashiba had climbed them himself and found them steep, treacherous, and overgrown with brush or bamboo.

But here lay the flaw in the defense case. If the tsunami had truly been unimaginable, something that had not even crossed the minds of the teachers at the school, then why give any thought at all to the need to escape from one, any more than from an asteroid impact or zombie apocalypse?

Yoshioka's cross-examination of Kashiba lingered on this contradiction. He pressed the principal for details about the precursor earthquake on March 9. A tsunami warning had been issued that day too, but for a wave of no more than twenty inches— scarcely noticeable to a casual observer, and incapable of causing damage. Nonetheless, as the children waited in the playground, Junji Endo, third in the school hierarchy, had conscientiously gone down to the river to scan its waters and confirm that nothing was amiss.

Kashiba was asked about an exchange that he'd had that day with Endo and Ishizaka, his deputy. Details of this conversation had been let slip by the principal himself; it was one of the choicest of the revelations that came out of the "explanatory meetings." After the children had returned safely to their classrooms, the three men had talked for several minutes about the evacuation, and the lessons to be learned from it. "We discussed what we should do if a tsunami reached Okawa Elementary School," Kashiba told the court. "In such circumstances, could we escape by climbing up behind the bamboo grove? As it's rough and steep, perhaps we couldn't. We didn't reach a conclusion."

He was shown a set of photographs that he had taken himself from the hill behind the school. It had been a blazing day of summer at the beginning of the long holiday. The photographs showed the red-roofed school set among the colorful jumbled roofs of the village, with the shining river and rice fields beyond. They had clearly been taken from a good way up the slope—a slope that, Kashiba insisted, was too dangerous for children to climb, even to save their lives.

"Take a look at these pictures," Yoshioka told the witness. "Photographs one and two were taken by you on the twenty-first of July 2009."

"I remember it," said Kashiba.

"How did you get up there?" Yoshioka asked him.

"I think that I climbed up behind the back of the little hut and through the bamboo grove."

"The route you walked—children could climb up there too, couldn't they?"

"I think that would be very dangerous."

"What was your physical condition when you took those pictures?"

The principal paused for a moment. "I weigh eleven stone," he said. "With a height of five foot one."

A moment passed in which this information registered with the court, along with the visual image of the short, pudgy man standing at the witness stand.

"At such a height and weight," asked the lawyer, "wouldn't it be easier for a child to climb than for you?"

The starkest evidence of all that the school had, in fact, anticipated the disaster was in the emergency manual itself.

Earlier versions of the document had adapted the basic template to strike out all references to tsunamis, on the basis that they were irrelevant to Okawa school. But beginning in 2007, these had been restored. The teacher who carried out the task was the deputy principal, Toshiya Ishizaka.

The section labeled "On the occurrence of an earthquake" was renamed "On the occurrence of an earthquake (tsunami)." In a list of actions to be taken, the instruction "collect information" became "collect information (also tsunami-related)." And Ishizaka had added a new directive among the list of tasks to be ticked off by teachers during an earthquake evacuation: "confirm the occurrence of a tsunami, and lead the school to the place of secondary evacuation." The place of secondary evacuation was added, but with wording unchanged from the template: "in case of tsunami: vacant land near school, or park, etc."

Kashiba's obvious discomfort in the witness stand reached its peak in the discussion of the emergency manual. At first he found himself unable to recall why the revisions had been undertaken at all. Yoshioka reminded him: the education board had summoned a meeting of principals at which they had been instructed to review their procedures. The logic of the changes seemed

221

inescapable. The manual had formerly made no mention of tsunamis. It had been changed to make provision for a tsunami. Why? Because there was a danger of tsunamis. With every question, Yoshioka seemed to tighten his grip on Kashiba; with every answer, he wriggled in the lawyer's grasp. At one moment, Yoshioka furiously reminded him of the risk of perjury.

"What prompted these revisions?" the lawyer asked.

"Deputy Principal Ishizaka added them," Kashiba said, "so I don't know."

"During the time you were in charge at the school, three additions to the manual were made."

"Perhaps, I think, awareness about tsunamis was gradually increasing."

"So you came back from the principals' meeting and told Mr. Ishizaka what to do."

"I just never expected a tsunami to reach the school at all," said Kashiba. "So I thought it would be fine if we just put the word in."

"But if you thought a tsunami would never come, why did you bother to put any word in at all?"

"We were told to put in the word 'tsunami,' so we did."

"But why did you support putting it in?"

"I thought . . . it would be fine."

The atmosphere in the courtroom was strained and grave. At various points there was stifled weeping from the seats where the families sat. But on hearing from the principal that their children had been protected from a tsunami by nothing stronger than words, the parents broke into bitter and incredulous laughter.

THERE MAY BE GAPS IN MEMORY

Sometimes Tetsuya Tadano wanted to be a policeman when he grew up, and sometimes he wanted to be a firefighter. He loved judo and swimming, but his mum often had to nag him to do his homework. In other words, he was a conventional, playful eleven-year-old boy. But of all the people I met, it was Tetsuya who had the greatest love and fascination for Okawa Elementary School, an enthusiasm close to passion.

Everyone else emphasized the school's ordinariness and normality, as if this absence of qualities enlarged the grossness of the tragedy. But in Tetsuya's eyes, it was a wondrous place, not so much for its pupils and teachers, whom he loved and respected, as for its physical eccentricities. Most Japanese schools are flat-roofed cubes, which vary only in their size. Okawa Elementary School was the work of an architect of ambition and imagination. The main building was constructed not as an angular block, but on a curving perpendicular; from it projected a secondary wing, which spread into a twelve-sided pavilion. Tetsuya talked about the inner courtyard where the children rode

their unicycles,* and the pond where they threw insects for the bloated ornamental carp. Planted along the front of the school were cherry trees, which every April put out a foam of pink blossoms. On one outer wall, the pupils had painted pictures of the children of the world in the national dress of their respective countries. Tetsuya described the view from the upper classrooms of the paddy fields and the river, and the play of the elements on the building's materials. "When the weather was fine," he said, "the roof was red. But when it rained, the color changed into this blend of purple and blue, a dark blue. And the whole building looked fantastic."

Before March 11, 2011, Tetsuya lived with his family in Yachinaka, the hamlet immediately behind Kamaya. His father, Hideaki, worked at the paper mill in Ishinomaki. He had fled from the tsunami to a hill in the center of the city. When the waters receded, he borrowed a bike and pedaled to the big inland sports center where the refugees from the Okawa area had gathered. There Hideaki learned the fate of the school and his village. But there, almost alone among the weeping parents, he found his own son, Tetsuya, scratched and battered, with a patch over his injured right eye—but alive.

Tadano was head of the local volunteer fire corps, which went into action at times of natural disaster as an auxiliary to the professional fire brigade. Fathers of children from the school were exempted from duty in Kamaya, on compassionate grounds, but he led his men anyway, lifting bodies out of the mud. His wife, Shiroe, was found five days after the disaster, his father after eight days, and his nine-year-old daughter, Mina, the day after that.

Father and son moved out of the sports center to the home of

---

* Unicycles, along with wooden stilts, are a feature of Japanese elementary schools: the idea is to promote good balance.

Hideaki's sister. Later they found a house of their own on the outskirts of Ishinomaki. They often went back to the site of where they had lived. All that was left of the family home—all that remained of any of the houses in Kamaya—was the outline of its concrete foundation. Even the doctor's clinic, the husk of which had outlasted the wave, had quickly been bulldozed. Only the school survived to show that there had ever been a village here at all—cracked, windowless, exposed in places to the elements, but still recognizable.

Upon its ruin, a remarkable feat had been performed. Early on, soldiers and recovery workers had removed the rubble of trees, cars, and broken houses that enmeshed the building, but the work had not ended there. The school's interior, and its contents, which had been churned and befouled by the inrushing water, had been tenderly sifted and restored, as if awaiting the return of children and teachers. The small desks with their iron legs had been lined up in rows. There were heaps of miscellaneous objects: a sewing machine, abacuses, a recorder, and a wall clock, its hands suspended at 3:37. Outside each classroom was a row of hooks still labeled with the names of the children whose coats had once hung there.

Tetsuya took comfort in his visits to the school. So much had changed, so suddenly, that his old life—and the lives of his mother, sister, grandfather, schoolmates—flickered in his mind sometimes, with the insubstantiality of a dream. The presence of the school assured him that he, and they, had lived. Memory lived on in its walls and spaces. During one of his wanderings through the deserted classrooms, Tetsuya uncovered a dictionary bearing the name of his little sister, Mina, written in her own childish handwriting.

Then one day his father told him that the city government would soon reach a decision about the future of the surviving

buildings. The consensus was that the remaining structures should be demolished, the site leveled, and all traces of Okawa Elementary School removed from the earth.

All along the northeast coast, those who had survived the tsunami were considering how to deal with what it left behind. Not the mundane mess of broken houses and commercial buildings, which was steadily being heaped and cleared, but the symbolic ruins: those sites of particularly acute or vivid tragedy, as well as the jarring juxtapositions thrown up by the wave's force. There was the Disaster Prevention Center in Minami-Sanriku, where a young woman named Miki Endo famously remained at her post, dutifully broadcasting evacuation warnings, even as she, and forty-two of her colleagues, were swallowed up. There was the *No. 18 Kyotoku-maru*, a 200-foot fishing boat, which was deposited in a residential street in the port of Kesennuma; and the *Hamayuri*, a 190-ton catamaran that came to rest on the roof of a hotel in Otsuchi. And then there was the "miracle pine" of Rikuzen-Takata, the single lonely survivor of a coastal forest of seventy thousand trees, and the object of intense efforts to keep it alive. There was a precedent in Japan for preserving ruins associated with death and disaster: the Atomic Bomb Dome in the city of Hiroshima, a former public hall whose skeletal shell is a place of international pilgrimage and a world-famous symbol of the horrors of nuclear war.

Local campaigns were established to preserve these relics, but they were controversial and divisive. To some people, the tsunami ruins were emblems of survival and hope, and a necessary warning to future generations of the power of the sea. To many others, they were reminders of a horror they were struggling to forget. Some pointed out the value of such sites as tourist attrac-

tions, in towns that now had less than ever to draw visitors from outside; for others, that was exactly the reason why the ruins should be expunged. "A lot of people want to pray for the souls of the dead in a calm, peaceful, silent environment," Naomi Hiratsuka told me. "They don't want pitying eyes upon them. The bodies of some of the children were recovered from inside the school—that's the kind of place it is. You don't want buses parking there, and sightseers on package tours."

The arguments also turned on money, and on the irrationality, as some people saw it, of devoting resources to maintaining ruins at a time when many people still lacked permanent homes. But they also seemed to express opposing convictions about the best way of dealing with mental trauma: whether to face it, articulate it, and struggle to accept it—or to thrust it out of view.

As time passed, the supporters of preservation lost several of their battles. The hulks of the *Kyotoku-maru* and *Hamayuri* were hoisted away and scrapped. The surviving iron frame of the Minami-Sanriku Disaster Prevention Center was condemned to demolition. Salt in the soil slowly killed the roots of the miracle pine.* A survey of the families of children who died at Okawa school revealed that 60 percent of them wanted it to be razed. "If you remain silent, it will definitely go," Hideaki Tadano told Tetsuya. "If you want to speak out, the time to speak out is now."

Of the seventy-eight children who were caught up in the water, only four had come out alive. Three of them disappeared from view, anxiously protected from scrutiny by their families. Te-

---

* After it died, the authorities in Rikuzen-Takata spent ¥150 million (£1.2 million, or $1.9 million) on cutting the tree up, hollowing it out, and reassembling it with fake twigs and needles.

tsuya's father, Hideaki, used to see one of them from time to time; he was struck by an air of anguished repression about the boy, as if he had been instructed not to speak, or even to think, about the fact of his escape from death. Only Tetsuya chose to talk publicly about his experience. To journalists, he was a gift—a child of the tsunami, both a victim and a survivor, authentically boyish in manner, but lucid, articulate, and, on the face of it, remarkably undamaged by what he had seen. Okawa Elementary had been re-established in another school and Tetsuya attended it with the other survivors, most of them children who had been picked up by parents or grandparents in the fifty-one minutes between earthquake and wave. He spoke willingly about the experience of being caught in the tsunami and the unanswered questions about what had happened and why. His father was vigilantly alert to his son's mental state, but encouraged these engagements. There was no systematic provision of mental-health care for the children of Okawa Elementary School: for Hideaki, Tetsuya's conversations with sympathetic reporters amounted to a kind of therapy. "And it was all easier," Hideaki told me, "with other people around. There was a restaurant where we all used to go as a family, and to go there with a TV producer, all talking about what they were going to film, was fun. To go there alone, just Tetsuya and me— that was too sad, because of all that we remembered."

Hideaki was aware of an atmosphere of unvoiced disapproval from the community of the bereaved, and he understood it very well. "I am the father of a survivor," he said, "but I am also the father of a child who died at the school. Plenty of people—the kind of people who have lost two or three children—they don't want to turn on the television and see the faces of the children who survived." But no one, surely, had a greater right to express his opinion than Tetsuya?

He began talking to journalists about the fate of the school

buildings, and his belief that they should be saved. He made a speech on the subject at a public event in Sendai. With his father, he took the bullet train to Tokyo to give talks at two famous universities. A handful of other young people began speaking up in support of Tetsuya—former pupils at the school whose younger siblings had died there, including the surviving daughters of Katsura Sato and Sayomi Shito, and Amane Ukitsu, the sixth-grade girl whose mother had picked her up just in time. The group of six children began to meet every week to discuss tactics and muster their resolve. "The Atomic Bomb Dome in Hiroshima was preserved because people took action," Amane said. "Nothing changes until somebody stands up."

Early in 2014, Tetsuya spoke at a symposium at Meiji University in Tokyo. It was a solemn and intimidating occasion, the biggest gathering he had ever addressed. "I lost my mother and sister in the tsunami," he told the audience, a strong, increasingly tall boy, but still with the tender skin of a child. "And my grandfather, who used to look after me. The grief did not come immediately, but now, at last, I feel the sadness and the pain."

He talked about the word *gareki*, meaning "rubble" or "debris," and used to refer to the detritus of the tsunami. To most people, it was a neutral, colorless term, unthinkingly employed; but for Tetsuya, it hurt to hear it. "Our possessions," he said, "are now called *gareki*. Until the disaster, they were part of our life. Now, they contain our memories. I don't like to hear all those things referred to as 'rubble.'" And now the school, where he had been so happy, and where his friends and sister had died, was also to be treated as *gareki*. "If the school is demolished, people in the future will not know what happened here," he said. "I don't want the building to be destroyed."

It was a matter of concern to his father that even in the early days after the tsunami, Tetsuya rarely wept or showed signs of

being overcome by emotion. But after delivering these words to the university audience, he began to slump in his seat; Hideaki had to lead him off the podium to a quiet room. Asked what was wrong, he laid his head on the table. "I started thinking about how everyone died, and how they must have felt," he said. "Thinking about that, I felt very heavy."

The final decision about the school lay with the mayor of Ishinomaki. In February 2016, he called a public meeting to debate the question of the school's future. At this, Tetsuya did not appear in person, but he recorded a video message, pleading for the school to be preserved. Naomi Hiratsuka's husband, Shinichiro, was one of those who argued passionately for it to be demolished. A wrenching and unbridgeable gulf separated the opposing sides; whatever the decision, the result would be pain. To some, the ruin of the school represented the destruction of their beloved children; to others, it was their last surviving trace.

The following month, the mayor made his decision. The school would be preserved, and a memorial park built around it. But a thicket of trees would be planted so that those who chose to could pass by without ever looking the ruin in the face.

Two weeks after the testimony of Kashiba, the former principal, a second hearing was held at which further witnesses were sworn in and examined. To spare them the ordeal of a court appearance, Yoshioka, lawyer for the families, decided not to call as witnesses any of the surviving children. But Miwae Ukitsu, the mother of the sixth-grade girl, Amane, did give evidence. She had been off work and at home on the day of the earthquake; she recounted how she had immediately driven the two miles to the school after hearing the tsunami warning on the radio. She went straight to her daughter's teacher, Takashi Sasaki, who was

standing in the playground with his class. "I told him, 'On the car radio, I heard that the height of the tsunami is getting higher, so please run up the hill quickly,'" she said. "I took his left arm, and I pointed at the hill with my right arm, and I said, 'There's a tsunami coming, run up the hill. Twenty feet high, they said.' I was upset, I was shouting loudly. He was completely unconcerned—he told me to calm down. He patted my right shoulder, and said, 'Calm down, ma'am.'"

Mr. Sasaki asked Mrs. Ukitsu to take Amane home. The girl was weeping uncontrollably and it was upsetting the other children. Her mother was struck by this, for Amane was not a tearful or touchy child. As Amane explained later, she had heard her two classmates, Yuki Sato and Daisuke Konno, arguing with the teacher.

Sir, let's go up the hill.

We should climb the hill, sir.

If we stay here, the ground might split open and swallow us up. We'll die if we stay here!

And she was thinking of a dream she had had a few days before, of all of her friends caught up in a churning, chaotic swirl. Remembering the nightmare, she became uncontrollably afraid.

The nineteen families who went to court did so for different reasons, and with varying degrees of alacrity and hesitation. For some, the prospect of a financial payout, after years of grief and hardship, was like rain after drought. For others, the idea of placing a value on the lives of their dead children was unbearably distasteful. But everyone I met agreed on one thing: the most important thing was not the money, but the prospect of uncovering the truth about what had happened at the school. These

declarations began to puzzle me after a while—for the families, after years of investigation, knew a great deal already.

The speedy evacuation from the school buildings, the long sojourn in the playground; Sasaki's offhand confidence, Ishizaka's indecisiveness; and then the panicked flight into the mouth of the tsunami—all of this has been established in documents and eyewitness accounts. The board of education might slither and swerve around the question of responsibility, but it was clear what had taken place and who had failed. What further "truth" remained to be uncovered? When I put this question to Sayomi Shito, she answered with a single word: "Endo."

After his single appearance at the first of the explanatory meetings, Junji Endo had gone to ground. With him, in the eyes of many of the parents, the truth had also vanished from view. This was the point of going to court—to force Endo out of hiding and compel him to come to the witness stand, where he would finally give voice to the evasive truth. "It's very simple," said Yoshioka. "There is one living adult witness who was present at the school. The families want to know in his own words exactly what happened to their children in those last moments, how they were washed away by the tsunami, how they died."

Endo continued to insist that he was psychologically unfit to appear in court. The judges, if they chose, had the power to order his appearance, and Yoshioka requested that they do this. In the meantime, he attempted to manage the expectations of his clients. To win their case, he pointed out, they had to show that the teachers could have foreseen a tsunami—Endo might be useful in achieving this, but there were other routes to proving the same thing. Even if he did appear as a witness, it was likely that, having been coached by the city's lawyers, his evidence would be vague and misleading. The parents nodded their understanding, but

the lawyer knew how much was invested in the hope of seeing and hearing this one man.

What exactly was it, I asked Sayomi Shito, that she expected to learn from Endo that she didn't already know, or couldn't guess?

"Everything that happened then."

"Such as what?"

"What kind of sky it was," she said. "How the wind was blowing. What kind of atmosphere there was. What the mood was among the children. Did the teachers seriously try to save their lives? Did the children feel cold? Did they want to go home? How was my child? Who was the last person to talk to her? Who was beside her when she ran away? Was she holding hands with anyone? Even knowing all of this, none of it will bring Chisato back. But everything that happened then—that is what I want to know."

The last hearing of the Sendai District Court was on April 21, 2016. Afterward, the lawyers made their final written submissions. The document prepared by the city of Ishinomaki was twenty-three pages long; lawyers for the second defendant, the government of Miyagi Prefecture, presented just nine pages. Yoshioka submitted a four-hundred-page book, dense with diagrams, graphs, statistics, and legal argument. He was a calm, poised man, but afterward he seemed to be as close as such a personality could ever get to jubilation. "I was talking about it with my colleague, and we can't think of a single reason why we might lose," he told me. "Not one—and that's a rare thing." From first filing to last submission, the case had taken two years and three months. By the standards of Japanese justice, Yoshioka said, that was "extremely quick."

But the chief judge ruled against calling Junji Endo as a witness.

He was not obliged to set out his reasons, but Yoshioka took it to be a good sign. The plaintiffs, it implied, had successfully argued their case by other means. The judges did not need another witness to persuade them; and they would, in any case, have been reluctant to impose upon a man diagnosed with mental illness.

"As long as he's alive, I believe that he will cross our lives again at some point," said Sayomi. "It may not be in court. But we will have a chance to meet him, and listen to what he has to say. It's not just Endo whose life has gone to pieces. He's not the only one suffering mentally. I don't just mean that our lives have changed. I mean inside our heads. Since that day, everyone has something wrong with them."

PART V

GONE ALTOGETHER

BEYOND

CONSOLATION OF THE SPIRITS

The Reverend Taio Kaneta, priest and exorcist, described to me the night after the tsunami, a moment remembered with intense clarity by people all over northern Japan. His inland temple had been untouched by the water, but the earthquake had knocked out power and light across Tohoku. For the first time in a century of human development, the land was in a state of historic, virgin darkness. No illuminated windows blazed upwards to obscure the patterning of the night sky; without traffic lights, drivers stayed off the unlit streets. The stars in their constellations and the blue river of the Milky Way were vivid in a way that few inhabitants of the developed world ever see. "Before nightfall, snow fell," Kaneta said. "All the dust of modern life was washed by it to the ground. It was sheer darkness. And it was intensely silent, because there were no cars. It was the true night sky that we hardly ever see, the sky filled with stars. Everyone who saw it talks about that sky."

Kaneta was personally safe, and isolated by the power failure from a full understanding of what had happened. But he recognized that the world had changed. He had learned enough about

the unprecedented magnitude and submarine epicenter of the earthquake to know that a tsunami must have followed. The closest stretch of coast to his temple was Shizugawa Bay, thirty miles away. His mind was filled with an image of the waters of the bay, awash with bodies. "A magnitude 9.2 earthquake," he said. "When something that powerful occurs, the Earth moves on its axis. So many people, all over Tohoku, were looking up at the sky on that night, filled with intense feelings. And looking at the stars, I became aware of the universe, the infinite space all around and above us. I felt as if I was looking into the universe, and I was conscious of the earthquake as something that had taken place within that vast expanse of empty space. And I began to understand that this was all part of a whole. Something enormous had happened. But whatever it was, it was entirely natural; it had happened as one of the mechanisms of the universe.

"It's engraved in my mind: the pitiless snow, and the beautiful shining, starry sky, and all those countless dead bodies drifting onto the beach. Perhaps this sounds pretentious, but I realized that when I began my work, giving support to people whose lives had been destroyed, I had to attend to the hearts of human beings and their suffering and anguish. But I also had to understand those sorrows from the cosmic perspective."

He experienced at that time a sensation of dissolution, of boundaries disappearing. It was the enactment of a Buddhist concept: *jita funi*, literally "self and other: undivided"—the unity of being apprehended in different times and places by mystics of all religions. "The universe wraps everything up inside it, in the end," Kaneta said. "Life, death, grief, anger, sorrow, joy. There was no boundary, then, between the living and the dead. There was no boundary between the selves of the living. The thoughts and feelings of everyone who was there at that moment melted into one. That was the understanding I achieved at that time, and it was

what made compassion possible, and love, in something like the Christian sense."

It was a unique, unrecoverable moment. A catastrophe had occurred. But because it was so new, was still unfolding in fact, no one could reckon its breadth and its height. In the Kitakami River, Teruo Konno was clinging to his raft. The mothers of Okawa Elementary School were listening to the reassuring broadcast on the radio, confident that they would see their children the next day. Standing beneath the stars, Kaneta glimpsed the scale and horror of what had happened, but he did so imaginatively, and in his imagination the disaster took on the lineaments of a profound spiritual truth. It would be a long time before he possessed such clarity again.

Of all the people I encountered in Tohoku, none made a stronger impression than Taio Kaneta. It was not his Buddhism that interested me the most—the fact of his being a priest often seemed incidental to who he was, no more than an interesting detail of personality. He was a natural teller of stories, a man of learning and intellectual honesty, and of rich empathy. And he had that gift of imagination that I had been seeking for myself—the paradoxical capacity to feel the tragedy on the surface of the skin, in all its cruelty and dread, but also to understand it, to observe from a position of detachment, with calm and penetration. Kaneta did not jump back from the disaster, as I always did—back on the bullet train, back to Tokyo, back to my desk on the tenth floor. He was immersed in the necessity of dealing with the corpses of the dead, although he had lost none of his own loved ones. He allowed the catastrophe to change his life, but he did not become its victim. He was strong enough to admit doubt, and confusion, and his own physical and mental weakness. It was these qualities

that enabled him to console the living, and to communicate with and command the dead. But there was a mental cost for those who straddled the boundary between the two worlds. In Kaneta's case, it would almost break him.

When the funerals were done, and after the possessing spirits had been driven out of Ono, Kaneta turned to face what the tsunami had left behind and looked for ways of making himself useful. In Buddhism, the forty-ninth day after death marks the moment when the departed soul enters the afterlife. He gathered a group of fellow priests, Shinto and Buddhist, as well as a Protestant pastor, to perform a ritual march to the town of Shizugawa, a town almost completely obliterated.

They set out in the morning from a temple inland. The Shinto priests wore their extravagant black lacquered hats; the Buddhists were red-robed and shaven-headed; the pastor had his dog collar and silver cross. The landscape through which they walked was broken and corrupt with decay. Bulldozers had cleared ways through the rubble, and piled it into looming mounds of concrete, metal, wood, and tile. The heaps had been incompletely searched; cadavers were folded inside them, unrecovered and invisible, but obvious to everyone who passed. "There were strange smells," said Kaneta, "of dead bodies and of mud. There was so much rubble, and mementos of people's lives still lying around on the ground. We had to take care where we stepped to avoid trampling on photographs."

The procession of vividly dressed men moved through the ruins, holding aloft a placard bearing characters meaning "Consolation for the Spirits." They walked for four hours. Machines were pawing at the rubble as they passed. Workers in hard hats picked at the debris and waved them gruffly away from the caterpillar tracks. The men of religion began to feel self-conscious. They began to suspect that, rather than helping, they were an unwel-

come obstruction to the clean-up operation. But there were ordinary people here too, standing about with a dazed air, or picking at the rubble of their former homes. "They were looking for the bodies of their loved ones," said Kaneta. "When they saw us marching past, they turned and bowed their heads. They were praying desperately to find their loved ones. Our hearts were so full when that happened. I had rarely been more conscious of suffering."

As they marched, Kaneta and his group had intended to chant sutras and sing hymns. But here, among the mess and stench, their voices failed them. "The Christian pastor was trying to sing hymns," said Kaneta. "But none of the hymns in his book seemed right. I couldn't even say the sutra—it came out in screams and shouts." The priests lurched uselessly through the rubble in their rich robes, croaking the scriptures, getting in the way. "And when we got to the sea," said Kaneta, "when we saw the sea—we couldn't face it. It was as if we couldn't interpret what we were seeing."

He said, "We realized that, for all that we had learned about religious ritual and language, none of it was effective in facing what we saw all around us. This destruction that we were living inside—it couldn't be framed by the principles and theories of religion. Even as priests, we were close to the fear that people express when they say, 'We see no God, we see no Buddha here.' I realized then that religious language was an armor that we wore to protect ourselves, and that the only way forward was to take it off."

Monku stood for the Japanese word "complaint" and the English word "monk," but there was a third allusion in the name of Café de Monku, the mobile event that Kaneta organized for survivors of the wave, to offer refreshment, companionship, and counseling by stealth. "I love jazz," he said, "and above all I love Thelonious

Monk. Bebop—such brilliant, peculiar music. Loose phrasing, those dissonant sounds. It seemed to me that it reflected what people's minds were like after the disaster—the tempo of people's minds and hearts. It was the perfect music for the occasion." At Café de Monku, Kaneta took off his priest's robes—in the struggle to help the survivors of the disaster, a jazz fan was as much use as a Buddhist.

The "temporary residences" were laid out in rows on vacant land on the margins of the inland towns. Kaneta would arrive with a group of priests and helpers and set up in the community meeting room. They would brew tea and coffee, set out cakes and biscuits. The inhabitants of the metal huts would begin to arrive, most of them elderly. Kaneta would stand up and address the room, a tall, smiling, bespectacled figure, dressed in a simple indigo tunic. He would welcome everyone, introduce his helpers, and make teasing jokes. "Mr. Suzuki is here to give you a massage around the shoulders, if you want one," he said. "Ah, what a massage! You should try it. His massage is so relaxing that you may actually find yourself slipping into the next world. But you needn't worry if that happens—we have lots of priests on hand."

Hot drinks would be poured, and plates of food passed around. Trays were set out with lengths of colored cord and beads of glass; the old people would sit on the floor at the low tables and string Buddhist rosaries. The priests inscribed and blessed *ihai* memorial tablets, for those who had lost them. There were more jokes and chuckling; but often Kaneta was to be seen sitting apart with one person or another, engaged in a private and visibly tearful conversation. Thelonious Monk would be playing.

Everyone in Japan was looking for consolation. The more time passed, the harder it became to find. After the immediate struggle for survival and the arduous weeks in the evacuation centers, the homeless were dispersed across the country in the

homes of relatives, in rented accommodations, and in the grim temporary residences. But the period of acute crisis, in some ways, had been the easy part. When survivors moved out of the cramped but cheerful communal shelters to the relative privacy of the metal containers, grief and loss rose up like a second wave.

"Immediately after the tsunami, people were worried about surviving for the next hour," said Naoya Kawakami, a Protestant pastor whom I met at Café de Monku. "Then they got to the shelters and worried about getting through the day. Things settled down, they were provided with food and something to sleep on, and they were anxious about the next fortnight. Then they were given temporary homes and their lives were secure, in a sense. They were not going to starve or freeze. But after the practical problems were resolved, the anxiety they felt was as strong as ever. It stretched ahead indefinitely into the future. It could no longer be soothed by just giving them things. The things will never be enough."

The metal boxes were lonely and sterile after the companionable crowding of the evacuation centers, but as the years passed, they were made cozy. Flowers and ornamental cauliflowers were planted; neighbors became friends. But then permanent homes became available, and the new communities began to shrink and break up. The homes were awarded by lottery—those who won moved to new purpose-built apartments; those who lost were left behind, at least until the next allocation. "Some people lose, and keep on losing," one of the priests told me. "They have an acute sense of abandonment. Sometimes they wake up and find that their neighbors, the winners, have disappeared without saying a word. They're too embarrassed to go and say their goodbyes."

Pastor Kawakami said, "In the beginning, they could talk about their anxieties, and how they could be resolved. 'I need a rice ball for my child.' 'I need a cardboard box to put my possessions

in.' People have those now. But they still have their anxiety, and the anxiety that remains is too big to speak of. It comes out in anger, in the breakdown of relationships, between individuals and between groups. There is resentment, disharmony, a failure of understanding. These are people of goodwill, but they are becoming stubborn. So many people are seeing ghosts these days, and it's because of trauma. People talk of seeing ghosts, but what they're talking about are troubles back home."

Japanese had been dying in tsunamis as long as the Japanese islands had existed. And every tsunami had brought forth ghosts. One of them was recorded in a famous old book of Tohoku folklore called *The Tales of Tono*. It told the story of a man named Fukuji who survived the Sanriku tsunami of 1896, and who lived with his two surviving children in a shack on the site of the family house. One moonlit summer night, he got up to relieve himself on the beach. "This night, the fog hovered low," the book records, "and he saw two people, a man and a woman, approaching him through the fog." The woman was his wife. The man was another villager, who had been in love with her, until the woman's family had chosen Fukuji as her husband.

As if in a dream, Fukuji followed the couple and called out his wife's name. She turned to him, smiling, and said, "I am married to this man now." Fukuji, half- or fully asleep, struggled to understand. "But don't you love your children?" he said. The woman's pale face became paler, and she began to weep. Fukuji, uncomprehending, looked miserably at his feet. His wife and her lover moved soundlessly out of sight. He started to follow them, and then remembered that both his wife and the man had died in the tsunami. "He stood on the road thinking until daybreak and

went home in the morning," the story ends. "It is said that he was sick for a long time after this."

No one knew the literature and folklore of Tohoku better than Masashi Hijikata, and he understood immediately that after the disaster, hauntings would follow. "We remembered the story of Fukuji," he said, "and we told one another that there would be many new stories like that. Personally, I don't believe in the existence of spirits, but that's not the point. If people say they see ghosts, then that's fine—we can leave it at that."

Hijikata was born in Hokkaido, Japan's northernmost island, but he had come to Sendai as a university student, and had the passion of the successful immigrant for his adopted home. He ran a small publishing company whose books and journals were exclusively on Tohoku subjects. It was Hijikata who explained to me the politics of ghosts, and the opportunity, as well as the risk, they represented for the people of Tohoku.

"We realized that so many people were having experiences like this," he said. "But there were people taking advantage of them. Trying to sell them this and that, telling them, 'This will give you relief.'" He met a woman who had lost her son in the disaster, and who was troubled by the sense of being haunted. She went to the hospital: the doctor gave her antidepressants. She went to the temple: the priest sold her an amulet and told her to read the sutras. "But all she wanted," Hijikata said, "was to see her son again. There are so many like her. They don't care if they are ghosts—they want to encounter ghosts.

"Given all that, we thought we had to do something. Of course, there are some people who are experiencing trauma, and if your mental health is suffering, then you need medical treatment. Other people will rely on the power of religion, and that is their choice. What we do is to create a place where people can accept the fact

that they are witnessing the supernatural. We provide an alternative for helping people through the power of literature."

Ghosts were not only inevitable, they were something to celebrate, part of the rich culture of Tohoku. Hijikata revived a literary form that had flourished in the feudal era: the *kaidan*, or "weird tale." *Kaidan-kai*, or "weird-tale parties," had been a popular summer pastime, when the delicious chill imparted by ghost stories served as a form of preindustrial air-conditioning. Hijikata's *kaidan-kai* were held in modern community centers and public halls. They would begin with a reading by one of his authors. Then members of the audience would share experiences of their own—students, housewives, working people, retirees. He organized *kaidan*-writing competitions, and published the best of them in an anthology. Among the winners was Ayane Suto, whom I met one afternoon at Hijikata's office.

She was a calm, neat young woman, with heavy black glasses and a drooping fringe, who worked in Sendai at a care home for the disabled. The fishing port of Kesennuma, where she grew up, had been one of the towns worst hit by the tsunami. Ayane's family home was beyond the reach of the wave, and her mother, sister, and grandparents were untouched by it. But her father, a maritime engineer, worked in an office on the town's harbor front, and that evening he didn't come home.

"I thought about him all the time," Ayane said. "It was obvious something had happened. But I said to myself that he might just be injured—he might be lying in a hospital somewhere. I knew that I should prepare for the worst. But I wasn't prepared at all."

Ayane passed painful days in Sendai, clearing up the mess caused in her flat by the earthquake, thinking constantly about her father. Two weeks after the disaster, his body was found.

She arrived back at her family home just before his coffin was carried in. Friends and extended family had gathered, most of

them casually dressed—everything black, everything formal, had been washed away. "He hadn't drowned, as most people did," Ayane said. "He died of a blow to the chest from some big piece of rubble. In the coffin you could only see his face through a glass window. It had been a fortnight, and I was afraid that his body might have decayed. I looked through the window. I could see that he had a few cuts, and he was pale. But it was still the face of my father."

She wanted to touch his face for the last time. But the casket and its window had been sealed shut. On it lay a white flower, a single cut stem placed on the coffin's wood by the undertaker. There was nothing unusual about it. But to Ayane it was extraordinary.

Ten days earlier, at the peak of her hope and despair, she had gone to a big public bathhouse to soak in the hot spring water. When she came out, she retrieved her boots from the locker, and felt an obstruction in the toe as she pulled them on. "It was a cold feeling," she remembered. "I could feel how cold it was, even through my socks. And it felt soft, fluffy." She reached in and removed a white flower, as fresh and flawless as if it had just been cut.

A minor mystery: How could such an object have found its way into a boot inside a locked container? It faded from her mind until that moment in front of her father's coffin, when the same flower presented itself again. "The first time, I'd had the feeling that this might be a premonition of bad news," Ayane said. "Dad might not be alive anymore, and this might be a sign of his death. But then I thought about it later, about the coolness of the flower, and the whiteness of the flower, and that feeling of softness against my toe. And I thought of that as the touch of my father, which I couldn't experience when he was in his coffin."

Ayane knew that the flower was just a flower. She didn't believe in ghosts, or that her dead father had sent it to her as a

sign—if such communication was possible, why would a loving parent express it in such obscure terms? "I think it was a coincidence," she said, "and that I made something good of it. When people see ghosts, they are telling a story, a story that had been broken off. They dream of ghosts because then the story carries on, or comes to a conclusion. And if that brings them comfort, that's a good thing."

Committed to print as a *kaidan*, published in Hijikata's magazine, it took on ever greater significance. "There were thousands of deaths, each of them different," Ayane said. "Most of them have never been told. My father's name was Tsutomu Suto. By writing about him, I share his death with others. Perhaps I save him in some way, and perhaps I save myself."

Once the tsunami's victims had been treated, fed, and sheltered, the struggle began to prevent an invisible secondary disaster of anxiety, depression, and suicide. A survey carried out a year after the disaster revealed that four out of ten survivors complained of sleeplessness, and one in five suffered from depression. There was a surge in alcoholism, and in stress-related conditions such as high blood pressure. It was a struggle to measure the crisis because of the difficulty in compiling accurate data—in the town of Rikuzen-Takata, for example, most of the social workers who would have carried out the surveys had drowned.

Café de Monku, so simple in form, came to seem an essential emergency measure. The good it did to the tsunami refugees was obvious from their faces. Requests were coming in from all over Tohoku; Kaneta and his priests were setting out their tea and biscuits once a week or more. But he also had a busy temple to run, and all the routine obligations of a town priest—funerals, memorial ceremonies, visits to the sick and lonely, mundane

tasks of administration. To everyone who knew him, it was obvious that he was taking on too much; hesitantly, and then with greater urgency, friends and family cautioned him to rest. But his presence, as comforter, organizer, and leader, had become indispensable to so many people; there seemed to be no way to extricate himself from their need. The physical collapse that came at the end of 2013 was inevitable and overwhelming.

Painful blisters erupted on his skin. He was so exhausted that he could hardly get out of bed. For weeks he did nothing except sit in front of the television and strum on his guitar. "I don't remember what I watched," Kaneta said. "I watched in a stupor. I didn't even listen to jazz. I would just play a chord on my guitar, something I liked the sound of, and then another one, and while I was doing that I would fall asleep. I was a step away from depression. I had to stop doing everything, or else."

It was the culmination of three years of physical, psychological, and spiritual crisis, but two things served as immediate triggers. One was a series of speeches that Kaneta gave in different parts of the country about the experience of the disaster. Like Sayomi Shito's husband, Takahiro, he traveled outside the zone of disaster in the hope of communicating to the outside world the pain and complexity of the situation there. Like Takahiro, he came away with the crushing sense of having failed to express himself or to have been understood.

The second experience was set in motion by a young woman whom I will call Rumiko Takahashi. She had telephoned Kaneta one evening in a state of incoherent distress. She talked of killing herself; she was shouting about things entering her. She too had become possessed by the spirits of the dead; she begged the priest to help her.

SAVE DON'T FALL TO SEA

The Sendai District Court delivered its verdict on October 26, 2016. I took the bullet train up that morning from Tokyo. It was a warm, piercingly bright day of early autumn. Five and a half years had passed since the tsunami, and there was no obvious sign that such an event had ever taken place. The towns and cities of Tohoku were humming with the money that was being injected into the region for its reconstruction. One hundred thousand people still lived in metal houses, but these upsetting places were tucked away out of sight of the casual visitor. None of the towns destroyed by the wave had been rebuilt, but they had been scoured completely of rubble. Coarse, tussocky grass had overgrown the coastal strip, and those ruins that poked through it looked more like neglected archaeological sites than places of continuing pain and despair.

The court building was a short taxi ride from the station. Inside, I joined a line and drew a lucky ticket for the public seats. An hour remained until the hearing began. I stood outside at the front of the courthouse, where reporters and photographers

were milling lazily; a ripple of animation passed through them at the arrival of a procession, slowly making its way through the sunshine. It was the plaintiffs in the case, the mothers and fathers of the Okawa children, walking along the pavement, three abreast. Apart from Naomi Hiratsuka, all the parents I had got to know best were there. They wore black. Several carried framed photographs of their sons and daughters. The three men at the front held a wide banner. Around its margins were the faces of the children, the twenty-three children named in the case, photographed at home, at school, or playing outside, laughing, smiling, or solemn. In the center was a sentence of Japanese, the characters carefully hand-painted with an ink brush: *We did what our teachers told us.*

It was a profoundly dignified spectacle. The group entered the courthouse and split into smaller groups, as plaintiffs and defendants, lawyers, journalists, and members of the public waited for the proceedings to get under way. There was no obvious anxiety or tension; there was comradely pleasure in the coming together of old allies and acquaintances. But everyone present was conscious of the possibility of defeat. Yoshioka had made his case as well as he could, but certain facts remained unalterable. The plaintiffs were a small group of individuals; the defendants were a city and a prefecture; and Japanese courts were conservative. "Whatever the verdict today," said Takahiro Shito, "it will just add to the sum of all the other experiences we have had up until now. It was our responsibility to do this, as parents. This is part of what it means to bring children into the world. Of course I'm worried about the verdict going against us. But if it does, it would mean that a school does not have to protect the lives of its pupils. And that should never be the case." The parents had just come from a meeting with their lawyer, Shito said. The delivery of the

verdict would take only a matter of moments, he had told them; it would be obvious in the first few seconds which way it was going to go.

The doors of the courtroom were opened, and everyone took their places. The five defense lawyers sat on the right, and on the left were the black-clad parents. I looked across at them from the public seats. How many hours I had spent talking to them over the years, in conversations filled with intense and sometimes unbearable detail. Grief was in their noses like a stench; it was the first thing they thought of when they woke in the morning, and the last thing in their minds as they went to sleep at night. They had spoken about each stage of the lives of their children, in childhood, infancy, even in gestation. They remembered the school, and the community of families of which it was the focus. They described the disaster and its unfolding, the blows of realization that followed, and the asphyxia of loss and of survival. Like the plot of a fiction, these remembrances culminated in belief in a mystery, in things missing, removed, and deliberately hidden— a conspiracy, in other words, that not only worsened the pain of grief but rendered it incomprehensible. It expressed itself in impotent, inward-turning anger, and in unanswered questions about particular individuals. Why did this one not do his job? Why did this one tell a lie? Why will that one not speak to us?

There had indeed been a cover-up, but of a pitifully unambitious and ill-executed kind: inconsistent, banal, and transparent. There was no grand plan, no mastermind—even to call it a conspiracy was to grant it a dignity and cunning that Kashiba and the mediocrities of the Ishinomaki Education Board never possessed. A group of unexceptional men had failed dismally. They didn't even try very hard to deny their failure, just to contain it within manageable bounds. They were stubborn, clumsy,

and charmless, personally and institutionally. But if Kashiba had fallen to his knees and confessed his negligence, and if Junji Endo had come forward and wept out his story once again—nothing that mattered would be significantly changed.

The true mystery of Okawa school was the one we all face. No mind can encompass it; consciousness recoils in panic. The idea of conspiracy is what we supply to make sense of what will never be sensible—the fiery fact of death.

Extinction of life: extinction of a perfect, a beloved child: for eternity.

Impossible! the soul cries out. *What are they hiding?*

A door opened noiselessly, and all at once the three judges—a young woman and two middle-aged men—were seated in their black gowns. The judge in the center began speaking, fast, quietly, and without inflection. The Japanese he used, formal and legalistic, was beyond my grasp. So I focused instead on the faces of the listening parents—there, surely, I would immediately be able to read the verdict, in their anger or jubilation. The faces looked intently at the judge. They frowned in concentration; their features were blank and expressionless. And then, as suddenly as it began, it was all over, and the occupants of the court were standing up and filing out.

The dark-clad parents were on their feet too. They exchanged no words or glances; they looked grave and even grim; they looked like people who had received deeply troubling news. And yet, towards the end, I thought I had been able to follow part of the judge's ruling, the part when he seemed to be ordering the defendants to pay what sounded like a very large sum of money.

I stepped out into the corridor where the Japanese reporters were huddled, comparing their notes. I had not misunderstood.

The Okawa parents had won their case—they had been awarded more than £11 million, or $13.4 million. All their children were still dead.

The final judgment ran to 87 pages. It surveyed in detail the actions taken by the teachers, and found no fault in their behavior immediately after the 2:46 p.m. earthquake. It was "not inappropriate," the judges insisted, to keep the children at school. For the first forty minutes that they waited in the playground, even after the first radio warnings, "it cannot be said that the teachers could foresee the danger of being hit by a tsunami." But then, at 3:30 p.m., the vans from the city office had careered past, blaring their frantic warning about the sea breaking over the beachside forest of pines. At that point, seven minutes before it eventually arrived, "the teachers could have foreseen the coming of a huge tsunami to Okawa Elementary School." The place of evacuation that was eventually chosen, the traffic island by the bridge, was "inappropriate." "The teachers," the judgment said, "should have evacuated the children up the hill at the back, which was unobstructed."

The damages—¥1.43 billion*—were less than the ¥2.3 billion that had been demanded, but still at the high end of those habitually awarded by the courts. Once legal costs were accounted for, the plaintiffs would receive some ¥60 million—about £470,000, or $570,000—for each child lost. Japanese judges were expert at forging compromise and delivering verdicts in which both sides won something of the argument, neither was humiliated, and vindication was impossible to tease out. This was not such a judgment. It was a decisive legal victory, an unambiguous assignment of responsibility,

---

* At the time, this was worth about £11.1 million, or $13.6 million.

which nonetheless completely failed to concern itself with the things that mattered to the parents the most.

It expressed no opinion about the actions of Kashiba, the principal, before or after the tsunami. It absolved the teachers from blame over the chaotic emergency manual. It was silent about the evasions of the board of education, about the disposal of the notes on the interviews with the children, about the untruths of Junji Endo, and about his failure to give an account of himself. A little while after the verdict, three of the fathers came before the cameras with another carefully hand-brushed placard. "We prevailed," it read. "The voices of the children were heard!" But there could hardly have been less sense of triumph; as they talked about it afterward, the families of the dead children expressed nothing stronger than relief at the absence of defeat.

"As far as the death of my daughter goes, we won, I suppose," said Hideaki Tadano. "But my son, Tetsuya, and me—we have been beaten. They've been beating us from the moment it happened, with their lies and their evasions. This verdict lets them get away with it—the falsifications, the hiding of evidence. That kind of thing should never be tolerated. I don't want a world in which that kind of thing is allowed."

"December is the time when the day is the shortest," said Reverend Kaneta. "And then midwinter comes, and the light begins to return. That was the moment for me. When the days began to get longer I recovered my energy. For three years, stress had been stored up inside me. It was pent-up. Over the winter, I let it go."

Months of precious inactivity healed Kaneta. With the crisis past, he returned to the life of his temple. The world around him was unchanged, still shadowed by grief and by ghosts. But the priest had been renewed. "For a long time, I felt that everything I

had learned had no reality," he said. "But the reality returned. It was a revival of my faith. When I was on the verge of collapse, it came back to me from a deeper level."

He began to rediscover the clarity that he had glimpsed in the starry sky on the first night of the disaster. The question with which he struggled—the question put most insistently by survivors—was the oldest one of all. "What does life mean, in the face of death?" Kaneta said. "That was what people wanted to know. An old woman told me, 'My grandchild was washed away before my eyes. I am ninety years old, and I lived. What am I supposed to make of that? Can you answer me, priest?' People who survived wanted to understand their survival. For a long time, I couldn't explain it to them."

Kaneta said, "What determined life or death? No Buddhist priest knows, no Christian pastor—not even the Pope in Rome. So I would say, 'There's one thing I can tell you, and that is that you *are* alive, and so am I. This is a certainty. And if we are alive, then there must be some meaning to it. So let's think about it, and keep thinking about it. I'll be with you as we think. I'll stay with you, and we will do it together.' Perhaps it sounds glib. But that is what I could say."

I asked Kaneta about Okawa Elementary School. He was a specialist in grief and suffering, and an instinctive ally of the small man and the underdog. The death of the children was the single grossest tragedy of the whole immense disaster, a distillation of its arbitrariness and horror. So it was striking, at first, to hear him talk of it in tones of such detachment.

He had often been to the school and prayed there; a nearby community of temporary homes had hosted Café de Monku. But the local priest had discouraged Kaneta and his team from ministering directly to the families of the children; and he knew none of them personally. "Of course I know that seventy-four

children died there," he said. "And that it was widely reported, and that the families brought a legal case. But I don't want to set what happened there apart from, or above, anywhere else. There are places all over this land, places little known or forgotten, where many people died, where many are grieving."

I asked him what kind of consolation a priest could offer to people such as the parents of Okawa school, and he was quiet for a moment. "You have to be careful," he said. "You have to be very careful in doing this to people who have lost their children. It takes long months, long years—it might take a whole lifetime. It might be the very last thing that you say to someone. But perhaps all that we can tell them in the end is to accept. The task of acceptance is very hard. It's up to every single person, individually. People of religion can play only a part in achieving that—they need the support of everyone around them. We watch them, watch over them. We remember our place in the cosmos, as we work. We stay with them, and we walk together. That's all we can do."

We were sitting in the priest's quarters of Kaneta's temple. His wife was pouring tea. Sunlight broke on the paper screens across the windows; the room smelled of incense and tatami mats. An everyday moment of beauty in a Buddhist temple in the heart of Japan: it was natural, in such a place, to assent to ideas of harmony, to acknowledge the existence of essential principles beyond the weak grasp of human thinking. There were few men whom I respected more than Kaneta. But in my gut, I rejected what he said.

I had had enough of Japanese acceptance; I was sick with a surfeit of *gaman*. Perhaps, at some level of superhuman detachment, the deaths of the Okawa children did make possible insight into the nature of the cosmos. But long before that remote point, in the world of creatures who lived and breathed, they were something else as well—an expression of human and institutional failure, of timidity, complacency, and indecision. It was

257

one thing to recognize a truth about the universe and man's small place within it; the challenge was how to do this without also submitting to the cult of quietism that had choked this country for so long. Japan had enough serenity and self-restraint. What it needed now were people like the Shitos and the Tadanos and the Suzukis: angry, scathing, determined people, unafraid to step out of the ranks and fight, even if all that the contest amounted to was the losing struggle with death.

How to balance affirmation of life with acceptance of its inevitable end? How to keep death in its place, to live under its regime, without submitting to it as a tyrant? As if in response to these unvoiced thoughts, Kaneta told a famous story about the Buddha. One day he was visited by a mother holding in her arms the body of her baby. The woman was grief-stricken and refused to accept the child's death. She had come to beg the famous teacher to perform a miracle and to bring the infant back to life. "Go out, and find a house where no son or daughter, no husband or wife, no father, mother, or grandparent has ever died," the Buddha told her. "Bring from there white mustard seeds, put the seeds into a gruel, feed them to your child, and his life will be restored."

The woman traveled from village to village, and from house to house, asking at each one if they had ever lost a loved one there. Everywhere she stopped she heard stories of heartbreak. Each one was different in its details, and all of them were the same. As she listened, the character of the woman's grief changed. It did not diminish. But in time it altered, from a black and suffocating mass to a form bright and crystalline, through which she was able to recognize death, not as the contradiction of life, but as the condition that makes it possible. She buried her child and went back to thank the Buddha. "By the time she returned to him," Kaneta said, "he didn't need to explain."

There is no tidying away of loose ends to be done in a story

about the deaths of young children, about the annihilation of a coast—only more stories to be told, and retold in different ways, and tested like radioactive material for the different kinds of meaning they give out. Stories alone show the way. "This is consolation," Kaneta said. "This is understanding. We don't work simply by saying to people, 'Accept.' There's no point lecturing them about dogma. We stay with them and walk with them until they find the answer on their own. We try to unthaw the frozen future. People feel as if they have staggered into a fantastic land of disaster and pain. But it is not a place of fantasy. It is the universe we inhabit, and the only life we have on these islands. Volcano, earthquake, tsunami, and typhoon—they are our culture, they are as much a part of Japan as the rich crops in the fields. Everything that was built over a hundred years was destroyed by the tsunami. But in time it will be built again."

Up and down I traveled between Tokyo and the disaster zone, for six years. My son—the small kicking creature on the scanner's screen—was born, and grew. His older sister grew up too, and before long she was entering Japanese elementary school herself, as the single blond-haired, blue-eyed child in the year's new intake. It was on a different scale from little Okawa—a big Tokyo school, reassuringly positioned on a hill and separated from the sea by miles of dense inner city. But, institutionally, the two were identical. Both had a head and deputy head, teachers of diverse ages and experience, a municipal education board, an emergency manual. Both had sports days and graduation ceremonies and disaster drills. Like the children in Okawa, my daughter wore a round hat and a badge bearing her name in Japanese, and carried one of the distinctive square rucksacks. The atmosphere at the school was warm and benign; the staff exuded assurance and

professionalism. But there are some situations that cannot be tested or drilled for. It was impossible not to wonder how these teachers might react in the face of extremity; or to forget the image of the hats, badges, and rucksacks of the Okawa children being hauled out of the mud.

I kept in touch with some of the people I had got to know in the northeast.

Tetsuya Tadano flourished in high school and became captain of its judo team. He always kept with him a photograph of his lost classmates. "If I carry it in my bag," he said, "I feel as if they are having lessons with me."

His father, Hideaki, teamed up with Toshiro, the husband of the art teacher Katsura Sato, in conducting guided tours of the school. Toshiro had been a teacher too, an employee of the Ishinomaki board of education. Like his wife, he had walked away from his career after the death of their daughter, Mizuho. Now he led groups of adults, and children from schools all over the country, around the school grounds. He showed them photographs of the children in the playground, now a patch of dried mud. He pointed to the path up the hill, which they could so easily have taken. He showed them Mizuho's name still there below the hook where she used to hang her coat, and on the black memorial stone erected at the back of the school. On the tour that I attended, many of the participants ended it in tears. "This," Hideaki said to me, "this is why we must preserve the school."

Naomi Hiratsuka continued to work at the school where Koharu would have gone. Her middle child, Koharu's brother, was autistic; sometimes Naomi imagined herself giving up teaching and establishing a new career, helping families with similar children. Miho Suzuki and her husband, Yoshiaki, finally bought a new house and moved out of their metal hut. The sad chill that had established itself between Miho and Naomi lingered, but

both went to the site of the school from time to time, where Masaru Naganuma, their comrade during long weeks searching the mud, was still looking for his seven-year-old boy, Koto. Naganuma took no part in the action against the city, and refused all requests to talk to journalists. But his determination was unquenchable. He still spent virtually every day searching, alone or with his elderly father, digging ground that had repeatedly been worked over before. With every month that passed, the chances of finding any trace of his son dwindled; and Masaru knew this. "Five years, ten years—to him it's nothing," Naomi said. "Masaru will keep looking for the rest of his life. He says that he cannot die. Even when the moment for his death comes, he cannot go."

Sayomi Shito's mother and father had been ailing before the disaster; after the loss of their granddaughter, their decline accelerated. They died in 2015, three months apart; their *ihai* and portraits were added to that of Chisato on the household shrine. The burden of caring for two infirm and confused parents compounded Sayomi's anguish and her grief. She was treated for depression. One day, she was at the supermarket, where she overheard the conversation of two younger mothers. It was evident from the way they spoke that they lived inland and had been completely unscathed by the disaster; they were talking, Sayomi realized, about the parents of Okawa Elementary School.

"If that happened to *me*," said the first woman, "I couldn't go on living."

"I *know*—me neither," said the second. "I would definitely kill myself."

Sayomi said, "I had prayed so often that I could die and Chisato could live. I knew that I should have gone to the school and taken her home. Or stayed there and died with her. When I heard that conversation, I felt that they were saying to me, 'Why are you alive?'"

She dropped her shopping basket and ran back to her car. She drove onto the straight road that ran along the river, heading in the direction of the sea. The car accelerated until it was traveling much too fast for the narrow carriageway. Sayomi was looking at the river. She was imagining how small a movement of the steering wheel would be necessary to swerve across the bank and into the water.

Her son, Kenya, her oldest child, was sitting in the car next to her.

As she drove, in agony and shame, an awareness came to her of what it would mean to kill her son as well as herself. She pulled over suddenly and leaped out. She started to clamber over the bank and towards the water. "I was thinking to myself that it was so strange, ridiculous really, that Chisato was dead and I was still alive," she said. "How could that be? Why was I still living? I was making for the river, because I wanted to be in the water, just like Chisato was."

She became aware that Kenya was beside her, gripping her arm so tightly that it left a bruise. "Mum," he was saying to her. "Mum, Mum. If you die, what will become of those of us left behind?"

One day, Reverend Kaneta told me the story of his last exorcism, the experience that had robbed him of his peace of mind. We sat in the room where the sun struck the screens. Lined up on the tatami were dozens of small clay statues, which would be handed out to the patrons of Café de Monku. They were representations of Jizo, the bodhisattva associated with kindness and mercy, who consoles the living and the dead.

It was in this room, Kaneta told me, that he had first met

Rumiko Takahashi, the twenty-five-year-old woman who had telephoned him in a frenzy of suicidal despair. Late that evening, a car pulled up at the temple with her mother, sister, fiancé, and, limp with exhaustion, Rumiko herself.

She was a nurse from the city of Sendai—"a very gentle person," Kaneta said, "nothing peculiar or unusual about her at all." Neither she nor her family had been hurt by the tsunami. But for weeks, her fiancé said, she had been assailed by the presence of the dead. She complained of someone, or something, pushing into her from a place deep below, of dead presences "pouring out" invisibly around her.

Rumiko herself was slumped over the table. She stirred as Kaneta addressed the creature within her. "I asked, 'Who are you, and what do you want?'" he said. "When it spoke, it didn't sound like her at all. It talked for three hours."

It was the spirit of a young woman whose mother had divorced and remarried, and who found herself unloved and unwanted by her new family. She ran away and found work in the *mizu shobai*, or "water trade," the nighttime world of clubs, bars, and prostitution. There she became more and more isolated and depressed, and fell under the influence of a morbid and manipulative man. Unknown to her family, unmourned by anyone, she had killed herself. Since then, not a stick of incense had been lit in her memory.

Kaneta asked the spirit, "Will you come with me? Do you want me to bring you to the light?" He led her to the main hall of the temple, where he recited the sutra and sprinkled holy water. By the time the prayers were done, Rumiko had returned to herself. It was half past one in the morning when she and her family left.

Three days later, she was back. She complained of great pain

in her left leg; and, once again, she had the sensation of being stalked by an alien presence. The effort of keeping out the intruder exhausted her. "That was the strain, the feeling that made her suicidal," Kaneta said. "I told her, 'Don't worry—just let it in.'" Rumiko's posture and voice immediately stiffened and deepened; Kaneta found himself talking to a gruff man with a barking, peremptory manner of speech. He was a sailor of the old Imperial Navy who had died in action during the Second World War after his left leg had been gravely injured by a shell.

The priest spoke soothingly to the old veteran; after he had prayed and chanted, the man departed, and Rumiko was at peace. But all of this was just a prologue. "All of the people who came," Kaneta said, "and each one of the stories they told, had some connection with water."

Over the course of a few weeks, Reverend Kaneta exorcised twenty-five spirits from Rumiko Takahashi. They came and went at the rate of several a week. All of them, after the wartime sailor, were ghosts of the tsunami.

For Kaneta, the days followed a relentless routine. The telephone call from Rumiko would come in the early evening; at nine o'clock her fiancé would pull up in front of the temple and carry her out of the car. As many as three spirits would appear in a single session. Kaneta talked to each personality in turn, sometimes over several hours. He established their circumstances, calmed their fears, and politely but firmly enjoined them to follow him towards the light. Kaneta's wife would sit with Rumiko; sometimes other priests were present to join in the prayers. "Each time she would feel better, and go back to Sendai and go to work," Kaneta told me. "But then, after a few days, she'd be overwhelmed

again." Out among the living, surrounded by the city, she would become conscious of the dead, a thousand importunate spirits pressing in on her and trying to get inside.

One of the first was a middle-aged man who, speaking through Rumiko, despairingly called the name of his daughter.

"Kaori!" said the voice. "Kaori! I have to get to Kaori. Where are you, Kaori? I have to get to the school, there's a tsunami coming."

The man's daughter had been at a school by the sea when the earthquake struck. He had hurried out of work and driven along the coast road to pick her up, when the water had overtaken him. His agitation was intense; he was impatient and suspicious of Kaneta.

The voice asked, "Am I alive or not?"

"No," said Kaneta. "You are dead."

"And how many people died?" asked the voice.

"Twenty thousand people died."

"Twenty thousand? So many?"

Later, Kaneta asked him where he was.

"I'm at the bottom of the sea. It is very cold."

Kaneta said, "Come up from the sea to the world of light."

"But the light is so small," the man replied. "There are bodies all around me, and I can't reach it. And who are you anyway? Who are you to lead me to the world of light?"

The conversation went around and around for two hours. Eventually, Kaneta said, "You are a father. You understand the anxieties of a parent. Consider this girl whose body you have used. She has a father and mother who are worried about her. Have you thought of that?"

There was a long pause until finally the man said, "You're right," and moaned deeply.

Kaneta chanted the sutra. He paused from time to time when

the voice uttered choked sounds, but they faded to mumbles and finally the man was gone.

Day after day, week after week, the spirits kept coming—men and women, young people and old, with accents rough and polished. Rather than being angry or vengeful, they were confused and panicked at their sudden immersion in a world of darkness and cold. They told their stories at length, but there was never enough specific detail—surnames, place names, addresses—to verify any individual account, and Kaneta felt no urge to. One man had survived the tsunami, but killed himself after learning of the death of his two daughters. There was a young woman who had tried to escape the water, but could not run fast enough because she was heavily pregnant. There was an old man who spoke in thick Tohoku dialect. He was desperately worried about his surviving widow, who lived alone and uncared for in one of the desolate tin huts. In a shoebox she kept a white rope, which she would contemplate and caress. He feared what she planned to use it for.

Kaneta reasoned and cajoled, prayed and chanted, and in the end each of the spirits gave way. But days or hours after one group of ghosts had been dismissed, more would stumble forward to take their place.

One night in the temple, Rumiko announced, "There are dogs all around me—it's loud! They are barking so loudly I can't bear it." Then she said, "No! I don't want it. I don't want to be a dog." Finally she said, "Give it rice and water to eat. I'm going to let it in."

"She seemed to think it would do something terrible," Kaneta said. "She told us to seize hold of her, and when the dog entered her, it had tremendous power. There were three men holding on

to her, but they were not strong enough and she threw them off. She was scratching the floor, and roaring, a deep growl." Later, after the chanting of the sutra, and the return to her peaceful self, Rumiko recounted the story of the dog. It had been the pet of an old couple who lived close to the Fukushima Dai-ichi nuclear power plant. When the radiation began to leak, its owners had fled in panic with all their neighbors. But they forgot to unchain the dog, which slowly died of thirst and hunger. Later, when it was much too late, the spirit of the animal observed men in white protective suits coming in and peering at its shriveled corpse.

In time, Rumiko became able to exercise control over the spirits; she spoke of a container, which she could choose to open or close. A friend of Kaneta's, who was present at one of the exorcisms, compared her to a chronically ill patient habituated to vomiting: what at first was painful and disgusting became, over time, familiar and bearable. Eventually Rumiko reported being able to brush the spirits away when they approached her. She was still conscious of their presence, but at a distance, no longer shoving and jostling her, but skulking at the room's edge. The evening telephone calls and late-night visits became less and less frequent. Rumiko and her fiancé married and moved away from Sendai; and, to his extreme relief, Kaneta stopped hearing from her.

The effort of the exorcisms was too much. This was the moment when his friends and family worried about him most. "I was overwhelmed," he said. "Over the months, I'd become accustomed to hearing the stories of survivors. But all of a sudden, I found myself listening to the voices of the dead."

Most difficult to bear were the occasions when Rumiko was possessed by the personalities of children. "When a child appeared," Kaneta said, "my wife took her hand. She said, 'It's Mummy—it's Mummy here. It's all right, it's all right. Let's go together.'" The first to appear was a tiny nameless boy, too young to understand what was being said to him, or to do more than call for his mother over and over again. The second was a girl of seven or eight years old. She kept repeating, "I'm sorry, I'm sorry." She had been with her even younger brother when the tsunami struck, and tried to run away with him. But in the water, as they were both drowning, she had let go of his hand; now she was afraid that her mother would be angry. She said, "There's a black wave coming, Mummy. I'm scared, Mummy. Mummy, I'm sorry, I'm sorry."

The voice of the girl was terrified and confused; her body was drifting helplessly in the cold water, and it was a long struggle to guide her upwards towards the light. "She gripped my wife's hand tightly until she finally came to the gate of the world of light," Kaneta recalled. "Then she said, 'Mum, I can go on my own now, you can let go.'"

Afterward, Mrs. Kaneta tried to describe the moment when she released the hand of the young-woman-as-little-drowned-girl. The priest himself was weeping for pity at her lonely death, and for the twenty thousand other stories of terror and extinction. But his wife was aware only of a huge energy dissipating. It made her remember the experience of childbirth, and the sense of power discharging at the end of pain, as the newborn child finally enters the world.

An easing of walls,
A shuddering through soles:
A petal loosens, falls.

In the room, alone:
It begins, then it has gone.
Ripples outlast stone.

Rain-smell stirs the heart;
Nostrils flare. A breath. We wait
For something to start.

—ANTHONY THWAITE

NOTES

This is a true story, based in large part on the accounts of the individuals named and quoted in its pages, and on my own observations. Other sources are recorded below.

Among the various authors I have consulted, I am indebted above all to Masaki Ikegami. Without his painstaking reporting, it would have been much more difficult to piece together events at Okawa Elementary School during and after the disaster.

Japanese names are given in the Western order: given name first, family name last. Conversions of Japanese yen are approximate, and based on the exchange rate prevailing at the time. On March 11, 2011, one pound was worth about ¥131, or $1.50.

xvii *18,500 people had been crushed, burned to death, or drowned*: The most commonly cited figures for casualties of the disaster are those published by Japan's National Police Agency, which counts separately the number of people killed and those officially regarded as missing. The former includes only those for whom a death certificate has been issued; but at this late stage, all those in the latter category can also be assumed to be dead. On March 10, 2017, there were 15,893 dead and 2,553 missing, a total of 18,446. See http://www.npa.go.jp/archive/keibi/biki/higaijokyo_e.pdf.

The separate count by the Fire and Disaster Management Agency records a significantly higher figure—19,475 dead and 2,587 missing, a total of 22,062. This includes those who died after the disaster from causes related

to it, such as sick people whose health deteriorated after they were forced to move precipitately from hospitals, and suicides. See http://www.fdma .go.jp/bn/higaihou/pdf/jishin/154.pdf.

PROLOGUE: SOLID VAPOR

12 *It knocked the Earth ten inches off its axis; it moved Japan*: Kenneth Chang, "Quake Moves Japan Closer to U.S. and Alters Earth's Spin," *The New York Times*, March 14, 2011.

12 *The earthquake and tsunami caused more than $210 billion of damage*: Jeff Kingston (ed.), *Natural Disaster and Nuclear Crisis in Japan* (Abingdon: Routledge, 2012).

12 *Japan's remaining nuclear reactors—all fifty of them—were shut down*: On the morning of March 11, 2011, Japan had fifty-four functioning nuclear reactors. Four of the six at Fukushima Dai-ichi were rendered unusable by the tsunami; by May 2012, all the others had been shut down due to public opposition. Ongoing efforts are being made to restart them, but the political and technical challenges are great. As of March 2017, only three were in operation.

13 *Farmers, suddenly unable to sell their crops, committed suicide*: Richard Lloyd Parry, "Suicide Cases Rise After Triple Disaster," *The Times* (London), June 17, 2011; and Richard Lloyd Parry, "Tepco Must Pay Damages over Woman's Suicide After Fukushima Leak," *The Times* (London) online, August 26, 2014, http://www.thetimes.co.uk/article/tepco-must-pay -damages-over-womans-suicide-after-fukushima-leak-vsm5tgbmh83.

14 *"All at once . . . something we could only have imagined was upon us"*: Philip Gourevitch, *We Wish to Inform You That Tomorrow We Will Be Killed with Our Families* (New York: Picador, 1998), 7.

HAVING GONE, I WILL COME

18 *her son's graduation ceremony from middle school*: The Japanese school system is modeled on that of the United States. Children go to primary, or elementary, school from ages six to twelve, middle school from twelve to fifteen, and senior high school from fifteen to eighteen.

22 *connecting Okawa in the south with the Kitakami district on the northern bank*: The district on the south bank of the river, a sub-municipality of

the city of Ishinomaki, is officially called Kahoku. Okawa is an older name for the area, but for ease of understanding, I have used it as a general term for the catchment area of Okawa Elementary School. It is pronounced with a long *o*, close to English "ore-cow-uh."

JIGOKU

44 *She went on: "He lifted up one of the blankets . . .":* In this passage I have drawn on my own interviews with Sayomi Shito, and on Chris Heath's fine article "Graduation Day," *GQ* (U.S. edition), July 1, 2011.

ABUNDANT NATURE

55 *the meeting point, deep beneath the ocean, of the Pacific and North American tectonic plates:* For an accessible account of the workings of earthquakes and tsunamis, see Bruce Parker, *The Power of the Sea* (New York: St. Martin's Press, 2010).

59 *"People cried and screamed . . .":* This is my adaptation of a translation from the *Nihon Sandai Jitsuroku* [*The True History of Three Reigns of Japan*] of 901 A.D., which appears in Jeff Kingston (ed.), *Tsunami: Japan's Post-Fukushima Future* (Washington: Foreign Policy, 2011), 10.

59 *Geologists found layers of fine sand:* For the history of earthquakes and tsunamis on the Sanriku coast, see K. Minoura et al., "The 869 Jogan Tsunami Deposit and Recurrence Interval of Large-Scale Tsunami on the Pacific Coast of Northeast Japan," *Journal of Natural Disaster Science* 23, no. 2 (2001): 83–88; and Masayuki Nakao, "The Great Meiji Sanriku Tsunami," Failure Knowledge Database, Hatamura Institute for the Advancement of Technology, 2005, http://www.sozogaku.com/fkd/en/hfen/HA1000616.pdf, accessed March 2017.

60 *On May 22, 1960, a 9.5-magnitude earthquake:* Parker, *Power of the Sea*, 151–152.

62 *the spiky-finned, bull-headed sculpions: Cottus pollux*, the Japanese fluvial sculpion or sculpin.

62 *"We had so much from the river":* quoted in Masaki Ikegami, *Ano toki, Okawa shogakko de nani ga okita noka* [What Happened That Day at Okawa Elementary School?] (Tokyo: Seishisha, 2012), 25.

63 *Three hundred and ninety-three people lived in Kamaya:* Ibid., 23.

THE OLD AND THE YOUNG

77 *one of the disaster's oldest victims*: Remarkably, Shimokawara was probably not the very oldest person to die in the tsunami. According to the Ministry of Health, Labour and Welfare, twenty-five of those confirmed dead were one hundred or older, three of them men, and twenty-two of them women.

80 *Fifty-four percent of those who perished were age sixty-five or older*: Ministry of Health, Labour and Welfare, "Jinko dotai tokei kara mita Higashi Nihon daishinsai ni yoru shibo no jokyo ni tsuite" ["On Mortality Caused by the Great East Japan Disaster Based on Demographic Statistics"] (Tokyo, 2011), http://www.mhlw.go.jp/toukei/saikin/hw/jinkou/kakutei11/dl/14_x34.pdf, accessed March 2017. People of seventy-five and older made up a third of the dead; a man in his forties was more than twice as likely to have perished as one in his twenties.

81 *In the Indian Ocean tsunami that struck Indonesia*: Richard Lloyd Parry, "The Town Left Without Women," *The Times* (London), January 12, 2005.

81 *Out of the 18,500 dead and missing, only 351—fewer than one in fifty— were schoolchildren*: "Over 110 Schoolchildren Die or Go Missing in Tsunami After Being Picked Up by Parents," *Mainichi Daily News*, August 12, 2011.

83 *a man named Teruyuki Kashiba*: I made repeated requests to speak to Mr. Kashiba, but received no response.

EXPLANATIONS

86 *"Good evening to you all," he croaked*: Gakko KyoikuKa, Ishinomaki-shi kyoiku iinkai jimukyoku, "Kaigi-roku," Okawa shougakko hogosha setsumeikai [School Education Section, Secretariat of Ishinomaki City Board of Education, "Proceedings of Meeting," in "Explanatory Meeting for the Parents of Okawa Elementary School"], April 9, 2011.

88 *He rewrote the plan to require escape up a steep hill*: Information from Katsura Sato.

94 *Tricky old bastard*: In Japanese, *Tanuki oyaji*. Literally, "father raccoon dog"—the raccoon dog being proverbially unreliable and deceitful.

GHOSTS

103 *"There are no eyes, no ears, no nose, no tongue"*: This is my adaptation of several translations of the Heart Sutra found on DharmaNet, http://www .dharmanet.org/HeartSutra.htm, accessed March 2017.

107 *academics at Tohoku University began to catalogue the stories*: See Hara Takahashi, "The Ghosts of the Tsunami Dead and *Kokoro no kea* in Japan's Religious Landscape," *Journal of Religion in Japan* 5, no. 2–3 (2016): 176–198.

107 *the true faith of Japan: the cult of the ancestors*: My account of the cult of the ancestors owes much to Robert J. Smith, *Ancestor Worship in Contemporary Japan* (Stanford University Press, 1974).

108 *"The dead are not as dead there as they are in our own society"*: Herbert Ooms, review of Robert J. Smith's *Ancestor Worship in Contemporary Japan*, in *Japanese Journal of Religious Studies* 2, no. 4 (1975): 317–322.

WHAT IT'S ALL ABOUT

116 *The water had reached a height of thirty-five meters here*: Figures for the height of the tsunami are taken from Tsuyoshi Haraguchi and Akira Iwamatsu, *Higashi Nihon Daishinsai Tsunami Shosai Chizu/Detailed Maps of the Impacts of the 2011 Japan Tsunami* (Bilingual, Tokyo, 2011).

PART 3: WHAT HAPPENED AT OKAWA

My account of the events at Okawa Elementary School on March 11 draws on multiple sources, including Ikegami, *Okawa Elementary School*; author interviews with Toshinobu Oikawa and Tetsuya and Hideaki Tadano; Japanese television interviews with Tetsuya Tadano, in the personal collection of Hideaki Tadano; official documents of Ishinomaki city; the final report of the Okawa Elementary School Incident Verification Committee; summary documents supplied by Sayomi and Takahiro Shito; and documents submitted to Sendai District Court by Kazuhiro Yoshioka.

THE LAST HOUR OF THE OLD WORLD

127 *the Okawa school bus was waiting in the parking lot*: "Gakko mae ni basu taiki" ["Bus Was Waiting in Front of School"], *Kahoku Shinpo* [newspaper], September 8, 2011.

128 *"It was shaking very slowly from side to side"*: *Children of the Tsunami*, BBC2 broadcast, March 1, 2012.

128 *the city authorities would compile a minute-by-minute log of the events of that afternoon*: Ishinomaki-shi kyoiku iinkai jimukyoku, "Okawa shogakko tsuika kikitori chosa kiroku," Okawa shogakko kyoshokuin no goizoku-sama he no 3.11 ni kansuru kikitori-chosa no setsumeikai no kaisai ni tsuite [Secretariat of Ishinomaki City Board of Education, "Records of additional hearings concerning Okawa Elementary School" in "Concerning the holding of an explanatory meeting for the bereaved families of Okawa Elementary School teachers on the hearing relating to 3.11"].

131 *The Education Plan*: Ishinomaki-shi kyoiku iinkai jimukyoku, "Heisei 22 nendo kyoiku keikaku Okawa shogakko (bassui)" [Secretariat of Ishinomaki City Board of Education, "Fiscal Year 2010 Education Plan Okawa Elementary School (Extracts)"], 81, 145–146.

134 *"I kept looking at the cars arriving and wondering, 'Is Mum going to come?'"*: *Children of the Tsunami*, BBC2 broadcast, March 1, 2012.

140 *"Manno-chan was right next to me"*: *Children of the Tsunami*, BBC2 broadcast, March 1, 2012.

141 *an elderly man named Kazuo Takahashi*: Takahashi's story is told in Ikegami, *Okawa Elementary School*, 187–193.

THE RIVER OF THREE CROSSINGS

159 *The 118-second film*: It can be viewed at https://www.youtube.com/watch?v=DW0dqWR4S7M, accessed March 2017.

IN THE WEB

166 *Tokyo will be shaken by an earthquake...*: For background on the coming Tokyo earthquake, see Peter Hadfield, *Sixty Seconds That Will Change the World* (London: Sidgwick & Jackson, 1991), and Peter Popham, *Tokyo: The City at the End of the World* (Tokyo: Kodansha, 1985).

166 *Seismologists point out that it is not, in fact, as simple as this*: Rather than committing themselves to predictions, seismologists offer probabilities. A study by the Earthquake Research Institute of Tokyo University in 2012 calculated that there is a 70 percent chance that Tokyo will be struck by an earthquake of magnitude 7 or higher by 2042. "Researchers Now Predict 70 Percent Chance of Major Tokyo Quake Within 30 Years," *Mainichi Shimbun*, May 25, 2012.

167 *an earthquake under Tokyo could kill as many as 13,000 people*: Richard Lloyd Parry, "Quake Experts Shake Tokyo with Forecast of 13,000 Dead," *The Times* (London), December 15, 2004.

167 *a tremor originating in one fault sets off earthquakes in two more*: Richard Lloyd Parry, "Japanese Make Plans to Survive Overdue Treble Quake," *The Times* (London), September 13, 2010.

167 *an earthquake and tsunami originating in the Nankai Trough*: Richard Lloyd Parry, "Million Victims from Next Tsunami, Japan Disaster Experts Warn," *The Times* (London) online, August 31, 2012, http://www.thetimes .co.uk/article/million-victims-from-nexttsunami-japan-disaster-experts -warn-gc3tx7vpw8s.

168 *only a tiny proportion of the victims was killed by the earthquake itself*: *Kahoku Shinpo* newspaper tallied ninety people who were killed by the earthquake rather than the tsunami. It is impossible to know exactly how many people died in collapsing houses, which were then inundated by the wave, but the overall number must be relatively low. "Daishinsai— yure no gisei 90 nin cho" ["Great Disaster—There Were More Than 90 Victims from the Earthquake"], *Kahoku Shinpo*, May 17, 2013.

169 *"Why does it not upset people more"*: Popham, *Tokyo*, 28.

170 *"Far from being dull to the dangers"*: Popham, *Tokyo*, 27, 28–29.

171 *"Now I will tell how Octavia, the spider-web city, is made"*: Italo Calvino, *Invisible Cities*, tr. William Weaver (London: Vintage, 1974 [1972]), 67.

WHAT USE IS THE TRUTH?

177 *Kashiba claimed that immediately after the disaster*: Ikegami, *Okawa Elementary School*, 91–92.

179 *"If it was such a big quake that so many trees fell down"*: Ikegami, *Okawa Elementary School*, 89.

180 *"He wore a check suit"*: Ikegami, *Okawa Elementary School*, 211.

181 *Endo wrote two letters*: Ishinomaki-shi kyoiku iinkai jimukyoku,

"2011-nen 6-gatsu 3-nichi zuke, Endo Junji kyoyu kara no Kashiba kocho ate FAX," Okawa shogakko kyoshokuin no goizokusama he no 3.11 ni kansuru kikitori-chosa no setsumeikai no kaisai ni tsuite [Secretariat of Ishinomaki City Board of Education, "FAX from teacher Junji Endo to headmaster Kashiba dated June 3, 2011" in "Concerning the holding of an explanatory meeting for the bereaved families of Okawa Elementary School teachers on the hearing relating to 3.11"].

182 *The men of the Ishinomaki city government were not villains*: This section draws on Ikegami, *Okawa Elementary School*, 113–127.

183 *a signed statement of apology addressed to the parents*: Ishinomaki-shi kyoiku iinkai jimukyoku, "Kashiba kocho shazaibun," Okawa shogakko kyoshokuin no goizoku-sama he no 3.11 ni kansuru kikitori-chosa no setsumeikai no kaisai ni tsuite [Secretariat of Ishinomaki City Board of Education, "Letter of Apology by Headmaster Kashiba" in "Concerning the holding of an explanatory meeting for the bereaved families of Okawa Elementary School teachers on the hearing relating to 3.11"].

186 *Its findings were published in a two-hundred-page report*: Okawa Elementary School Incident Verification Committee, Okawa shogakko jiko kensho hokoku-sho [Okawa Elementary School Incident Verification Report] (Tokyo, 2014), http://www.mext.go.jp/b_menu/shingi/chukyo/chukyo5/012/gijiroku/__icsFiles/afieldfile/2014/08/07/1350542_01.pdf, accessed March 2017. See also "Report on tsunami-hit school should be used as disaster-prevention textbook," *Mainichi Shimbun*, February 28, 2014.

186 *The committee was funded by the city at a cost of ¥57 million (£390,000)*: "Okawasho kensho-i saishu hokokushoan ni rakutan suru izoku" ["Bereaved Families Disappointed at the Final Report of the Okawa Elementary Verification Committee"], *Shukan Diamondo* (*Weekly Diamond*), January 22, 2014.

187 *Shigemi Kato . . . was promoted*: Ikegami, *Okawa Elementary School*, 112.

THE TSUNAMI IS NOT WATER

191 *"The Japanese people rose from the ashes"*: Naoto Kan, "Japan's Road to Recovery and Rebirth," *International Herald Tribune*, April 16, 2011.

199 *"The children were murdered by an invisible monster . . . It has no human warmth"*: Ikegami, *Okawa Elementary School*, 20. The rest of the quotations in this passage are from my interviews with Sayomi and Takahiro Shito.

PREDESTINATION

210 *she was evolving into what Japanese call* hotoke-sama: For more on the *hotoke-sama*, see Smith, *Ancestor Worship in Contemporary Japan*, 50–56.

THERE MAY BE GAPS IN MEMORY

226 *the symbolic ruins*: Richard Lloyd Parry, "Tsunami Survivors Face Dilemma over Its Haunting Ruins," *The Times* (London), August 24, 2012; Eugene Hoshiko, "Legacies of a Disaster Dot Japan's Tsunami Coast," Associated Press, March 10, 2016; "Residents Divided over Preservation of Remains 5 Years After Disaster," *Kyodo News*, March 10, 2016.

229 *"The Atomic Bomb Dome in Hiroshima was preserved"*: "Alumni of Tsunami-Devastated Miyagi School Ask for Support to Preserve Building," *Mainichi Shimbun*, December 5, 2014.

229 *Tetsuya spoke at a symposium at Meiji University*: Recording in the collection of Hideaki Tadano.

CONSOLATION OF THE SPIRITS

244 *the story of a man named Fukuji*: Kunio Yanagita, *The Legends of Tono*, tr. Ronald A. Morse (Lanham: Rowman & Littlefield, 2008 [1910]), 58–59.

SAVE DON'T FALL TO SEA

250 *None of the towns destroyed by the wave had been rebuilt*: Zoning regulations were introduced, which banned the construction of residential property in areas inundated by the wave. Businesses could still operate there, but homes were to be relocated inland or to higher ground.

253 *nothing that mattered would be significantly changed*: This is not to say that the actions of the education board are to be excused. Masaki Ikegami's trenchant conclusion is worth quoting at length: "What the City Board of Education should have done from the beginning was to listen thoroughly and carefully to the parties involved, reliably document and record everything, disclose information obtained in the investigation to the bereaved families, . . . verify the facts one by one, and investigate the truth.

Furthermore, they should sincerely apologize for sacrificing the lives of children under the management of the school, and discuss punishment of officials who have been neglectful in their responses and oversight. On top of that, they should make public the lessons learned from the worst such accident in history to parties such as prefectural boards of education and the Ministry of Education, and create the opportunity to reconsider fundamentally disaster management in Japan. These actions should be performed with speed, and shared with the bereaved families to the greatest extent possible. By acting in such a lackadaisical and untransparent manner, the City Board of Education has made the problem worse" (Ikegami, *Okawa Elementary School*, 83).

255 *But there could hardly have been less sense of triumph*: It was further undermined a few days later, when the defendants announced that they would appeal against the verdict in the High Court. The plaintiffs responded by making an appeal of their own, on the grounds that the damages awarded were inadequate. A verdict is expected in 2018.

261 *Masaru knew this*: Masaru Naganuma declined to speak to me. This account is based on conversations with Naomi Hiratsuka and Miho Suzuki.

267 *A friend of Kaneta's, who was present at one of the exorcisms*: The religious studies scholar, Hara Takahashi, who corroborated Kaneta's account.

ACKNOWLEDGMENTS

Many of the people who helped me the most in the writing of this book are named in its pages: I thank all of those who agreed to talk to me, sometimes repeatedly over the course of several years, and often at times of overwhelming grief. Among those who are not named, I am grateful to Kazuyoshi Abe, Yuko Kaneta, Akio Kumagai, Akemi Miura, Minoru Ota, Tsugio and Mayumi Nakamura, and Ken Sakashita.

For practical, professional, intellectual, and personal support of diverse kinds, I thank Lucy Alexander, Regis Arnaud, Lucy Birmingham, Peter Blakely, Azby Brown, Kyle Cleveland, Jamie Coleman, Margot and Bill Coles, Martin Colthorpe and the Japan Foundation, the Currie family, Alissa Descotes-Toyosaki, Toby Eady, Max Edwards, Natasha Fairweather and the Rogers, Coleridge & White, the Foreign Correspondents' Club of Japan, Dan Franklin and Penguin Random House, Rob Gilhooly, Mandy Greenfield, Takahashi Hara, Kuni Hatanaka, Jennifer Joel and ICM Partners, Chris Jue, Nagisa Kato, Angela Kubo, Leo Lewis, the Lloyd Parry family, Justin McCurry, Sean McDonald and Farrar, Straus and Giroux, Hamish Mackaskill and the English Agency Japan, Levi McLaughlin, David McNeil, Koichi Nakano, the staff of Oiwake Onsen, Kyoko Onoki, David Pearce, Peter Popham, Roger Pulvers, Zaria Rich, Junzo Sawa, Shuji Shibuya, Iwayumi Suzuki, Jeremy Sutton-Hibbert, Bunei Takayama, Chika Tonooka, Rick Wallace, and Fiona Wilson.

From the beginning, my employer, *The Times*, energetically sponsored my reporting of the disaster and graciously gave me time off for writing and research. I thank my colleagues there, past and present, especially the late

ACKNOWLEDGMENTS

Richard Beeston, James Harding, Anoushka Healy, Roland Watson, and John Witherow. Sections of this book first appeared in the *London Review of Books*. Among the editors, I thank especially Daniel Soar and Mary-Kay Wilmers.

There are numerous charitable organizations for victims of the tsunami. The Momo-Kaki Orphans Fund helps children who have lost their parents: www .momokaki.org.

INDEX

Page numbers in *italics* refer to illustrations or maps.

Buddhists (*cont.*)
secret cults of, 54; unity of being of, 238–39; Zen, 98; *see also* Café de Monku; temples, Buddhist
butsudan (household altars), 23, 107–109, 208

C

Café de Monku, 105, 241–43, 248, 256, 262
Calvino, Italo, 171
carelessness, 183–85
casualty figures, 11, 27, 167, 168, 271*n*
Chernobyl, 12
Chiba, Masahiko, 180, 198–99
Chiba Prefecture, 10
Chile, tsunami caused by earthquake in, 60, 80, 130, 139, 217
China, 192
Chive Island, 200
Christianity, 19, 107, 108, 239–41, 243, 256
compassion, 14, 239
construction regulations, Japanese, 7–8, 81–83, 88, 148, 167

cremation, 47, 80, 82–83, 105, 120, 174

D

detachment (feeling), 13–14, 100, 147, 239, 256, 257; professional, 13–14, 147
Disaster Counter-Measure Rooms, 7
domestic leave-taking, 19
dreams, 92, 95, 106, 115, 171, 205, 248; disturbing, 37, 231

E

earthquakes, xviii, 11–12, 30–31, 45, 81–82, 149, 221, 246, 259; children picked up from school after, 48, 90, 123, 134, 185, 228; electricity and communications system outages due to, 25–28, 66, 82, 89, 98, 123, 136, 182, 237; intensity and magnitude of, 4, 11, 60, 146–47, 182, 238, 277*n*; safety precautions during and

L

N

M

A Note About the Author

Richard Lloyd Parry has lived in Tokyo for twenty-two years as a foreign correspondent, first for *The Independent* and now as Asia editor of *The Times* (London). He has reported from twenty-eight countries, including Afghanistan, Iraq, and North Korea. His work has also appeared in the *London Review of Books, Granta,* and *The New York Times.* He is the author of *In the Time of Madness,* an account of black magic and violence in Indonesia in the late 1990s, and *People Who Eat Darkness: The True Story of a Young Woman Who Vanished from the Streets of Tokyo—and the Evil That Swallowed Her Up.*

DATE DUE